DATE DUE

GAYLORD			PRINTED IN U.S.A.

THE FOUNDING FORTUNES

MICHAEL PATRICK ALLEN

THE FOUNDING FORTUNES

A New Anatomy of the Super-Rich Families in America

T·T

TRUMAN TALLEY BOOKS
E. P. DUTTON
NEW YORK

Published in the United States by Truman Talley Books • E. P. Dutton,
a division of NAL Penguin Inc.,
2 Park Avenue, New York, N.Y. 10016.

Published simultaneously in Canada by
Fitzhenry and Whiteside
Limited, Toronto.

Library of Congress Cataloging-in-Publication Data
Allen, Michael Patrick.
The founding fortunes.
"Truman Talley Books"
Includes bibliographical references and index.
1. Wealth—United States. 2. Millionaires—
United States. I. Title.
HC110.W4A44 1987 332'.0973 87-9912
ISBN: 0-525-24569-3

W

DESIGNED BY STEVEN N. STATHAKIS

1 3 5 7 9 10 8 6 4 2

First Edition

for my mother, and in memory of my father

Contents

The Corporate Rich

The United States is a very wealthy nation, but much of its wealth is owned by a small minority of its citizens. According to the best estimates, less than 1 percent of the population owns roughly a quarter of all the personal wealth in the country, including half of the stocks and bonds owned by individuals. Furthermore, a large proportion of this wealth is owned by the members of a few hundred families. By and large, the members of these families are multimillionaires. Some of the richest, such as David Rockefeller and Henry Ford II, are worth hundreds of millions of dollars. A select few, like Gordon Getty or Paul Mellon, are even billionaires. Most of the rest, however, are worth somewhat less. In particular, many of the younger members of these families are currently worth only a few million dollars apiece. Although most of these individuals are not fabulously rich, their families are extremely wealthy. As a group, they comprise what Ferdinand Lundberg once labeled "the rich and the super-rich." Although many American families are relatively affluent, few are truly rich. Even among the affluent, the major asset of most families is usually the equity they have in their homes. The truly rich have equity in their homes, of course, but they also have substantial investments in stocks, bonds, and commercial real estate as well. These investments alone are usually sufficient to provide them with generous incomes. Indeed, the fundamental distinction between the truly rich and the merely affluent is that the rich receive enough income from their investments to be able to live out their lives in comparative luxury without the necessity of ever seeking gainful employment.

Much of the wealth owned by the richest families in America is corporate wealth. In fact, almost all of the really big fortunes in America were derived, at least initially, from the ownership of corporate stock of one kind or another. Indeed, most wealthy families owe the bulk of their fortunes to their original stockholdings in a single corporation. Large corporations often begin as small firms, owned and managed by the members of their founding families. As these firms grow into large corporations, the corporate stock owned by these founding families sometimes appreciates greatly in value. The corporate rich, then, consist of the members of wealthy capitalist families who amassed large fortunes from their original stockholdings in a family corporation. Of course, not all new companies become large corporations. To the contrary, a majority of new businesses fail within a few years. But a few, through either good management or good fortune, succeed beyond all expectations. The founders of these firms and those who invested in them at the outset often become very wealthy. For example, William R. Hewlett and David Packard founded their own electronic instruments firm in 1939 with an initial cash investment of $538. Forty years later, their stock in Hewlett-Packard was worth over $3 billion. Although billionaires are few and far between, many successful entrepreneurs have become multimillionaires. On the basis of his own analysis of the very rich, C. Wright Mills, an ardent critic of corporate capitalism, was forced to conclude that the American economic system was successful "as a machine for producing millionaires."

Despite the fact that they own a major share of all the personal wealth in the country, surprisingly little is known about the corporate rich in America. With only a few notable exceptions, they lead intensely private lives, which render them practically invisible. This lack of visibility is no mere accident. To the contrary, it is the result of a conscious strategy. In order to preserve their privacy, many wealthy individuals have chosen to lead lives of deliberate obscurity. They attempt to conceal their family ties and the extent of their wealth from everyone except other family members, close friends, and a few trusted business associates. With only a few exceptions, most of the members of the richest families in America are entirely unknown to the public at large. For example, as the result of the publicity generated by recent legal battles, Gordon Getty has become widely known as a billionaire. However, his equally rich brother, J. Paul Getty, Jr., remains virtually unknown. The reasons for this conscious pursuit of privacy through obscurity are obvious enough. Anyone with a few million dollars to spare is fair game for those in search of money. To begin with, the corporate rich are natural targets for professional fund-raisers from both charitable causes and political campaigns. They also attract un-solicited business propositions from wandering legions of hapless in-ventors and speculators. Last but certainly not least, they seek privacy for reasons of personal security. The scions of several wealthy families have fallen victim to kidnapping and extortion attempts. For the corporate rich, obscurity is often the cheapest and most effective form of security.

Although the corporate rich may be largely invisible to the rest of society, they are certainly not inconsequential. They may have relinquished their claim to celebrity status in order to safeguard their privacy, but they have not relinquished their wealth or the power inherent in that wealth. In a society in which money is easily trans-lated into power, the very rich are also very powerful. Although they would probably deny that their wealth and their family ties give them any special privileges, the corporate rich do exert a pervasive influence in social and political affairs at both the local and the national level. Sometimes this power is exercised directly in an overt and public fashion. For example, the members of wealthy families are well repre-sented among the major contributors to political campaigns, espe-cially those for national office. Before the enactment of recent cam-paign-finance reforms, it was not unusual for the corporate rich to give large sums of money to their favorite political candidates. For example, Richard M. Scaife, a grandson of Richard B. Mellon, one of the early investors in Gulf Oil and Aluminum Company of America, gave $1 million to the reelection campaign of President Nixon in 1972. The corporate rich also exert a powerful influence on American society in less direct and more subtle ways. Members of these wealthy capitalist families are, of course, directly involved in the economic activities of the country as a result of their positions as officers, directors, and principal stockholders in many major corporations. They also exert considerable influence on the formation of public policy through the activities of the large philanthropic foundations endowed and controlled by family members.

THE WEALTH PROBLEM

In general, there are two very different types of individuals among the corporate rich. There are those who have accumulated large fortunes and those who have simply inherited them. As a rule, public attention is focused on entrepreneurs who have amassed great wealth on their own. Depending on the particular historical circumstances and the general political climate, these wealthy entrepreneurs have either been venerated as brilliant "innovators" or condemned as avaricious "speculators." Needless to say, the distinction between the two is often somewhat arbitrary. As a rule, they are simply individuals who were early investors in companies that, as a result of either superior management or fortuitous circumstances, grew into large corporations. Despite the fact that successful entrepreneurs receive most of the publicity, they are a distinct minority among the corporate rich. In terms of sheer numbers of people, most of the corporate rich in America are inheritors. Although they may have made some money on their own, these inheritors owe the bulk of their wealth to gifts and bequests they received from relatives. The fabled entrepreneurs of this century, like John D. Rockefeller and Henry Ford, are gone, but their families and much of their fortunes endure. The Rockefeller and Ford fortunes, only slightly depleted by estate taxes and charitable bequests, are now owned by scores of individuals, all of them descendants of the founding entrepreneurs. None of these inheritors will ever be as rich, in real terms, as the founders of these fortunes, but most of them are nevertheless extremely wealthy. Indeed, the Rockefellers and the Fords remain among the wealthiest families of the corporate rich.

The distinction between entrepreneurs and inheritors is at the heart of the ambivalent attitudes that most Americans have about great wealth. This distinction is also apparent in government policies concerning the redistribution of wealth. It has never been a crime to be rich in America. In point of fact, the tax system actually encourages the initial accumulation of wealth. For example, there are no property taxes at the federal level on the ownership of stocks and bonds as such. As a result, individuals who have most of their fortunes invested in these types of securities pay no taxes at all on the bulk of their wealth. They pay federal income taxes only on the dividend and interest income that they receive from these securities. Until recently, even the profits that the corporate rich accrued from the sale of their stocks and bonds were not subject to the usual income taxes. Instead, these profits were taxed at the preferential rate accorded capital gains. Although the federal tax system does not hinder the accumulation of wealth, it does discourage the transfer of great wealth from one generation of family members to the next. The United States, like most advanced industrial societies, has created an elaborate system of gift and estate taxes. These taxes were never intended to raise much revenue, at least not at the federal level. Instead, federal gift and estate taxes were imposed primarily to prevent wealthy individuals from transferring their entire fortunes to their descendants. Consequently, these taxes are formally progressive, such that large intergenerational transfers of wealth are subject to higher gift and estate tax rates than small transfers.

Laws are a reflection, albeit an imperfect one, of the dominant normative principles of a society. The very fact that the United States has progressive gift and estate taxes to limit the intergenerational transfer of wealth provides concrete proof of the popular sentiment in the country concerning the inheritance of large fortunes. Although most Americans accept the accumulation of great wealth by successful entrepreneurs as an inevitable consequence of the free-enterprise system, they do not accept the inheritance of this wealth by the progeny of these entrepreneurs with the same equanimity. To begin with, inherited wealth on a large scale is seen as an affront to the principle of equal opportunity, as it provides a select few with almost insurmountable material advantages. Moreover, the fact that wealth can be translated into economic and political power is viewed by many as a threat to the democratic principle of "one man, one vote." Indeed, it was largely the fear of a "hereditary plutocracy" that led to the passage of the first nominal estate taxes in 1916. However, really progressive gift and estate taxes did not gain widespread public support until after the onset of the Great Depression. In his message to Congress calling for the passage of more progressive gift and estate taxes in 1935, President Roosevelt declared unequivocally that "inherited economic power is as inconsistent with the ideals of this generation as inherited political power was inconsistent with the ideals of the generation that established our government." Although the taxes designed to prevent the inheritance of great wealth have been revised many times since that time, they have never been repealed.

The existence of formally progressive gift and estate taxes has given rise to the popular belief that the corporate rich are a dying breed in America. According to the conventional wisdom, wealthy capitalist families have been driven to the brink of extinction by a system of progressive taxation that prevents the inheritance of wealth on a large scale. In point of fact, the corporate rich are alive and well in America. Despite widespread popular support, gift and estate taxes have failed to reduce substantially, let alone eliminate entirely, the inheritance of great wealth in America. A careful enumeration of the wealthiest individuals in the country demonstrates that a clear majority of them are inheritors. The failure of the tax system to prevent the inheritance of these fortunes is attributable primarily to the development of a series of often elaborate strategies for avoiding these taxes. Unlike tax evasion, which involves an element of criminal fraud, tax avoidance is simply the reduction of taxes by strictly legal means. Members of the corporate rich have retained some of the best lawyers in the nation to devise means for avoiding gift and estate taxes. As a matter of fact, the various strategies devised to circumvent these taxes have been so successful that one tax expert has termed the estate tax a "voluntary tax." The clear implication is that most wealthy individuals can, with only a modicum of sound legal advice, succeed in passing on most of their wealth to their progeny. Consequently, the corporate rich in America have the best of both worlds. While popular sentiment against the inheritance of large fortunes is assuaged by the existence of formally progressive transfer taxes, the actual inheritance of great wealth continues almost unabated.

It is hardly surprising to discover that there are so many public misconceptions about the efficacy of the present system of gift and estate taxes. The scholar and the layman alike are often misled by news accounts that fail to disclose the true extent of inheritance within wealthy families. Whenever a rich entrepreneur dies, press accounts of his wealth are typically limited to a description of the estate filed for probate. Little attention is paid to the fact that much of the family fortune may have escaped probate altogether as the result of lifetime gifts. The major cause of such journalistic omissions is the financial secrecy maintained by almost all corporate rich families. There is the example of Haroldson L. Hunt, a relatively unknown Texas oilman before he was proclaimed as the richest American by both *Fortune* and *Life* magazines in 1948. Yet when Hunt died in 1974, his estate was initially appraised at only $55 million. Clearly, Hunt had succeeded in transferring most of his assets to his children before he died. However, because the centerpiece of the Hunt family fortune, Placid Oil Company, was a private company that did not issue reports to the public, it was impossible to estimate with any accuracy the total wealth of the Hunt family. The full extent of the Hunt family fortune was not revealed until six years later, when the family mortgaged most of its assets, including Placid Oil, in order to repay debts incurred by three family members in the silver futures market. Altogether, the family was able to pledge assets worth $3.2 billion as collateral for this loan.

The fact that H. L. Hunt was able to transfer the bulk of his wealth to his children during his lifetime demonstrates some of the

7

limitations of the present system of gift and estate taxes. Furthermore, the Hunts are hardly unique in this regard. Most of the wealthiest capitalist families in America have succeeded in perpetuating their fortunes over successive generations. In the case of the Hunt family, this feat of tax avoidance was accomplished largely through the use of a device known as a *generation-skipping trust.* In 1935, just before more progressive gift and estate taxes were due to take effect, H. L. Hunt created a series of trusts for his children. Over the years, he transferred most of his assets, including all of the stock in Placid Oil and a number of lucrative oil leases, to these trusts. Under the terms of the trusts, his six children were to receive all of the income produced by these assets during their lifetimes while the assets themselves were preserved for his grandchildren. Moreover, because his children do not legally own the assets held by these trusts, the Hunt grandchildren will eventually receive these assets without any estate taxes. In this way, Hunt safeguarded the bulk of his fortune from estate taxes for two generations. Moreover, generation-skipping trusts are but one of a number of tax-avoidance strategies employed by corporate rich families. Other strategies for circumventing or reducing gift and estate taxes include the use of lifetime gifts, family holding companies, and low-interest loans. Most of the other wealthy capitalist families in America, like the Rockefellers, du Ponts, Mellons, and Gettys, have used these and other tax-avoidance techniques to preserve their fortunes for several generations.

FAMILY AND FORTUNE

For most Americans, the notion of "family" corresponds to the sociological concept of the nuclear family consisting solely of parents and their children. Indeed, many Americans have only limited information about or contact with the members of their extended family, comprising such collateral relatives as aunts, uncles, and cousins. Sociologists have attributed this decline in the strength of such kinship ties to the fact that the extended family no longer performs very many important functions for individual family members. Although it has all but disappeared in much of modern American society, the extended family is a vital entity among the corporate rich. By and large, the members of these families are aware of their kinship ties to a large number of collateral relatives. Indeed, they may have occasional contact with many of them at family reunions, weddings, and funerals. There are many reasons for the survival of the extended family or kinship group among the corporate rich. The most important, of course, concerns wealth. In his classic study, *America's Sixty Families,* Ferdinand Lundberg declared unequivocally that "the family today, in no slighter degree than two or three centuries ago or in imperial Rome, is supreme in the governance of wealth—amassing it, standing watch over it, and keeping it intact from generation to generation." A somewhat less impassioned observer of the American upper class, E. Digby Baltzell, put it much more succinctly when he described wealth as the "fertilizer of family trees."

The extended family persists among the corporate rich precisely because it still performs a number of vital functions for the members of these families. To begin with, kinship ties serve to delimit clearly which family members have a legitimate claim to part of the family fortune. Indeed, the primacy of the family in all matters pertaining to wealth is nowhere more evident than in the matter of inheritance. Of course, individuals who possess great wealth usually execute elaborate wills stipulating the exact distribution of their estates. For example, William Randolph Hearst, the newspaper magnate, left a will that was 125 pages in length. However, even when individuals with great wealth die without a valid will, their property and their progeny are protected by the rules governing intestate succession. Each state has laws that provide detailed directions for the distribution of estates among family members in the absence of a will. In general, these laws decree that an estate must be distributed to the spouse and children of the deceased. If there is none, then it typically reverts to his or her parents or siblings. Finally, if there are no surviving parents or siblings, then the estate is distributed among collateral relatives. The bizarre circumstances surrounding the estate of the reclusive billionaire, Howard R. Hughes, Jr., provide a case in point. Because he apparently died without a valid will and without a wife, children, surviving parents, or siblings, his estate was eventually distributed among twenty-one cousins. It did not matter that Hughes never knew most of the heirs to his estate. All that mattered to the courts were their claims to kinship.

The inheritance of wealth provides an important economic basis for the maintenance of kinship ties among the corporate rich. Because most large fortunes are composed, at least initially, of stock in a single corporation, the members of a wealthy capitalist family often share a common financial fate. Although family members may eventually sell some of this stock and reinvest the proceeds in other securities, diversification may be delayed for many years in order to avoid unnecessary capital-gains taxes. Consequently, the members of these families are typically linked to one another for a long period of time because of their shared economic interests. Moreover, the members of corporate rich families are usually bound together by a number of legal arrangements designed to avoid gift and estate taxes. As George E. Marcus, an anthropologist concerned with inheritance, has observed, "the transference of wealth to descendants combined with the effort to conserve capital has required the internally motivated reproduction of the family in formal terms, through the use of such legal instruments as trusts, foundations, and holding companies." In other words, informal family ties are reinforced by formal legal arrangements. In many cases, family cohesion is also facilitated by the existence of a family office that handles the financial affairs of family members. For example, the twenty-three grandchildren of John D. Rockefeller, Jr., are inextricably linked to one another by a series of trusts, which hold most of the family fortune; by their common ownership of Rockefeller Group Inc., a family holding company for their real estate and broadcasting properties; and by a family office, Rockefeller Family Associates, which handles their personal finances.

To some extent, the existence of elaborate legal arrangements involving trusts and holding companies has rendered the notion of individual wealth virtually obsolete. For all practical purposes, most family fortunes are owned by families and not by individuals. For example, J. Paul Getty was heralded by the press as a certifiable billionaire. After all, he held a majority of the stock in Getty Oil Company. He also received almost all of the dividend income from this stock, as much as $29 million a year. Despite the fact that this stock was worth at least $2 billion at the time of his death in 1976, J. Paul Getty was never really a billionaire. The reason, of course, is that most of the Getty Oil stock he controlled was not really his. Instead, he held roughly $1.3 billion of this stock as the sole trustee of a trust established by his mother. He voted all of the stock held by the trust and received virtually all of the dividends from it, but, in the eyes of the law at least, he did not own it. Indeed, J. Paul Getty and even his sons were only lifetime income beneficiaries of this trust: they were entitled to all of the income produced by the trust assets during their lifetimes, but they could not touch the principal. If the stock belonged to anyone, it ultimately belonged to the sixteen grandchildren of J. Paul Getty. According to the terms of the trust, however, they will not receive this stock until the trust is dissolved upon the death of the last income beneficiary. In view of the fact that J. Paul Getty, his sons, and his grandchildren all enjoyed benefits of one kind or another from this trust, its assets were, in some sense, the collective property of the entire family.

Wealthy capitalist families usually possess more than mere fortunes; they also possess "symbolic family estates." In the words of one expert on kinship patterns in America, Bernard Farber, "symbolic estates derive from the fact that individuals inherit and accumulate not only property but relatives." For example, the great-grandchildren of John D. Rockefeller inherit not only part of the Rockefeller fortune but also a complex network of relationships with aunts, uncles, and cousins who are also Rockefellers. These social bonds between family members are reaffirmed during periodic family reunions as well as on such occasions as weddings and funerals. Family members usually strive to maintain their symbolic family estates primarily because they derive much of their social status as individuals from the social status accorded their family as a whole. For example, family ties are especially important whenever members of these wealthy capitalist families seek acceptance into the inner circles of the upper class. As

E. Digby Baltzell observed in his book *Philadelphia Gentlemen,* "the upper class concept refers to a group of families, whose members are descendants of successful individuals." Moreover, the process of gaining unqualified membership in the upper class, through the accumulation and maintenance of an appropriate symbolic family estate, may require several decades. The grandchildren and great-grandchildren of John D. Rockefeller have gained acceptance into the most exclusive institutions of the American upper class, but it took the family almost two generations to overcome the stigma originally associated with the creation of its fortune.

The importance of symbolic family estates is nowhere more evident than in the choice of names. It is common practice among the corporate rich to commemorate the founder of the family fortune by perpetuating his name in subsequent generations. Consequently, it is not unusual to find a namesake of the founder among his grandchildren or great-grandchildren. One result of this form of ancestor worship is the sometimes confusing use of generational numbers. The scions of some of the more prominent capitalist families include Harvey S. Firestone III, Robert W. Johnson IV, J. Paul Getty III, Richard J. Reynolds III, Eli Lilly III, Henry J. Kaiser III, and Clinton W. Murchison III, to name but a few. The record in this field may be held by Marshall Field VI, the great-great-great-grandson of the founder of the department store chain of the same name. Scions of wealthy families with dynastic names can, of course, ignore them when it suits their purposes. Two such scions who entered electoral politics, Senator John D. Rockefeller IV of West Virginia and Senator Henry J. Heinz III of Pennsylvania, prefer to be called "Jay" and "Jack," respectively, at least by their constituents. The maintenance of symbolic family estates through the use of family names sometimes occurs, albeit in somewhat modified form, even among the female descendants of a wealthy entrepreneur. In these cases, the children receive the maiden name of their mother as their middle name. Some of the more notable examples of this practice include Richard Mellon Scaife, Lammot du Pont Copeland, Arthur Ochs Sulzberger, Thomas Watson Buckner, and Edward Harriman Gerry.

FAMILY AND FIRM

The capitalist family, comprising a wealthy entrepreneur and his descendants, is something of an anachronism in the modern corporate economy. Of course, the entrepreneur himself is considered a heroic figure in the folklore of capitalism. After all, accepted economic theory argues that it is the entrepreneur, not the professional manager, who is the source of innovation in the capitalist economic system. However, even the most innovative and capable entrepreneurs eventually outlive their usefulness. In an economy dominated by large, bureaucratic corporations, the aging entrepreneur can sometimes become a serious threat to the prosperity and continued survival of the firm. The classic example of this pattern is, of course, Henry Ford. He is celebrated in American business history as the individual most responsible for perfecting the assembly-line method of production and for providing the public with reliable and affordable transportation. He was largely responsible for creating the Ford Motor Company and guiding it through a turbulent period of expansion to become one of the largest firms in the entire world. In his later years, however, Henry Ford almost succeeded in destroying the company he had built by refusing to change the design of his automobiles to meet the innovations introduced by his competitors. His intransigence undoubtedly cost the company much of its market share during a critical phase in the development of the automobile industry. More recently, Steven P. Jobs, one of the founders of Apple Computer Inc., left the company after the board of directors concluded that his autocratic behavior as chairman had jeopardized the profitability of the corporation.

If the individual entrepreneur seems out of place within the large corporation, the position of his descendants is even more anomalous. The capitalist family that retains major stockholdings as well as positions of authority within an established corporation is often seen as an undesirable but unavoidable remnant of an earlier economic age. According to the tenets of conventional economic wisdom, all large corporations eventually succumb to a "managerial revolution" in which the actual control of the firm is quietly wrested from the founding family by professional managers. As a result of such a revolution, the descendants of the founder who still have major stockholdings in the firm are eventually relegated to the rather mundane task of collecting their dividends while the more important chore of managing the firm is left to others. The notion of a managerial revolution has a certain appeal, particularly to professional managers seeking to free themselves from the fetters of family control. However, the available evidence suggests that the managerial revolution may be one of the most protracted revolutions in history. There are still a number of large corporations that have descendants of their founders as their principal stockholders. Several studies have shown that roughly a quarter of the largest industrial corporations in America are subject to some form of family control. In most of these cases, family members also serve as officers or directors of the corporation. In light of this evidence, one noted researcher, Maurice Zeitlin, has concluded that the managerial revolution is nothing more than a plausible and convenient "pseudofact."

In its simplest form, the notion of a managerial revolution implies that there is a separation of ownership and control in the large corporation. In other words, it is assumed that those individuals who own most of the stock in a corporation are no longer the individuals who control it. This theory is predicated on two patently questionable assumptions. To begin with, it assumes that there is a gradual dilution of family stock ownership as the firm issues new stock to the public in order to finance its expansion. It also assumes that the stock in the corporation held by the founding family is dispersed among a large number of family members, rendering the coordination of these stockholdings difficult at best. Presumably, the dilution and dispersion of family stockholdings serve to erode the power of the family and allow professional managers to assume effective control of the firm. The logic of this theory seems almost incontrovertible. Like most theories, however, it does not always work in practice. Many corporations are able to finance their expansion largely from retained earnings or debt without the necessity of issuing additional stock to the public. At the same time, the stock in the corporation held by members of the founding family may be concentrated by an interwoven network of trust funds, holding companies, and family offices. There are many firms in which the stockholdings of the founding family have been neither diluted nor dispersed to any great extent. As a result, many of these corporations are still controlled by members of their founding families.

The inclination of corporate rich families to control or even manage their corporations for generations is not an act of mere perversity. In many cases, a wealthy capitalist family may have the vast bulk of its fortune invested in the stock of a single company. Consequently, family members may feel compelled to exercise some control over the firm simply to protect their investment. Although individual family members may gradually diversify their investment portfolios, tax considerations often dictate against such a strategy, at least in the short term. In all probability, the stock in the family corporation held by family members has appreciated greatly in value since they received it through gifts or inheritances. Whenever this stock is sold, the difference between the original cost of the stock and its present market value becomes subject to capital-gains taxes. For tax purposes, then, it is often advisable to defer any diversification until the stock in the family corporation has been revalued for tax purposes as the result of a transfer by gift or inheritance. In addition, the attachment of family members to the stock of the family corporation may be as much sentimental as financial. In many ways, the success of a wealthy capitalist family and the success of its firm are inextricably linked. Having risen from mere affluence to great wealth within a generation or two as a result of the appreciation in the market value of their stockholdings, family members may be understandably reluctant to sell all of their stock in the family corporation. Last but not least, family members may derive a great deal of power and prestige from the fact that their family controls a major corporation.

It is not difficult to find many examples of firms in which the managerial revolution is more of an abstract theory than a concrete fact. One example is the Weyerhaeuser family and its long involvement with the Weyerhaeuser Company. The original Weyerhaeuser Timber Company was formed in 1900 by Frederick Weyerhaeuser, who served as its first president. In the years that followed, all four of his sons served as officers or directors of the company. Later, four grandsons also served as officers or directors. Largely as the result of acquisitions, the proportion of Weyerhaeuser Company stock held by members of the Weyerhaeuser family has declined from approximately 20 percent in 1937 to around 12 percent today. Inasmuch as this amount of Weyerhaeuser stock is worth in the neighborhood of $450 million, the family obviously has a sizable stake in the future of the company. George H. Weyerhaeuser, a great-grandson of the founder, is now president of the company, and a second cousin serves as a director. The Weyerhaeusers are not typical of all capitalist families, but they do serve to point out the obvious limitations of any theory positing an imminent managerial revolution. It is not all that unusual to find grandsons and even great-grandsons of wealthy entrepreneurs serving as officers or directors of some of the largest corporations in America. To the Weyerhaeusers, one may add such familiar family and company names as du Pont, Firestone, Ford, Dow, Heinz, Hearst, Coors, and Timken. In each of these cases, the founding family retains a substantial investment in the corporation.

In short, a cursory review of the available evidence confirms that reports of the demise of family capitalism, even among the largest corporations, are somewhat premature. Most of the firms controlled by capitalist families may well be on the road to a managerial revolution, but such a revolution may be many years off. Family participation in the management and direction of a large corporation may, under certain circumstances, extend over a period of several decades. Even if family capitalism is on the decline among older corporations in mature industries, it appears to be on the rise among newer corporations. Some of the fastest growing and most profitable companies in America, many of them in burgeoning industries, are subject to some degree of control by their founding families. Drug companies such as Eli Lilly and Company, The Upjohn Company, Baxter Travenol Laboratories Inc., A.H. Robins Company Inc., and SmithKline Beckman Corporation have members of their founding families as major stockholders. Members of these same families often serve as officers and directors of these firms as well. The same can be said for electronics and computer companies such as Texas Instruments Inc., Hewlett-

Packard Company, Motorola Inc., Intel Corporation, and Wang Laboratories Inc. In retailing, companies such as Dayton Hudson Corporation, Nordstrom Inc., The Limited Inc., Petrie Stores Corporation, and Wal-Mart Stores Inc. are controlled to some extent by members of their founding families. Last but not least, several major media companies, such as Knight-Ridder Inc., The Washington Post Company, The Times Mirror Company, Dow Jones and Company Inc., and The New York Times Company, are still subject to family control.

WEALTH AND POWER

The conscious pursuit of obscurity by many members of the corporate rich has rendered them practically invisible to the public at large. Nevertheless, they continue to exercise a pervasive and significant influence in American politics. The power inherent in great wealth is especially evident in the arena of campaign financing. As early as 1937, Ferdinand Lundberg documented that individuals from wealthy capitalist families were regular and substantial contributors to the campaigns of presidential candidates. He also confirmed that the bulk of these contributions went to the candidates of the Republican party. This financial bond between presidential candidates and wealthy campaign contributors has remained virtually unchanged for several decades. According to Herbert E. Alexander, a prominent scholar of campaign financing, the members of just twelve wealthy families contributed at least $3.6 million to the presidential campaign of 1972. Of course, most of these funds went to the Republican party. Indeed, the disclosure of illegal contributions during that campaign eventually forced Congress to pass a series of campaign-financing reforms in 1974. Although these reforms limit the amount of money that individuals can contribute directly to a candidate for federal office, they still permit individuals to contribute to a number of political action committees, even if they all endorse the same candidate. Moreover,

17

individuals are allowed to spend an unlimited amount of money on independent advertisements and commercials. Despite the intent of recent campaign-financing reforms, then, the members of the corporate rich are still a major source of political campaign contributions.

The power of wealth is all too obvious whenever the scion of a wealthy capitalist family seeks elected office. Political campaigns at both the state and the national levels have become so expensive that the rich possess an often decisive advantage over their less affluent opponents. Recent campaign-financing reforms did not place any limits on the amount of money that candidates can spend on their own campaigns. Senator John C. Danforth of Missouri, a member of the family that founded Ralston Purina Company, and Senator Henry J. Heinz III of Pennsylvania, a great-grandson of the original H. J. Heinz, were both able to rely on their own financial resources during their initial campaigns. In many cases, the scions of wealthy families who enter electoral politics also benefit from the immediate name recognition accorded their family. This combination of personal wealth and name recognition enabled three members of one corporate rich family, two brothers and their nephew, to win gubernatorial campaigns in three different states: Nelson Rockefeller in New York, Winthrop Rockefeller in Arkansas, and John D. Rockefeller IV in West Virginia. The voters were unlikely to forget a candidate named Rockefeller. It did not matter to them that much of this name recognition was probably attributable to the stigma once associated with that name. Although the scions of wealthy capitalist families usually win their elections, there are exceptions. For example, Mark Dayton, the great-grandson of the founder of Dayton Hudson, was defeated in his recent bid for the Senate. However, his defeat was probably the result of his somewhat radical views, which alienated even some members of his own family. Money cannot always buy high office, but it is rarely a serious hindrance.

Wealthy capitalist families also exert a powerful influence on American society in less direct and more subtle ways. They are, of course, directly involved in the economic activities of the nation as a result of their position as principal stockholders in many major corporations. Members of corporate rich families often serve as officers and directors of these corporations. Consequently, these families often exercise effective control over some of the largest and most powerful corporations in the world. Through these corporations, they are able to influence policies, at both the local and the national levels, that affect their economic interests. Members of the corporate rich often exert a great deal of influence at the local level, even in large cities. For example, Henry Ford II, as chairman of Ford Motor Company, was instrumental in the development of the huge Renaissance Center in downtown Detroit. Indeed, he saw to it that Ford Motor Company became one of the earliest and largest investors in this development. The political process operates in much the same way at the national level. During that same period, for example, Henry Ford II organized a national campaign against the passage of stringent federal automobile safety and pollution standards. In order to get media coverage of the industry position, Ford sought the assistance of an old acquaintance, Arthur O. Sulzberger, the scion of another corporate rich family and the publisher of *The New York Times*. The most influential newspaper in the country soon printed a front-page story that detailed the opposition of the industry to this legislation. As a result of this campaign, Congress passed only relatively lenient safety and pollution standards for automobiles.

The corporate rich also exercise considerable influence at both the local and the national levels through the activities of the large philanthropic foundations endowed and controlled by their families. These foundations dispense hundreds of millions of dollars each year to an array of public institutions and charitable organizations. As trustees and officers of these foundations, the corporate rich often direct resources to those projects that are most consistent with their economic interests. At the local level, foundations can generate much goodwill for a corporation and its founding family by donating large sums of money to charitable organizations that serve the community. For example, the Lilly Endowment, which is a major stockholder in Eli Lilly and Company and which still has a descendant of the founder among its trustees, has contributed generously to hospitals and charities in the city of Indianapolis. Foundations also enable the corporate rich to exercise considerable influence at the level of national politics.

These families may use foundation money to support policy groups that espouse their own brand of political ideology. In recent years, for example, conservative institutions such as the American Enterprise Institute, the Hoover Institution, and the Heritage Foundation have received large donations from foundations, like the Richardson Foundation and the John M. Olin Foundation, which are controlled by families with extremely conservative social and political views. Many of the policy advisers to President Reagan once received grants, either directly or indirectly, from these same foundations.

Debates about the economic and political power of wealthy capitalist families typically revolve around the question of whether or not these families comprise a "ruling class." In its most extreme form, the ruling class thesis argues that there exists a cohesive group, comprising the corporate rich and their allies, which effectively controls government at every level. There can be little doubt that, as a result of their shared economic interests, the corporate rich constitute a distinct social class. The crucial issue is whether this capitalist class rules in the sense that it exercises a decisive influence in American politics. Some evidence for the ruling class thesis is found in the fact that members of the corporate rich often occupy important positions in American society. However, only a few of the scions of the wealthy capitalist families ever seek a career in either business or politics. Consequently, most of the positions of authority in government and business are filled by members of a managerial elite chosen primarily on the basis of their expertise and experience. Nevertheless, proponents of the ruling class thesis assert that this managerial elite is, in the final analysis, nothing more than an instrument of the capitalist class because these elites and the organizations they represent have the same economic interests as the members of the capitalist class. For example, both the capitalist class and the managerial elite within large business corporations advocate minimal regulation and taxation by the federal government. They also share a common interest in the maintenance of corporate profits by sustaining the growth of the entire economy.

In recent years, political sociologists have focused their attention on some of the mechanisms by which the capitalist class exercises its power in American society. One of these mechanisms involves the ability of the corporate rich to control the political agenda in such a way as to prevent issues contrary to their economic interests from gaining any degree of public legitimacy. They are able to exercise such a degree of ideological hegemony because much of the news available to the population at large is produced by large media corporations, many of which are controlled directly by wealthy capitalist families. For example, several of the most influential newspapers in the country, including *The New York Times, The Washington Post,* the *Los Angeles Times,* and the *Chicago Tribune,* are owned by corporations that are still subject to some degree of control by their founding families. These and other large media corporations also own and operate most of the radio and television stations in the major metropolitan markets. Needless to say, these newspapers and radio and television stations do not devote much attention to issues and policies that challenge the fundamental economic interests of the corporate rich and the large corporations that are the basis of their wealth and power. In short, Americans live in a democratic society in which the political agenda has been set by organizations subject to the control of a small but powerful minority. As G. William Domhoff puts it, "legally, the government is of all of us, but members of the upper class have the predominant, all-pervasive influence."

SURVIVAL STRATEGIES

It is not so much the existence of corporate rich families, as it is their persistence over several generations, that raises important issues of public policy. Some of the wealthiest and most powerful families in America today, such as the Rockefellers and the Fords, were also extremely wealthy and powerful over a half century ago. As families, their role in the economic and political affairs of the country has diminished only slightly in recent decades. Indeed, most corporate rich families have managed to keep their fortunes virtually intact for generations despite the existence of formally progressive gift and estate taxes. However, the emergence of each new generation has invariably transformed the kinship structure of these families. Most of the established corporate rich families are much larger than they were even a generation ago. Families that were once composed largely of siblings are now composed primarily of individuals who are no more than cousins to one another. As a result of the continual redistribution of wealth within these families, the members of each new generation have less wealth than the members of previous generations. Similarly, the family companies that provided the bases for these family fortunes have generally grown into large corporations. Although founding families have remained principal stockholders in many of these corporations, most of them have gradually relinquished the actual management of these corporations to others. In short, time has taken its toll on the corporate rich. Each successive generation of family members has been forced to adapt to a series of inexorable historical developments.

The historical evolution of corporate rich families can perhaps best be understood in terms of the theory of *social reproduction* advanced by the renowned French sociologist, Pierre Bourdieu. He was one of the first researchers to note that the members of wealthy capitalist families employ strategies of social reproduction in order to enhance and perpetuate their position in society. According to this perspective, the status of individuals depends on the degree to which they possess three distinct forms of capital. The first type of capital, of course, is *economic capital* in the form of property. Economic capital is essential because it determines the ability of an individual to accumulate other forms of capital. Another form of capital is *cultural capital,* which consists essentially of the patterns of speech, dress, and behavior typical of the upper class in a society. In his study of upper-class society in Philadelphia, for example, E. Digby Baltzell discovered differences in both accent and word usage, as well as differences in dress, which serve to distinguish members of the upper class from the rest of the population. A third form of capital is *social capital,* which consists of the network of social contacts accumulated by an individual. In other words, social capital comprises ties to friends and relatives. For example, another observer of upper-class society in Philadelphia, Nathaniel Burt, noted that each member of the upper class has a position within a web of social contacts in which "everybody is related and connected to each other."

The distinction between various forms of capital explains the basic relationship between the capitalist class and the upper class in America. By virtue of their position as major stockholders in large corporations, corporate rich families are at the heart of the capitalist class. In the words of Karl Marx, these families represent the *grande bourgeoisie,* the richest and most powerful segment of the capitalist class. As such, they are not to be confused with the members of the considerably less affluent and less powerful *petite bourgeoisie,* which consists of countless small businessmen and merchants. Despite their enormous wealth, corporate rich families are not always incorporated into the upper class. Although there is much overlap between the capitalist class and the upper class, membership in the upper class is a matter of social status rather than mere wealth. Indeed, many established upper-class families possess relatively modest fortunes. Conversely, some of the wealthiest individuals in the country are not welcome within certain upper-class social circles. Within the social upper class, with its emphasis on the prestige and status of a family, the size of a family fortune is less important than its age. As Nathaniel Burt observed of upper-class society in Philadelphia, "inherited money is better than made money." If the members of a corporate rich family aspire to high social status, they must be prepared to accumulate cultural and social capital commensurate with their economic capital. In short, nothing succeeds like money, manners, and connections.

In order to accumulate the appropriate cultural capital, members of wealthy capitalist families often send their children to expensive private schools, beginning with local day schools. Most large metropolitan areas have private day schools that are roughly the educational equivalent of public elementary schools. However, the most important stage in the accumulation of cultural capital is attendance at a preparatory school. Prep schools are the educational, if not the social, equivalents of high school. They provide their students with all of the

23

educational advantages that money can buy, including small classes and posh instructional and recreational facilities. Prep schools are generally boarding schools, where students live in dormitories during the school year, although most accept a few day students from the local area. There are literally scores of prep schools scattered across the country, but a few are better than most, at least in terms of their prestige. Only a few of the most established, like Phillips Exeter, St. Paul's, and Groton, are genuine citadels of upper-class culture. Although several private prep schools now accept girls as well as boys, many girls still attend exclusive finishing schools, such as Foxcroft, St. Timothy's, and Miss Porter's. Prep schools and finishing schools provide their students with cultural capital by inculcating them with the values and norms of the upper class. According to E. Digby Baltzell, "these private educational institutions serve the latent function of acculturating the members of the younger generation, particularly those not quite to the manor [sic] born, into an upper-class style of life."

Another step in the accumulation of cultural capital is attendance at a suitable elite private university. The private university provides many of the same functions of the exclusive prep school, except that it does so on a larger scale and at a more selective level. The most prestigious universities are still those associated with the revered Ivy League. However, even some Ivy League schools are better than others, at least with respect to their prestige value. In terms of attendance by the scions of upper-class families, the most exclusive universities are Princeton, Yale, and Harvard. Only slightly less prestigious are a number of private universities such as Pennsylvania, Stanford, Cornell, and Brown. Although elite private colleges and universities are generally known for their stringent admissions standards, exceptions are routinely made for the scions of wealthy families, particularly those from families that have contributed or might someday contribute generously to the school. Even within the confines of these exclusive schools, the scions of upper-class families are often segregated from their less affluent peers by their membership in even more exclusive "eating clubs" and secret societies. As E. Digby Baltzell notes, "an intricate system of exclusive clubs, like fraternities on less rarefied American campuses, serves to insulate the members of the upper class from the rest of the students at Harvard, Yale, and Princeton." At Harvard there are a handful of prestigious eating clubs such as the Porcellian, A.D., and Fly. Not to be outdone, Yale has its prestigious secret societies such as Scroll and Key, and Skull and Bones.

Private schools provide their students with more than just cultural capital. They also provide them with valuable social capital in terms of the friendships and acquaintances that students form with their classmates, many of whom are also the scions of wealthy and socially prominent families. In short, attendance at an exclusive prep school and acceptance into an exclusive club at a private elite university provide an individual with valuable social contacts that can be relied on in later life. Social capital can also be accumulated, of course, by marriage into another wealthy or socially prominent family. This matrimonial strategy for accumulating social capital accounts, at least in part, for the high degree of endogamy within the upper class. In the end, only those individuals who possess the appropriate cultural and social capital, as well as sufficient economic capital, are likely to gain acceptance into the most exclusive circles of upper-class society. Perhaps the final validation of membership within the American upper class occurs when the scions of these wealthy families gain acceptance to one or more exclusive metropolitan social clubs or country clubs. Of course, the most exclusive social clubs are those located in the oldest metropolitan cities, such as New York, Boston, and Philadelphia, but there are comparable clubs of roughly equal status at the local level in other major cities, such as Pittsburgh, Chicago, and San Francisco. In New York, the most exclusive clubs are The Links and the Knickerbocker; and the Philadelphia and Rittenhouse clubs enjoy comparable status in Philadelphia. In other cities, a country club such as the St. Louis Country Club, the Woodhill Country Club in Minneapolis, or the Everglades Club in Palm Beach may become the center of the local upper-class society.

In general, the strategies of social reproduction designed to accumulate the necessary cultural and social capital encompass more than one generation. As a rule, the process of elevating a nouveau

25

riche capitalist family to the status of an established "old wealth" family commonly requires a couple of generations. For example, John D. Rockefeller gave hundreds of millions of dollars to charity, but he was considered an undesirable arriviste by most members of the American upper class because the family bore the stigma of its association with the infamous Standard Oil Trust. In addition to his famous philanthropic activities, John D. Rockefeller took a number of steps to ensure that his children and grandchildren would not be denied access to the upper class. His son, John D. Rockefeller, Jr., attended several prep schools before being sent to Brown University. Moreover, in order to avoid any social stigma, the son was never connected officially with any of the Standard Oil companies, even though the family was the largest stockholder in those corporations. As a result of these steps, as well as his marriage into a socially and politically prominent family, John D. Rockefeller, Jr., became accepted as a provisional member of upper-class society. His children, of course, were even more secure in their acceptance within the upper class. The grandsons of the original founder of the family fortune attended exclusive preparatory schools and elite private universities. Several of them eventually gained acceptance to the most exclusive social clubs. In some cases, the integration of the Rockefeller grandchildren into the upper class was expedited by marriages with the scions of other socially prominent upper-class families.

HIDDEN FORTUNES

Very little is known with certainty about most corporate rich families or their fortunes. The reason, of course, is that the members of these families want all the advantages of being rich without any of the disadvantages of being famous. As a rule, the members of wealthy capitalist families refuse to divulge even the most rudimentary details of their wealth. Moreover, the secrecy that surrounds many of the largest fortunes often extends to the families that own these fortunes as well. In order to maintain their anonymity, the members of corporate rich families typically refuse to disclose even basic biographical information about themselves. Many of the richest Americans are not listed in *Who's Who in America,* simply because they refuse to provide the editors of this directory with any biographical information. One extreme example of this obsession with secrecy is the Mars family, which owns and manages Mars Inc., one of the largest food companies in the country. Although the company spends heavily to advertise its products, Forrest E. Mars and his three children, who control almost all of the stock in the company and are its only directors, have not granted any interviews to journalists in many years. There are not even any current pictures available of Forrest Mars or his children. Other corporate rich families that have demonstrated a similar obsession with secrecy include the Lillys, Pews, Klebergs, and Basses. As a result, some of the wealthiest families in America have achieved almost complete anonymity, despite the fact that they exercise enormous power as a result of their control over many major corporations and philanthropic foundations.

The first obstacle to any systematic analysis of the corporate rich is one of identification. In order to identify the wealthiest capitalist families in America, it is necessary to examine systematically those reports issued by large corporations that contain information about their directors and principal stockholders. All large corporations with more than five hundred stockholders are required to comply with the disclosure requirements imposed by the Securities and Exchange Commission. To begin with, these corporations are required to disclose the amount of stock owned or controlled by each of their directors. They are also required to disclose the identities of their principal *stockholders of record,* defined as any person or institution that owns or controls more than 5 percent of any class of corporation stock. This requirement to identify major stockholders of record does not necessarily reveal the identities of the beneficial owners of that stock. For example, proxy statements issued by The Gannett Company over the past several years have disclosed that about 10 percent of its common stock was held of record by Lincoln First Bank of Rochester but did not identify the beneficial owners of this stock. An analysis of earlier

27

reports issued by The Gannett Company reveals that most of this stock is held in a series of trusts for the benefit of the widow and two children of Frank E. Gannett, the founder of the company. The identities of the beneficial owners of this stock were revealed in 1969 only because Caroline W. Gannett, the widow of the founder, served as a director of the corporation at the time.

Furthermore, the stockholdings disclosed by individual directors are often misleading simply because they are required to reveal only the number of shares owned or controlled by them and the members of their immediate family. The regulations promulgated by the SEC define *immediate family members* as those individuals who share the same household with the director. Normally, this requirement includes only the stockholdings of the director, his or her spouse, and their minor children and excludes the stockholdings of their adult children. For example, William L. McKnight, as the chairman of Minnesota Mining and Manufacturing Company, disclosed that he and his wife owned 7.6 percent of the company stock as of 1972. He did not disclose the stockholdings of his adult daughter, Virginia McKnight Binger, because she maintained her own household. Only after his son-in-law was elected as a director the following year was it disclosed that Virginia McKnight Binger and her immediate family held another 1.6 percent of the stock in Minnesota Mining and Manufacturing Company. Moreover, these disclosure requirements do not usually pertain to collateral relatives such as siblings and cousins. For example, two of the current directors of Dow Chemical Company are grandchildren of its founder, Herbert H. Dow. According to a recent proxy statement issued by the company, these two directors own only about 1 percent of the stock in Dow Chemical. However, earlier disclosures by the company indicate that twelve other members of the Dow family, most of them either siblings or cousins of these two directors, probably own at least another 5 percent of Dow Chemical stock.

Information about the stockholdings of founding families is also revealed in the prospectuses that corporations must file whenever their principal stockholders sell part of their stock to the public through secondary offerings. The SEC requires that the sale of a large block of stock by the principal stockholders of a public company must be conducted through a registered secondary offering instead of through private sales. Furthermore, the prospectus issued in connection with such a secondary offering must disclose the stockholdings of any principal stockholders as well as the stockholdings of those individuals and institutions participating in the stock offering. For example, when The Upjohn Company, a large pharmaceutical firm, applied for a listing on the New York Stock Exchange in 1958, it filed a prospectus for a secondary offering of its stock held by several family members as well as a few minority stockholders. In addition to providing information on the financial condition of the company, this prospectus revealed that the descendants of the founder, William E. Upjohn, and his nephew owned over 71 percent of the Upjohn stock at the time. It also listed the exact stockholdings of thirty-four individuals, most of them members of the Upjohn family, as well as the stockholdings of twenty-two fiduciary agents for various family trusts, estates, and foundations. Subsequent secondary offerings of Upjohn stock in later years revealed the stockholdings of still other members of the Upjohn family. The reports issued by the company over the past several years indicate that, even after selling roughly $280 million in company stock, family members probably still own nearly 30 percent of Upjohn stock.

In the absence of secondary offerings, it is necessary to infer the proportion of company stock held by the founding family from the stockholdings disclosed by those family members who serve as directors of the family corporation. However, these inferences must be based on information about the exact position of these individuals within the family as a whole. Fortunately, it is usually possible to glean the requisite information from biographical articles, family histories, obituaries, and other genealogical records. For example, recent proxy statements issued by Cabot Corporation, a specialty chemical company, have indicated only that three of its directors owned roughly 5 percent of its stock. These reports failed to mention that these directors were all grandsons of Godfrey L. Cabot, the founder of the company. Indeed, a complete genealogy of the Cabot family shows that there are seventeen Cabot grandchildren. On the basis of this genealogical information, as well as information revealed in a secondary offering of Cabot stock by several descendants of the founder in 1968, it is possible to infer that the Cabots still own about 45 percent of Cabot stock. Similarly, proxy statements issued in recent years by Potlatch Corporation, a forest-products firm, have only indicated that four of its directors owned close to 7 percent of its stock. These reports did not indicate that these four directors were all either descendants or the spouses of descendants of Frederick Weyerhaeuser. Only after another company proposed to acquire Potlatch did the company disclose that members of the founding family still owned roughly 40 percent of its stock.

In many cases, it is possible to trace the stockholdings of a company founder and his descendants over several decades. Any such historical analysis of the specific stockholdings and aggregate wealth of a family must take into account the effects of any stock distributions, the cumulative dividend income paid on such stock, the proceeds received from stock sales, and the taxes paid by family members. For example, as the result of numerous stock splits, the $3 million in International Business Machines stock held by Thomas J. Watson and his wife in 1938 would now be worth over $1.4 billion. Moreover, the Watson family would have received over $480 million in dividends on their IBM stock during that same period. These initial estimates of the wealth of the family are only heuristic because the Watsons, like most corporate rich families, have diversified much of their fortune by selling some of their stock in the family corporation and reinvesting the proceeds in other stocks, bonds, and real estate. In point of fact, the extent of diversification by a founding family can often be deduced from secondary offerings by individual family members or inferred from private sales of company stock reported by those members of the founding family who serve as directors of the corporation. In addition, information obtained from corporate reports can be collated with information on charitable bequests and estate taxes obtained from probate records. In the case of the Watson family, for example,

Thomas J. Watson, his wife, both of his sons, and the husbands of both of his daughters served as directors of IBM at one point or another. Indeed, the available evidence indicates that the Watsons gradually sold over half of their IBM stock over the past three decades. As a result, the entire Watson family is actually worth only about $800 million today.

2

Three
Dynasties
in
Transition

Fame and fortune may be transitory phenomena, but for some families, especially the richest of the corporate rich, wealth and the fame that is often attached to it have a more enduring quality. For the past half century or more, three families have loomed larger than all the rest among the corporate rich in America. They are, of course, the Rockefellers, du Ponts, and Mellons. All three were, without any doubt, among the wealthiest families in America during the 1930s. Despite a precipitous decline in the stock market, which deflated their fortunes, they did not share the privations experienced by millions of families during the Great Depression. According to one official government estimate, the Rockefellers, du Ponts, and Mellons were worth altogether over $1.2 billion in 1937. This estimate was based solely on the value of their principal stockholdings in major corporations and did not include the value of other stocks, bonds, bank accounts, real estate, and personal property owned by family members. These families have been almost forgotten in recent years. Only those family members with political ambitions, like John D. Rockefeller IV and Pierre S. du Pont IV, have attracted much public attention. Although they have gained a measure of obscurity in recent years, neither the families nor their fortunes have disappeared. In point of fact, they are still extremely wealthy. Precise figures are not available, but these three families are almost certainly worth together over $15 billion today. In short, it appears that these three families have succeeded in gaining an almost permanent niche among the corporate rich in America.

It is precisely the continuity of families like the Rockefellers, du Ponts, and Mellons and their fortunes over successive generations that makes them the closest equivalents to dynasties that America is ever likely to produce. Like all dynasties before them, these families have possessed great wealth and have occasionally exercised the often enormous power inherent in such wealth. Because of their prominence in American society, each of these dynasties has been the subject of more than one history. Although these family histories provide intriguing glimpses into the lives of the corporate rich in America, they usually fail to provide much detailed information about their wealth and the manner in which that wealth has been transmitted from one generation to the next. In particular, these accounts only rarely mention any of the strategies that family members have adopted to avoid taxation and to retain a measure of control over family companies. Like all families, these three corporate rich families have become larger and less cohesive as kinship groups over time. Consequently, the wealth held by them has been redistributed among a larger number of family members with each passing generation. In order to cope with these common problems, corporate rich families have often resorted to very similar strategies for perpetuating their fortunes. It is only by observing the historical evolution of a number of wealthy capitalist families that it is possible to understand the problems they have faced and the efficacy of the various strategies they have employed to resolve them. These problems are nowhere more difficult and the adaptive strategies more elaborate than among the Rockefellers, du Ponts, and Mellons.

THE ROCKEFELLER FAMILY

No other family in recent American history has engendered as much public adulation or provoked as much public condemnation as the Rockefellers. The mere mention of their name conjures up images of power and wealth on a colossal scale. The man who accumulated this fortune was, of course, John D. Rockefeller. In the last years of his life, he was portrayed in the press as a wizened old miser who amused himself in the midst of the Great Depression by doling out dimes to children. In his heyday, however, J. D. Rockefeller was the epitome of the shrewd and utterly ruthless "robber baron." Although he is now celebrated as a great philanthropist for his endowment of the Rockefeller Foundation and a number of smaller charities, his most notable achievement was certainly the creation of the formidable Standard Oil Trust. He and his partners succeeded in creating the largest monopoly in the country by using a series of predatory business tactics to destroy their competitors. At the height of its power around 1900, the Standard Oil Trust controlled over 80 percent of the oil refining capacity in the United States. J. D. Rockefeller alone had a 24 percent interest in this trust. After several years of litigation, the Supreme Court finally called for the dissolution of the Standard Oil Trust in 1911. As a result of this decree, the participants in the trust received their proportionate share of the stock in the various Standard Oil Companies held by the trust. Consequently, J. D. Rockefeller soon became the largest single stockholder in a half dozen of the largest oil companies in America. By 1913, his stockholdings in these oil companies were reportedly worth $900 million.

For all this, John D. Rockefeller was surprisingly poor when he died in 1937. The man who had once been proclaimed the richest man in the world left an estate of only $26 million. Of this, $16 million went to state and federal taxes. The man who had built the mighty Standard Oil Trust died with only one share of common stock in any Standard Oil company, a certificate for the first share issued by the predecessor Chevron Corporation. In order to account for this state of comparative poverty, a family spokesman explained that J. D. Rockefeller had given $530 million to charity during his lifetime. The bulk of this went, of course, to family philanthropies such as the Rockefeller Foundation and the Rockefeller Institute. If there was any public concern about the financial security of the Rockefeller family, it was laid to rest three years later with the publication of a report issued by the Temporary National Economic Committee appointed by President Roosevelt. In this study of the concentration of stock ownership among the two hundred largest nonfinancial corporations in America, it was disclosed that the Rockefellers held stock worth $274 million in six oil companies, including the predecessors of such giant corporations as Exxon, Mobil, Amoco, and Chevron. Moreover, this was only a partial estimate of their wealth, as it did not include any of their stockholdings in other companies or their holdings of bonds and real estate.

This report also disclosed that the members of the Rockefeller family did not share equally in the Rockefeller fortune. Of the $274 million in oil stocks held by the descendants of John D. Rockefeller, almost $250 million was held by his only son, John D. Rockefeller, Jr., and his children. The three daughters of J. D. Rockefeller, Sr., got much less. Two of his daughters, Alta Rockefeller Prentice and Edith Rockefeller McCormick, were the income beneficiaries of trusts that held oil stocks worth a relatively modest $24 million in 1939. The children of his third daughter, Bessie Rockefeller Strong, who had died several years earlier, received $9 million in cash and bonds from his estate in the form of a trust. Perhaps because he wished to keep the bulk of his fortune in one piece, J. D. Rockefeller, Sr., decided to give almost all of his enormous wealth to his son. He apparently felt that his son was the only one adequately prepared for the task of managing such a fortune. After all, J. D. Rockefeller, Jr., had worked for his father ever since his graduation from Brown University. Beginning in 1917, J. D. Rockefeller, Sr., began transferring large amounts of stock and cash to his son. Within five years, he had given him securities then worth roughly $400 million. Because there were no federal gift taxes at the time, the Rockefeller fortune was transferred from one generation to the next virtually intact. Although he soon became the largest stockholder in the various Standard Oil companies, J. D. Rockefeller, Jr., never served as an officer or director of any of them. He was content to let others run the companies for him while he devoted himself to managing the massive Rockefeller fortune and overseeing the various Rockefeller philanthropies.

One of the most important decisions that J. D. Rockefeller, Jr., made as the head of the family was to diversify the Rockefeller fortune. This decision may have been motivated in large part by a desire to remove from the family the stigma associated with the Standard Oil Trust. Although the Rockefellers attempted to dissociate themselves from the former Standard Oil companies, they remained major stockholders in them for many years following the dissolution decree. The full extent of their control over these companies was revealed in 1928, after the president of Amoco was charged with perjury by a Senate committee. When he refused to resign, J. D. Rockefeller, Jr., initiated a proxy contest in order to assert his control over the company. Even though he won the contest easily, the bitter struggle for control brought the family more unwanted publicity. In the years following the death of his father, J. D. Rockefeller, Jr., quietly began selling much of his stock in the Standard Oil companies and reinvesting the proceeds in a diversified portfolio of stocks and bonds. He also directed some of the Rockefeller fortune into real estate. In the midst of the Great Depression, he invested $125 million in the construction of Rockefeller Center, a giant complex of fourteen office buildings constructed on three city blocks in the middle of Manhattan. Although he borrowed $45 million to finance part of the construction, J. D. Rockefeller, Jr., was able to raise the rest of the funds simply by selling some of his oil stocks.

John D. Rockefeller, Jr., and his wife raised their six children in an atmosphere of almost puritanical morality. Despite the fact that they were constantly surrounded by a small army of servants, governesses, and bodyguards, J. D. Rockefeller, Jr., insisted that his children learn a sense of responsibility, particularly in matters of money. Consequently, he required all of them to keep an account book of their weekly allowance and expenditures, just as he had done as a child. He also kept their allowances low so that they were forced to perform menial chores in order to earn extra money. Despite this enforced frugality, the children were inevitably raised in an environment of quiet but uncompromising luxury. Home was a huge nine-story town house in New York City, not far from Central Park, but weekends were often spent at Pocantico, the lavish 3,500-acre estate in the Hudson River Valley built by their grandfather. The estate had its own golf course, stables, riding paths, swimming pool, and squash court. Part of every summer was spent at the large mansion their father built at Seal Harbor, Maine. There they often played with children from other prominent and wealthy families, including the children of Edsel Ford. All of the children were sent to exclusive private schools, and the five boys eventually attended elite private universities. Even after they reached maturity and went their own ways, the children of J. D. Rockefeller, Jr., maintained a degree of family unity. Four of his sons eventually built separate homes on the sprawling grounds of the Pocantico estate, where they took turns visiting their father for Sunday dinner.

While the family was gaining national recognition for its charitable contributions, J. D. Rockefeller, Jr., was busy safeguarding the rest of the family fortune from the threat of gift and estate taxes. He was particularly quick to react to the progressive "wealth tax" proposed by President Roosevelt in 1934. In December of that year, only a few days before the imposition of the new gift taxes, he established massive trusts, each worth approximately $20 million, for his wife and six children. These trusts, which consisted initially of stock in the various Standard Oil companies, were typical generation-skipping trusts. His wife and children were to receive the income from these trusts during their lifetimes, but the assets held by these trusts were preserved for his grandchildren. According to the terms of the trusts, they are not to be dissolved until the death of the last of the four grandchildren of J. D. Rockefeller, Jr., who were alive at the time of their creation in 1934. Only then will the trusts be dissolved and their assets distributed, without any gift or estate taxes, among the grandchildren of J. D. Rockefeller, Jr., or their survivors. In 1952, J. D. Rockefeller, Jr., created another series of smaller trusts to provide his grandchildren with independent incomes while their parents were still alive. The resulting legal labyrinth of overlapping trusts was a masterpiece of tax avoidance. When he died in 1960, J. D. Rockefeller, Jr., left an estate of $160 million, which was split between the Rockefeller Brothers Fund and his second wife. In this way, there were virtually no estate taxes levied against his estate.

Of the six children of J. D. Rockefeller, Jr., the best known was Nelson Rockefeller. He was, without any doubt, the most sociable and energetic of the five brothers. Despite the fact that he suffered from a reading disorder, he graduated with honors from Dartmouth. Soon after his graduation, Nelson went to work for his father at the newly constructed Rockefeller Center. He later served as assistant secretary of state under President Roosevelt and under secretary of Health, Education and Welfare under President Eisenhower. In 1958, Nelson was elected to the first of his four terms as governor of New York. He never hesitated to use family money to finance his political campaigns. Between 1958 and 1970, Nelson contributed just over $1 million to his own gubernatorial and presidential campaigns. In a convincing display of family solidarity, his parents, brothers, and sister contributed another $14 million to these same campaigns. When he was later asked about these family contributions to his various campaigns, he lamented that "it is very difficult for a Rockefeller to raise any money for a campaign." Finally in 1974, after four unsuccessful attempts to become the presidential nominee of the Republican party, Nelson Rockefeller was nominated vice president of the United States by President Ford, who had been nominated to the same office by President Nixon.

Only two of the brothers demonstrated any interest in business. One of them, of course, was David Rockefeller, the youngest of the five brothers. After his graduation from Harvard, David spent two years at the London School of Economics before going on to the University of Chicago for his Ph.D. in economics. He later joined Chase Manhattan Bank as an assistant manager, but was soon promoted to the rank of vice president. Within nine short years, he was vice chairman, a post he held for five years, until he was appointed president of the bank. His rapid advancement was assisted, no doubt, by the fact that the Rockefeller family was a major stockholder in the bank. As chairman of one of the largest banks in the world, David Rockefeller became an important figure in the arena of international finance. In recent years, David has augmented his fortune by investing in several large real estate developments, including L'Enfant Plaza in Washington, D.C., and Embarcadero Center in San Francisco. The other brother to enter business was Laurence Rockefeller. Within a few years of his graduation from Princeton, Laurence bought a seat on the New York Stock Exchange and declared himself a "venture capitalist." He was fascinated by aviation and became one of the original investors in both Eastern Airlines and the forerunner of McDonnell Douglas. By 1975, he had made a total of $48 million from his investments in seventy new companies. Laurence also managed to combine his abilities as a businessman with his interest in conservation. The result was Rockresorts, a chain of exclusive resort hotels with developments bordering on national parks in such locales as Hawaii and the Virgin Islands.

The eldest brother, John D. Rockefeller III, avoided both business and politics. After his graduation from Princeton, he became involved with several family philanthropies, including the Rockefeller Foundation. Over the years, he developed a genuine interest in a series of charitable causes. He was instrumental in the formation of several civic organizations, including the Population Council, but his most ambitious project was the construction of Lincoln Center. As its first chairman, J. D. Rockefeller III gave $10 million of his own money to the project and convinced other family members and foundations to donate another $34 million. The only rebel among the brothers was Winthrop Rockefeller. He dropped out of Yale after his freshman year and went to work as a roughneck in the Texas oil fields. In the years that followed, Winthrop earned a reputation as a playboy. He also developed a serious drinking problem. His estrangement from the rest of the family was further exacerbated after he married and quickly divorced a young actress. To establish his own identity, he moved to Arkansas, where he built Winrock Farms, a 31,400-acre farming and ranching operation. Thirteen years later he became the first Republican governor of the state since Reconstruction. Almost forgotten among the five famous Rockefeller brothers was their older sister, Abby Rockefeller Mauze. She led an extremely private life interrupted only by the publicity of two divorces. Nevertheless, she participated in most of the financial and philanthropic ventures initiated by her brothers.

It is ironic that, as a direct result of their political power, the financial affairs of the Rockefellers are more public than those of any other corporate rich family in America. In his confirmation hearings for vice president, Nelson Rockefeller and his financial advisers were forced to provide the House Judiciary Committee with a detailed, albeit conservative, accounting of the Rockefeller fortune. To begin with, Nelson disclosed that he and his wife had a net worth of $62 million, about half of that in art. In addition, Nelson was the sole income beneficiary of two trusts worth a total of $116 million, even in the depressed stock market of 1974. Moreover, his wife and six children held securities and were the beneficiaries of still other trusts holding securities worth another $39 million. In all, Nelson and his branch of the Rockefeller family were worth at least $218 million. Later in the confirmation hearings, a representative of Rockefeller Family and Associates, the family investment office, provided the committee with a summary of the stockholdings of the entire Rockefeller family. The descendants of John D. Rockefeller, Jr., and their spouses, eighty-four individuals in all, were worth slightly more than $1 billion in securities. This figure excluded real estate and personal property, including jewelry and art, worth at least another $200 million. Most of this fortune, $738 million to be exact, was held by trusts created by John D. Rockefeller, Jr.

By 1980, four of the grandchildren of John D. Rockefeller had passed away. Winthrop Rockefeller died of cancer in 1973. In his will, he left most of his estate, appraised at $81 million, to a charitable trust. This trust later sold Winrock Farms to Winthrop Paul Rockefeller, his son by his first marriage. Abby Rockefeller Mauze too died of cancer three years later. She left the bulk of her estate to a charitable lead trust, which would pay all of its income to charity for thirty-five years, after which the principal would be distributed free of taxes to her grandchildren. The eldest brother, John D. Rockefeller III, died in an automobile accident on the family estate at Pocantico in 1978. His will stipulated that part of his art collection, worth about $25 million, be donated to two museums. The rest of his approximately $100 million estate, after estate taxes, went to a trust for his wife and children. Later that same year, Nelson Rockefeller died of a heart attack under somewhat mysterious circumstances while in the company of a young female assistant. His personal estate was valued at approximately $66 million. Most of his art collection went to museums, and his share of the Pocantico estate was given to the federal government as part of a park. The rest of his estate, after taxes, went to a trust for the benefit of his second wife and their two sons. Upon the death of their parents, of course, the children of the two Rockefeller brothers and their sister immediately became the income beneficiaries of the massive trusts created by John D. Rockefeller, Jr., in 1934.

As the children of J. D. Rockefeller, Jr., fade from the scene, they are being replaced, on a somewhat less obtrusive scale, by their children. It is the cousins, the twenty-two surviving grandchildren of J. D. Rockefeller, Jr., who will eventually inherit the bulk of the family fortune. The best known of all the cousins is, not surprisingly, a namesake of the founder of Standard Oil. John D. Rockefeller IV, or Jay as he prefers to be called, became interested in politics while serving on the staff of the Peace Corps soon after his graduation from Harvard. After a brief stint in the State Department, he decided to enter politics at the state level, as his uncles Nelson and Winthrop had done so successfully. He also decided to go a state where his wealth might be appreciated rather than scorned. Jay Rockefeller moved to West Virginia in 1964 and, two years later, was elected to the state legislature. In 1976, he was elected governor. After two terms as governor, he was elected to the Senate in 1984. Like his uncles, he did not hesitate to use his wealth to further his political career. In all, Jay spent over $20 million of his own money on his last two campaigns alone. By and large, the cousins are a diverse group. Several of them are actively involved in civic and philanthropic organizations. Although none of the rest has pursued a career in politics, some of the cousins have contributed generously to various political causes. Only one of them, Rodman Rockefeller, the eldest son of Nelson Rockefeller, works for any of the family corporations.

Although the Rockefeller family may never again have the

wealth or the unity of purpose that it once possessed, it will remain a potent political and economic force for generations to come. The Rockefeller cousins no longer see each other frequently, but many of them meet twice each year at reunions to discuss family matters. The matter of common interest to all of them, of course, is Rockefeller Family and Associates, the family office that administers most of their wealth. In the meantime, the Rockefeller fortune continues to grow, slowly but surely. The investments of the family have increased greatly in value since the nomination hearings for Nelson Rockefeller in 1974. The market value of their stockholdings in major corporations has, in all likelihood, risen from $653 million in 1974 to over $1.7 billion. These totals exclude the family stockholdings in Rockefeller Group Inc., the holding company for their real estate and broadcasting properties. In a complex financial transaction designed to raise additional cash, Rockefeller Group recently sold a 71.5 percent interest in twelve buildings in Rockefeller Center to the public for $1.3 billion. Rockefeller Group still retains a full or half interest in four other buildings in Rockefeller Center as well as Outlet Company, which owns and operates seven television and four radio stations, and Cushman and Wakefield Inc., a real estate management firm. The total net worth of Rockefeller Group is at least $2.5 billion. In addition, individual family members probably own at least another $500 million in municipal bonds, real estate, and art. In all, the Rockefellers are now worth close to $5 billion.

THE DU PONT FAMILY

Of all the corporate rich families in America, few are richer and none is older than the du Ponts. The founder of this prolific and sometimes profligate clan was Pierre S. du Pont de Nemours, a prosperous French businessman who migrated to this country in 1800. At last count in 1977, there were about sixteen hundred du Ponts. Although they share a common ancestry, they do not all share in the du Pont fortune. Most du Ponts are at least somewhat affluent, but only a couple of hundred of them are truly rich. Indeed, most du Ponts no longer have any affiliation with the giant chemical company of the same name. For the first hundred years of its existence, E.I. du Pont de Nemours and Company was simply a family partnership owned by those family members who were actively engaged in the business of making munitions and explosives. The foundation for the present concentration of wealth within a few branches of the du Pont family was laid in 1902 when three young cousins, Alfred I. du Pont, T. Coleman du Pont, and Pierre S. du Pont II, bought majority control of the company from four older cousins. In all, they acquired 72 percent of the Du Pont stock for $12 million in promissory notes. The du Pont fortune was consolidated even further thirteen years later when Pierre organized a holding company, later to be known as Christiana Securities, to buy out Coleman, the largest stockholder in the company, for $14 million in cash and notes. This stock purchase, which gave Pierre effective control of Du Pont, was later challenged in the courts by his cousin Alfred. The ensuing legal battle, which Pierre eventually won, created a family feud that lasted for decades.

As a result of these two transactions, the bulk of the du Pont fortune is held by the descendants of the brothers and sisters of Pierre S. du Pont II, a great-great-grandson and namesake of the first du Pont to migrate to America. More than any other person, it was Pierre who oversaw the growth of Du Pont into a giant corporation. He also managed to accumulate much of the current du Pont fortune. After his father was killed in an explosion at a Du Pont plant, the young Pierre apparently decided that it was his responsibility, as the oldest son, to ensure the welfare of his eight siblings. As he had no children of his own, Pierre proceeded to amass a fortune of staggering proportions, only to distribute most of it to his brothers and sisters and their children. For example, when Pierre first organized Christiana Securities in 1915 to buy out Coleman du Pont, he brought in two brothers and the husbands of two sisters as major stockholders. Eight years later, Pierre organized another holding company, Delaware Realty and Investment, to which he transferred the bulk of his holdings in both Du Pont and Christiana Securities. He then distributed the stock in this holding company equally among his brothers and sisters, as well as the children of two deceased brothers, in exchange for an annuity of $900,000 a year for him and his wife. By 1938, the stock in Delaware Realty and Investment alone was worth $145 million in Du Pont stock. In addition, Pierre and his brothers and sisters owned other stock in Christiana Securities worth another $141 million in Du Pont stock.

The Du Pont Company grew and prospered under the leadership of Pierre du Pont. As John Gates, a historian of the du Pont family, observed, "he was, to be sure, the right man at the right time in the right place, and he was surrounded by other right men in the right places, but Pierre made it all happen." As a result of soaring munitions sales during World War I, Du Pont Company profits increased almost sevenfold between 1914 and 1918. Even before the war was over, Pierre used some of these profits to diversify the company into the production of paints, dyes, and chemicals. In search of another investment opportunity for the remainder of the wartime profits, he also engineered the purchase by Du Pont of a 23 percent stake in General Motors in early 1918. For the next several years, Pierre was to exercise enormous economic power as the president of both Du Pont and General Motors. By the time he died in 1954, his brothers and sisters had produced thirty-four children, many of whom had children of their own. It was a large family, to be sure, but he had provided it with a large fortune. The stock in Delaware Realty and Investment was then worth $858 million in Du Pont stock. His brothers and sisters and their children also held stock in Christiana Securities worth another $629 million in Du Pont stock. In all, this branch of the du Pont family alone owned, either directly or indirectly through holding companies, over 26 percent of the stock in Du Pont in 1954. Moreover, the family was actively involved in the management of the company, with eight family members serving as either officers or directors.

Although Pierre du Pont was an extremely astute businessman, he was aided and abetted throughout by other family members. When he stepped down as president of Du Pont in 1919, Pierre was succeeded by his younger brother, Irénée du Pont. Following family tradition, Irénée graduated from M.I.T. with a degree in chemical engineering before joining Du Pont. Although he did not possess Pierre's genius for organization or finance, Irénée proved to be an effective chief executive officer with an undeniable talent for making money. For example, it was Irénée who initiated the du Pont family investment in the U.S. Rubber Company. In 1927, he organized a syndicate of family members, which purchased almost 30 percent of the stock in U.S. Rubber. Not surprisingly, the company soon became the largest supplier of tires to General Motors. As a result of his early participation in Christiana Securities, Irénée became extremely wealthy. He bought a sixty-foot yacht and built Granogue, a lavish 500-acre estate outside Wilmington, Delaware. However, his most extravagant purchase was Xanadu, a $2 million oceanfront estate in Cuba, where he raised pet iguanas. When he died in 1966 at the age of eighty-four, Irénée left an estate of approximately $200 million. Of this, $90 million went to taxes, $32 million went to a family foundation, and $64 million went into trusts for his children. However, he had already given his children the bulk of his stock in Christiana Securities. In all, Irénée du Pont was survived by eight children and thirty-seven grandchildren. Altogether, they are worth approximately $800 million.

When Irénée du Pont resigned as president of Du Pont in 1928, he was succeeded by Lammot du Pont, the youngest of the three brothers. In a family in which eccentrics were common, Lammot was almost in a class by himself. He was the first and probably the last president of Du Pont to ride to work on a bicycle. At home, he often chopped firewood or sharpened knives for recreation. His main contribution to the company was the commitment of substantial funds for research and development. This effort eventually led to several profitable discoveries by Du Pont chemists, including the invention of nylon in 1938. Along the way, Lammot accumulated a fortune that finally eclipsed the considerable fortune amassed by his brother Irénée. Although he did not flaunt his wealth on the same scale as Irénée, he did permit himself the minor extravagance of a ninety-six-foot yacht. Lammot was also a family man of sorts. In all, he had ten children by his four wives. Because of the size of his family, he took great care to minimize the taxes on his estate. When he died in 1954, he left an estate of only $75 million. In his will, he took full advantage of the tax laws and left half of his estate, tax free, in trust for his wife. He also stipulated that the remainder of his estate, after taxes, was to go into a series of trusts for his children. Of course, Lammot had already placed the vast bulk of his fortune in trusts for his descendants. His ten children and twenty-seven grandchildren are worth, in the aggregate, roughly $1 billion.

Perhaps the richest of all the nephews and nieces of Pierre du Pont was Lammot Copeland. He owed this distinction to the fact that he was the only child of Louisa du Pont Copeland, the older sister of Pierre du Pont. His father, Charles Copeland, was an investment banker who later served as the secretary of Du Pont. Lammot joined the company after graduation from Harvard, and, because he was talented and because he was a du Pont, he rose quickly through the managerial ranks at Du Pont to become president and later chairman. He resigned as chairman in 1972, not long after it was disclosed that his son, Lammot Copeland, Jr., had filed for bankruptcy, listing liabilities of almost $60 million against assets of only $26 million. The son had become involved in a number of questionable business ventures and had incurred massive debts, largely by guaranteeing loans to several unprofitable companies. Lammot Copeland, Sr., lent his son over $8 million in order to bail him out but to no avail. In the end, they decided that bankruptcy was the quickest and the cheapest way out of an impossible situation. Although both father and son lost several million dollars in the settlement, neither of them was severely affected by the bankruptcy. Under Delaware law, the creditors were unable to invade the trust established for Lammot Copeland, Jr., which held approximately $14 million in Du Pont and Christiana Securities stock. Lammot Copeland, Sr., who died in 1983, had three children who are probably worth close to $400 million.

Most of the descendants of the other brothers and sisters of Pierre S. du Pont are also quite wealthy. Pierre's youngest sister, Margaretta du Pont, married Robert R. M. Carpenter, who developed a close relationship with the childless Pierre. He eventually served as a vice president and director of Du Pont. One of their four children, Robert

R. M. Carpenter, Jr., gained national attention in 1943 when he purchased the Philadelphia Phillies baseball team for about half a million dollars. His son, Robert R. M. Carpenter III, gained even more attention when he sold the team for more than $30 million in 1981. The four children of Ruly and Margaretta du Pont Carpenter eventually had eleven children of their own. Overall, the Carpenter branch of the du Pont family is worth at least $500 million. Although the descendants of the other two sisters and two brothers of Pierre du Pont are not quite so rich as their cousins, most of them are nevertheless very wealthy. Neither of Pierre's two other sisters, Mary and Isabella du Pont, or their respective husbands, William W. Laird and H. Rodney Sharp, was ever a major stockholder in Christiana Securities, other than through Delaware Realty and Investment. Neither was any of the children of his two older brothers, William and Henry du Pont, both of whom died before the creation of Christiana Securities. Consequently, the children of Mary du Pont Laird, Isabella du Pont Sharp, Henry B. du Pont, and William K. du Pont owe the bulk of their wealth to the shares of Delaware Realty and Investment, which they or their parents received from Pierre S. du Pont in 1925. These four brothers and sisters had twelve children and twenty-seven grandchildren, who are worth, in the aggregate, about $1.2 billion.

Despite their great wealth, the du Ponts have established very few charitable foundations comparable to those created by other corporate rich families. This limited philanthropy may be due to the fact that the du Pont family was much larger than most of these families almost from the outset. The greatest philanthropic gesture by any member of the family was the creation of Alfred I. du Pont. One of the most dynamic and colorful members of the entire du Pont clan, it was Alfred who encouraged Pierre and Coleman to join him in purchasing majority control of Du Pont in 1902. However, after Pierre gained control of the company by buying out Coleman, Alfred severed his ties with many members of the du Pont family. He resigned as a director of Du Pont and moved to Florida, where he began amassing large tracts of undeveloped land. When he died in 1935, Alfred left most of his estate to the Alfred I. du Pont Testamentary Trust. Almost all of the income from this trust went to his wife until her death in 1970.

The primary income beneficiary of the trust is now a hospital for crippled children located on the grounds of his Nemours estate in Delaware. In addition to large blocks of General Motors and Du Pont, the main asset held by the trust is a 74 percent interest in St. Joe Paper Company, which, in turn, controls Florida East Coast Railway and owns over a million acres of timberland in Florida and Georgia. In 1979, the trust conservatively valued its assets at $1.1 billion. The only other major du Pont foundation is the Longwood Foundation, which was created out of the residual estate of Pierre S. du Pont. This foundation, with assets of $112 million in 1983, is devoted to the maintenance of his Longwood estate outside Wilmington, Delaware, as a public garden.

As a group, the heirs of Pierre S. du Pont are the richest members of the du Pont clan, but they are by no means the only ones to share in the du Pont fortune. The other really wealthy branch of the clan consists of the descendants of William du Pont, a first cousin once removed of Pierre. William inherited a relatively small block of Du Pont stock from his father, Henry du Pont, one of the four du Pont cousins who retained a minority interest in the company after selling out to Pierre, Alfred, and Coleman du Pont in 1902. Although William resigned as a director after Pierre gained control of the company, he kept his Du Pont stock. With his cousin, Alfred I. du Pont, he also founded the Delaware Trust Company to compete with the Wilmington Trust Company controlled by Pierre and his relatives. When William died in 1928, his will stipulated that his entire estate be placed in trust for his two children. By 1937, this trust held over $32 million in Du Pont stock alone. His son, William du Pont, Jr., established a national reputation as a horse breeder while his daughter, Marion du Pont, gained some notoriety by marrying and later divorcing the actor Randolph Scott. When William du Pont, Jr., passed away in 1966, his five children each received over $50 million from the trust created by their grandfather. Because their aunt, Marion du Pont Scott, never had children, they also received her share of the trust, probably worth another $60 million apiece when she died in 1983. In all, the William du Pont branch of the family is probably worth at least $600 million.

By and large, the younger du Ponts, the grandnephews and

grandnieces of Pierre du Pont, have led private lives. Certainly the best known grandnephew is Pierre S. du Pont IV, the former governor of Delaware, who prefers to be called "Pete" by his constituents. His father, Pierre S. du Pont III, once served as a vice president and director of Du Pont. Pete too joined the company soon after graduation from Harvard Law School but quit after seven years. He then decided to enter politics by running unopposed for a seat in the Delaware legislature. It was something of a feat, inasmuch as the du Pont name was almost as great a liability in Delaware electoral politics as the du Pont fortune was an asset. With the help of a professional campaign-management firm, Pete was elected to three terms as the sole member of the House of Representatives from Delaware before being elected governor of the state in 1976. When he first entered the House of Representatives in 1971, he released a list of his stockholdings; it was a relatively modest portfolio worth less than $2.2 million. He did not reveal, however, the value of trusts for his benefit, which probably account for the bulk of his personal wealth. Only one of the heirs of Pierre S. du Pont still works for Du Pont. H. Rodney Sharp III, who is a grandson of Isabella du Pont Sharp, is a manager in charge of the computer operations division for the company. However, unlike most lower-echelon managers, he is also a director of Du Pont. By and large, the other descendants of Pierre S. du Pont have pursued independent activities, ranging from coin collecting to horse breeding. All of them are able to subsist quite nicely on the income from their trust funds and investments.

Despite the fact that it grew to become one of the largest corporations in America, Du Pont has remained, until relatively recently at least, a family enterprise. The heirs of Pierre du Pont have not only held a controlling block of Du Pont stock, they have also been active in the management and direction of the company for several decades. Several of Pierre's nephews and even a few of his grandnephews have served as officers and directors of Du Pont. In recent years, however, the du Ponts have been content to let others manage the company for them. Lammot Copeland was the last member of the du Pont family to serve as president. The gradual withdrawal of the family from active control of the company was accelerated by the dissolution of the pyramid of holding companies created by Pierre to consolidate the stockholdings of the family. Delaware Realty and Investment was merged into Christiana Securities in 1961 through an exchange of stock. Sixteen years later, Christiana Securities itself was merged into Du Pont in exchange for Du Pont stock. In explaining the decision to merge Christiana into Du Pont, Irénée du Pont declared cryptically that "the original reasons for establishing Christiana have run their course and no longer prevail." In point of fact, these mergers were motivated primarily by a desire to reduce the income taxes paid indirectly by family members through these holding companies. As the result of the merger between Du Pont and Conoco in 1981, the heirs of Pierre S. du Pont currently control only about 12 percent of the stock in Du Pont. However, three members of the du Pont family still serve as directors of the company.

The du Pont family, which eventually comprised 34 first cousins and at least 107 second cousins, is the largest of the corporate rich families in America. As a result, the current du Pont fortune is distributed among a large number of individuals who are only distantly related to one another. The only entity that represents the interests of the entire family is Wilmington Trust Company, which is controlled by the du Ponts and which provides them with various financial and fiduciary services. Nevertheless, the family as a whole has slowly divided itself into a number of separate branches. The only cohesive kinship groups are now those involving the descendants of each of the eight brothers and sister of Pierre du Pont, most of whom are either siblings or first cousins to one another. Even today, the mainstay of the du Pont fortune is the Du Pont stock distributed to family members and their trusts after the dissolution of Christiana Securities in 1977. This stock has a current market value of roughly $1.8 billion. Another major asset is the General Motors stock distributed to family members after the divestiture by Du Pont of its General Motors stockholdings beginning in 1962. The market value of this stock is now about $800 million. Moreover, these major stockholdings represent only part of the du Pont fortune. For example, the heirs of Pierre du Pont received over $1.5 billion in dividends from Christiana Securities alone in the years between 1925 and 1977. Although some of this income went to income taxes and to maintaining a comfortable standard of living, much of it was undoubtedly reinvested in stocks, bonds, and commercial real estate. As a result, the heirs of Pierre S. du Pont alone are now worth at least $4 billion.

THE MELLON FAMILY

Of the three big dynasties, certainly the least well known is the Mellon family. This relative obscurity is somewhat paradoxical in light of the fact that the Mellons are, without much doubt, the wealthiest of these three families. Unlike most other corporate rich families, whose fortunes stem primarily from their investments in a single company or industry, the Mellons have been major stockholders in a number of otherwise unrelated firms. They were once major stockholders in Gulf Oil Company, and their principal investments still include large stockholdings in such major corporations as Aluminum Company of America, Mellon National Bank, Koppers, General Reinsurance, and First Boston Corporation. This diversified fortune was compiled by two brothers, Andrew W. and Richard B. Mellon. In the words of David E. Koskoff, a family biographer, they made "one of the most unlikely and one of the most successful partnerships in history." They were as unlike in appearance as they were in temperament: A. W. Mellon, the older of the two, was thin and extremely shy, whereas his brother, R. B. Mellon, was stocky and gregarious. According to this same biographer, "about the only thing the two seemed to have in common was their incessant acquisitiveness." They may have inherited this trait from their father, Thomas Mellon, a Pittsburgh banker whose firm, T. Mellon and Sons, would later form the nucleus of the present-day Mellon National Bank. Using the modest fortune amassed by their father as a foundation, A. W. and R. B. Mellon went on to accumulate several fortunes of their own.

The Mellon brothers started out as bankers, but they soon became venture capitalists as well. Whenever an especially promising company came to T. Mellon and Sons for a loan to finance expansion, the Mellons would also buy a large block of stock in the company. By virtue of their position as both major creditors and principal stockholders, they were usually able to exercise control over these companies. In this manner, the Mellon brothers amassed their first real fortune in a new industry: aluminum. In 1889, Andrew W. Mellon was approached by a group of investors representing the Pittsburgh Reduction Company, a firm formed to exploit a newly developed process for refining aluminum. T. Mellon and Sons extended the firm, later to be renamed the Aluminum Company of America, a line of credit, and A. W. Mellon purchased some stock in the company. The Mellons gradually increased their stockholdings in the growing firm from about 12 percent in 1894 to over 26 percent by 1917. Although both Mellons served as directors of the company, they left the actual management of the firm to others. As the company increased its control over the burgeoning aluminum industry, the Mellons increased their control over the company. By 1937, the Mellon family controlled 35 percent of the common stock of Aluminum Company of America, as well as 24 percent of its preferred stock, worth a total of $72 million in the depressed stock market of the period.

The accumulation of a fortune in aluminum was but a prelude to the accumulation of an even larger fortune in oil. In 1901, James M. Guffey, a veteran oilman, came to T. Mellon and Sons for a loan to continue his drilling operations near Beaumont, Texas. Later that same year, using money lent by the Mellons, Guffey and his associates brought in the first major oil well in the state of Texas. However, they soon needed more money to develop the field and to construct a pipeline for transporting the oil. In order to raise the necessary capital, the Mellons organized the J.M. Guffey Petroleum Company, which acquired the interests of Guffey and his associates in the new field. Andrew W. and Richard B. Mellon also bought 13 percent of its stock. In the years that followed, they helped the company finance the construction of an oil refinery on the Gulf Coast and new exploration activities in Oklahoma. However, Guffey soon demonstrated his limitations as a manager, and the Mellon brothers were forced to send their cousin, William L. Mellon, to Texas in order to restore the company to profitability. During this period, Guffey borrowed heavily from the Mellons, pledging his stock in the company as collateral. In 1907, the Mellons reorganized the J.M. Guffey Petroleum Company and its affiliates as the Gulf Oil Company. They also increased their stockholdings in the new company, largely by canceling their loans to Guffey in exchange for the stock they held as collateral. By 1939, the Mellon family, including William L. Mellon, controlled 70 percent of the common stock in Gulf Oil, worth $240 million.

Although Gulf Oil and Aluminum Company of America were to become the cornerstones of the Mellon family fortune, the "incessant acquisitiveness" of the Mellon brothers led them to invest in a number of other promising companies as well. While they were consolidating their control over Gulf Oil and Alcoa, Andrew W. and Richard B. Mellon were also investing heavily in several other large corporations including Koppers, a chemical firm; Carborundum, an abrasives company; and Pullman, the railroad car manufacturer. Their 52 percent stake in Koppers alone was worth $37 million by 1939. In most cases, the pattern of investment and control was the same. The Mellon brothers began by lending money to small companies in need of capital for expansion. However, they often bought enough stock in these companies to become their controlling stockholders. They then asserted active control over these firms, serving as directors and appointing capable and trusted associates as managers. In 1902, T. Mellon and Sons itself was converted, through a series of mergers with affiliated banks and trust companies, into Mellon National Bank. The Mellon brothers emerged with 42 percent of the stock in the new bank holding company. They also owned all of the stock in both Mellon Securities and Mellon Indemnity, two companies that had been investment and insurance affiliates of Mellon National Bank.

Having succeeded in amassing one of the most monumental fortunes in American history, the Mellon brothers soon set about safeguarding it from the estate taxes. For example, Andrew W. Mellon created Coalesced Company and Richard B. Mellon created Aloxite Corporation as family holding companies in order to transfer most of their assets to their children. By the time he passed away in 1933, Richard B. Mellon had already given the bulk of his stock in the various Mellon enterprises to his two children, Richard K. Mellon and Sarah Mellon Scaife. Nevertheless, he left an estate of about $86 million, the bulk of which, after payment of relatively modest estate taxes, was divided equally among his wife and children. Perhaps because he had served as the secretary of the Treasury in three consecutive administrations, Andrew W. Mellon knew more about estate taxes and how to avoid them. When he died in 1937, he left an estate of only $37 million, all of which he bequeathed to a family foundation. Of course, he had already transferred the bulk of his stock in the Mellon companies to his two children, Paul Mellon and Ailsa Mellon Bruce. Because the Mellon brothers were equal partners in most of their business ventures, their children inherited almost equal fortunes. By 1939, Richard K. Mellon and Sarah Mellon Scaife were worth $156 million in the stock of just three companies: Gulf Oil, Aluminum Company of America, and Koppers. Their cousins, Paul Mellon and Ailsa Mellon Bruce, were worth $136 million in the stock of these same three corporations. These two branches of the Mellon family also held large blocks of stock in several other enterprises such as Mellon National Bank, Carborundum, and Pullman.

With the passing of the Mellon brothers, the task of overseeing the extensive investments of the family fell largely to Richard K. Mellon, the son of Richard B. Mellon. He was not only the eldest of the four wealthy Mellon cousins but also the only one to show any interest in business or the affairs of the Mellon companies. After flunking out of Princeton his first term there, R. K. Mellon went to work for his father at Mellon National Bank, where he became a vice president when he was only twenty-nine years old. When his father died four years later, he took over as president. He later resigned that post, but he never lost interest in the Mellon companies. He continued to serve as a director of Gulf Oil, Aluminum Company of America, Koppers, and Mellon National Bank for many years. Moreover, his involvement with these firms was far from passive. When a reporter asked him about his occupation, he once replied, "I hire company presidents." Although he was actively involved in the redevelopment of downtown Pittsburgh, R. K. Mellon actually lived at Rolling Rock Farms, an 18,000-

acre estate near Ligonier, fifty miles outside the city. When he died in 1970, he left an estate of over $226 million. He bequeathed half of it to his wife, and the other half to his Richard K. Mellon Foundation. In this way, all of it escaped federal estate taxes. The bulk of his fortune had been transferred into a series of massive trusts for his children many years earlier.

The only Mellon in a position to challenge Richard K. Mellon as the head of the Mellon financial empire was his equally wealthy cousin, Paul Mellon. As the only son of Andrew W. Mellon, he had been encouraged from an early age to enter business, but he was never able to generate much enthusiasm for the mundane details of finance and industry. After graduating from Yale, where he became known primarily as a poet, he went on to Cambridge. On returning to America, Paul admitted to reporters, "there are other members of our family who are far more fitted than I am to look after the family interests." Nevertheless, he kept a promise he had made to his father and went to work for Mellon National Bank. Within a couple of years, Paul was a director of several of the Mellon companies. After his father died, however, Paul gradually resigned all of his directorships and turned over his business affairs to a staff of financial advisers. He then retired to Oak Spring, his 4,000-acre estate near Upperville, Virginia. The estate also houses Rokeby Stables, a highly successful horse-breeding operation. In addition to breeding and racing thoroughbred horses, he has gained considerable attention as an art collector. In 1967, Paul gave most of his collection of English art, valued at over $35 million, to Yale University. He threw in another $10 million to build a special museum to house the collection. Paul has yet to part with his collection of French impressionist and postimpressionist art, which is undoubtedly the biggest and best collection in private hands.

Richard K. Mellon and Paul Mellon controlled only half of the fortune left by their fathers. The other half was held by their sisters. Sarah Mellon, the sister of Richard K. Mellon, married Alan Scaife, the scion of an established Pittsburgh family. Over the years, he served as a director of several Mellon companies and foundations. By all accounts, Sarah was intelligent but extremely shy. As one of the richest women in the world, she became accustomed to being cared for by servants. According to her own daughter, "she did not know how to cook; she couldn't drive." Although she devoted the requisite amount of time to her art collection and her philanthropies, Sarah found more pleasure in entertaining and traveling. When she died in 1965, she left $66 million to her Sarah Mellon Scaife Foundation. Ailsa Mellon, the sister of Paul Mellon, married David K. Bruce, a young foreign service officer. Soon after their marriage, Ailsa Mellon Bruce was stricken by an undiagnosed illness that rendered her, in the words of her husband, a "semi-invalid." They were eventually divorced, and David Bruce went on to a distinguished diplomatic career. After the divorce, Ailsa became almost a recluse. At one time, she owned three apartments in New York, two houses in Connecticut, an estate on Long Island, and a residence in Palm Beach. Ailsa apparently took a great deal of interest in her philanthropies and her art collection, much of which she donated to the National Gallery of Art. When she died in 1969, she left the bulk of her estate, valued at $570 million, to her Avalon Foundation. This foundation was later merged with two smaller foundations established by her brother to form the giant Andrew W. Mellon Foundation.

At this point, much of the Mellon fortune is in the hands of the six grandchildren of Richard B. Mellon and the three grandchildren of Andrew W. Mellon. On the Richard B. Mellon side of the family, perhaps the wealthiest members of this generation are the two children of Sarah Mellon Scaife. Her son, Richard M. Scaife, is a newspaper publisher, but he has gained prominence primarily for his political largesse. A conservative Republican, Richard Scaife has given roughly $144 million of family money to various political organizations. The other members of this branch of the Mellon family include the four children of Richard K. Mellon. They control the massive Richard King Mellon Foundation, and one of the sons, Seward Prosser Mellon, serves as a director of Mellon National Bank. On the Andrew W. Mellon side of the family, Ailsa Mellon Bruce had only one child, Audrey Bruce Currier. Under the tutelage of her husband, Stephen Currier, she became an early financial contributor to the civil rights movement. Both of the Curriers were lost at sea aboard a private airplane in 1967, and their three children are now the sole beneficiaries of several substantial trusts. Paul Mellon, the brother of Ailsa, has two children. His son, Timothy Mellon, has gained notoriety recently by buying three marginal railroads for $44 million in order to create Guilford Transportation, a railway system with over 2,500 miles of track in six Northeast states. Catherine Mellon, the daughter of Paul Mellon, married and eventually divorced John Warner, who later married and divorced the actress Elizabeth Taylor.

Not all members of the Mellon family are rich. Among the descendants of Thomas A. Mellon, only two of the brothers, Andrew W. and Richard B. Mellon, were brought into the bank. The two other brothers became wealthy, but they did not amass great fortunes. Consequently, their descendants must contend with the disadvantages of the Mellon name without the advantages of the Mellon wealth. The only exceptions are the children of William L. Mellon, the nephew of A. W. and R. B. Mellon. William Mellon served his uncles well when he went to Texas in 1902 to manage and oversee their investments in the burgeoning oil industry. He was eventually made chairman of Gulf Oil and accumulated a relatively small block of stock in the company. By 1937, his 4 percent stake in Gulf Oil was worth over $12 million. It was a small fortune by Mellon standards, but it was enough to provide for his four children. One of them, William L. Mellon, Jr., astounded other members of the family when he announced that he had decided to follow the example of Albert Schweitzer. He sold his ranch in Arizona and went back to school, at age thirty-seven, to become a doctor. After his graduation from Tulane University Medical School in 1953, he and his wife moved to Haiti, where they built a hospital for the poor. Altogether, the descendants of William L. Mellon, Sr., may now be worth as much as $300 million.

Over the past several decades, the Mellon fortune has become increasingly diversified as the family has sold much of their stock in the original Mellon companies and reinvested the proceeds in other stocks, bonds, and real estate. Nevertheless, the vast bulk of the Mellon fortune can be traced to large family stockholdings in Gulf Oil. In 1937, the 70 percent of Gulf Oil stock owned or controlled by the

Mellons was worth $240 million. In the decades that followed, however, the Mellons gradually disposed of much of this stock through a series of public offerings and countless private sales. In the six secondary offerings of Gulf Oil held by the Mellons since 1943, family members sold Gulf stock worth over $350 million. As a result, by the time of the last public offering in 1972, the Mellons and their foundations had reduced their stake in Gulf Oil to about 21 percent. If the proceeds from these stock sales were subsequently reinvested in diversified portfolios of stocks and bonds, they would now be worth at least $1.1 billion. This total excludes, of course, the stock portfolios of the various Mellon foundations. By 1984, when Gulf Oil was acquired by Chevron, members of the Mellon family probably owned no more than 12 percent of the company, for which they received at least $1.5 billion in cash. This is the latest in a series of cash infusions received by the Mellons. For example, family members received roughly $150 million between 1951 and 1961 for their stock in Alcan Aluminum, which they were forced to sell as the result of an antitrust settlement. Similarly, the Mellons received over $100 million for their remaining 20 percent stake in Carborundum when it was acquired by another company in 1978.

Although the Mellons have systematically diversified their investment portfolios, some of the original Mellon companies still constitute part of the family fortune. For example, the Mellons have kept much of their stock in Aluminum Company of America. The only public stock offering by the family occurred in 1972, when several family members and foundations sold about a third of their stake for $96 million. At present, the Mellons probably own about 17 percent of the stock in Aluminum Company of America, worth close to $500 million. Similarly, the Mellons have retained almost all of their stock in Mellon National Corporation. As the result of recent mergers, the Mellons now probably own no more than 23 percent of the stock in Mellon National, worth about $350 million. The Mellons also own about 10 percent of Koppers, currently worth $60 million. In general, the four cousins held roughly equal shares in the various Mellon companies but there were a few notable exceptions. As the result of an exchange of stock within the family in 1933, Richard K. Mellon and Sarah Mellon Scaife wound up the sole owners of two family financial companies, Mellon Indemnity and Mellon Securities. In 1946, these two companies were merged into General Reinsurance Company and First Boston Corporation, respectively. As a result of these mergers, the heirs of Richard K. Mellon and Sarah Mellon Scaife currently own about 6 percent of First Boston and 4 percent of General Reinsurance. Altogether, these two investments are now worth just over $210 million.

Although the Mellons no longer exert active control over their companies, family members or their advisers continue to serve as directors of such major corporations as Aluminum Company of America, Mellon National, Koppers, General Reinsurance, and First Boston. The only entity capable of coordinating the financial affairs of the family at present is Mellon National Bank, whose trust department still administers much of the family fortune. Foundations endowed by members of the family are also large stockholders in many of the original Mellon companies. The largest of these foundations is the Andrew W. Mellon Foundation with assets of $816 million in 1981. The only two other large Mellon foundations are the Richard King Mellon Foundation, with assets of $357 million in 1983, and the Sarah Scaife Foundation, with assets of $112 million in 1981. Family members and their associates serve as trustees and officers of these foundations. As a rule, however, the Mellons now prefer to be passive investors. As one of the younger Mellons put it, "in families like ours what life becomes is holding on to what you've got." So far, the Mellons have succeeded in holding on to the bulk of their fortune. The stock in the original Mellon companies still owned by the family is now worth $1.1 billion. In addition, their proceeds from various stock sales, after appreciation, come to over $3.2 billion, most of this from their Gulf Oil stock. Last but not least, family members have received at least $2.1 billion in dividend income since 1937 from their stock in Gulf Oil, Aluminum Company of America, and Mellon National alone. Altogether, the Mellons are now worth at least $6 billion.

CONTINUITY AND CHANGE

There can be little doubt that the three major dynasties of a half century ago are still alive and quite wealthy today. Indeed, their massive fortunes have appreciated greatly over the decades, although perhaps only enough to keep pace with inflation. Even today, however, only a handful of corporate rich families control as much wealth as the Rockefeller, du Pont, and Mellon families. Income and estate taxes have, of course, taken their toll on these fortunes, but they have hardly eliminated them. The continuity of these fortunes over the past several decades is largely attributable to the fact that these families did not hesitate to employ elaborate legal strategies to avoid these taxes. In particular, the members of corporate rich families often resorted to the creation of generation-skipping trusts. They also created family holding companies to avoid estate taxes and consolidate the stockholdings of family members, although most of these holding companies were dissolved once they had served their purpose. In general, parents employed a variety of legal maneuvers to transfer much of their wealth to their children and grandchildren long before they died. Only after their heirs were provided for did they bequeath their residual estates to family foundations. In this way, they were able to avoid estate taxes and keep the last remains of their wealth under family control. As a result, these families now exercise enormous social and political power by virtue of their control over large family foundations.

The most significant consequence of the historical evolution of corporate rich families has been the change in their relationship to those companies that were the original sources of their fortunes. The Rockefellers long ago severed their ties with the various Standard Oil companies and have concentrated their attention in recent years on Rockefeller Group, the family holding company for their real estate and broadcasting properties. Similarly, although various members of the du Pont family remained actively involved in management of Du Pont Company until relatively recently, they are now content to have several family members serve simply as directors. Last but not least, the Mellons, who only rarely became involved as managers of the companies they controlled, have family financial advisers represent them as directors. As a rule, these families have largely relinquished the management of the family firms to others, although family members and their financial advisers often continue to serve as directors. Nevertheless, the current investment strategy among these three corporate rich families is clearly one of diversification. Stock in the original family companies has gradually been sold, and the proceeds have been reinvested in diversified portfolios that contain a combination of growth stocks for long-term capital appreciation as well as municipal bonds for tax-free income.

The fortunes of these three dynastic families and the relationships of these families to their companies have been altered in the past several decades largely as a result of fundamental transformations in their structures as families. They are larger and more complex as kinship groups than ever before. In the past five decades, two new generations of family members have reached maturity. In the late 1930s, the du Pont clan consisted of a few aging siblings and scores of adult cousins. Today, it is now a clan comprising well over a hundred adult members, most of whom are only first and second cousins to one another. Similarly, the Mellon family once consisted primarily of four cousins who were still young adults. It now comprises primarily a few second and third cousins. In the Rockefeller family, there were only six young siblings and their father. Currently, most of the Rockefellers are first cousins. Despite the large size of these families and the remoteness of their kinship ties, family members have managed to maintain a strong sense of family unity, largely because of their common economic interests. These kinship ties are also reinforced by a number of shared institutional arrangements involving family investment offices, family trusts, and family foundations. However, these family ties become more tenuous with each successive generation. Indeed, as these families have developed into large and complex clans, they have become divided into a series of smaller and more cohesive branches. Of course, none of the younger members of these families will ever be as rich as their parents because, with the passing of each generation, their family fortunes have been redistributed among a larger number of family members.

Despite these differences between these families, which stem from differences in their size and complexity as kinship groups as well as differences in the composition and distribution of their fortunes, the individual members of these families have led very similar lives. In particular, the members of each successive generation of family members have confronted similar situations and problems. To begin with, the children and many of the grandchildren of the entrepreneurs who amassed these family fortunes were sent to the most exclusive private schools. Later, they attended elite private universities, even though they did not always graduate. By and large, the members of the second and third generations of these families also married well. With only a few notable exceptions, most of them married the scions of other wealthy and socially prominent families. In short, the implicit agenda for members of the second generations of these families involved the accumulation of cultural and social capital commensurate with their economic capital. Although the same expectations existed for members of the third generation as well, they were much less urgent. Finding themselves at or very near the pinnacle of wealth and status in American society, the members of subsequent generations have been content to draw on the social and cultural capital, as well as the economic capital, amassed by their parents and grandparents. They have sometimes shunned the most exclusive prep schools and colleges and married individuals from families that were neither especially prominent nor wealthy.

3

The
Test of
Time

Families like the Rockefellers, du Ponts, and Mellons are hardly typical, even of the corporate rich. Over the past several decades, the members of these families have paid substantial estate taxes and endowed large foundations and have still managed to preserve huge fortunes for their heirs. It may be that they have survived the ravages of time simply because they possessed incredibly large fortunes from the outset. Much less is known about other corporate rich families of the past half century, particularly those with fortunes that were not on quite the same scale as those of the Rockefellers, du Ponts, and Mellons. There are a number of such lesser corporate rich families. Although a few of these families, such as the Fords and Woolworths, have famous names, relatively little is known about them and how they have fared over the years. Indeed, some of the most celebrated of the wealthy capitalist families of the past few decades have quietly slipped into deliberate obscurity in recent years. Other families, such as the Pitcairns and Clarks, never achieved celebrity status. Despite the fact that they never possessed the huge fortunes of the Rockefellers, du Ponts, and Mellons, the members of these lesser corporate rich families were wealthy enough to confront many of the same problems faced by the members of the three major dynasties. In particular, they faced the prospect of seeing their nevertheless substantial fortunes depleted by progressive gift and estate taxes. Consequently, they adopted a series of strategies to safeguard their fortunes over the course of several generations similar to those employed by the three big dynasties. In general, the composite history of these lesser corporate rich families contains important lessons concerning the perpetuation of wealth and privilege in America.

There has never been, of course, any official roster of the corporate rich in America. For the most part, the members of the wealthiest capitalist families have succeeded in maintaining their anonymity. There exists, however, some information about those families that were among the wealthiest a half century ago. The most reliable source of information is a government study of the concentration of stock ownership, conducted by the Temporary National Economic Committee, which identified those families that were major stockholders in the largest nonfinancial corporations during the 1930s. In all, this committee identified just over a dozen families whose stockholdings in major American corporations were worth at least $50 million in 1939. Information from other sources confirms that these families were among the wealthiest in the nation during this time period. For example, Ferdinand Lundberg, in his classic study, *America's Sixty Families,* was able to identify the richest families in America by using published income tax returns. Specifically, he used published reports of the federal income tax returns filed by those individuals with the largest incomes in 1924 to estimate the aggregate wealth of entire families. Using these two sources, it is possible to identify ten corporate rich families of the period that ranked just behind the Rockefellers, du Ponts, and Mellons in terms of their aggregate wealth. Some of these families, such as the Fords, McCormicks, Reynoldses, Dukes, and Woolworths, have names that are vaguely familiar. Others, such as the Pews, Harknesses, Pitcairns, Hartfords, and Clarks, are less well known. In either case, each of these families was worth no less than $50 million in the midst of the Great Depression. Some of them, of course, were worth considerably more.

THE COST OF CONTROL

Those corporate rich families of the 1930s that developed into business dynasties did not always find it easy to maintain control over their family corporations. In the case of the Ford family, the cost of control was significant. It has been forgotten that the Fords were once richer than the Rockefellers, du Ponts, or Mellons. The source of their wealth, of course, was the Ford Motor Company. In 1937, members of the Ford family owned over 92 percent of the stock in the company, worth somewhere in the neighborhood of $580 million. Any estimate of their wealth is necessarily imprecise simply because there was no market for Ford Motor Company stock at the time. However, the net asset value of the company, the stated value of its assets minus its liabilities, was $624 million. The only stock in the company that was not owned by members of the Ford family was held by the Ford Foundation. The founder of this massive fortune was Henry Ford, one of the most innovative entrepreneurs in the history of American business. With no guide but his own intuition, he created a company that eventually became one of the major forces in a gigantic and highly profitable industry. Although Henry Ford was an acknowledged business genius, his preoccupation with maintaining control over the company he founded cost his family most of its fortune. By refusing to transfer the bulk of his wealth to his descendants before the enactment of progressive gift and estate taxes, he left most of the family fortune exposed to these taxes. As a result of this miscalculation, the Fords became, almost involuntarily, some of the greatest philanthropists of all time.

Henry Ford built his first automobile in a shed behind his home in Detroit in 1896. Not content with his first model, he promptly sold it and began building an improved version. In the next several years, he organized two automobile companies that were eventually dissolved after investors lost faith in his ability to make them any money. Finally in 1903, Henry Ford and several investors incorporated the Ford Motor Company. The investors, including John and Horace Dodge, contributed a little over $56,000 in cash and materials to the enterprise in exchange for almost 75 percent of its stock. Henry received the remaining 25 percent of Ford Motor Company stock in exchange for his designs and patents. Two years later, a dispute arose between Henry and several of the original investors over his strategy of concentrating exclusively on the mass production of inexpensive automobiles. He bought their 33 percent of the stock in Ford Motor Company for a total of $231,000 and became, for the first time, the majority stockholder in the company that bore his name. Fourteen years later, another dispute erupted between Henry and his remaining stockholders, led by the Dodge brothers, over the distribution of surplus profits. In order to resolve the dispute and gain absolute control over the company, he and his family borrowed money to buy out the remaining investors and their heirs for almost $104 million. In a span of sixteen years, Henry Ford had not only built the Ford Motor Company into a major corporation, he had also bought out all of his original investors.

The destiny of the Ford family was also shaped by the fact that Henry Ford had only one child, Edsel Ford. Almost from the outset, Henry treated his son as a junior partner in the business. After graduation from prep school, Edsel joined the company instead of going to college. Four years later, at the age of twenty-five, he was appointed company president. Although Henry gave Edsel a large block of Ford Motor stock, he refused to consider any other tax-avoidance strategies that might diminish his absolute control over the company. As a result, he failed to safeguard the bulk of the family fortune from estate taxes. At age seventy-two, he still owned over half of the stock in Ford Motor Company. His son owned most of the rest. None of it was held by any of his four grandchildren. Edsel was quick to understand the threat that the progressive gift and estate taxes enacted in 1935 posed to both the family and the company. He realized that the family might someday be forced to sell a substantial block of Ford stock just to pay estate taxes. They might even lose control of the company altogether. Appalled at the prospect of losing complete control of his company, Henry finally agreed to an ingenious plan in which the common stock of Ford Motor Company was split into two classes. Five percent of the company stock was designated voting stock, and the remainder was designated nonvoting stock. Henry and Edsel Ford then executed complementary wills, each bequeathing all his voting stock to other family members and all his nonvoting stock to a new entity to be called the Ford Foundation. In this way, most of the family fortune would eventually go to charity in order to avoid estate taxes, but the family would still retain absolute control over the company.

Henry Ford despised the ostentation of upper-class society. His son, however, was determined to enjoy the privileges inherent in his wealth. Edsel Ford began by marrying Eleanor Clay, the scion of a prominent Detroit family. Later, he built a massive lodge at Seal Harbor, Maine, where his children played each summer with children of other wealthy families, including those of John D. Rockefeller, Jr. He even sent his three sons to elite private universities, although only one of them bothered to graduate. After a prolonged illness, Edsel died of stomach cancer in 1943 at the age of forty-nine. A few days later, Henry Ford announced that he was resuming the presidency of Ford Motor Company. The family had good reason to fear what might become of the company. The founder of the family fortune was almost eighty years old and showed the effects of at least one stroke. As Ford Motor Company was engaged in war production, the government agreed to discharge Henry Ford II from the Navy so he could help his grandfather manage the company. Although he often indulged his grandchildren when they were young, Henry steadfastly refused to bring any of them into the company. True to form, the elder Ford refused to delegate any responsibility to his grandson. As a last resort, Eleanor Ford threatened to sell the voting stock she had inherited from her husband to outsiders unless her son were appointed president. Tired and sick, Henry Ford at last relinquished control of the company he had created four decades earlier. He died four years later. As the result of the bequests from the estates of both Henry and Edsel Ford, the Ford Foundation eventually wound up with essentially all of the nonvoting stock in Ford Motor Company. However, the Fords kept absolute control of the company by virtue of the fact that they owned all of its voting stock.

The Ford Motor Company prospered in the years following World War II. As the company grew larger and more profitable, the Ford Foundation was frequently denounced as an instrument of the company and the Ford family. Although the foundation held 95 percent of the stock in Ford Motor Company, it had no vote in electing any of the directors. This nonvoting stock could not be sold to the public because it was not listed on any exchange. Moreover, the New York Stock Exchange refused to list any stock that did not have at least limited voting rights. After extensive negotiations with foundation trustees and a cadre of investment bankers, the Ford family agreed to relinquish its complete control of the company in exchange for a larger share of the outstanding common stock. In the subsequent financial reorganization of the company, the Ford family received all of the new Class B stock, which represented 12 percent of all the stock in Ford Motor Company. The Ford Foundation received all of the new nonvoting Class A stock. The company charter was amended so that both classes of stock could be converted into voting common stock and sold to the public. However, the Ford family insisted that the Class B stock retain preferential voting rights, initially casting at least 40 percent of the votes, as long as a substantial proportion of it was held by the members of the family. In early 1956, Ford Motor Company common stock was listed on the New York Stock Exchange for the first time when the Ford Foundation sold a large block of Ford Motor stock for $642 million. Over the next several years, the foundation sold all of its stock in the company. Today, it has assets of $3.4 billion.

The Fords eventually severed their ties with the Ford Foundation, but they have not relinquished their control over the Ford Motor Company. Henry Ford II served as chairman of the company for many years until his resignation in 1980. His younger brothers, Benson and William Ford, both served as vice presidents and directors for many years. Moreover, Edsel Ford II and Walter B. Ford III, two great-grandsons of the founder, hold managerial positions with the company. The current president of Ford Motor Company is not a family member, but it is quite possible that one of the great-grandsons of Henry Ford will one day serve as either president or chairman. The family still casts 40 percent of the votes, and both Henry and William Ford continue to serve as directors. In recent years, the Fords have sold roughly $300 million of their Ford Motor stock. However, as the result of large stock repurchases announced by Ford Motor Company in 1985, their remaining stockholdings, which are currently worth over $800 million, will represent close to 9 percent of the outstanding stock in the company. In addition, the family has received roughly $900 million in dividend income from its Ford stock since 1946. Much of the money received from the stock sales and dividend income has undoubtedly been reinvested elsewhere. For example, William Ford purchased the Detroit Lions professional football team in 1964 for a mere $6 million. The family fortune is currently administered by a family office known simply as Ford Estates. In recent years, this office has invested heavily in real estate projects designed to shelter the incomes of family members from taxes. Altogether, the four grandchildren and thirteen great-grandchildren of Henry Ford are now worth at least $1.5 billion.

PROLONGED PROSPERITY

A few other business dynasties have also managed to keep much of their wealth intact over the last several decades. Indeed, the success of these families in perpetuating their fortunes over at least two generations may be due, at least in part, to the fact that they were able to retain some control over their family corporations. One example of such a pattern is the Pitcairn family of Philadelphia. John Pitcairn, the founder of this family and its fortune, came to America from Scotland as a child and began his career in business as a clerk for the Pennsylvania Railroad. In 1883, he and several associates organized the forerunner of PPG Industries Inc., a major producer of glass, paint, and chemicals. He was president of the company for several years and later served as its chairman. Even though he married relatively late in life, John Pitcairn had three sons. In fact, he was fifty-six years old when his last son was born. He was also one of the founders of a new religious sect in America, the General Church of New Jerusalem. In his later years, he donated large sums of money to the church. When he died in 1916, John Pitcairn left an estate of roughly $20 million. Seven years later, the three brothers created Pitcairn Company, a family holding company whose main asset was a large block of stock in the company founded by their father. By 1938, Pitcairn Company held 34 percent of the stock in PPG Industries, worth almost $64 million. This family holding company was to have a profound effect on the family and its fortune. Indeed, it enabled the Pitcairns to retain some semblance of family unity as well as effective control over PPG Industries for several decades.

The Pitcairns were an unusual family even by the somewhat eccentric standards of the corporate rich. All three brothers went to New Church Academy, a private religious school founded by their father, before they attended the University of Pennsylvania. One son, Theodore Pitcairn, entered the ministry and served as a missionary in Africa for a number of years. On returning to the United States, he became a leader of the General Church of New Jerusalem. An avid art collector, he gained national attention in 1966 when he sold part of his substantial collection in order to finance his religious activities. For example, he sold three paintings, two by Van Gogh and one by Monet, for a little over $2 million. Altogether, he had paid less than $30,000 for all three paintings forty years earlier. His brother, Raymond Pitcairn, spent several years studying cathedral architecture in the United States and Europe in order to prepare himself for the task of designing and building a large Gothic cathedral for the General Church of New Jerusalem in Bryn Athyn, outside Philadelphia. The youngest son, Harold Pitcairn, was an aviation enthusiast who contributed to the early development of the helicopter. Both Harold and Raymond Pitcairn did serve as directors of PPG Industries, but neither of them ever served as officers. They were apparently content to leave the mundane task of running the company to others. The last of the three brothers, Theodore Pitcairn, died in 1973. One of their most enduring legacies was a family of enormous size. The three Pitcairn brothers had a total of twenty-four children among them, some of whom turned out to be almost as prolific as their parents. For instance, Raymond Pitcairn alone had forty-nine grandchildren.

This large family was held together, at least in part, by the family holding company. Pitcairn Company gradually disposed of some of its PPG Industries stock over the years in order to diversify its investment portfolio, but it still held over 25 percent of the stock in the company as of 1972. That same year, it sold a large block of PPG Industries stock, representing 10 percent of the stock in the corporation, to the public for $90 million. Even though they had disposed of over half of their stock in PPG Industries, the Pitcairns did not immediately relinquish their control over the company. Two officers of Pitcairn Company, including a husband of one of the granddaughters of John Pitcairn, continued to serve as directors of PPG Industries for several years. Finally, in 1985, the family decided to dispose of its remaining investment in the company. PPG Industries agreed to purchase the 15 percent of its stock still held by the Pitcairns for $529 million, half in cash and the remainder in installment notes. Pitcairn Company, which held roughly 13 percent of the stock in PPG Industries by then, received $438 million. The rest of the stock was sold by a family investment fund, three family foundations, and an estate. In all, PPG Industries proved to be a lucrative investment for the Pitcairns. Between 1938 and 1985 alone, the corporation paid over $320 million in dividends to their holding company. In part, because of the large number of heirs in each generation, relatively little of the Pitcairn fortune has gone to philanthropies. The three foundations endowed by the Pitcairn brothers and their families had assets of less than $22 million by 1982. Altogether, the Pitcairn family is now worth at least $600 million.

At least one other corporate rich family has managed to hold on to much of its fortune and retain control over its family corporation for the past few decades. The Pew family of Philadelphia is almost as rich today as it was about a half century ago, even allowing for inflation. The family fortune is derived, almost entirely, from stockholdings in a single firm, Sun Company Inc. This corporation, a large domestic oil company, was founded in Ohio in 1886 by Joseph N. Pew. However, it did not become a major oil company until 1902, when it bought leases in a newly discovered oil field near Beaumont, Texas. Even though it is not well known to the public, the Pew family must be counted as one of the most prolific and successful business dynasties in American history. Sun Company has been managed and directed by the descendants of Joseph N. Pew for over half a century. After the death of the founder in 1912, the company was run by his three sons. His eldest son, J. Newton Pew, Jr., served as its chairman for several decades. Another son, J. Howard Pew, served as president of the company during much of this period. In later years, three of the four grandsons and even a great-grandson of the founder served as either officers or directors of the company. Although two nephews of Joseph Pew served as officers and directors of the company as well, the vast majority of its stock has been held by Joseph N. Pew and his descendants. In 1938, his four living children and nine grandchildren held 69 percent of the common stock in Sun Company, worth in excess of $75 million. His nephews, J. Edgar Pew and John G. Pew, who were both directors of the company at the time, held less than $2 million in Sun Company stock.

Few wealthy families have pursued their privacy as avidly as the Pews. Moreover, they have succeeded in avoiding publicity despite the fact that several family members, especially the children of the founder, have been generous contributors to various conservative political causes. As early as 1936, for example, the Pews gave $514,000 to the Republican party, almost as much as the du Ponts, in a vain effort to prevent the reelection of President Roosevelt. Between 1956 and 1972, various members of the Pew family gave over $873,000 to the presidential campaigns of successive Republican candidates. The conservative political views of the Pew family are reflected in the activities of their family foundations. The oldest and largest among the family foundations is the Pew Memorial Trust, which was established in 1948 by the four living children of Joseph N. Pew with an initial endowment of $50 million in Sun Company stock. Eight years later, they organized the Glenmede Trust Company and named it the sole trustee of the Pew Memorial Trust. In the past, the recipients of its largesse have included conservative political organizations such as the Christian Anti-Communist Crusade and the Freedoms Foundation of Valley Forge as well as fundamentalist religious groups such as the Billy Graham Evangelical Association. In recent years, the Pew children have endowed several large foundations of their own, including the Mabel Pew Myrin Trust, the J. N. Pew, Jr., Charitable Trust, and the J. Howard Pew Freedom Trust. True to family tradition, these foundations have provided funds for a number of neoconservative policy research institutions. As of 1982, the Pew Memorial Trust held assets worth $900 million, and five other foundations endowed by the Pews held assets worth another $430 million.

The Pews have not hesitated to use their family foundations to consolidate their control over Sun Company. Six family members serve as directors of Glenmede Trust Company, which, in turn, serves as the sole trustee for all of the foundations endowed by the Pew family. In various fiduciary capacities, the Glenmede Trust Company held 27 percent of the stock in Sun Company as of 1985. In order to consolidate the investments held by individual family members, the Pews also created a family office, which is located just across the hall from the offices of the Glenmede Trust Company in the Sun Company headquarters building. This office provides family members with a variety of financial and legal services. At present, one member of the Pew family, a great-grandson of the founder, serves as a director of Sun Company. Although there is only one family member on the board of directors of the corporation, there is little doubt that the family is still in control. In 1980, the Pews forced the chairman of Sun Company to resign simply because they disagreed with his diversification strategy for the company. According to R. Anderson Pew, one of two family members on the board of directors at the time, "if there is a disagreement about the way the company is run, we don't sell our stock, we change the management." Despite the fact that a relatively large share of the Pew fortune eventually went to charitable foundations, members of the Pew family and trusts for their benefit still own approximately 6 percent of the stock in Sun Company, now worth over $300 million. The Pews have also received roughly $350 million in dividends on their Sun Company stock since 1938. Altogether, the nine grandchildren of Joseph H. Pew and their children are now worth well over $500 million.

FAMILIES IN DECLINE

Even the most successful business dynasties cannot be maintained forever. Those corporate rich families that develop into dynasties are usually able to maintain control of the family corporation for only a few generations. Some of the most established capitalist families inevitably enter a period of decline. Such is the case with the McCormick family of International Harvester fame. Cyrus H. McCormick is still celebrated as the inventor of the mechanical harvester, despite the fact that the basic design was first developed by his father. Nevertheless, Cyrus McCormick was responsible for perfecting the machine and manufacturing and marketing it in large numbers. With the help of his two brothers, William and Leander McCormick, he established the McCormick Reaping Machine Company in Chicago in 1848. In the years that followed, Cyrus and his children bought out the other members of the McCormick family. Finally, in 1902, they merged the firm with several others to form International Harvester. For the next several decades, the company was controlled and managed by the descendants of Cyrus McCormick. The eldest son of the founder, Cyrus H. McCormick, Jr., was the first president of the new company and, when he resigned sixteen years later, he was succeeded by his brother, Harold F. McCormick. For many years after the merger, the McCormicks remained the largest stockholders in International Harvester. As of 1937, the descendants of Cyrus McCormick held 32 percent of the common stock and 20 percent of the preferred stock in the company, worth at least $111 million. With Harold McCormick as chairman and his nephew, Cyrus H. McCormick III, as a director, the future of the McCormick dynasty seemed secure.

Despite its controlling interest in International Harvester, the McCormick family soon showed signs of failure as a dynasty. Although Cyrus McCormick left a large family, three sons and two daughters, it was a family with more than its share of problems. One of the daughters, Virginia McCormick, became mentally ill at an early age and was eventually placed in the care of a small army of nurses and servants on her estate in Pasadena, California, for the rest of her life. The youngest son, Stanley McCormick, joined his brothers at

International Harvester as company comptroller for a short time. However, soon after his marriage, he began to show signs of mental illness as well. He was later declared incompetent and spent the rest of his life in his own personal mental institution on his estate in Santa Barbara, California. The best-known member of the family was Harold McCormick, who first gained notoriety by marrying Edith Rockefeller, the daughter of John D. Rockefeller. It was an unconventional marriage from the start. At one point, Edith took their three children and moved to Switzerland for eight years. On his own, Harold soon fell in love with a young Polish opera singer, Ganna Walska. After divorcing Edith, he married Ganna Walska, but she left him after only two years, taking over $5 million of his International Harvester stock with her. Despite the often sensational publicity concerning his personal affairs, Harold McCormick served as chairman of the company until his death in 1941.

The McCormick family not only failed to maintain itself as a dynasty; it came close to disappearing as a family altogether. Indeed, the second generation almost failed to reproduce itself. Neither Virginia nor Stanley McCormick had any children, and their brothers and sister produced only six children between them. As a result, the McCormicks were able to maintain direct control of International Harvester for only three generations. Harold McCormick was eventually succeeded as both president and chairman of the company by his son, H. Fowler McCormick. Another grandson of the founder, Cyrus McCormick III, served as a vice president and director of the company. However, the McCormick family almost disappeared in the fourth generation. Of the six grandchildren of the founder, only two had children of their own. Another granddaughter, Muriel McCormick Hubbard, adopted children, but they were eventually placed in a foster home after a bitter family fight to have her declared an unfit mother. In all, there were only seven members of the McCormick family in the fourth generation, four of them adopted and only one of them named McCormick. One of them, Anne Blaine, married Gilbert A. Harrison, who later purchased the *New Republic,* a magazine of political commentary. The last McCormick to serve as chairman of International Harvester, Brooks McCormick, was not a descendant of Cyrus McCormick at all. Instead, he was a great-grand-nephew whose mother, Marion Deering McCormick, was the grand-daughter of the other principal founder of the company, William Deering.

The McCormick fortune declined over time as well, although not quite so precipitously as the family. Harold McCormick, of course, even managed to augment the family fortune for a while by marrying into the Rockefeller family. Their three children eventually inherited not only their share of the McCormick fortune but a small part of the Rockefeller fortune as well. With so many members of the family failing to produce any heirs, much of the family fortune was eventually redistributed among other family members. For example, when Virginia McCormick died without any heirs in 1941, her $21 million estate was divided among her four brothers and sisters. When Stanley McCormick passed away six years later, his brothers and sister filed suit to have his will, which left his entire estate to his wife, declared invalid on the grounds that he was mentally incompetent to execute a valid will. The judge ruled that the wife, Katharine Dexter McCormick, was the sole heir to his $35 million estate because the will had been executed before Stanley had been officially declared incompetent. When she died many years later, Katharine left her entire estate, by then worth roughly $30 million, to the Massachusetts Institute of Technology. The McCormicks undoubtedly sold much of their remaining International Harvester stock, in order to create more diversified investment portfolios, soon after Fowler McCormick resigned as chairman of the company in 1951. As a result, the family fortune was not depleted by the precipitous decline in the value of International Harvester stock several years later. Altogether, the remaining descendants of Cyrus McCormick are now probably worth somewhat less than $100 million.

Another family that has almost disappeared from the ranks of the corporate rich is the Clark family. Since it was never known to the public as one of the wealthiest families in America, its decline has gone almost unnoticed. In a very real sense, the Clark fortune stems from an allegation of patent infringement. The founder of this fortune,

Edward Clark, was working for a New York law firm in 1851 when he was approached by a young inventor by the name of Isaac M. Singer. Singer held several patents on the sewing machine, but he was also being sued for infringing upon the patents of others. Because Singer was short on cash, Clark agreed to defend him on the condition that he be made an equal partner in the firm. When the company was incorporated twelve years later, Clark and Singer split 82 percent of the stock in Singer Manufacturing Company. Isaac Singer contributed over twenty patents to the company, but Edward Clark, as president of Singer, was largely responsible for the growth and profitability of the firm. He expanded the company into foreign markets, developed the system of exclusive Singer sales outlets, and initiated installment purchases. When he died in 1882, Edward Clark left the bulk of his estate, valued at $25 million, to his only surviving son, Alfred C. Clark. Alfred Clark was, in turn, survived by four sons of his own. By 1939, the Clark dynasty seemed secure. The three surviving sons of Alfred Clark and their children owned, directly or indirectly, 28 percent of the stock in Singer Manufacturing Company, worth $57 million. Moreover, one of the sons, Stephen C. Clark, served as a director of the company.

It soon became apparent, however, that the Clark family was not destined to remain a business dynasty. The major barrier was simply a lack of heirs. Two of the three sons of Alfred Clark failed to produce any children of their own. Furthermore, neither of them demonstrated much of an interest in the Singer Company. The eldest son, Robert S. Clark, devoted much of his time and money to his art collection. When he died in 1957, he left an estate valued at $84 million. After payment of $31 million in state and federal estate taxes, half of his estate went into a trust for his wife and the remainder was split between the Robert S. Clark Foundation and the Sterling and Francine Clark Art Institute. The art institute received his entire art collection, which included no fewer than thirty paintings by Renoir in addition to many paintings by Homer. Another brother, F. Ambrose Clark, was known primarily as a breeder and owner of racehorses. As a young man, he had even ridden as a jockey until injuries convinced him to pursue more sedate activities. He once admitted, "I'm not a money-maker and all I know is horses." When he died, he bequeathed a considerable portion of his estate to his Clark Foundation. The only son to produce any heirs was Stephen Clark. Although he served as a director of Singer Company for many years, he is probably best known as the founder of the Baseball Hall of Fame, which he located near the family estate in Cooperstown, New York. Stephen Clark had four children and five grandchildren. One of his sons, Stephen C. Clark, Jr., was the last member of the family to serve as a director of Singer Company.

Because of the shortage of heirs, much of the Clark fortune went to charities. The two family foundations are the Clark Foundation, with assets of $113 million in 1980, and the Robert S. Clark Foundation, with assets of $28 million. At least two descendants of the founder serve as trustees of the Clark Foundation. With only one exception, the few remaining members of the Clark family have generally receded into obscurity in recent years. The exception is Anne Labouisse, a great-granddaughter of Edward Clark, who married Martin Peretz, then an assistant professor at Harvard. Anne and Martin Peretz have used at least part of her share of the Clark fortune to fund a variety of political causes. In 1972, they gave over $275,000 to the presidential campaign of George McGovern. Two years later, Martin Peretz purchased the *New Republic* for $380,000 from Gilbert A. Harrison, the husband of a great-granddaughter of Cyrus McCormick. He appointed himself editor in chief the following year. As late as 1960, the two surviving Clark brothers still owned or were the beneficiaries of trusts which owned over 24 percent of the stock in Singer Company, worth almost $70 million. Eight years later, Stephen C. Clark, Jr., one of the four great-grandchildren of the founder, Edward Clark, held $14 million in Singer Company stock. The Clarks probably began selling off much of their Singer stock, in order to diversify their investment portfolios, even before Stephen Clark, Jr., resigned as a director of the company in 1970. The primary members of the Clark family include a great-grandson and five great-great-grandchildren of the founder. The family fortune, which is currently administered by a family office known as Clark Estates, is now probably worth just under $100 million.

LAPSED CONTROL

Sometimes a corporate rich family may produce the male heirs required to establish a business dynasty but those heirs may have little or no interest in the business affairs of the family company. This is the case with the Duke family. The Duke fortune was founded by two brothers, James and Benjamin Duke, who got their start in the tobacco business in North Carolina around 1874. By all accounts, James B. Duke was an aggressive and innovative businessman whose marketing talents were complemented by the financial and managerial skills of his brother, Benjamin N. Duke. In 1890, the Duke brothers helped organize the forerunner of American Brands, the largest cigarette company in the United States at the time. From there, they went on to amass a second fortune in the electric power industry. In 1905, James and Benjamin Duke organized the Duke Power Company, a utility that supplies electricity to most of both North and South Carolina. Despite their business achievements, the Dukes are probably best known for their association with Duke University. For many years, Benjamin Duke contributed generously to Trinity College in Durham, North Carolina. In 1925, James Duke created the Duke Endowment and turned over to it $40 million in Duke Power stock. The endowment stipulated that the income was to be distributed among a number of schools, hospitals, and churches in the region. However, $6 million of the principal was reserved for Trinity College, on the condition that it change its name to Duke University. Needless to say, that task was quickly accomplished.

James Duke left an estate worth $86 million when he died in 1925. In his will, he bequeathed $17 million to charity and the remainder, after the payment of relatively modest estate taxes, to his wife and daughter. As a result, Doris Duke, his thirteen-year-old daughter, became one of the wealthiest and most celebrated heiresses in America. By 1939, she and trusts for her benefit owned Duke Power stock worth at least $14 million. Her mother, Nanaline Inman Duke, and her stepbrother, Walker F. Inman, owned Duke Power stock worth at least another $5 million. When Benjamin Duke died four years later, he left an estate of less than $8 million. However, he had already transferred most of his wealth to his two children, Angier and Mary Duke. Either directly or indirectly through trusts, they and their children owned Duke Power stock worth at least $11 million in 1939. Altogether, the Duke family held almost 53 percent of the stock in Duke Power. The Duke Endowment, of which Doris Duke was a permanent trustee, held another 38 percent. In addition, members of the Duke family held stock in Aluminum Company of America worth $6 million in 1939. Last but not least, they also owned stock in various tobacco companies, including American Brands Inc. and BAT Industries Inc., then worth in the neighborhood of $12 million. Both Doris Duke and Walker F. Inman served briefly as directors of Duke Power, but neither of them became involved in its management. Instead, Doris Duke devoted her early years to the pursuits and pastimes of café society. At one time, she owned homes in New York, Paris, Hollywood, Long Island, and Hawaii. After two celebrated marriages that ended in divorce, she retreated to Duke Farms, her 2,200-acre estate near Princeton, New Jersey.

In contrast to their once flamboyant cousin, the two children of Benjamin Duke led relatively quiet lives. They gained admittance to upper-class society by marrying the scions of a prominent Philadelphia family. Angier B. Duke married Cordelia Biddle, and his sister, Mary L. Duke, later married his brother-in-law, Anthony J. Drexel Biddle, Jr. Although both marriages eventually ended in divorce, they each produced two children. The most conspicuous of these children has been Angier Biddle Duke, who has served as an ambassador to several countries. The three other grandchildren of Benjamin Duke have generally pursued such genteel avocations as philanthropy and horse breeding. Much of the Duke fortune is probably still invested in Duke Power stock. For example, in 1961, Doris Duke still held over 6 percent of the stock in Duke Power, and a trust of which she is the primary income beneficiary held another 8 percent. Because she has no children, much of the Duke Power stock held in trust for her will someday revert to Duke University. Over the years, the stock in Duke Power has provided the Duke family with a generous income. Doris Duke alone has received at least $120 million in dividends from Duke Power since 1938. The descendants of Benjamin Duke have also prospered in the past few decades. For example, when Mary Duke Biddle died in 1960, she left an estate of $60 million. Most of this estate went to charity because she had already placed much of her fortune in trusts for the benefit of her two children. Her brother, Angier B. Duke, drowned in a yachting accident at the age of thirty-nine. However, his two sons are also the beneficiaries of substantial trusts. In all, the Duke family is now probably worth in the neighborhood of $300 million.

Another family that did not participate actively in the management of the family company after the death of the founder is the Reynolds family of North Carolina. Although the Reynoldses have been principal stockholders in R.J. Reynolds Industries Inc. for many years, only one of the children of the founder ever served as a director of the corporation. The company was founded in 1875 by Richard J. Reynolds and his brother, William N. Reynolds. Like many other successful entrepreneurs, R. J. Reynolds married late in life and, as a result, was fifty-six years old when his first child was born. When he died in 1918, R. J. Reynolds left an estate of about $60 million, much of it in R.J. Reynolds Industries stock. In his will, he stipulated that the bulk of his estate was to be divided among his four children but that their inheritances were to be held in trust until they turned twenty-eight years of age. By 1938, the descendants of R. J. Reynolds owned or were the beneficiaries of trusts that owned stock in R.J. Reynolds Industries worth $41 million. His brother, William N. Reynolds, and his wife owned stock in the company worth another $16 million. Altogether, the Reynolds family owned over 12 percent of the stock in the company. Because the children of R. J. Reynolds were still minors when he died, the task of safeguarding the Reynolds family and its fortune fell to his brother, William Reynolds. Indeed, for many years after the death of R. J. Reynolds, William Reynolds was the only member of the Reynolds family with any association with R.J. Reynolds Industries. Indeed, he served several years as president and later chairman of the company.

Because William Reynolds had no children of his own, his logical successor as president of R.J. Reynolds Industries was Richard J. Reynolds, Jr., the eldest son of the founder. However, Richard Reynolds showed little interest in the company. He dropped out of college after his second year and took up aviation. In 1927, he declared that he was leaving the country and would not return for seven years, until he was old enough to claim his inheritance. He spent three of these years sailing the Atlantic on his own ship. After receiving his inheritance in 1934, R. J. Reynolds, Jr., bought a 44,000-acre plantation on Sapelo Island, off the Georgia coast. Only in his later years did he develop any real interest in business. For example, he became a major stockholder and director of Delta Air Lines at the age of forty-three. It was during this same period that he finally joined the board of directors of R.J. Reynolds Industries. In all, Richard Reynolds was married four times and had seven children. He died of cancer in Switzerland in 1964. The other son of the founder, Z. Smith Reynolds, did not have an opportunity to become involved with the company. His death in 1932, at the age of twenty, was finally ruled a suicide, despite evidence of foul play. Because he had not yet received his inheritance when he died, his widow and his first wife both went to court to secure part of his trust for their respective children. In the end, an agreement was reached in which his trust, which was then worth roughly $28 million, was used to establish separate trusts for his two children and to fund the Z. Smith Reynolds Foundation. Richard Reynolds became the first president of the foundation, and his sisters, Mary Reynolds Babcock and Nancy Reynolds Bagley, became trustees.

The Reynolds family no longer has any direct involvement with R.J. Reynolds Industries. Richard J. Reynolds, Jr., was the last member of the family to serve as a director of the company. Indeed, the only member of the family to achieve any notoriety of late is Smith W. Bagley, the son of Nancy Reynolds Bagley. An early supporter of President Carter, Smith Bagley entertained the president on the family's 1,800-acre plantation on St. Simons Island, off the coast of Georgia. In 1979, he and several former business associates were charged with stock manipulation. He was acquitted by a jury later that same year. Because a substantial portion of the Reynolds fortune has gone to charity, the family has remained involved with the activities of its foundations. Various family members still control six separate family foundations that had total assets of $162 million in 1980. The Reynolds family undoubtedly began selling some of its R.J. Reynolds Industries stock after Richard Reynolds resigned as a director in 1949. Nevertheless, members of the Reynolds family and foundations endowed by them still owned over 6 percent of R.J. Reynolds Industries stock as of 1971. Of course, family members have used the proceeds from the sale of their R.J. Reynolds Industries stock to create more diversified investment portfolios. Richard Reynolds, for example, owned 10 percent of the stock in Delta Air Lines when he resigned as a director in 1957. Because three of the four children of R. J. Reynolds have passed away, most of the family fortune is now owned by his sixteen grandchildren and their children. Altogether, the Reynolds family is now probably worth in excess of $400 million.

Sometimes the failure of a corporate rich family to maintain control over the family corporation can adversely affect its fortune. This is the case with the Hartford family and its fortune. The founder of this fortune, George H. Hartford, began his business career as a clerk in a tea store. He helped expand the business into a chain of eleven tea stores, and, in 1867, he was made a junior partner in the firm. By the time his partner died in 1901, the company owned 198 stores selling groceries as well as tea. In order to settle the estate of his partner, George H. Hartford had the firm incorporated as the Great Atlantic & Pacific Tea Company Inc. He then convinced the heirs of his former partner to accept $1,250,000 in preferred stock as their share of the company, while he took only $150,000 in preferred stock plus all of the common stock, ostensibly worth only $700,000. The company, known simply as A&P, grew to become the largest grocery chain in the country. Along the way, it introduced many innovations in order to reduce both prices and costs, such as selling store brand items at discounts from popular brand items. It was not entirely an individual achievement, however. His two eldest sons, George and John Hartford, entered the business as soon as they got out of school and were instrumental in the expansion of the chain. They made a formidable business combination. George, who was chairman, devoted himself to the financial details, and John, who was president, concentrated on marketing. They were among the first to appreciate the advantages of larger stores, the forerunners of the modern supermarket, and they soon began closing small stores and opening larger ones. By 1951, A&P owned and operated 4,700 stores, most of them supermarkets.

For the first few decades at least, the Hartford family and its fortune seemed secure. George Hartford had five children, including three sons who worked for the company. As late as 1939, family members owned all of the voting common stock, almost 70 percent of the nonvoting common stock, and nearly 60 percent of the preferred stock in A&P. Together the children and grandchildren of the founder held stock in A&P worth at least $105 million, most of it through a family holding company. Although they were extremely competent businessmen, neither John nor George Hartford did much to safeguard the perpetuation of a Hartford dynasty at the Great Atlantic and Pacific Tea Company. John A. Hartford was married three times, twice to the same woman, but he had no children. His brother, George L. Hartford, had a daughter, but she died early in life. The only other source of heirs to carry on at A&P were the descendants of their other brother and two sisters. The youngest of the brothers, Edward V. Hartford, served for many years as the company secretary, but later he devoted most of his energies to developing various inventions. His son, Huntington Hartford, worked for the company for a while before he was fired by his uncle, John Hartford, for taking off half a day to attend the Harvard-Yale football game. Other relatives of the founder, including a son-in-law, another grandson, and the husband of a granddaughter, eventually became officers and directors of the company, but none of them ever rose to the post of president. Indeed, the other members of the Hartford family were deprived of their opportunity to control the corporation.

When John A. Hartford died in 1951, he willed almost his entire estate to his own Hartford Foundation. Similarly, when George L. Hartford died without any heirs six years later, he too left most of his estate to the Hartford Foundation. The following year, the Hartford family decided to dissolve their family holding company and list their A&P stock on the New York Stock Exchange. After the various classes of stock were consolidated into a single class of common stock, the Hartford Foundation was left with 34 percent of A&P stock, and the remaining members of the Hartford family held another 48 percent. It was at about this time that the fortunes of the Hartford family took a turn for the worse. When he left his estate to the Hartford Foundation, John Hartford stipulated that the president of A&P serve also as the president of the foundation. Consequently, the management of the company, with its control of the stock held by the Hartford Foundation and the support of a few members of the Hartford family, became insulated from the profit constraints felt by the managements of other grocery chains. In the years that followed, A&P suffered a gradual but prolonged decline in both sales and profits. Some of the members of the Hartford family tried to force changes in the management of the company, but they were unsuccessful. With the profits of the company in decline, the value of A&P stock plunged from $55 a share in 1959 to only $35 a share in 1969. Ten years later, when the Hartford Foundation and several members of the Hartford family finally sold most of their A&P stock to a foreign investment group, they had to settle for less than $8 a share.

Of the six grandchildren of George H. Hartford who eventually received a share of the family fortune, the best known was Huntington Hartford. Named George Huntington Hartford II, in honor of his grandfather, Huntington Hartford gained notoriety for his lavish standard of living and his misfortunes in business. In an interview published in 1961, he claimed that he was worth a mere $70 million. He found many uses for his money. He owned homes in Florida, California, New York, England, and France, as well as a hundred-foot yacht. In 1959, he bought the greater part of a small island in the Bahamas, where he built an exclusive resort for "discriminating" vacationers. After investing a total of $30 million in his Paradise Island resort, he was forced to sell his interest in the project for less than $2 million. His unprofitable investments in his Gallery of Modern Art, the publication of *Show,* a magazine of the arts, and an automated parking garage cost him at least another $17 million. His only really successful business venture was his initial investment in Oil Shale Corporation in 1959. By the time Huntington Hartford resigned as chairman of the company nine years later, his stock in Oil Shale Corporation was worth over $5 million. He now claims to be worth less than $10 million. Those members of the family who sold most of their A&P stock in the decade following the dissolution of the family holding company in 1959 were able to preserve most of their fortunes. However, two family members who held on to much of their stock saw their combined stockholdings in the company decline in value from over $180 million to less than $25 million in twenty years. Altogether, the six grandchildren of George Hartford and their respective children are probably worth less than $200 million today.

CUT SHORT

Not all corporate rich families develop into business dynasties. Indeed, some of them do not even survive as families. The Harkness family is an example of the virtual disappearance of a wealthy capitalist family. Although he was virtually unknown to the public at large, Edward S. Harkness was one of the richest men in America in 1938. He owed his great wealth to the fact that he inherited almost all of the fortune amassed by his father, Stephen V. Harkness, an early partner in the Standard Oil Company. His father, a successful distillery owner in Ohio, had invested in the oil-refining business in 1865 at the urging of Henry M. Flagler, the husband of his niece. As a result of this initial investment, he became one of the major stockholders in the Standard Oil Company. His son, Edward S. Harkness, had already inherited a considerable fortune when, in 1917, he inherited another $36 million from the estate of his older brother, Charles W. Harkness, who had no children of his own. His fortune was enlarged even more ten years later when he inherited $93 million from his mother's estate. Over the years, Edward Harkness developed a reputation for being both an astute financier and an unstinting philanthropist. As a financier, he invested heavily in railroads and became a major stockholder in the Southern Pacific, Union Pacific, New York Central, and Illinois Central railroads. He was also a major stockholder in several oil companies, including Exxon, Chevron, and Mobil. By 1938, his stock-holdings in just eight major companies, four oil companies and four railroads, were worth a total of $74 million.

Despite his success as a financier, Edward S. Harkness became known primarily as a philanthropist. It was a commitment instilled in him by his mother, Anna Harkness. After the death of her older son, Anna Harkness gave a total of $9 million to Yale University to construct a group of residence halls as a memorial to him. A few years later, she donated over $10 million to endow a charitable foundation to be known as the Commonwealth Fund. In all, her contributions to the Commonwealth Fund would eventually exceed $38 million. Edward Harkness became, of course, the first president of the Commonwealth Fund. Like his elder brother, Edward Harkness and his wife, Mary Stillman Harkness, never had any children. Reserved and modest by nature, he did not flaunt his immense wealth. Nevertheless, he did permit himself a few luxuries, such as a 135-foot yacht and a mansion in New York City. When he died in 1940, he left the bulk of his estate, over $55 million, in trust to several charities, including the Commonwealth Fund, with the income from this trust to be paid to his wife during her lifetime. When she died in 1954, Mary Harkness left a separate estate of $20 million, much of which eventually went to the Commonwealth Fund. In all, Edward Harkness, his mother, and his wife gave over $81 million to the Commonwealth Fund. The only surviving members of the Harkness family are the descendants of the three children of Lamon V. Harkness, an older half-brother to Charles and Edward Harkness. However, Lamon Harkness never inherited as much wealth as Edward Harkness.

Some corporate rich families fail to develop into business dynasties simply because of a shortage of male heirs. In the case of the Woolworth family, for example, the founder had no sons to perpetuate family control of the company. The Woolworth fortune was amassed by Frank W. Woolworth, one of the originators of the discount variety store. After a couple of failures as a storekeeper, Frank Woolworth opened his first successful variety store in 1879. With the help of his brother, C. Sumner Woolworth, he opened another store the following year. During the next three decades, Frank Woolworth established over three hundred stores across the nation. In 1911, he decided to merge his chain of stores with those owned by several competitors, including Seymour Knox and Fred M. Kirby, to form F. W. Woolworth Company. As a result of this merger, he received over half of the stock in a company that owned more than six hundred stores in the United States and England. During this same period, he spent almost $14 million of his own money to build the sixty-story Woolworth Building in New York. When Frank Woolworth died in 1919, his wife, who had just been declared mentally incompetent, inherited an estate conservatively valued at $31 million. When she died five years later, the Woolworth fortune, then worth almost $60 million, passed to their heirs with only minimal estate taxes. One-third of the estate went to Barbara Hutton, the only child of the late Edna Woolworth Hutton, one of the daughters of Frank Woolworth. The remainder of the estate was split between his two surviving daughters, Helena Woolworth McCann and Jessie Woolworth Donahue.

Despite the fact that Frank W. Woolworth had no sons, his family did not completely relinquish control of the company after his death. Even though women were a rarity in American business at the time, Jessie Woolworth Donahue and Helena Woolworth McCann both served as directors of F. W. Woolworth Company for a number of years. Their uncle, Sumner Woolworth, was the chairman of the company during this period. Altogether, the various members of the Woolworth family still owned over 10 percent of F.W. Woolworth Company, worth $36 million, in 1939. At that point, Barbara Hutton was no longer a major stockholder in the company. Because she was only twelve years old when she inherited her share of the Woolworth fortune, her father had been appointed as her guardian. In this capacity, Franklyn Hutton had liquidated her Woolworth stock and had invested the proceeds in other stocks and bonds. After all, he was the brother of Edward F. Hutton, the founder of a major brokerage house. When Barbara Hutton finally came into her inheritance in 1933, it was worth $42 million. In the years that followed, Barbara Hutton became a socialite known primarily for her many failed marriages. Her husbands included a Russian polo player, a Danish count, a Lithuanian prince of questionable nobility, a German baron, a Laotian artist, a notorious playboy from the Dominican Republic, and the famous actor Cary Grant. She had only one child, Lance Reventlow, who died in an airplane crash at the age of thirty-seven. Barbara Hutton died in 1972, unmarried and alone. By then, she had managed to spend almost all of her inheritance.

By and large, the Woolworths were more interested in the social activities of the upper class than in the business affairs of the F.W. Woolworth Company. Helena Woolworth, the eldest of the three daughters of Frank Woolworth, married Charles E. F. McCann, a lawyer from a prominent New York family. They built a lavish estate on Long Island and maintained slightly less opulent homes in New York and Palm Beach. Helena Woolworth McCann raised prize-winning roses while her husband built a substantial art collection. He also found time to sail their 247-foot diesel yacht. They had a son, Frazier McCann, and two daughters, Constance McCann Betts and Helena McCann Guest Charlton. When she died in 1938, Helena Woolworth McCann left most of her remaining stock in F.W. Woolworth Company, worth over $8 million, to her three children. She had created a trust for them three years earlier, composed mainly of Woolworth stock, which was reportedly worth $15 million. The other daughter of Frank Woolworth, Jessie Woolworth, married James P. Donahue, a man of relatively modest means. They had two sons, James and Woolworth Donahue, neither of whom had any children. Like her sister, Jessie Woolworth Donahue maintained an estate on Long Island, as well as homes in New York and Palm Beach. After her husband committed suicide, she became a recluse. Although various members of the Woolworth family maintained large stockholdings in F.W. Woolworth Company for at least two decades, none of the grandchildren of Frank Woolworth ever served as an officer or director of the company. The remaining members of the Woolworth family now share a fortune that is probably worth somewhat less than $100 million.

ALIVE AND WELL

On the basis of the fragmentary evidence at hand, it must be concluded that most of the corporate rich families of the 1930s are still quite wealthy. Of course, these families and their fortunes have changed a great deal over the years. To begin with, most of the individuals who were among the corporate rich a half century ago have passed away. They have been replaced within the ranks of the corporate rich by their children and grandchildren. Their descendants are still members of the corporate rich because their family fortunes were transferred virtually intact from one generation to the next. Nevertheless, time has taken its toll. Most of these corporate rich families are much larger today than they were in the 1930s. As a result, the younger members of these families are often less wealthy than their parents and grandparents. As these wealthy families grew in size, their fortunes were divided among more and more heirs. To the extent that the aggregate wealth of a family failed to grow apace with the growth of the family itself, the individual members of the family became less wealthy with each succeeding generation. However, there is considerable diversity among these families in terms of their size and complexity. Indeed, some wealthy families have almost disappeared altogether, whereas others have been reduced to only a handful of members. In some cases, the shortage of heirs has served to concentrate the remaining family fortune into a few hands. Conversely, other corporate rich families have grown very large. In these cases, the family fortune has been dispersed among a large number of family members.

The diversity among these corporate rich families as kinship groups is matched only by the diversity in the development of their fortunes. In this regard, it must be noted that the major corporate rich families in America during the 1930s were families that had been wealthy for at least two and often three generations. By 1939, only two of the wealthy entrepreneurs who had amassed these fortunes were still alive: Pierre S. du Pont and Henry Ford. In most cases, the wealthiest capitalist families in America at that time comprised the children and grandchildren of the entrepreneurs who had passed away years before. This fact suggests a peculiar characteristic about the wealth-accumulation process: The fortunes created by wealthy entrepreneurs may not reach their full scope during their lifetime. There are several plausible explanations for this pattern. All of the fortunes owned by corporate rich families consisted primarily of stock in one or more companies founded by the original entrepreneur. Although this entrepreneur may have experienced great success in his lifetime, his company may continue to grow and prosper for several decades after his death. In short, it may take more than one generation for a company to saturate its markets. As a result, many entrepreneurs may not live long enough to see their companies reach their full potential as major corporations with established positions in their industries. In this same vein, it must be noted that the successful entrepreneurs who founded these large fortunes often began their families relatively late in life. All of them were thirty years old before they had children, and many of them waited until they were over forty years old before they became parents.

By and large, most of the major fortunes of the 1930s have grown even larger over the past half century. However, the growth of these fortunes has generally failed to keep pace with inflation. In addition, taxes have taken their toll. None of these fortunes has been entirely eliminated by gift and estate taxes, but they have all been reduced to some extent as the indirect result of these taxes. In many cases, a substantial portion of the family fortune has been transferred to philanthropic foundations controlled by family members in order to avoid estate taxes. At the same time, fortunes which were once composed primarily of the stock in family corporations have been diversified. Much of the stock in family firms has been sold and the proceeds invested in diversified portfolios containing a variety of stocks and bonds. Usually, this process of diversification has proceeded slowly to avoid unnecessary capital-gains taxes. In other instances, fortunes have been greatly reduced in value by changes in stock market valuations attributable to changes in the profitability and growth of the family corporations. In a few cases, the decline in the family fortune has been precipitous. Another consequence of this diversification effort is that most of the corporations controlled by these families during the 1930s are no longer under family control. Even among those firms in which the founding family retains significant stockholdings, family members are no longer active in their daily management. Instead, family control has become relatively passive with only one or two family members serving as directors of the firm.

In general, these developments are not entirely unexpected. They mirror many of the changes that have occurred in even wealthier families such as the Rockefellers, du Ponts, and Mellons. Some decline in the fortunes of these families was inevitable. After all, they were the wealthiest of the corporate rich families in America simply because they were major stockholders in corporations that had very large market valuations. These market valuations were based on the fact that these corporations had experienced inordinately high levels of growth and profitability over the years. In the years that followed, these firms became mature corporations that dominated large but highly saturated markets. They were not able to grow at the same rate as in the past, and their market valuations declined as a result. Consequently, these corporate rich families were probably at the height of their wealth and power by the 1930s. Most of them had not been among the wealthiest capitalist families in America in the decades preceding the 1930s and, as a rule, they were not among the wealthiest capitalist families in the decades to come. In the pantheon of the corporate rich, they were soon to be eclipsed by other families, whose fortunes were on the rise. Nevertheless, any report of the demise of these families and their fortunes is surely premature. Although the corporate rich families of the 1930s have entered a period of gradual decline, they are still very rich, and, if history is any guide, they will probably remain very rich for many decades to come.

4

All
in the
Family

Corporate rich families are different from less affluent families. In particular, the members of wealthy capitalist families often possess a sense of family identity and an awareness of kinship ties that are virtually unique in contemporary American society. This emphasis on family and kinship is attributable to the fact that these families control large fortunes. Indeed, the distribution of wealth within each family has important implications for the structure of the family and the activities of its members. To begin with, the fortunes held by corporate rich families are based, at least initially, on their stockholdings in corporations founded by one or more family members. Consequently, the descendants of these founders have a common economic interest in the profitability and growth of particular firms. Furthermore, the corporate rich often employ elaborate strategies for preserving their fortunes as well as their control over family corporations. In order to keep gift and estate taxes to a minimum, for example, parents typically transfer most of their wealth to their children during their own lifetimes. These intergenerational transfers of wealth often entail complex legal and financial arrangements. As a result, the members of wealthy capitalist families are typically bound together into cohesive kinship groups by a series of family trusts, family offices, family holding companies, and family foundations. In short, the strategies developed by these families to ensure the transmission of their fortunes from one generation to the next have major consequences for the structure of these families as kinship groups.

The members of corporate rich families invariably accumulate symbolic as well as material capital. In short, they inherit not only economic wealth but social status as well. Individuals born into these families involuntarily become part of a network of relatives, both living and dead, whose history is inextricably linked to the history of a major corporation. Consequently, their positions within that family network define, to a large extent, their positions within the society at large. In the final analysis, it is the existence of an estate that is both material and symbolic in nature that gives the corporate rich family its unique character. Of course, the ownership of great wealth has many important implications for the activities of individual family members. In particular, it has a significant impact on the position of women in these families. Although almost all of the entrepreneurs who have amassed large fortunes have been men, women have generally inherited wealth equally with men in recent years. As a result, some of the wealthiest individuals in America have been the widows and daughters of successful entrepreneurs. Despite the fact that they are often excluded from management positions in family corporations, these women can still influence the policies of these firms by virtue of their positions as major stockholders. Last but not least, the ownership of great wealth also has an effect on such fundamental processes as mate selection. It is not coincidental that many members of corporate rich families marry scions of other wealthy or socially prominent families.

CHARITY BEGINS AT HOME

One of the most distinctive features of the corporate rich family is the systematic manner in which parents, over a period of many years, transfer most of their wealth to their children and grandchildren. Because the present system of gift and estate taxes is somewhat more lenient toward lifetime gifts than posthumous bequests, there is a real incentive for wealthy individuals to transfer assets to their progeny while they are still alive. Consequently, it is not unusual for wealthy individuals to give most of their fortunes to their heirs long before they die. An extreme example of this pattern is Henry Crown, who amassed a fortune in real estate and corporate stock, including a 20 percent stake in General Dynamics Corporation, which is now worth in excess of $600 million. Over the years, he has succeeded in transferring most of his personal fortune into a network of trusts, partnerships, and holding companies owned largely by his children and grandchildren. By the time he was eighty-four years old, he could boast: "I personally own very little. I've already given most of it away." As a result of such lifetime gifts, it is not at all unusual for even the wealthiest entrepreneurs to leave relatively small estates. John D. Rockefeller, for example, had given away almost all of his fortune either to his family or to charity before he passed away. Similarly, his only son and principal heir, John D. Rockefeller, Jr., managed to give the bulk of his wealth to his own children before he died. Almost identical patterns of lifetime transfers can be found among other corporate rich families such as the Mellons, du Ponts, Gettys, and Hunts.

In order to reduce gift and estate taxes to a minimum, it is sometimes necessary for wealthy parents to begin transferring their assets, especially corporate stock, to their children even before they are adults. Because corporate stock typically appreciates over time, gift and estate taxes can be reduced by giving this stock to children before it has appreciated in value. For example, John D. Rockefeller, Jr., established a series of trusts for his wife and children in 1934, when his youngest child was only nineteen years old. The primary assets of these trusts were stock in three Standard Oil companies worth almost $74 million. By the time John D. Rockefeller, Jr., died in 1960, this stock had appreciated in value to over $303 million. The estate taxes on $303 million in 1960 would have been much greater than the gift taxes on $74 million in 1934. In fact, the imposition of more progressive gift and estate taxes in 1935 forced other corporate rich families to adopt similar strategies. A number of large family trusts were established in 1934 by such wealthy individuals as Andrew W. Mellon, J. Paul Getty, and H. L. Hunt. Lifetime transfers of assets to children can also serve as a means of reducing income taxes for wealthy parents. Even with the best tax advice, the corporate rich often pay substantial income taxes. Children, however, are typically in lower income-tax brackets than their parents. As a result, the tax liability of the family as a whole can be reduced by distributing income-producing assets, such as corporate stock, more or less equally among all the members of the family.

Most of the intergenerational transfers of wealth among the corporate rich involve the use of generation-skipping trusts. In such an arrangement, parents irrevocably transfer certain assets to a trust for the benefit of their children and grandchildren. The children, who are usually the income beneficiaries of the trust, are entitled to receive all of the income produced by these assets for life. The grandchildren, who are usually the remaindermen of the trust, receive these assets only after the death of the last surviving income beneficiary. The widespread use of generation-skipping trusts has enabled most corporate rich families to protect the bulk of their fortunes from gift and estate taxes. In the case of the Rockefeller family, for example, the largest single family holding, Rockefeller Group Inc., is owned almost entirely by the trusts that John D. Rockefeller, Jr., created for his children in 1934. Indeed, fully three-quarters of the $1.03 billion in securities owned by the Rockefeller family in 1974 was held in trusts. Similarly, almost all of the fortune accumulated by Texas oilman H. L. Hunt is held by a series of generation-skipping trusts. In 1935, as a means of avoiding future gift and estate taxes, H. L. Hunt placed all of the stock in Placid Oil, to which he later transferred his most lucrative oil properties, into a series of trusts for his six children by Lyda Bunker Hunt. A similar maze of trusts encompassing most of the family fortune can be found in almost any corporate rich family.

In addition to often substantial tax advantages, trusts of this type contain inherent *spendthrift* provisions that prevent any dissipation of the principal until it is distributed to the remaindermen. In many states, for example, the assets of a trust cannot be invaded to satisfy the claims of creditors against an income beneficiary. When the young du Pont scion, Lammot du Pont Copeland, Jr., declared bankruptcy in 1972 with almost $60 million in liabilities and less than $26 million in assets, creditors were unable to invade the principal of his $14 million trust. Although he did agree to pay a small fraction of his debts over a ten-year period out of his income from this trust, the trust itself was not depleted by this financial debacle. Another advantage of trusts for corporate rich families is the fact that they are beyond the reach of spouses. Trust agreements usually limit the payment of either income or principal to the lineal descendants of the grantor with no provisions for the spouses of these descendants. In the event of a divorce, a trust is not counted as part of any property settlement, because the one spouse is simply an income beneficiary of the trust with no claim on its assets. For example, when Nelson Rockefeller divorced his first wife in 1962, after thirty-two years of marriage, her divorce settlement was based only on his personal wealth. The massive trusts established for him by his father, which provided most of his income, were not included as part of their community property. Similarly, when he died in 1978, his second wife did not receive anything from these trusts. Instead, they reverted to his children. Fortunately for her, she was already the income beneficiary of a smaller but substantial trust that Nelson had created out of his own funds.

Although progressive gift and estate taxes have largely failed to reduce the intergenerational transmission of wealth, they have had a profound impact on the structure of wealthy capitalist families. Before the enactment of progressive estate taxes in the early part of this century, most of the inheritors of great wealth did not receive the bulk of their inheritances until one or both of their parents had died. There were few tax incentives, at the time, for parents to give more than a modicum of wealth to their children by way of lifetime transfers. In this way, parents also retained the option of disinheriting any errant progeny. This ability to disinherit children gave parents considerable power within the family and resulted in hierarchically organized kinship groups in which wealthy parents were generally accorded a certain amount of deference by their children and grandchildren. However, the imposition of progressive gift and estate taxes changed all that. In order to avoid estate taxes that might deplete the family fortune, the corporate rich have been forced to transfer much of their wealth to their children by means of lifetime transfers. Children from wealthy capitalist families now receive most of their inheritances in the form of gifts from parents or grandparents who are still alive. One consequence of this pattern of lifetime transfers to children is a subtle change in the nature of family relations among the corporate rich. The children of the corporate rich are likely to achieve financial independence at a very early age as the result of becoming income beneficiaries of trusts established by their parents and grandparents. As Rachel Lambert Mellon, the wife of Paul Mellon, once lamented, "it's hard with children who are on the same economic level. They simply don't have to listen."

Patterns of inheritance, through either lifetime gifts or testamentary bequests, reveal the basic kinship patterns of wealthy capitalist families. The inheritances received by the relatives of a wealthy entrepreneur are usually dictated by their position within the kinship group as a whole. Conceptions of kinship are also reflected in the laws governing inheritance. Typically, the capitalist family is defined in terms of lineal descent. For certain purposes, the family may also include the spouses of these descendants, although the rights of spouses to share in the family fortune are usually restricted by the use of trusts. As a rule, this model of kinship does not include collateral relatives. Brothers and sisters of wealthy entrepreneurs do not receive much of the family fortune unless they were involved somehow in the family firm. Andrew W. Mellon and Richard B. Mellon, for example, did not bother to include their two older brothers in their business ventures. Consequently, some Mellon cousins eventually became billionaires whereas others never even became millionaires. Of course, collateral relatives may receive substantial inheritances whenever a wealthy individual is childless. Pierre S. du Pont II, for example, gave most of his fortune to his brothers and sisters and their children. In this same manner, Sid W. Richardson, who remained a bachelor all of his life, gave most of his oil properties to collateral relatives while he was still alive. In particular, he managed to transfer the bulk of his massive oil fortune to his only nephew and business partner, Perry R. Bass.

In actual practice, patterns of inheritance are affected by tax considerations as well as conceptions of kinship. The members of corporate rich families seek to reduce not only their own taxes but the taxes of their descendants as well. These tax considerations lead to some fairly standard patterns of lifetime gifts and inheritances. To begin with, most of the corporate rich give relatively little to their spouses in the way of lifetime transfers. The reason is simple. There are no tax benefits to such a transfer of wealth because husbands and wives typically file joint income-tax returns. However, these same individuals almost invariably make generous provisions for their spouses in their wills because estate taxes contain a marital exemption that allows at least half of any estate to pass directly to a spouse without any taxes. This marital exemption is based, of course, on the supposition that the assets accumulated by any individual are common property with his or her spouse. Assuming both husband and wife eventually bequeath their residual estates to their descendants, the marital exemption often serves to reduce the estate taxes on the overall family fortune because it is transferred to the succeeding generation in two installments. Because of the progressive nature of estate taxes, the aggregate taxes eventually paid on each half of the estate are usually smaller than the taxes that would have been assessed on the entire estate. By way of illustration, Richard K. Mellon left half of his residual estate, worth roughly $113 million in 1970, in trust for his wife. She was the lifetime income beneficiary of this trust. Only after her death ten years later were the assets held by this trust distributed among their children.

Aside from the special attention given spouses because of the marital exemption, most of the wealth held by the corporate rich that is not destined for charity is distributed, sooner or later, among their children and grandchildren. As Stanley Lebergott puts it: "In the most capitalistic of societies, during the most Byzantine stages of its decadence, the family still constitutes an island of primitive communism. The U.S. offers no exception." By and large, the wealth of parents is distributed equitably among their children and grandchildren. Specifically, the distribution of wealth within the family is usually *per stirpes,* with each branch of the family getting an equal share. Under this rule, if a child dies before receiving his or her inheritance, it is distributed among his or her children. In general, daughters inherit more or less equally with sons. In the past, of course, sons often inherited substantially more than daughters. John D. Rockefeller, Jr., for example, received much more of the family fortune than his three sisters. Other members of the corporate rich who gave more to their sons than their daughters include Edward H. Harriman of Union Pacific, Marshall Field III of Field Communications, and John T. Dorrance of Campbell Soup. The partial disinheritance of daughters is no longer common among the corporate rich. Unlike his father, John D. Rockefeller, Jr., gave his one daughter only slightly less than he gave each of his five sons. Similarly, the two daughters of H. L. Hunt each inherited approximately the same amount as each of their four brothers.

FROM FAMILY TO CLAN

It is a demographic inevitability that most families, even corporate rich families, become larger and more complex with each passing generation. Moreover, as these families grow in size and complexity, they become less cohesive as kinship groups. Of course, family unity is usually not a problem for the first few generations. As long as the founding entrepreneur or his wife is alive, there is little difficulty in maintaining the unity of the family. After all, children typically defer to their parents on matters that affect the entire family, particularly when those parents are both rich and powerful. Even in the second generation, the task of maintaining some semblance of family unity is not very problematic because the children of the founder usually share the sense of affinity that is common between brothers and sisters. In general, the strength of the kinship ties between siblings stems from the fact that they were raised together and consequently share many formative experiences in common. However, these kinship ties often become much more attenuated by the third generation. The members of this generation, many of whom are only first cousins to one another, do not possess the same sense of affinity that existed between their parents. Although cousins may share some common experiences, most of their lives have been spent apart with their own parents and siblings. By the third generation, the corporate rich family, primarily comprising the grandchildren of the founder, has usually become both large in size and complex in its structure. At the same time, it has also become less cohesive as a kinship group as a result of the attenuation of ties among family members.

Of course, corporate rich families vary considerably in both their size and complexity as kinship groups. Those families in which each descendant produces only a few progeny may remain relatively small even into the third and fourth generations. The Ford family, for example, is small in comparison to most other established capitalist families, largely because of the fact that Henry Ford had only 1 child, Edsel Ford. His 4 children, in turn, had only 13 children of their own. Conversely, those families in which there are a large number of children in each generation may become extremely large. One of the most prolific of all corporate rich families is the Pitcairn family. Although John Pitcairn, the founder of PPG Industries, had only 3 children, they provided him with 24 grandchildren. These grandchildren proved to be only slightly less prolific than their parents. At last count, they had produced 124 children of their own. The Ford family is not only smaller than the Pitcairn family; it is also less complex in terms of its structure as a kinship group. The 13 great-grandchildren of Henry Ford are all first cousins, whereas most of the 124 great-grandchildren of John Pitcairn are only second cousins to one another. Other factors being equal, the differences in the size and complexity of these families as kinship groups render it easier for the Ford family to maintain some sense of family unity than the Pitcairn family. Although the Fords can still be considered a family, the Pitcairns can only be considered a clan.

Even though strong kinship ties that extend beyond primary relatives, such as parents, siblings, and children, are not common in the United States, corporate rich families develop norms that emphasize the importance of kinship ties with secondary relatives. In such families, individuals are familiar with their grandparents, aunts, uncles, nieces, and nephews, as well as many of their first cousins. By and large, it seems that the development of such centripetal kinship norms depends on the existence of some common interest that both unifies the family and distinguishes it from other families. "The presence of a transcendent interest," asserts one kinship expert, "justifies the persistence of kinship structures beyond a single generation without regard to individual privation." In the case of the corporate rich family, this transcendent interest centers on the economic and social status of the family. Because the inheritance of stock in a family corporation is the defining characteristic of the corporate rich family, membership in the family is limited primarily to the lineal descendants of the founding entrepreneur. Of course, if more than one family member participated in the founding of the family firm, the boundaries of family are expanded to include their descendants as well. In short, the corporate rich family is composed almost exclusively of the heirs to the family fortune. This demarcation of the corporate rich family prevails because, in the final analysis, it is the fortune that unites and sustains the family. As one of the great-grandchildren of Frederick Weyerhaeuser noted, "wealth is what keeps the family together."

Wealth may well be the main bond that unites the corporate rich family, but it is not the only bond. In addition to inheriting a share of the family fortune, the descendants of a wealthy entrepreneur also inherit a position within the network of relatives that constitutes the corporate rich family. This network of relatives, both living and dead, represents what one researcher terms a "symbolic family estate." Anyone who inherits part of the du Pont fortune, for example, also inherits a role, however small, in an ongoing saga involving hundreds of relatives over a period of two centuries. Symbolic estates, like material estates comprising property, require some maintenance. Individual family members maintain these symbolic estates through the construction of family genealogies, the publication of biographies, and the oral transmission of personal anecdotes. Furthermore, family members have a personal stake in the perpetuation of this symbolic estate. As Bernard Farber observes, "regardless of where they live or the nature of their social world, they can utilize this symbolic estate to legitimate their social status." The emphasis on kinship ties among wealthy capitalist families is, of course, typical of the upper class in general. In the words of one keen observer of proper Philadelphia society, "the ultimate club is the family, not the immediate family circle but the total family of in-laws and connections—'kin.'" In this regard, the family is the most exclusive of all social clubs inasmuch as membership is predicated on either birth or marriage into the family. In the end, the extended capitalist family is more than a mere genealogical construction; it is a closely linked network of relatives with common economic interests and a collective social identity.

The focal point for the social identity of the corporate rich family is the founding entrepreneur. As the historian Edward Saveth points out, "it is the achieving individuals within the achieving family who become family history." Indeed, the practice of naming male scions after their illustrious forebears represents a form of ancestor worship for wealthy capitalist families. Several of these namesakes of famous entrepreneurs, such as Eli Lilly II; Harvey S. Firestone, Jr.; Henry Ford II; and William R. Hearst, Jr., have managed to achieve at least some measure of success as managers in companies founded by their fathers or grandfathers. Marshall Field V served as president of Field Communications, the company founded by his grandfather, Marshall Field III. The original family fortune, however, can be traced to the department store founded by his great-great-grandfather, the original Marshall Field. Sometimes the omission of a serial number may obscure the fact that a scion is a namesake of the founding entrepreneur. For example, Amory Houghton, Jr., who served for many years as the president of Corning Glass Works, is actually the grandson of another Amory Houghton, Jr., the founder of the company. In this same tradition, J. Paul Getty named his first son, George F. Getty II, after his father, the original founder of Getty Oil. He was also pleased when another son, Eugene P. Getty, decided to change his name to J. Paul Getty, Jr. Other namesakes of famous entrepreneurs, such as John D. Rockefeller IV, Pierre S. du Pont IV, and Henry J. Heinz III, achieved fame of their own in politics but only after adopting more pedestrian nicknames such as "Jay" Rockefeller, "Pete" du Pont, and "Jack" Heinz.

The symbolic significance of family names is nowhere more evident than among the female descendants of wealthy entrepreneurs. Although they usually take the family names of their husbands when they marry, many of them use their maiden names as middle names in order to retain their original family identities. For example, Marjorie Post, the daughter of the founder of General Foods, Charles W. Post, used Post as her middle name during each of her four marriages. Finally, she reverted to her maiden name after she divorced her last husband. Another example of this pattern is Marion Deering McCormick, a granddaughter of William Deering, one of the founders of International Harvester. Despite the fact that she had married into the celebrated McCormick family, she was quick to point out her own family identity by saying, "I myself am a Deering." Other prominent heiresses who maintained their original family identities include Sarah Mellon Scaife, Abby Rockefeller Mauze, and Elinor Medill Patterson. Moreover, the daughters of wealthy entrepreneurs often give their family names as middle names to their own children. For example, Anna Deere Wiman, one of the granddaughters of John Deere, the founder of Deere & Company, named her sons Charles Deere Wiman and Dwight Deere Wiman. Arthur Ochs Sulzberger and Richard Mellon Scaife are also examples of this pattern. On occasion, a scion of a corporate rich family may even wind up with the family name as a first name. Edna Cargill MacMillan, the daughter of the founder of Cargill, Inc., named her second son Cargill MacMillan. In this same vein, Elinor Dorrance Hill, a daughter of the founder of Campbell Soup, named one of her daughters Dorrance Hill.

The identity and cohesion of the corporate rich family are also promoted by social contact and interaction among family members. To begin with, members of these families sometimes live near one another in the exclusive neighborhoods and suburbs of major American cities. Their neighbors typically include the scions of other wealthy and socially prominent families. There are strong centripetal forces that keep many of the scions of corporate rich families in close proximity to one another. For instance, those family members who are still actively engaged in the management and direction of the family firm must live within commuting distance of its corporate headquarters. Others may choose to remain in the same general vicinity because of the friendships they have established with the members of other wealthy and socially prominent families. In addition, the members of these families may derive a certain amount of status and power in the local area from their association with the family firm and any philanthropic foundations endowed by the family. For whatever reasons, the pattern of residential propinquity within corporate rich families often obtains even in the third and fourth generations. Some of the wealthiest scions of the Mellon family, for example, still live on family estates in the Ligonier Valley outside Pittsburgh. Similarly, several of the grandchildren and great-grandchildren of Henry Ford still live in Grosse Pointe Farms near Detroit. The estates and the houses of the children are rarely as large or opulent as those of their parents, but the locale is often the same.

As corporate rich families evolve, however, many family members eventually move away from their ancestral homes. Relocation can serve as a means of regaining a degree of anonymity for those family members who find their family identity more of a burden than an advantage. However, even the geographical dispersion of family members does not necessarily lead to the complete disintegration of the wealthy capitalist family as a kinship group. In order to maintain their kinship ties, many corporate rich families hold periodic family reunions. The Rockefeller family, for example, meets at least twice a year, at the family estate at Pocantico. Although not every member of the family comes to these meetings, many of them attend on a fairly regular basis. In the same manner, the descendants of Lunsford Richardson, the founder of the Richardson-Vicks Inc. subsidiary of The Procter & Gamble Company, have met every other year for the past five decades. Family meetings and reunions serve a dual purpose. First and foremost, they are social events that permit family members who live far apart to become reacquainted with one another. These meetings also give family members an opportunity to discuss common financial problems and the affairs of the family firm. The Weyerhaeuser family, for instance, schedules its annual family meeting to coincide with the annual meeting of the Weyerhaeuser Company. Family members typically meet on other occasions as well. Weddings involving the scions of corporate rich families are typically very large social events attended by a great many family members, including aunts, uncles, and cousins. Similarly, the funerals for members of these same families are also occasions for reuniting distant relatives.

Even as the corporate rich family evolves into a large and somewhat dispersed clan, it usually manages to maintain some semblance of family identity. Indeed, some of the younger scions of prominent capitalist families may feel their personal identity is almost eclipsed by their family identity. As one of the young Rockefeller cousins lamented, "within the family, one hardly ever talks directly about who we are without our Rockefeller identity." Nevertheless, the growing size and complexity of the wealthy capitalist family eventually erode the kinship ties between members of different branches of the family. By the fourth generation, the corporate rich family has typically evolved into a clan whose members are often no more than second cousins to one another. Rather than disintegrating altogether, however, large capitalist families often become segmented into a series of relatively distinct and cohesive branches. For example, the du Pont family, which is composed primarily of 34 first cousins and over 107 second cousins, has clearly reached the status of a clan. For all practical purposes, this clan is now segmented into eight distinct branches, each comprising the descendants of one of the brothers and sisters of Pierre S. du Pont. Most of the members of these branches are still first cousins to one another. Despite this attenuation and segmentation of kinship ties in older corporate rich families, some sense of family identity may still prevail. As Pierre S. du Pont IV, one of these second cousins, puts it, "there's still a bond of heritage holding us together, but I don't feel it as strongly as my father did, and my children don't feel it as strongly as I do."

TIES THAT BIND

The corporate rich family is more than simply a family. In the words of Maurice Zeitlin, the wealthy capitalist family is "a complex kinship unit in which economic interests and kinship bonds are inextricably intertwined." To begin with, there is a high degree of class homogeneity within corporate rich families. Whatever their differences and idiosyncrasies, individuals from these families inevitably occupy very similar positions within the American class structure. Consequently, these individuals have many economic and political interests in common with the members of other wealthy capitalist families. The class interests of these families include, most notably, the reduction of income and transfer taxes as well as the promotion of economic growth and corporate profitability. The great-grandchildren of John D. Rockefeller and the children of H. L. Hunt may not travel in the same social circles, but they nevertheless share many of the same class interests. In addition, the members of a particular corporate rich family share specific economic interests as the result of their common stockholdings in the family corporation. As a rule, the descendants of a wealthy entrepreneur have inherited a fortune composed, by and large, of a substantial block of stock in a single corporation. Consequently, the fate of a corporate rich family and its fortune are inextricably linked, at least initially, with the fate of the family firm. As a result, the corporate rich family is more than a kinship group. It also represents, in effect, a cohesive economic interest group.

Sometimes the members of the corporate rich family are united by the fact that much of their wealth is invested in family holding companies or private corporations whose stock is not traded on any exchange. Whenever a company is closely held by a family, it may be extremely difficult, if not impossible, for individual stockholders to dispose of their shares. Bechtel Corporation, Cargill Inc., Hallmark Cards, and Advance Publications are all examples of very large firms whose shares are so closely held by their founding families that they are not traded on any exchange. In most of these private companies, family members who want to sell out must either sell their shares to other family members or convince the corporation itself to buy back their stock. Even if the family fortune comprises corporate stock that is publicly traded on the major exchanges, this stock may be held by a family holding company. Several corporate rich families are bound together by such holding companies. Almost half of the stock in The Times Mirror Company owned by the Chandler family is held indirectly through a family holding company, Chandlis Securities. Other major examples of this pattern include the MGM/UA Entertainment stock held for the Kerkorian family by Tracinda Corporation, the Consolidated Papers Inc. stock held for the Mead family by Mead Securities, and the Amoco stock held for the Blaustein family by the American Trading and Production Company. Several other family holding companies, such as the Harbel Corporation owned by the Firestone family and the Midland Investment Company owned by the Hixon family, have been dissolved in recent years.

The shared economic interests of the corporate rich family are usually given concrete form by a series of institutions. In order to administer their finances, many corporate rich families have established family offices in one form or another. For example, the finances of the Ford family are administered by an entity known only as Ford Estates. These offices provide family members with financial advice and tax counsel as well as general accounting services. The size of the office is typically proportional to the size of the family, as well as the magnitude of its fortune. The Rockefellers maintain a family office, Rockefeller Family and Associates, which employs over two hundred clerks, accountants, lawyers, and financial advisers. For many years, the Mellons also had a central family office, T. Mellon and Sons, to handle their myriad investments. However, this central office was later dissolved, only to be replaced by separate family offices, such as Richard K. Mellon and Sons, for each branch of the family. Families with smaller fortunes require much smaller offices. The Weyerhaeusers, for example, manage with an office that has only thirty employees. Sometimes a trust company controlled by the family functions as a family office. The Wilmington Trust Company, for example, provides many of the services of a family office to the numerous heirs of Pierre S. du Pont. Other families that use trust companies as family offices include the Phippses with their Bessemer Trust Company and the Pews with their Glenmede Trust Company. In some cases, a family holding company serves as a family office. The Blaustein family of Baltimore uses its family holding company, American Trading and Production Company, to manage the various investments and business activities of the family.

There are a number of other institutional arrangements that serve to unite the corporate rich family. In particular, trusts established for family members often serve to centralize control over the entire family fortune. In the most extreme case, a wealthy individual may create a single large trust for the benefit of all of his or her descendants. Families in which the bulk of the family fortune was held for many years by a single trust include the Gettys of Getty Oil, the Klines of SmithKline Beckman, the Ordways of Minnesota Mining and Manufacturing, and the Medills of Tribune Company. A few corporate rich families, such as the Hearsts of Hearst Corporation and the Sulzbergers of The New York Times Company, are still bound together by such monolithic trusts. More often, a few key family members serve as the trustees of a series of separate trusts for the benefit of many different family members. For example, Arthur A. Houghton, Jr., and his cousin Amory Houghton have served for four decades as trustees of over a dozen trusts for the benefit of their children and various nieces, nephews, and cousins. Most of the Houghton family fortune, including almost all of its $340 million in Corning Glass Works stock, is held by these trusts. The existence of family trusts, family holding companies, and family offices serves to reinforce kinship ties among the members of corporate rich families. Indeed, George Marcus, an observer of kinship patterns among wealthy capitalist families, concludes, "a legally devised plan to transfer and conserve patrimonial capital in one generation becomes in the next generation an organizational framework for extended family relations."

Although the common financial interests shared by the members of a wealthy capitalist family usually serve to maintain some semblance of unity among its members, these same financial interests can also create bitter family feuds. Such disputes often erupt whenever some of the members of a family are deprived of the opportunity to control their share of the family fortune. One of the most celebrated instances of this problem involved the Getty family. In 1934, J. Paul Getty convinced his mother, Sarah C. Getty, to put most of her Getty Oil stock in a trust for the benefit of him and his children. The original trust agreement named J. Paul Getty as its sole trustee. By the time J. Paul Getty died in 1976, this trust was worth $1.3 billion. In 1982, Gordon Getty, the youngest son of J. Paul Getty, became the sole trustee of the trust. Neither of the other two sons of J. Paul Getty nor any of his sixteen grandchildren had any control over the trust, even though they were all beneficiaries. In 1985, Gordon Getty decided to sell the 40 percent of Getty Oil stock held by the Sarah Getty Trust to Texaco Inc. for a little over $4 billion. This decision led to a series of family disputes concerning the administration of the trust. Three nieces of Gordon Getty filed suit to block the sale, but to no avail. A few months after the transaction was completed, three other nieces filed suit to have Gordon Getty removed as the sole trustee of the trust. Lawyers for all twenty-six descendants of J. Paul Getty recently agreed on a plan to divide the family trust into a series of smaller trusts. In this way, each branch of the Getty family would be able to control its own share of the Getty fortune.

Family feuds over the control of portions of a family fortune can last for decades. One of the most protracted family disputes occurred in the otherwise staid and intensely respectable Phipps family. In 1955, Esmond B. Martin, one of the seventeen grandchildren of Henry Phipps, sued his uncle as the trustee of his trust fund, for an accounting of his share of the family holding company, Bessemer Securities. Charging his uncle and other family members with abrogating their fiduciary responsibilities, Esmond Martin sought personal control over his 5 percent share of the $280 million in stocks, bonds, and real estate held by Bessemer Securities. He was opposed not only by his cousins but also by his brothers, one of whom threatened to sell the family estate, where Esmond lived, out from under him. Not one to be easily deterred, Esmond has spent nearly $3 million over the past three decades in legal fees in various suits against the family holding company and those members of the family who manage it. Perhaps because the bulk of its fortune is concentrated in a labyrinth of trusts administered by a family trust company, the Phipps family has witnessed several family confrontations. In the latest family row, Ogden M. Phipps, Jr., displaced his second cousin, Frederick E. Guest II, as chairman of Bessemer Securities with the promise of instigating a more aggressive investment policy. However, this most recent skirmish within the Phipps family for control of the family holding company was merely a continuation of a conflict that began a few years earlier when Frederick Guest deposed the father of Ogden Phipps as chairman of Bessemer Securities.

Family disputes often involve money as well as power. One of the most celebrated family feuds in recent years involved the descendants of Alice King Kleberg, most of whom are heirs to the massive King Ranch in Texas. Several years ago, two grandsons of Alice King Kleberg sold their stock in King Ranch Inc. back to the corporation. Belton K. Johnson and his half-brother, Robert R. Sheldon, decided to sell out because they disagreed with the financial policies being pursued by the corporation, which is owned entirely by fifty or so members of the Kleberg family. Belton K. Johnson alone received $70 million for his 12 percent interest in the ranch and its oil royalties. The two half-brothers later brought suit against the family corporation, seeking approximately $60 million in restitution. In their suits, they claimed that their cousins misled them about the value of their King Ranch stock by failing to mention the prospect of a settlement with Exxon that increased the oil royalties paid to the ranch.

A similar dispute has surfaced recently among the descendants of Hugh R. Cullen, the Texas oilman who founded Quintana Petroleum. Two of his grandsons, Erico and Ugo di Portanova, recently filed suit against three aunts over their administration of his estate.

The brothers claim that the aunts acted illegally when they sold a large block of Quintana stock held by the estate of Hugh Cullen to their own husbands and two other nephews at a bargain price in 1964. The di Portanovas argued that this transaction deprived them of the opportunity to share fully in a family fortune that has been estimated at over $1 billion. In the interim, the two brothers manage to survive on the roughly $6 million income they receive each year from various family trusts and investments managed by the other members of the Cullen family.

Family disputes among the corporate rich often turn into protracted legal battles that provide the grist for sensationalistic articles in major newspapers and national magazines. Because so little is known about the affairs and dealings of wealthy capitalist families, except for those details that are made public in the course of these legal proceedings, it is generally assumed that these families are somehow prone to feuds. In point of fact, feuds and disagreements are exceptions to the rule among the corporate rich. Most of these families manage to maintain at least a modicum of unity. Indeed, the absence of discord among wealthy capitalist families is remarkable in view of the enormity of the financial stakes. Moreover, the members of these families typically have the resources to pursue even the most frivolous litigation. In any event, these disputes are usually perceived by the participants as internal family affairs. As such, they do not necessarily impair the ability of the family to act as a cohesive kinship group whenever some display of unity is required to preserve the family fortune and maintain control over the family firm. For example, William C. Ford disagreed with Henry Ford II over his decision to fire Lee Iacocca as president of Ford Motor Company. Henry Ford was, of course, chairman of the company at the time, but William Ford was a director and its largest single stockholder. Nevertheless, William Ford reluctantly backed his brother for the sake of family unity. As one knowledgeable observer of the Fords put it, "when it gets down to a confrontation, it's still the family against the world."

FOR LOVE AND MONEY

Another distinctive characteristic of corporate rich families is the extent to which they are intermarried with other wealthy and socially prominent families. Of course, marriage has always been one of the most expedient means of gaining social status. Around the turn of the century, for example, it was fashionable for young American heiresses to marry European aristocrats. Perhaps the most celebrated of these marriages was that between Consuelo Vanderbilt, the daughter of William K. Vanderbilt III, who controlled the New York Central Railroad, and Charles Spencer-Churchill, the ninth Duke of Marlborough, in 1895. Over the next several years, many other wealthy capitalist families, including the Whitneys, Woolworths, Phippses, Blaffers, Fields, Manvilles, Johnsons, and Guggenheims, also became related by marriage to various aristocratic families. In some cases, very large dowries were exchanged for titles of dubious authenticity. Marriages of this type became much less common after the turn of the century, but they were not unknown. Several decades later, for example, Marcia Stranahan, an heiress to the Champion Spark Plug fortune, married Prince Youka Troubetzkoy. At about the same time, Boyce Schulze, an heiress to the Newmont Mining fortune, married Prince Alexander Hohenlohe. In virtually every case, it was a female descendant of a wealthy American family who married the male descendant of an aristocratic family. For their part, men from wealthy American families demonstrated very little interest in marrying into the European aristocracy.

Although marriages between American heiresses and European aristocrats eventually fell out of fashion, similar alliances between "new wealth" and "old families" within the United States became almost commonplace. There are many plausible explanations for the prevalence of marriages between the scions of corporate rich families and the descendants of socially prominent families. To some extent, they can be viewed simply as exchanges of wealth for status. The members of socially prominent families often welcomed marriages with the scions of wealthy capitalist families in order to replenish their somewhat depleted family fortunes. As Stephen Birmingham notes in his study *The Right People,* "family money is a thing that, from generation to generation, must not only be preserved, but must also be enriched and fed and nourished from time to time, from whatever sources are at hand." At the same time, the members of wealthy capitalist families welcomed marriages with the scions of socially prominent families because they expedited the acceptance of family members into the social circles of the upper class. For example, the social status of the entire Duke family was quickly elevated after it was linked by marriage, not only once but twice, to the established Biddle family of Philadelphia. In this same manner, John D. Rockefeller, Jr., helped accelerate the acceptance of the Rockefeller family into the American upper class when he married Abby Aldrich, the daughter of a U.S. senator whose family could trace its roots in America to the arrival of the *Mayflower.* The Aldrich family also gained from this alliance. Nelson Aldrich, the brother of Abby Aldrich Rockefeller, was later appointed chairman of Chase Manhattan Bank.

The most heralded marriages, however, have been those involving the scions of two corporate rich families. In the first few decades of this century, there were many instances of intermarriage between wealthy capitalist families. Indeed, one observer felt justified in proclaiming that eventually "all the big American proprietors will be blood relatives." There was ample reason, at the time, to fear the consolidation of corporate wealth within a single network of interrelated families. After all, many of the largest American corporations were affiliated with one another by virtue of the fact that their controlling families were related to one another by marriage. The Moore family of the American Can Company was related to the Hanna family of Hanna Mining, which, in turn, was related to the Medill family of the *Chicago Tribune.* Similarly, the Milbank family of Southern Railway was related to the Duke family of Duke Power, which, in turn, was related to the Ordway family of Minnesota Mining and Manufacturing. This trend may have reached its peak with the marriage of Edith Rockefeller, the daughter of John D. Rockefeller, to Harold F. McCormick, the son of Cyrus McCormick. Needless to say, the press treated the event more as a corporate merger between the Standard Oil companies and the International Harvester Company than a marriage. In recent years, instances of marriage between the scions of two corporate rich families have become much less common. However, the pattern is far from obsolete. For example, Alida Rockefeller, a great-granddaughter of John D. Rockefeller, recently married Mark Dayton, a great-grandson of the founder of the Dayton Hudson department store chain.

In a few instances, scions of corporate rich families have even married other members of the same family. The du Ponts, for example, were notorious for marrying cousins. A few years after he took over as chairman of E.I. du Pont de Nemours and Company, Pierre S. du Pont II married a first cousin, Alice Belin. The wedding was held in New York, because marriages between first cousins were illegal in both Delaware, where the groom lived, and Pennsylvania, the home of his bride. In marrying a cousin, Pierre was simply following a family tradition of sorts. For example, his early partners in the company, T. Coleman du Pont and Alfred I. du Pont, had both married distant cousins. Similarly, two of his brothers, Irénée du Pont and Henry B. du Pont, married second cousins. According to one family historian, there were no fewer than fourteen consanguineous marriages among the descendants of the original Pierre S. du Pont de Nemours. Despite the example set by the du Ponts, marriages between the members of the same family are rare even among the corporate rich. The almost incestuous degree of intermarriage within the du Pont family can be attributed in part to the fact that the family was so old that it had grown into an extremely large clan comprising scores of distant cousins. Moreover, many members of this large and diverse clan lived near one another on large estates outside Wilmington, Delaware. In fact, many of these cousins met at a private school that the du Ponts had established for their children.

In addition to those explanations involving the exchange of wealth and status, there are many reasons for the degree of intermarriage among wealthy and socially prominent families. For a variety of reasons, most marriages are between individuals who have similar social class characteristics. This general pattern is simply carried to its logical extreme among individuals from corporate rich and upper-class families. To begin with, children from these families typically live in the same neighborhoods and, as a result, often travel in the same rather constricted social circles. For example, the marriage of William C. Ford, a grandson of Henry Ford, to Martha P. Firestone, a granddaughter of Harvey S. Firestone, was probably facilitated by the fact that their grandfathers were close friends who spent their vacations together. Similarly, children from upper-class families often attend private schools where they are able to interact with one another both in school and at social exchanges with other schools. Although propinquity and social interaction are important factors that serve to delimit the marriage market for the scions of corporate rich families, economic considerations are inevitably involved in the process of mate selection. Any marriage involving individuals of unequal wealth raises the possibility that the less affluent spouse is marrying for money rather than love. As one observer puts it, "love among the rich is different simply because the rich are rich, and for no other reason." Most wealthy parents are acutely aware of the financial stakes involved whenever one of their children marries someone from a less affluent family.

Although intermarriages between corporate rich families receive much publicity, they are the exception to the rule. Most scions of wealthy capitalist families marry individuals from less affluent families. The Rockefeller brothers, for example, generally married women from families that were affluent but hardly rich. Indeed, given the magnitude of the Rockefeller fortune, it was almost inevitable that they would marry women who were not their economic equals. In almost every case, however, the Rockefeller wives came from families that were socially prominent. Some of the wives of the Rockefeller brothers were from families that had been accepted into the social upper class while John D. Rockefeller was still a struggling clerk in Cleveland. The pattern is much the same in the Mellon family. The children of Andrew W. Mellon and Richard B. Mellon generally married individuals from families that were socially prominent but did not possess great wealth. Paul Mellon married the daughter of a prominent surgeon; and his sister, Ailsa Mellon, married the son of a U.S. senator. Richard K. Mellon married the daughter of the president of a major corporation; and his sister, Sarah Mellon, married the scion of a more established but less wealthy business family. With only minor exceptions, this pattern obtains in other corporate rich families as well. By and large, the scions of these families marry individuals from families that are socially prominent but only modestly wealthy. The social status of these spouses is reflected in the fact that many of them have been educated at exclusive private schools and universities.

In order to maintain the social status of the wealthy capitalist family as well as the security of its fortune, parents may discourage their children from marrying anyone from a family of modest means. There is the example of Winthrop Rockefeller, the only one of the five Rockefeller brothers to marry someone from a socially obscure family. Although his wife was very attractive, having once been named Miss Lithuania in Chicago, her only claim to social status was her previous marriage to the scion of a prominent Boston family. Most of the members of the Rockefeller family disapproved of the marriage. In fact, the only family member to attend the wedding was his brother, Laurence Rockefeller. As G. William Domhoff notes in his study, *The Higher Circles,* marriage outside the group is generally restricted to fellow students at elite private colleges and universities as well as a few beautiful actresses and models. However, he also notes that these deviations may be fortuitous because they "have the happy consequence of infusing more brains and beauty into the privileged class." In general, class homogamy may be less prevalent among the members of the third and fourth generations of wealthy capitalist families than it was among the members of preceding generations. After all, once the members of the second generation of a corporate rich family have integrated the family into the American upper class, either by intermarriage or by other means, members of succeeding generations are much less insecure about their social status. Several of the great-grandchildren of John D. Rockefeller, Jr., for example, have married individuals from relatively prosaic backgrounds. There have been similar deviations among the younger members of the Mellon and Ford families as well.

A WOMAN'S PLACE

Women from corporate rich families are very different from women from less affluent families. In a society in which many women still occupy subordinate or otherwise dependent positions, women from corporate rich families enjoy considerable independence. Indeed, there is a degree of sexual equality among the corporate rich, at least in matters of wealth. This fortunate situation stems from the fact that women have generally inherited wealth equally with men in recent years. Consequently, half of all the millionaires in America are women. In fact, women have been among the wealthiest members of the corporate rich. Some, like Sarah Mellon Scaife and Abby Rockefeller Mauze, were scions of corporate rich families. They inherited from their parents fortunes that were roughly equal to those inherited by their brothers. Others, like Constance Mellon Burrell, the widow of Richard K. Mellon, and Martha B. Rockefeller, the widow of John D. Rockefeller, Jr., married scions of corporate rich families. They inherited substantial estates from their husbands. In fact, the present tax system encourages the creation of wealthy widows insofar as it permits any estate to pass to a surviving spouse free of estate taxes. Despite their financial independence, however, women within the corporate rich occupy a position that is more than a little incongruous. Although they possess great wealth, they are often denied the power that is usually associated with such wealth. For example, very few of the women who are major stockholders in large corporations serve as either officers or directors of those corporations.

Whatever the sources of their wealth, the opportunities available to the women of corporate rich families are immense. They are able to choose any career without the necessity of choosing one at all. A few wealthy heiresses, such as Doris Duke and Barbara Hutton, devoted much of their lives to the highly publicized pursuits and pastimes of what was then known as "café society." However, Doris Duke and Barbara Hutton, both of whom lost parents at an early age, were hardly representative of other wealthy heiresses. In point of fact, they both had female cousins, of generally comparable wealth, who led relatively staid and private lives. Like other members of the corporate rich, most wealthy women seek the security afforded by almost complete obscurity. Obviously, women who have inherited great wealth, like their male counterparts, have had little incentive to work. Indeed, only a few have seriously pursued careers of any kind. Nedenia Hutton Robertson, the daughter of Marjorie Post and Edward F. Hutton, gained fame as an actress under the name of Dina Merrill, but she was an exception to the rule. Most of the women from corporate rich families are content to volunteer their services to various charitable and civic activities. Moreover, these women usually limit their involvement to raising funds for civic projects rather than performing direct service work. Many of them are members of local chapters of the Junior League, a service organization that, in many cities at least, is the most socially exclusive club available to women. One of the two founders of the Junior League was Mary Harriman Rumsey, whose father, Edward H. Harriman, controlled the Union Pacific Railroad.

Until relatively recently, the highest echelons of American business have been a largely male preserve. There have been, of course, a few successful women entrepreneurs such as Estee Lauder and Mary Kay Ash. Nevertheless, women who were born into corporate rich families have rarely been encouraged to seek managerial positions with the family corporations, despite the fact that they are often destined to become major stockholders in those firms. Indeed, it has only been in the past few decades that women have served even as directors of major corporations. The exceptions have been women who happened to become controlling stockholders in particular firms. For example, when John T. Dorrance, the founder of Campbell Soup Company, died in 1930, his wife was elected as a director. Ethel M. Dorrance could hardly be ignored, inasmuch as she was a trustee and a beneficiary of a trust that held virtually all of the stock in Campbell Soup. Similarly, Marjorie Post was elected as a director of General Foods Corporation after the death of her father, Charles W. Post. After all, she was the largest single stockholder in the company with over 8 percent of its stock. During this same period, Helena Woolworth McCann and Jesse Woolworth Donahue became directors of F.W. Woolworth Company under similar circumstances. More recently,

Joan Kroc became a director of McDonald's Corporation after the death of her husband, Raymond Kroc. As the primary heir of the founder of the company, she became its largest stockholder.

With the influx of women into business in recent years, wealthy women are no longer precluded from serving as directors and even officers of major corporations. One of the first women to become the chairman of a large American corporation through inheritance was Katharine Meyer Graham. She was the daughter of Eugene Meyer, Jr., one of the founders of Allied Chemical Corporation, who later purchased *The Washington Post.* Katharine Meyer married Philip L. Graham, who was subsequently named publisher of the newspaper by her father. In 1948, Eugene Meyer transferred all of the voting stock in The Washington Post Company to a trust for the benefit of his daughter and her husband. When her husband committed suicide in 1963, Katharine Graham suddenly inherited control of one of the largest and most influential media corporations in the country. Although she had no previous experience in the newspaper business, she quietly assumed the duties of publisher. In her first meeting with the editorial staff, she said: "This has been, this is, and this will continue to be a family operation. There is another generation coming, and we intend to turn the paper over to them." In the years since, her eldest son, Donald Graham, has become an officer and director of The Washington Post Company, but Katharine Graham has chosen to remain in control. More recently, Helen Copley took over as chairman of Copley Press after the death of her husband, James S. Copley. Having inherited a controlling block of stock in the family corporation, she asserted her control over the newspaper chain after convincing its president to take early retirement "in order to travel."

Although they only rarely serve as corporate officers or directors, women can nevertheless exercise considerable power over the policies of family corporations by virtue of their positions as principal stockholders. There is the example of Eleanor Ford, the widow of Benson Ford, who forced her aging father-in-law to resign as president of the company he had founded. Henry Ford finally appointed her eldest son, Henry Ford II, president of Ford Motor Company, but only after she threatened to sell her shares in the company to outsiders. A more recent case involves the reclusive Doris Duke and her influence within Duke Power Company. Although she resigned as a director of the company several decades ago, Doris Duke has remained one of its principal stockholders. She is also a lifetime trustee of the Duke Endowment, a foundation created by her father that owns a large block of the stock in Duke Power. In 1974, Duke Power became mired in a prolonged and violent strike by the United Mine Workers against a coal mine in Kentucky, owned by one of its subsidiaries. Doris Duke felt that the company ought to settle the strike, perhaps because she felt that the labor problems were detracting from the reputation of her family. Whatever the reasons, she did not hesitate to telephone the president of Duke Power in order to urge him to settle with the union. With public opinion running against the company and one of its major stockholders demanding a resolution to the dispute, Duke Power finally came to terms with the union. In both cases, women who had inherited large stockholdings in a company were able to exert some degree of control even though they were not directors of the company.

In a few instances, women who were major stockholders in family firms have had their husbands appointed as officers or directors. For example, William Butterworth, the husband of one of the daughters of Charles Deere, was appointed president of Deere & Company after the death of his father-in-law in 1907. Almost a half century later, William A. Hewitt, the husband of one of the great-granddaughters of Charles Deere, was appointed president of the company after the death of his father-in-law, Charles Deere Wiman. There is little doubt that managerial careers of both men were abetted by the fact that their wives and other members of the Deere family were controlling stockholders in the company. Similarly, Iphigene Ochs Sulzberger, who inherited control of The New York Times Company from her father, Adolph Ochs, had her husband, Arthur H. Sulzberger, appointed publisher of the newspaper. Although she refrained from becoming overly involved in the daily operations of *The New York Times,* she did not hesitate to make her views known to its editors. According to David Halberstam, a former reporter with the newspaper, "it was her family's paper, not her husband's, and she could raise a decisive voice." More recently, Ronald W. Miller, the husband of one of the two daughters of Walt Disney, served for several years as president of Walt Disney Productions. He resigned recently after other major stockholders, led by Roy O. Disney, a cousin of his wife, expressed dissatisfaction with his performance. In order to avoid a rift within the family, his sister-in-law, Sharon Disney Lund, was later elected as a director of the company.

The only area of public life in which women from corporate rich families are represented in any significant numbers is philanthropy. It is not uncommon to find women serving as trustees and officers of family foundations. Many of these women are wives or daughters of the founders of these foundations. Even the reclusive Abby Rockefeller Mauze served as a trustee of the Rockefeller Brothers Fund, despite the fact that her father named the foundation after her five brothers. There are even a few foundations in which the widow or daughter of the founder serves as president. The largest foundation run by a woman at present is the McKnight Foundation with assets of over $500 million. The president of this foundation, Virginia McKnight Binger, is the only child of the founder, William L. McKnight. Whatever their official positions with these foundations, women from corporate rich families sometimes exercise considerable influence over foundation policies. A case in point involved Josephine Hartford Bryce, one of the granddaughters of George H. Hartford, the founder of the Great Atlantic and Pacific Tea Company. In a radical departure from their policy of funding only medical research, she convinced the other trustees of the John A. Hartford Foundation, which was endowed by two of her uncles, that it should contribute $2 million to the construction of the Lincoln Center for the Performing Arts. The trustees, most of whom were past and present officers of the company, may have agreed to her request simply because they needed her shares of A&P stock, in conjunction with the shares held by the foundation, to maintain their absolute control over the grocery store chain.

5

Family
Business

Most of the business corporations in America, even the very largest, were once small companies. They were the creations of entrepreneurs who provided them with much of their initial investment capital and managerial expertise. During the first few decades of their existence, these firms were typically owned and managed by a small group of individuals, many of whom were related to the founder by blood or marriage. In this sense, then, almost all corporations began as family businesses. However, as these small firms grew into large corporations, the ties binding them to their founding families became increasingly tenuous. Over a period of several decades, the descendants of the founder were often reduced to the status of minority stockholders. Consequently, the management of these corporations on a daily basis became the almost exclusive domain of managers who had no kinship ties to their founding families. However, not all the wealthy capitalist families have disappeared simply because their firms grew into large corporations. Founding families are still major stockholders in a number of large corporations. As a result, they are usually able to exercise considerable power in the management of these companies. In some cases, the president or chairman of a major corporation is a member of the founding family. More often, one or more descendants of the founder serve as directors of the corporation. The fact that these families are no longer majority stockholders in these firms has only slightly diminished their power.

The perpetuation of family control in large corporations is not merely a historical accident. Corporate rich families must resolve certain problems if they are to retain control over their corporations for more than one or two generations. In particular, they must ensure that at least some family members remain involved in the management and direction of these firms. In most cases, the son of the founder is able to maintain active family control over the corporation by succeeding his father as chief executive officer. Of course, other family members may serve as officers and directors as well. However, founding families often relinquish active control of their corporations after a couple of generations. At that point, they may exert only passive control. Although they no longer serve as officers of the corporation, descendants of the founder may continue to serve as directors. In this way, founding families are able to exercise effective control over large corporations even though they are only minority stockholders. Alternatively, a few corporate rich families are able to maintain absolute control over their corporations simply because these firms never issued stock to the public at large. Private corporations offer their owners certain advantages in terms of avoiding both taxes and publicity. Nevertheless, most corporate rich families eventually relinquish their control over those corporations that formed the basis of their original fortunes. In the end, they either sell their stock in the family firm for cash or exchange it for stock in a larger and more diversified corporation.

UNFINISHED REVOLUTIONS

According to accepted economic doctrine, the large corporation is the epitome of rational organization. In such an organization, family ties are simply irrelevant; corporate managers are chosen solely on the basis of their business expertise. The transformation of a small company, owned and managed by a founding entrepreneur and his descendants, into a large corporation, owned by countless small stockholders and run by managers who have only small stockholdings in the company, is neatly encapsulated in the concept of the *managerial revolution.* The onset of this revolution has been celebrated, albeit somewhat prematurely, by social theorists for a variety of reasons. To begin with, it is believed that corporations controlled by autonomous managers are more "socially responsible" than corporations controlled by their founding families. Several theoretical arguments have been advanced to suggest that managers who are not major stockholders in their corporations are less obsessed with the maximization of profits than members of the founding families that own large blocks of the stock in those corporations. Despite its popularity, there is precious little evidence to support this proposition. The managerial revolution is also credited with stripping wealthy capitalist families of much of their social, economic, and political power. Deprived of their institutional power base in family corporations, corporate rich families are no more powerful than other families, even though they still possess most of their original wealth. Once again, the evidence for this assertion is equivocal at best. Indeed, the facts at hand suggest that the managerial revolution is, in many corporations at least, largely unfinished.

The inexorable demotion of the capitalist family from its privileged position as the principal stockholder in a large corporation to the almost powerless status of minor stockholder is usually attributed to a number of developments. First, it is assumed that the stockholdings of a founding family become diluted as a result of corporate growth. As the family company grows, it typically raises capital for expansion by selling new shares of its stock to the public at large. Alternatively, the company may grow through mergers in which it issues new shares of its stock in exchange for the stock of other companies. In either case, the issuance of additional stock invariably results in a dilution of the original equity position of the founding family. Second, it is assumed that the stockholdings of the founding family in the corporation become more dispersed over time. With each passing generation, the company stock once owned by the founding entrepreneur is generally redistributed among a growing number of children, grandchildren, and great-grandchildren. Last but not least, it is assumed that the stockholdings of the family in the corporation are reduced as family members seek to diversify their investment portfolios. Family members often attempt to reduce the risks of having almost their entire fortune invested in the stock of a single corporation by selling some of their shares in the family firm and reinvesting the proceeds in bonds, real estate, and the stock of other companies. In the end, the result is presumably the same: the corporate rich family eventually loses control of the firm that was the original source of its fortune.

One of the attractions of the theory of the managerial revolution is that it is based on a logic that seems almost irrefutable. Nevertheless, this logic is often at odds with the hard facts of American business history. The difficulty arises from the fact that not all corporations conform to the assumptions of the theory. To begin with, the stockholdings of the founding family in a corporation are not always diluted by the issuance of additional stock. Some corporations have been able to meet the bulk of their capital requirements from retained earnings. These companies may borrow money from time to time in order to finance expansion, but they are able to retire their loans from the resultant increases in their profits. For example, International Business Machines has become one of the largest corporations in the world in the matter of a few decades. In 1937, the company ranked 185th among all nonfinancial corporations in the United States in terms of its assets. Today, IBM ranks well among the top ten. This growth has been financed primarily from retained earnings. Although IBM has borrowed heavily at times to finance the development of its products, it has issued relatively little stock in the past several decades. As a result, there has been very little dilution of the equity position of the original stockholders. In 1937, Thomas J. Watson and his family owned just over 2 percent of the outstanding IBM stock. Those initial stockholdings, after twelve stock splits and eighteen stock dividends, would still represent almost 2 percent of the total stock in the company.

Of course, not all corporations are able to finance their growth entirely from retained earnings. In particular, corporations that operate in capital-intensive industries are typically forced to issue additional stock in order to meet their capital requirements. Steel companies, oil companies, and public utilities are but a few examples of companies that are often unable to finance their growth entirely from retained earnings. The history of Duke Power Company demonstrates how the equity position of a founding family can be diluted by the issuance of additional stock. In 1924, James B. Duke created the Doris Duke Trust for the benefit of his daughter and other members of the Duke family. By 1939, this trust held 14 percent of the stock in Duke Power. Although the trust has not sold any of its original Duke Power stock, the company has issued millions of shares of additional stock over the years in order to finance its growth. As a result, the equity position of the Doris Duke Trust has declined to the point that its Duke Power stock now represents only about 2 percent of the outstanding stock in the company. One consequence of this steady dilution of stockholder equity is that the Duke Power stock held by this trust and the individual members of the Duke family has not appreciated much in the past several decades. The Duke Power stock held by the Doris Duke Trust was worth a little over $9 million in 1939. This same stock, even after three stock splits, is currently worth only about $72 million. Moreover, as the equity position of the Duke family has eroded over the years, the family has relinquished most of its control over the company.

Many of the wealthiest corporate rich families in America owe the bulk of their fortunes to their initial investments in companies that have grown very large without issuing much additional stock. Whenever retained earnings have been sufficient to finance expansion, there has been very little dilution of the initial equity position of the founding family. For example, there has been little dilution of the original equity positions held by those families that founded many of the major drug companies and electronics firms. Although these industries have relatively high capital requirements, at least in terms of research and development expenditures, both industries enjoy comparatively high levels of profitability. Consequently, they have been able to finance much of their expansion from retained earnings. In drug companies such as Eli Lilly and Company, The Upjohn Company, Johnson & Johnson, and SmithKline Beckman, the original stockholdings of the founding families have not been greatly diluted over the years. Similarly, in electronics firms such as Intel Corporation, Texas Instruments, Hewlett-Packard, and Motorola, there has been very little dilution of the equity positions of the founding families, even though these companies have grown enormously during the past several years. In a few other industries, such as retailing, corporations have not required large infusions of capital in order to expand their operations. The stockholdings of the founding families in such companies as Dayton Hudson Corporation, Wal-Mart Stores, Nordstrom Inc., and The Limited have not been diluted much because of their rapid growth. As a result of this lack of dilution, many of the companies in these industries are still under the control of their founding families.

According to the theory of the managerial revolution, the control that the founding family exerts over the family corporation may also become eroded as the stockholdings of the family are dispersed among a growing number of family members. By the third generation, for example, the original stockholdings of the founder may be owned by a large number of individuals who are no more than cousins to one another. Given this dispersion of the stock held by the descendants of the founder of the company, it may be difficult for family members to act in concert as a unified group. For example, the Weyerhaeuser family currently comprises almost thirty second cousins and well over eighty third cousins. Although the dispersion of stock in the family corporation among a large number of family members does render it more difficult for the family to act in unison, the theory of the managerial revolution neglects the fact that most corporate rich families have developed a series of strategies for maintaining some semblance of family unity, at least with respect to financial matters. In many cases, the stockholdings of family members are concentrated by the use of trusts, holding companies, and family offices. For example, the Weyerhaeusers maintain a family office that handles the financial affairs of family members. Moreover, much of the stock in Weyerhaeuser Company owned by family members is held in trusts. Most of this is voted by a small number of key family members who serve as trustees of these trusts. Finally, these families are also able to maintain their identity and coordinate their financial affairs by organizing periodic family reunions. The Weyerhaeusers, for example, hold a large meeting every year.

Last but not least, the theory of the managerial revolution asserts that corporate rich families eventually lose control over their family corporations simply because of the inevitable diversification of their fortunes. According to this view, family members eventually sell much of their stock in the family firm and use the proceeds to create more diversified investment portfolios. There are, of course, some tax advantages associated with diversification. For example, part of the proceeds from the sale of stock in the family corporation may be invested in real estate. At least part of any large fortune is usually invested in real estate simply because the depreciation allowance on buildings allows the members of corporate rich families to shelter much of their income from taxes. Similarly, part of these proceeds may be invested in state and municipal bonds that provide these same individuals with tax-free income. Finally, the remainder of the proceeds may be invested in the stock of growth companies that provide only modest dividend income but generous capital appreciation. A large portion of any fortune is typically invested in corporate stock as a hedge against inflation. Of course, the exact timing of any diversification effort is often determined by tax considerations. For example, diversification may be delayed until the stock in the family firm has been revalued for tax purposes, as the result of either lifetime gifts or testamentary bequests, in order to avoid unnecessary capital-gains taxes. In any event, a corporate rich family may postpone diversification as long as it is able to safeguard its fortune by exercising control over the family firm. Members of the Weyerhaeuser family, for example, have sold very little of their stock in Weyerhaeuser Company over the past several decades.

In the end, however, most corporate rich families eventually diversify their stockholdings in the family corporation. As they sell their stock in this corporation, they also relinquish their control over it. The Rockefeller family provides a classic illustration of this process. John D. Rockefeller was, of course, one of the founders of the Standard Oil Trust. For several decades after the dissolution of this trust, the Rockefeller fortune consisted primarily of stock in several Standard Oil companies. Specifically, one of the most valuable investments held by John D. Rockefeller, Jr., and his family in 1938 was their 16 percent stockholding in the forerunner of Mobil Oil Corporation. This block of stock was worth over $76 million at the time. It also represented fully 30 percent of the total value of the known family stockholdings in the two hundred largest nonfinancial corporations in 1938. Clearly, the Rockefeller fortune was not yet very diversified and, as a result, the family was still able to exercise effective control over several of the original Standard Oil companies. However, in the years that followed, John D. Rockefeller, Jr., supervised the almost complete diversification of the Rockefeller fortune. Much of the stock in the oil companies was sold and the proceeds reinvested in real estate, mainly Rockefeller Center, as well as corporate stocks and bonds. By 1974, the stockholdings of the Rockefeller family in Mobil Oil Corporation represented less than 2 percent of its total outstanding stock. This block of stock, which was worth a little over $51 million at the time, represented only about 6 percent of all the corporate stock held by the Rockefeller family.

The theory of the managerial revolution is capable of explaining precisely how most large corporations eventually come to be controlled by autonomous managers rather than their founding families. However, the transformation of any corporation from family control to management control is contingent upon a series of factors. By and large, it is possible for the founding family to determine the pace of this transformation. For example, the family may avoid opportunities for expansion of the family firm that might entail a dilution of their equity position. Similarly, the family may create holding companies and trusts that serve to restrict the dispersion of its stockholdings in the family corporation. Finally, family members may choose to limit the diversification of their investment portfolios and to retain much of their original stockholdings in the family corporation. As a result, roughly a quarter of all major industrial corporations are still subject to some degree of family control. Nevertheless, most corporate rich families eventually relinquish their control over their family corporations. In the end, they do so because they recognize that it is no longer in their best interests to maintain such close associations with these corporations. The loss of control over the family firm, on the one hand, deprives family members of much of their economic and political power. On the other hand, the absence of any identification between a corporate rich family and a major corporation makes it easier for family members to achieve some degree of anonymity.

THE CHANGING OF THE GUARD

The entrepreneur is a revered figure in the folklore of American business. Entrepreneurs are venerated because they are responsible for the creation of new firms that have developed and exploited innovative products and services. In return, these founders are permitted to exercise almost absolute control over their corporations. In addition to the fact that they are often principal stockholders, founders exercise considerable authority within these corporations because they were largely responsible for their initial growth and profitability. For example, after the death of his son and successor, Henry Ford decided to resume the presidency of Ford Motor Company, even though he was eighty years old and showing signs of senility. No one in the company was able to challenge his authority. Indeed, one indication of the power that founders exercise within their firms is the fact that they often continue to run them well beyond the normal retirement age for chief executive officers. For example, Armand Hammer, the founder and chairman of Occidental Petroleum Corporation, was still in control of the company at the age of eighty-eight, despite the fact that he owned less than 1 percent of the stock in the company. Similarly, William S. Paley still exercised almost absolute control over CBS Inc. until he was eighty-four years old. Other founders of major corporations who exerted active control over those corporations until they were at least seventy years old include Ray Kroc of McDonald's Corporation, J. Willard Marriott of Marriott Corporation, Edwin H. Land of Polaroid Corporation, and James S. McDonnell, Jr., of McDonnell Douglas Corporation.

Of course, family control does not necessarily end with the death of the founder. There are a large number of corporations in which the founding family has maintained active control of the firm for at least two generations by appointing a family member to succeed the founder as president. It is common for the son of a founder to assume the presidency of the family firm from his father. In many cases, the father maintains the line of succession by assuming the role of chairman so that the son can become president. For example, J. Willard Marriott was sixty-four years old when he appointed his son, J. Willard Marriott, Jr., president of Marriott Corporation. At the same time, he stated, "I expect to be around for a long time as chairman." He was still chairman of the company when he died two decades later. More recently, the president of Wang Laboratories resigned after it became clear that An Wang, the founder and chairman of the company, intended to appoint his son, Frederick A. Wang, as his eventual successor. Sons who have succeeded their fathers as presidents of family corporations include J. Paul Getty of Getty Oil, Edgar F. Kaiser of Kaiser Industries, Donald Danforth of Ralston Purina, John T. Dorrance of Campbell Soup, Willard H. Dow of Dow Chemical, and Harvey S. Firestone, Jr., of Firestone Tire & Rubber, to name but a few. More recent examples of chief executive officers who are sons of the founders of major corporations include Robert W. Galvin of Motorola, John P. Thompson of The Southland Corporation, William Wishnick of Witco Corporation, Michael G. O'Neil of GenCorp Inc., and Barron Hilton of Hilton Hotels Corporation.

After two generations of active participation in the management of the family corporation, a corporate rich family typically recruits someone from outside the family to serve as chief executive officer. Nevertheless, it is not unusual for a grandson of the company founder to serve as the chief executive officer of the family corporation. Examples of this pattern include William K. Coors of Adolph Coors Company, Fred M. Kirby II of Alleghany Corporation, Arthur O. Sulzberger of The New York Times Company, William R. Timken, Jr., of The Timken Company, and Charles M. Pigott of PACCAR Inc. Until relatively recently, this group also included Henry Ford II of Ford Motor Company, H. J. Heinz II of H.J. Heinz Company, Charles W. Ireland of Vulcan Materials Company, Eli Lilly II of Eli Lilly and Company, and Ralph Lazarus of Federated Department Stores. In almost every case, these individuals succeeded their own fathers as chief executive officers of family-controlled companies. Alternatively, the founding family may appoint someone from outside the family as president while a member of the family continues to serve in the less demanding but more powerful position of chairman. For example, Otis Chandler, the grandson of the founder of The Times Mirror Company, resigned as president of the company but retained the position of chairman. Similarly, Henry J. Heinz II, the grandson of the founder of H.J. Heinz Company, stayed on as chairman after resigning as president.

Although it is not uncommon for the sons and even grandsons of founders to serve as chief executive officers of major corporations, it is rare for a family to provide the chief executive officers for a large corporation for more than three generations. A notable exception is the Weyerhaeuser family. George H. Weyerhaeuser, the president of Weyerhaeuser Company, is a great-grandson of Frederick Weyereyerhaeuser, the founder of the company. The company has been managed as well as controlled by the family since it was incorporated in 1900. The ability of the Weyerhaeusers to maintain active control of Weyerhaeuser Company for a such a prolonged period of time can be traced to a series of factors. The Weyerhaeusers have been careful to avoid diluting their equity position in the company. They have also refrained from selling much of their Weyerhaeuser stock. However, the most important factor may simply be the number of male heirs within the family. Frederick Weyerhaeuser had four sons and seven grandsons, most of whom were involved with the family company at one time or another. In all, at least nine members of the family have served as officers or directors of the company. Other family members served as officers and directors of other family-controlled corporations such as Potlatch Corporation. There are only a few chief executive officers of major corporations who are members of the fourth generation of the founding family. In addition to George Weyerhaeuser, this select group includes August A. Busch III of Anheuser-Busch Companies Inc.; W. L. Lyons Brown, Jr., of Brown-Forman Inc.; and Arthur Houghton, Jr., of Corning Glass Works.

In most family-controlled corporations, the management of the company is passed from father to son. Consequently, not all of the male members of a corporate rich family have the same chance of being chosen to serve as president of the family firm. As a rule, these families develop fairly clear lines of succession. There is the example of the Cabot Corporation, a major chemical company, which has been managed as well as controlled by members of the Cabot family for almost a century. Godfrey L. Cabot purchased the predecessor of the present Cabot Corporation in 1882. In later years, three of his sons, as well as his son-in-law, worked for the company in various capacities. However, only one of them, Thomas D. Cabot, chose a career with Cabot Corporation. In the years that followed, several of the grandsons of the founder also served as officers and directors of the company. Nevertheless, Thomas Cabot selected his own son, Louis W. Cabot, as his successor. Whenever possible, fathers choose their own sons to succeed them as chief executive officers of family corporations. One consequence of this pattern is that those descendants of the founder who do not pursue careers with the family company also render it much more difficult for their own children to pursue such careers. In short, a descendant of the founder often requires the sponsorship of another family member in order to advance rapidly through the managerial ranks of the corporation. For example, George Weyerhaeuser had a distinct advantage over most of his cousins in his career with Weyerhaeuser Company, because both his father and his grandfather had been presidents of the company.

.   .   .

Despite the fact that members of corporate rich families serve as managers of many family corporations, most of the corporations that are still controlled by their founding families are not actively managed by family members. After two or three generations of management by family members, most of these firms quietly slip into a more passive form of family control. Instead of a family member serving as either president or chairman of the company, one or more family members serve simply as directors. There are several reasons for this transition from active management to passive direction. In many cases, the family stockholdings in the company have become so diluted or dispersed that no member of the family can assert a legitimate claim to the position of chief executive officer. Sometimes, there may not be any family members with the expertise required to manage a large corporation. In a few cases, family members actually have demonstrated their limitations as managers. For example, Daniel C. Searle succeeded his father, John G. Searle, as chief executive officer of the family pharmaceutical firm, G.D. Searle and Co., in 1966. However, after a decade of declining profitability, the family installed an outsider as president in 1977. Daniel Searle, his brother, and his brother-in-law resigned their managerial positions with the firm. They continued to serve as directors because they still controlled over 31 percent of Searle stock. Seven years after they relinquished active control of the company, the Searles announced their intention to diversify their fortune by selling their Searle stock. The company was acquired by Monsanto Company in 1985.

The decision of a founding family to delegate the management of the family corporation to individuals who are not members of the family is a critical point in the evolution of the family and the corporation. Once the family has relinquished active control over the company, it is difficult for any member of the family to become its chief executive officer. Different families have different reasons for delegating the management of their companies to others. It may be, of course, that there are no suitable successors to the chief executive officer within the family. More often, the family will relinquish active control of the corporation simply because no family member wishes to assume the responsibilities of being the chief executive officer of a large corporation. Indeed, the descendants of the founder are often so wealthy that there is no financial incentive for them to assume a managerial position with the company. Paul Mellon, for example, could have pursued a managerial career with any number of companies in which he was a major stockholder, but he chose to pursue the more genteel life of an art collector, horse breeder, and philanthropist. His cousin, Richard K. Mellon, served for several years as a director of Gulf Oil, Aluminum Company of America, and Mellon Corporation. However, he was content to hire others to manage these corporations. Similarly, David Rockefeller was the only one of the five sons of John D. Rockefeller, Jr., who chose a managerial career with a major corporation. His brothers all worked briefly for various Rockefeller companies, but they eventually chose vocations as politicians, philanthropists, and investors.

Consequently, in most of the corporations that are still controlled by their founding families, this control is passive rather than active. Specifically, a corporate rich family may still be the principal stockholder in the corporation and one or more family members may serve as directors, but, more often than not, the chief executive officer of the company is not a member of the family. In such a situation, family control is reduced to safeguarding the family investment in the company from gross managerial incompetence. Although family control over a corporation is greatly attenuated whenever the chief executive officer of the company is not a member of the founding family, it can be reinforced by having more than one family member on the board of directors. For example, the children and grandchildren of Herbert H. Dow still controlled at least 6 percent of the stock in Dow Chemical Company in 1972. Two grandsons of the founder, both of whom once worked for the company, now serve as directors. One of them, Herbert D. Doan, was the last member of the Dow family to serve as president of Dow Chemical. The Donnelleys of R.R. Donnelley and Sons, the Bancrofts of Dow Jones & Company, the Danforths of Ralston Purina Company, the Chandlers of The Times Mirror Company, and the Daytons of Dayton Hudson Corporation are but a few examples of families that have delegated the management of family corporations to others but have kept at least two family members on the board of directors. The du Ponts, for example, appointed someone from outside the family as chief executive officer of E.I. du Pont de Nemours and Company many years ago. However, at least four members of the du Pont family are still directors of Du Pont.

Family control is, of course, most tenuous whenever the founding family has only one representative on the board of directors. This is the least effective level of family control because other directors may simply ignore the director representing the founding family. However, even one director from the founding family may be sufficient to exercise control if the proportion of company stock held by the family is sufficiently large. For example, John G. Ordway, Jr., has been, for several years, the only member of the Ordway family on the board of directors of Minnesota Mining and Manufacturing Company. His grandfather, Lucius P. Ordway, was one of the original founders of the company. Although he is only one of several directors, he is one of the most powerful directors of the company simply because he and other members of the Ordway family still own approximately 7 percent of the stock in the company. Similarly, Arthur P. Hixon is the only member of the Hixon family on the board of directors of AMP Incorporated, the electrical equipment manufacturer. Nevertheless, he undoubtedly wields more power than the other directors because the Hixon family owns about 12 percent of the stock in AMP. However, the fact that only one member of the founding family remains on the board of directors is usually a sign that the family has largely relinquished its control over the corporation. In general, family participation in the management and direction of a company is proportional to its stockholdings in the company. As the stockholdings of the founding family are diluted, dispersed, and diversified, the family ineluctably reduces its involvement in the management and direction of the company.

MINORITY RULE

It has long been recognized that, under certain conditions, a family can exercise effective control of a large corporation with much less than a majority of its stock. In many cases, a corporate rich family is able to elect directors and even appoint the senior officers of a corporation even though it owns only a small minority of the stock in that company. Indeed, minority control by a founding family can occur in even the largest corporations. As Adolf Berle and Gardiner Means observed as early as 1932, "the larger the corporation and the wider the distribution of its stock, the more difficult it appears to be to dislodge a controlling minority." They went on to suggest that 10 percent stock ownership was sufficient for a family to maintain control of a corporation. In recent years, however, researchers have concluded that even 5 percent stock ownership, in conjunction with representation on the board of directors, is usually sufficient to establish family control. In point of fact, there are many cases in which a family has been able to control a corporation with as little as 2 percent of its stock. Although a family can achieve a level of largely passive control over a corporation with a small minority of the stock and representation on the board of directors, active control can be assured only when the chief executive officer of the corporation is also a member of the controlling family.

The ability of a family to maintain control of a major corporation for a prolonged period of time with only a small fraction of its stock can be demonstrated by the case of the Watson family of International Business Machines. Thomas J. Watson is often described as one of the founders of the firm. In point of fact, he was hired as president of the company in 1914, three years after its formation by a group of financiers. In return for his services, Watson received a modest salary, a percentage of the profits, and an option on a small block of company stock. IBM, as it became known throughout the world, flourished under his guidance. In 1946, his eldest son, Thomas J. Watson, Jr., joined the company as an assistant to a vice president. The younger Watson was promoted to vice president and elected as a director the following year, even though he was only thirty-three years old. Two years later, the elder Watson appointed his other son, Arthur K. Watson, who was only twenty-nine years old, as a vice president as well. Although both sons had worked briefly as IBM salesmen after graduation from college, their meteoric rise within the corporation was clearly the result of nepotism. In 1955, just one year before he retired, Thomas J. Watson appointed his eldest son president. The Watsons never owned more than 3 percent of the stock in IBM, but they were able to maintain effective control of the company for several decades. During most of this period, there were at least two members of the family on the board of directors. Arthur K. Watson eventually joined his brother as a director of IBM, as did the husbands of their two sisters. The family exercised active control over the company until Thomas Watson, Jr., resigned as chairman in 1971.

Because minority control of a large corporation by a founding family is most effective whenever a member of the family also serves as either the chairman or president of the corporation, the members of corporate rich families must devote particular attention to the issue of managerial succession. Whenever a family controls a corporation with only a small minority of its stock, it is essential to maintain the line of succession from one member of the family to another. The influence of family ties in the matter of managerial succession can be demonstrated by the involvement of the Magowan family in the management of Safeway Stores, Incorporated. This grocery store chain was founded by Charles E. Merrill, who was also one of the founders of Merrill Lynch & Co. In 1955, Charles Merrill appointed his son-in-law, Robert A. Magowan, as chairman of Safeway Stores. At the time, the Merrill family probably controlled in excess of 10 percent of the stock in Safeway Stores. In 1971, a few years before he retired as chairman, Robert Magowan nominated one of his sons, Merrill L. Magowan, as a director of the company. Another son, Peter A. Magowan, who was one of the youngest vice presidents of Safeway, was elected to the board of directors a few years later. When Robert Magowan finally retired as chairman of Safeway in 1980, Peter Magowan was appointed as his successor, even though he was only thirty-seven years old. As a manager of a competing grocery store chain put it, "he wouldn't have the job if his name wasn't Magowan." It is unlikely that the Magowans themselves held much more than 2 percent of the stock in Safeway Stores at the time, although additional stock may have been held by other descendants of Merrill.

There are many other examples of corporate rich families that have been able to maintain passive control of major corporations for several decades even though they owned only a relatively small minority of the stock in those corporations. One of the most notable examples of this pattern involves the Harriman family and its long association with the Union Pacific Railroad. Edward H. Harriman gained control of the Union Pacific in 1901. By 1938, however, his descendants owned less than 3 percent of the stock in the company. His sons, W. Averell Harriman and E. Roland Harriman, both served as chairmen of the railroad for long periods of time. As late as 1974, the Interstate Commerce Commission ruled that the Harriman family and the associated investment banking firm of Brown Brothers, Harriman and Co. controlled the Union Pacific Corporation by virtue of the fact that they voted slightly more than 3 percent of its stock. At the time, two members of the Harriman family and another partner in Brown Brothers, Harriman were directors of Union Pacific. The Harriman family is still represented on the board of directors of the Union Pacific Corporation by Elbridge T. Gerry, Jr., the husband of one of the granddaughters of Edward Harriman. Similarly, the two sons of Ernest W. Woodruff were able to control the giant Coca-Cola Company for over half a century, despite the fact that they never owned more than 7 percent of its stock. One of those sons, Robert W. Woodruff, served as a director until he was ninety-two years old. Even at that age, he was able to veto decisions of the chairman of the corporation.

Although founding families may retain effective control of corporations through minority ownership, they are not able to exercise the absolute control that comes only with majority ownership. As a result, their corporations are invariably susceptible to merger and acquisition proposals from other corporations. Despite the fact that they control only a minority of the stock in these corporations, founding families are often able to resist unsolicited acquisition and merger offers. For

example, McGraw-Hill, Inc., a publishing company, received an un-
solicited acquisition offer from American Express Company in 1978.
At the time, roughly 25 percent of the stock in the company was held
by grandchildren and great-grandchildren of the founder, James H.
McGraw. The proposed acquisition failed after Harold W. McGraw,
Jr., the chairman of the company, managed to convince several of his
cousins that the price that they were being offered for their stock was
inadequate. Once the acquisition was rejected by the board of directors, McGraw-Hill proceeded to challenge the proposed acquisition in
court on antitrust grounds. Even if founding families cannot always
prevent the assimilation of their corporations by other corporations,
they are often in a position to influence the terms of any acquisitions
or mergers. Recently, the Richardson family, which owned or controlled over 36 percent of the stock in Richardson-Vicks Inc., rejected
an unsolicited acquisition offer from Unilever. Later, the family accepted a more lucrative offer from The Procter & Gamble Company.
In this particular case, the acquisition succeeded because family members who served as trustees of various family foundations and trusts
that owned large blocks of Richardson-Vicks stock felt a fiduciary
obligation to accept the final offer.

Not all corporations that are subject to minority control by their
founding families are equally susceptible to acquisition offers from
other corporations. Some founding families have taken elaborate
precautions to prevent other corporations from gaining control of
their family corporations. One of the most effective means of maintaining minority control of a corporation is to create different classes
of stock with differential voting power. For example, when The Washington Post Company first went public in 1971, it sold over $33 million
worth of Class B common stock. However, the corporation did not sell
any of its Class A common stock. Although both classes of common
stock receive the same dividend, they have differential voting power.
The Class A stock, which represents less than 20 percent of the
outstanding common stock in The Washington Post Company, elects
70 percent of the directors. As a result of the fact that most of this
Class A stock is held by family trusts in which Katharine Meyer
Graham has the sole voting power, she is able to elect a majority of

the board of directors even though she personally owns less than 5 percent of the outstanding common stock in The Washington Post Company. The Adolph Coors Company, which is controlled by the grandchildren and great-grandchildren of Adolph Coors, and Wang Laboratories, which is controlled by An Wang and his children, are two of the most recent cases of corporations in which the founding families have ensured their control by issuing to the public common stock that has only limited voting power.

PRIVATE AFFAIRS

Some corporate rich families have defied the theory of the managerial revolution by refusing to sell any stock in the family firm to the public. As a result, these companies remain privately owned by members of the founding family and a few of their trusted associates. Although relatively few major corporations are still private, these corporations provide the bases for some extremely large fortunes. Moreover, most of these corporations are almost entirely unknown outside the business community. For example, the largest private corporation in the world in terms of sales is undoubtedly Cargill Inc. Originally a grain trading firm, Cargill diversified into corn milling, animal feeds, resins, salt mining, soybean processing, and insurance many years ago. More recently, it has expanded into flour processing, steel manufacturing, poultry processing, and coal mining as well. Although the company does not release detailed financial reports, it has been estimated that Cargill had sales of $30 billion in 1985. Its net worth was probably in the neighborhood of $2 billion. The company, which is headquartered on a secluded estate near Minneapolis, deliberately avoids publicity. Approximately 85 percent of Cargill stock is owned by descendants of William W. Cargill. A majority of that is held by the six grandchildren and twenty-three great-grandchildren of John H. Macmillan, who married Edna Cargill, a daughter of the founder. Another large block of stock is held by the two children and three grandchildren of Austen Cargill, the younger brother of Edna Cargill Macmillan. The remaining stock is held by senior management officials who must sell their shares back to the corporation when they leave Cargill.

Other major private corporations include S.C. Johnson and Son, the manufacturer of household waxes, pest sprays, and toiletries; Bechtel Corporation, the international engineering and construction firm; Hearst Corporation, the newspaper and magazine publishing and broadcasting company; United Parcel Service, the parcel delivery firm; Hallmark Cards, the greeting card company; and Mars Inc., the candy and pet foods manufacturer. At last count, there were over 400 private companies whose stock was closely held by their founding families and employees with sales in excess of $200 million.

Although most private companies steadfastly refuse to release even the most rudimentary details of their finances, they are sometimes forced to disclose at least some information. For example, the exact value of Placid Oil Company, the oil-exploration firm created by H. L. Hunt, has been a closely guarded family secret for decades. Until recently, the company was owned entirely by trusts that the founder had created for the benefit of his six children by his first wife. Consequently, when three of the Hunt brothers required huge sums of cash to finance their speculations in the silver market in 1980, they had to convince their two sisters, who were also directors of Placid, to let them pledge most of the assets of the company as collateral for a loan to them. In return for mortgages on substantially all of its oil and gas properties in Louisiana, Mississippi, and the Gulf of Mexico, Placid Oil received a $2 billion line of credit from a consortium of banks. Their sisters later withdrew from the company. As a result of these departures and the debt incurred to repay the silver loans, Placid Oil now has a net worth of only about $1 billion.

There are many reasons why corporate rich families endeavor to keep their companies private. One advantage is that they are able to avoid any financial disclosures. Private corporations with fewer than 500 stockholders do not have to file periodic reports with the Securities and Exchange Commission. In this way, a corporation is able to keep secret both the magnitude and the sources of its profits. The founding family itself also benefits from this lack of disclosure. Because a private corporation is not subject to SEC regulations, it does not have to disclose the stockholdings of either its directors or its principal stockholders. In the case of a private corporation, therefore, the secrecy surrounding the wealth of the founding family is twofold. To begin with, there is no exact market value for a private company because it is extremely difficult to estimate the value of a company that is not required to disclose either its revenues or its profits. And even if it were possible to arrive at some valuation of a private company, there is no accurate information available on the distribution of its stock among the various members of the founding family. As a result of this veil of secrecy, the members of these corporate rich families enjoy comparative anonymity, even when they occupy positions of authority in these private corporations. For example, Stephen D. Bechtel, Jr., Samuel C. Johnson II, and Whitney Macmillan are almost unknown to the public at large despite the fact that all three are the chairmen of some of the largest corporations in the nation.

In addition to the benefits of secrecy, private corporations also offer distinct advantages to their founding families in terms of tax avoidance. Because family members typically own a majority of the stock in the corporation, the family is able to establish or modify the capital structure of the company in such a way as to reduce the gift and estate taxes of family members. For example, members of the eldest generation of the family may exchange some of their common stock in the company for preferred stock and give their remaining common stock to their children and grandchildren. There are distinct tax advantages to such an exchange. The preferred stock received by the members of the eldest generation provides them with an ample and stable income. However, this stock does not appreciate in value over time, because its dividends are fixed. The benefits of any future growth in the family company, such as increased dividends paid on the common stock and any resultant appreciation in its value, accrue to their children and grandchildren. As one tax expert, George Cooper, observes, "the preferred stock recapitalization as a technique to pass on future growth in a closely held corporation is old hat to estate planners." In any event, gift and estate taxes on the stock of a private corporation are often relatively low, inasmuch as there is no ready

144

market for these shares. Moreover, any attempt by tax assessors to assign a hypothetical market value to this stock must rely on financial statements provided by the company itself. It is not uncommon, therefore, for private companies to understate their profits. For example, Cargill Inc. eventually pleaded guilty to filing false tax returns in 1975 and 1976 that understated profits in those years by a total of $7 million.

Whenever a private family company sells shares to the public, it is a sign that the members of the founding family have arrived at a collective decision to relinquish their absolute control over the family firm. There are, of course, certain disadvantages associated with taking a family corporation public. The most obvious of these is that the family must dilute its equity position in the company and, consequently, its control over the company. Moreover, once a company sells some of its shares to the public at large, it must comply with the disclosure requirements of the SEC. Specifically, the company must issue annual reports concerning its management and its finances. In short, when a family corporation goes public, its founding family must go public as well. Specifically, members of the founding family who serve as directors or who are principal stockholders are forced to disclose the extent of their stockholdings in the corporation. For example, before Levi Strauss and Company went public in 1971, few people who were not members of the founding family knew much about its finances or the ownership of its stock. However, after the company went public, it had to file with the SEC reports that confirmed that at least half of the stock in Levi Strauss was held by the children and several collateral relatives of Walter A. Haas, the husband of one of the nieces of the original Levi Strauss. In particular, Walter Haas and his three children held stock in Levi Strauss worth in the neighborhood of $200 million by 1976. Several other collateral relatives, primarily a brother-in-law and a niece, owned Levi Strauss stock worth at least another $50 million.

Despite these problems, there are some advantages to both the company and the founding family from going public. The most obvious benefit stems from the fact that selling shares to the public enables the family corporation to use the proceeds to reduce corporate debt and finance expansion. At the same time, the family may use this opportunity to diversify its investments by selling some of its stock in the company. For example, when Levi Strauss first went public, the company was experiencing tremendous growth in the sales of its primary product, denim jeans. As Walter Haas explained, "we were growing so fast we just had to have equity money." In its initial public offering in 1971, the company sold newly issued stock, which represented slightly less than a 10 percent stake in the company, for $47 million. Almost half of the proceeds went to pay off short-term loans from banks. The remainder went to finance the construction of several new manufacturing plants. During the next several years, members of the Haas family and several family charities sold over $44 million worth of their Levi Strauss stock as well. In 1985, however, the Haases decided to take their company private again. Using the assets of the company as collateral, they and a few associates borrowed just over $1.4 billion to purchase all of the stock in Levi Strauss held by the public. Several family members sold $340 million of their stock to the new company as well. In the words of one family member, "a lot of us, particularly older family members, had to make sure our estates were liquid for estate tax purposes." The remaining family members received a 92 percent interest in the new private Levi Strauss in exchange for their remaining 20 percent of the stock in the old public Levi Strauss.

Sometimes the decision to take a company public is forced upon the founding family by circumstances beyond its control. In particular, it may be necessary for a corporate rich family to raise large sums of cash in order to pay the estate taxes of a family member. The payment of estate taxes can be especially problematic if the primary asset of the estate is a large block of stock in a private corporation for which there is no ready market. In such a situation, the family may resort to one of several options. If other family members have enough cash, they may purchase the stock in the private corporation from the estate. Alternatively, the private corporation, which may be controlled by the family, may repurchase this stock from the estate. In either case, the estate receives the required cash and the equity position of the founding family in the private corporation remains undiluted. However, if the estate tax obligations are larger than the cash reserves of both the family and the corporation, the estate may be forced to sell all or part of its stockholdings in the family firm to the public at large in order to raise the necessary cash. If this stock is purchased by a large number of individuals, the company may be compelled to comply with the disclosure requirements of the SEC. For example, the descendants of Adolph H. Coors took their family brewing company, Adolph Coors Company, public in order to pay estate taxes. As William K. Coors explained, "we decided to go public when we got a bill from the IRS for $50 million in inheritance taxes." In 1975, the family sold part of its stockholdings, representing roughly 12 percent of the outstanding nonvoting Class B common stock in Coors, for $127 million.

As long as a corporation remains private, members of the founding family may find it difficult to convert their stockholdings into cash because the shares of private corporations can be traded only on the over-the-counter market. Moreover, because private companies do not issue financial reports to the public, the value of the stock in these companies is often a matter of conjecture. Once a family corporation goes public, however, the fortune of the founding family becomes highly liquid. In other words, family members are readily able to convert all or part of their company stock into cash. Furthermore, a listing on a major exchange often increases the value of the stock in a private company. This was certainly the case when The Upjohn Company, a major pharmaceutical firm, went public in 1958. Before its first public offering, over 71 percent of the Upjohn stock was held by descendants and collateral relatives of the company founder, William E. Upjohn. As long as Upjohn remained a private company, the value of its stock and, consequently, the wealth of the Upjohn family was somewhat indeterminate. For purposes of gift and estate taxes, the company stock had been appraised at less than $12 a share before going public. But when members of the Upjohn family sold over 1.7 million shares of company stock in a public offering in 1958, they received $45 a share for their stock. This one transaction raised almost $78 million in cash for members of the Upjohn family. The stock offering also established that the remaining Upjohn stock still held by the family was worth another $374 million in the open market. As a result of taking their company public, the Upjohns were instantaneously and securely established as a major corporate rich family.

SELLING OUT

The members of a corporate rich family often decide, after decades of managing and directing the family corporation, to sever their ties with the company by selling their stock to another corporation. There are many reasons for selling out. To begin with, the founding family may no longer be able to provide the company with adequate management. There simply may not be any qualified family members with any interest in managing the firm. More often, the founding family simply decides to merge the company into another corporation as a means of diversifying its fortune. To the extent that the family fortune is invested in the stock of a single company, the welfare of the family hinges almost entirely upon the success or failure of that company. Moreover, the profitability of this company is often dependent on the economic conditions within a single industry. By selling out for cash or for stock in a larger and more diversified corporation, the family is able to achieve greater financial security. At the same time, large corporations are constantly in search of smaller companies with above-average growth rates or profit margins as merger partners. Indeed, many major corporations owe their present status as growth companies to a succession of mergers and acquisitions. Even a large and established corporation such as Procter & Gamble must attribute much of its present size and diversity to a series of acquisitions and mergers involving family-controlled companies with established brands such as Folgers coffee, Duncan Hines cake mixes, Charmin bathroom tissues, and Richardson-Vicks proprietary drugs.

The decision by a founding family to sell out to another company is often precipitated by a crisis of one kind or another. For example, the acquisition of Jos. Schlitz Brewing Company by Stroh Brewing Company was the result of a series of crises. For several decades Schlitz was one of the leading brewers in the nation. In recent years, it had been owned primarily by the grandchildren and great-grand-children of four Uihlein brothers, who had inherited the company from their uncle, Joseph Schlitz. By 1975, the Uihlein family still owned almost 75 percent of its stock and fourteen of the seventeen directors of the company were family members. However, the family was extremely large, comprising scores of second and third cousins. It also had a history of acrimonious disputes. Indeed, annual meetings of the company sometimes degenerated into family shouting matches. When Schlitz president Robert A. Uihlein, Jr., passed away in 1975, there were two other Uihleins serving as vice presidents of the com-pany. However, neither of them was acceptable to the entire family as a successor. At the very next annual meeting, family members began quarreling among themselves over the choice of a successor. In the years that followed, profits declined precipitously at Schlitz until the dividend on its common stock was first reduced and then elimi-nated altogether. Scores of Uihleins were suddenly deprived of their main source of income. By 1982, a majority of the Uihleins were more than willing to sell their stock in the company to Stroh Brewing. As a result of this merger, the family received roughly $330 million in cash. The Uihleins were reinstated to the ranks of the corporate rich, but their company disappeared as an independent brewer.

Other families have sold out for less pressing reasons. In most of these cases, family members have simply decided to retire from active participation in business. By and large, these are third- and fourth-generation corporate rich families that have grown very large. Conse-quently, they have little reason to refuse lucrative cash offers for their stock from other corporations. For example, when Oscar Mayer and Company was acquired by General Foods in 1981, the Mayer family had already relinquished active control over the company. Although the descendants of Oscar F. Mayer still held at least 54 percent of the Oscar Mayer stock and four members of the family served as directors, there were no Mayers working as managers for the company. The four Mayers on the board of directors, who were all grandchildren of the founder, had once served as managers, but none of the great-grand-children of the founder had any association with the company. In return for their stock in Oscar Mayer and Company, the members of the Mayer family received over $225 million in cash. The situation was much the same when the Beinecke family sold their remaining 43 percent of Sperry and Hutchinson stock to Baldwin United in 1981 for $145 million in cash. The company had been controlled and managed for over a half century by three brothers, Edwin, Frederick, and Walter Beinecke, and their descendants. Although one of the Beinecke cousins was still chief executive officer of the company and his son was a vice president, most family members considered the acquisition offer from Baldwin United too lucrative to refuse. Of course, both Beineckes resigned from Sperry and Hutchinson once it became a subsidiary of Baldwin United.

Perhaps the most important reason for a family to merge its company into a larger corporation is financial security. In many cases, virtually the entire fortune of a corporate rich family is based on its stockhold-ings in a single company. Moreover, this company may operate in a highly cyclical industry. Consequently, the fortune of the founding family may rise and fall with cyclical fluctuations in that particular industry. By merging the family company into a larger corporation with more diversified operations, the family may be able to achieve greater financial security. For example, Willard F. Rockwell, Jr., negotiated the merger in 1967 of Rockwell Standard, a manufacturer of automotive parts founded by his father and his uncle, into North American Aviation, a large aerospace firm, to form North American Rockwell. Six years later he engineered the merger of Rockwell Manu-facturing, a tool and equipment manufacturer that was almost 20 percent owned by the Rockwell family, into North American Rock-well to form Rockwell International Corporation. He explained the mergers by saying, "the best thing for my family and the stockholders was to give them the best security and marketability I could get." Similarly, Edmund W. Littlefield initiated the merger of Utah Interna-tional Inc., a mining and construction company founded by his grand-father, into General Electric Company in 1977 in order to provide members of the Wattis family with greater financial security. Utah International, which was almost 14 percent owned by the descendants of Edmund O. Wattis, depended on overseas mining operations for much of its profits. As a result of the merger, the Wattis family wound up with roughly 2 percent of the stock in one of the largest and most diversified corporations in the world.

The most critical element in any merger or acquisition is financing. In general, one company can purchase another by using cash, stock, or some combination of both. If a corporate rich family owns a significant block of stock in a company, the acquiring company may prefer to buy their stockholdings for cash. In this way, the selling family does not receive enough stock to make it the principal stockholder in the acquiring company. For example, when Texaco purchased Getty Oil in 1984, the management of Texaco insisted on a cash transaction because an exchange of stock would have given the Getty family enough Texaco common stock to control the company. In terms of tax avoidance, however, corporate rich families almost invariably prefer mergers involving an exchange of stock to acquisitions involving cash purchases of stock. Selling stock, which may have a low valuation for tax purposes, can expose family members to large capital-gains taxes. For example, the Sarah C. Getty Trust had to pay approximately $810 million in capital-gains taxes after it sold its Getty Oil stock to Texaco for $4.1 billion in cash and government securities. This huge tax liability resulted from the fact that its stockholdings in Getty Oil were valued at less than $4 million when the trust was created in 1934. Conversely, an exchange of stock in one company for stock in another, as the result of a merger, does not usually require the payment of any capital-gains taxes, because the tax code treats exchanges of stock differently from sales of stock.

In some cases, an acquiring company may issue preferred stock, with limited voting privileges, to the members of the family that controls the company being acquired. For example, when Malcolm McLean sold his privately owned Sea-Land Industries to R.J. Reynolds Industries in 1969, he received $160 million in preferred stock to prevent him from gaining control of R.J. Reynolds Industries. Similarly, Revlon issued preferred stock to Edwin C. Whitehead worth roughly $300 million in 1980 for his 84 percent of Technicon Corporation. Although he was given a seat on the board of directors, he was not able to control the company, because his preferred stock had only limited voting power. More recently, the Belfer family sold their 45 percent of Belco Petroleum to InterNorth in 1983 for $285 million in preferred stock. Once again, two members of the Belfer family were elected to the board of directors of InterNorth, but they do not control the corporation. Preferred stock is ideal for such acquisitions because the acquiring company is able to redeem it later at a fixed price. However, the strategy of financing an acquisition with preferred stock does not always succeed in maintaining the autonomy of management. For example, General Dynamics Corporation acquired Material Services Corporation from Henry Crown in 1959 for $116 million in preferred stock. After several years of disagreements with Crown, management decided to redeem his preferred stock in the company. Not one to be ignored, Henry Crown took the cash he received for his preferred shares and bought General Dynamics common stock. By 1970, the Crown family and their associates controlled 18 percent of General Dynamics common stock as well as six of the fourteen seats on the board of directors.

On a few occasions, the merger of a family-controlled company into another corporation may allow the founding family to gain active control of the combined company. This occurs whenever a corporate rich family receives as part of the merger so much common stock in the acquiring corporation that a family member is able to become the chief executive officer of the corporation. Such was the case after Robert O. Anderson merged his family-owned oil company into Atlantic Richfield Company. In 1963, Anderson sold Hondo Oil and Gas to the predecessor of Atlantic Richfield for $36 million in common stock. He was given a seat on the board of directors because, with over 5 percent of its common stock, he had become the largest stockholder in the company. Two years later, however, he assumed the position of chairman and chief executive officer. In this capacity, Anderson exercised unquestioned control over Atlantic Richfield for two decades, until he resigned as chairman in 1985. By that time, he and his family owned only about 1 percent of the outstanding Atlantic

Richfield stock. Similarly, Dwayne O. Andreas and his brother, Lowell W. Andreas, gained control of Archer Daniels Midland Company not long after their family firm, First Interoceanic Corporation, bought a 6 percent stake in the corporation in 1965. Both brothers were subsequently elected directors. Three years later, Archer Daniels Midland acquired First Interoceanic in an exchange of stock. As a result of this merger, the Andreas brothers wound up with over 16 percent of the stock in Archer Daniels Midland. By 1971, Dwayne Andreas was chairman and Lowell Andreas was president of the company.

Only rarely does a corporate rich family gain active control of a major corporation as the result of a merger. However, it is not unusual for a family to gain passive control in this way. In other words, whenever a family becomes the principal stockholder in a corporation as the result of a merger, it usually has little difficulty obtaining representation on the board of directors. For example, when the five grandchildren of Edward L. Doheny sold their oil properties to the predecessor of Unocal Corporation in 1959, they received $22 million in cash and almost $17 million in Unocal common stock. As a result of this merger, they became the largest stockholders in the company, with 11 percent of its stock. Within a few days of the merger, their stepfather was elected a director of Unocal. One of the Doheny grandchildren still serves as a director of Unocal, even though the family probably owns only about 4 percent of the stock in the company. Whether or not a corporate rich family is able to exercise some form of minority control over a corporation after a merger depends largely on how much stock they receive as a result of the merger. The merger between Time Inc. and Temple Industries in 1973 provides an illustration of this point. In this merger, the stockholders of Temple Industries received $153 million in Time common stock, of which half went to the descendants of Thomas L. Temple. Consequently, the Temples wound up with nearly 15 percent of the stock in Time. Two of the grandsons of Thomas L. Temple also became directors of Time. In this way, a somewhat obscure family from rural Texas gained effective control of one of the largest media companies in the nation.

6

Death
and
Taxes

Corporate rich families, by definition, possess great wealth. The members of these families also enjoy certain privileges associated with such wealth. To begin with, they are usually welcome among the most exclusive social circles of the upper class in America. In addition, some of them occupy positions of power in business, government, and civic affairs. Despite their individual achievements, the social status and power enjoyed by the members of these families are ultimately the products of their fortunes. Any diminution of a family fortune eventually diminishes the status and power of each member of the family. Consequently, the first priority of every wealthy capitalist family is the preservation of its fortune. Of course, there are many obstacles to the perpetuation of wealth. First and foremost, there is the obstacle presented by taxes. The tax system in the United States is formally progressive. In other words, individuals with large incomes are expected to pay disproportionately more in taxes than those with small incomes. The corporate rich, who derive large dividend incomes and capital gains from their stockholdings, are usually in the highest income-tax brackets. However, the greatest threat to the fortune of a corporate rich family is that posed by gift and estate taxes. These highly progressive taxes were designed specifically to reduce the intergenerational transmission of great wealth. Whenever wealthy individuals transfer valuable assets to others by way of lifetime gifts, they must pay substantial gift taxes. Similarly, whenever they bequeath valuable assets to their heirs, their estates are subject to substantial estate taxes.

The corporate rich have not acquiesced passively in the imposition of progressive gift and estate taxes. To the contrary, they have acted quickly and decisively to avoid these taxes whenever possible. For example, they have retained tax lawyers and financial advisers who, in turn, have devised often elaborate strategies for avoiding or reducing gift and estate taxes. Indeed, the distribution of wealth within the typical corporate rich family is purposely structured to avoid unnecessary taxes and to preserve the family fortune intact from one generation to the next. In order to avoid estate taxes, parents have been forced to distribute the bulk of their assets to their children in the form of lifetime gifts. More often than not, these gifts have taken the form of contributions to trusts that they have established for the benefit of their children and grandchildren.

Consequently, most of the wealth owned by a corporate rich family is usually held by a complex network of family trusts. In some cases, these families have also established private companies to hold and manage their investments. Furthermore, the financial structures of these holding companies have often been designed to reduce the impact of gift and estate taxes. As a result of these various tax-avoidance strategies, wealthy capitalist families have created elaborate legal arrangements for the administration of their fortunes. These formal arrangements, in turn, have influenced kinship patterns within these families.

THE WAR ON WEALTH

Despite their egalitarian ideals, Americans tolerated for many decades the inheritance of great wealth. Although several states enacted estate taxes as early as the Civil War, these taxes were nominal and were not intended to prevent the intergenerational transmission of wealth. Popular sentiment against the inheritance of great wealth did not develop until the emergence of large industrial fortunes in the late nineteenth century. Previous to that time, land was the main form of wealth. However, the formation of large corporations led to the creation of industrial fortunes so stupendous that they provoked widespread public condemnation. Public opinion was aroused by the fact that wealthy "robber barons" were able to pass their entire fortunes on to their children. For example, when Philip D. Armour, the founder of Armour and Company and an organizer of the notorious "Beef Trust," died in 1901, he left his son an estate reportedly worth $50 million. It was during this period that progressive politicians began to speak out against the evils of inherited wealth. One of the first national figures to condemn the inheritance of large fortunes was Theodore Roosevelt, a member of a moderately wealthy and decidedly upper-class family. In an address to Congress in 1906, President Roosevelt declared that "no advantage comes either to the country or to the individual inheriting money by permitting the transmission in their entirety of the enormous fortunes." Progressives argued for inheritance taxes as a means of achieving "equality of property" in order to assure equal opportunity among individuals. In this view, the scion of a wealthy family, by mere accident of birth, gained an unfair advantage in the "game of life."

Although Theodore Roosevelt and other progressive politicians campaigned for the passage of a federal inheritance tax, none was passed by Congress until the United States prepared to enter World War I. Faced with the enormous costs of military mobilization, Congress passed the first federal estate tax in 1916. It was originally a very modest tax with a maximum rate of 10 percent on estates in excess of $5 million. This tax was increased twice the following year in order to finance the war effort, until the maximum rate reached 25 percent on estates larger than $10 million. The corporate rich countered the passage of the increasingly progressive federal estate taxes by simply giving much of their wealth to their heirs, because there was no federal tax on gifts. Congress finally moved to remedy this situation in 1924 with the passage of the first federal gift tax. This tax reached a maximum rate of 25 percent on gifts larger than $10 million. At the same time, Congress also raised the estate tax to a maximum rate of 40 percent on estates of the same size. These reforms were vehemently opposed by the corporate rich. Four years later, yielding to a concerted lobbying effort, Congress cut the estate taxes by half and eliminated the gift tax entirely. But this was only a temporary reprieve. With the onset of the Great Depression, taxes on intergenerational transfers of great wealth gained renewed public support. Even Herbert Hoover, a steadfast conservative, advocated gift and estate taxes as a means of eliminating the "evils of inherited economic power." In 1932, Congress raised the federal estate tax to a maximum rate of 45 percent on estates in excess of $10 million. Also, a federal gift tax with a maximum rate of 33.5 percent on gifts of the same size was reinstated.

The war on wealth, which had raged back and forth inconclusively for almost three decades, took a decisive turn with the election of Franklin D. Roosevelt, a member of the same family that had produced Theodore Roosevelt. With the nation mired in the Great Depression, Congress voted in 1934 to raise both the gift and estate taxes to unprecedented levels. The estate tax was increased to a maximum rate of 60 percent on estates in excess of $10 million. At the same time, the gift tax rate was set at three-quarters of the estate tax rate. For example, the maximum gift tax rate was 45 percent on gifts larger than $10 million. Despite the imposition of these new taxes, many Americans still felt that the corporate rich were still too rich. Huey Long, a populist senator from Louisiana, began to gain national recognition with a radical program to redistribute wealth. In order to preempt any potential third-party challenge in the next election, President Roosevelt decided to adopt the issue as his own. In an address to Congress in 1935, he declared that "the transmission from generation to generation of vast fortunes by will, inheritance, or gift is not

consistent with the ideals and sentiments of the American people."
After considerable debate, Congress voted in 1935 to raise estate taxes
to seemingly confiscatory levels. The maximum estate tax rate was
increased to 70 percent on estates in excess of $50 million. Estates of
$10 million were taxed at the rate of 67 percent. The gift tax rate
remained at three-quarters of the estate tax rate. However, these tax
reforms were intended primarily to assuage public opinion rather than
redistribute concentrated wealth. In the words of one historian, Mark
H. Leff, "the New Deal tax system illustrated the limits to symbolic
reform."

Most corporate rich families reacted quickly to the tax reforms
of 1935. In fact, the tax legislation passed by the Congress provided
them with numerous opportunities to safeguard the bulk of their
fortunes. Although the legislation was signed into law by President
Roosevelt in September of that year, the new gift tax rates were not
scheduled to take effect until the beginning of 1936. In the interim,
there was a virtual stampede among the corporate rich to give much
of their wealth to their heirs while the more lenient gift taxes were still
in effect. With two full months left before the end of the year, the
Securities and Exchange Commission reported that directors and
principal stockholders of major corporations had given over $62 mil-
lion in stock to members of their families. Even this compilation was
incomplete, because it did not include gifts by other stockholders not
required to report to the SEC. It was reported, for example, that Jesse
I. Strauss and Percy S. Strauss, two of the three brothers who controlled R.H. Macy & Co. Inc., gave their children Macy stock worth
over $5 million. Similarly, Helena Woolworth McCann, the daughter
of Frank W. Woolworth, placed $11 million in Woolworth stock in
a series of trusts for her children. Among the richest of the corporate
rich families, the gifts were even larger. The four Mellon cousins,
Richard K. Mellon, Sarah Mellon Scaife, Paul Mellon, and Ailsa
Mellon Bruce, placed Gulf Oil stock in itself worth over $17 million
in trusts for their children. Not to be outdone, John D. Rockefeller,
Jr., gave his children, and trusts he had set up for their benefit, $27
million in Mobil Oil stock alone. In most cases, these gifts merely
augmented earlier gifts of comparable magnitude.

In general, the vicissitudes of gift and estate taxes are closely related to the state of the economy and the fiscal requirements of the federal government. The major increases in these taxes, as with other taxes, have typically occurred during periods of economic recession and military mobilization. For example, the highly progressive gift and estate taxes imposed during the Great Depression were raised once again as the United States prepared for World War II. In 1941, Congress raised the maximum estate tax rate to 77 percent on estates in excess of $10 million. Correspondingly, the maximum gift tax rate became 57.75 percent on gifts of the same size. These highly progressive gift and estate taxes remained in effect, virtually unchanged, for almost four decades. They were not altered significantly until the passage of new tax reforms in 1976. In that year, the differences between the gift and estate taxes were eliminated by the imposition of a *uniform transfer tax,* which taxed gifts and estates at the same rate. At the same time, the maximum transfer tax rate was set at 70 percent on gifts and estates in excess of $5 million. Moreover, this same legislation imposed a tax equivalent to the transfer tax on all generation-skipping trusts created after 1980. Although most of these tax reforms are still in effect, the tax rates on gifts and estates were drastically reduced after the election of Ronald Reagan in 1980. As part of his overall tax-reduction plan, President Reagan advocated a major reduction in the transfer tax. In 1981, Congress agreed to reduce the maximum transfer tax rate to 55 percent on gifts and estates in excess of $5 million. Federal taxes on intergenerational transfers of wealth are now at their lowest levels since the Great Depression.

Despite the fact that highly progressive gift and estate taxes have been in force for the past half century, most wealthy capitalist families have managed to hold on to the bulk of their fortunes. Even the richest of the corporate rich families have survived the onslaught of formally confiscatory gift and estate taxes relatively unscathed. There is, for example, the case of the Mellon family. According to an official government report, the entire Mellon family owned corporate stock worth at least $352 million in 1939. Over four decades later, the Mellon fortune is still largely intact. According to the best available

159

evidence, it appears that the Mellons are now worth nearly $6 billion. The situation is much the same with the Rockefellers, another major corporate rich family. According to this same government report, the main branch of the Rockefeller family owned corporate stock worth at least $249 million in 1939. Once again, the best available evidence indicates that the Rockefellers are now worth at least $5 billion. Both of these families employed an array of tax-avoidance strategies, such as lifetime gifts, generation-skipping trusts, and family holding companies, in order to preserve most of their fortunes. Other corporate rich families, like the du Ponts, Gettys, and Hunts, have used these same strategies with roughly equal success. The war on inherited wealth waged by the federal government for the past several decades has, to date, only slightly diminished most of the great family fortunes.

THE JOYS OF GIVING

One of the most effective strategies for avoiding estate taxes is to pay gift taxes instead. In short, the corporate rich are able to avoid estate taxes simply by reducing their estates through a program of lifetime gifts to their heirs. Indeed, for several decades, there was a clear tax incentive for wealthy individuals to make lifetime gifts instead of testamentary bequests inasmuch as the tax rate on gifts was only three-quarters of the tax rate on estates. From 1942 to 1976, the maximum marginal estate tax rate was 77 percent on estates in excess of $10 million. However, the maximum marginal gift tax rate during this same period was only 57.75 percent on gifts in excess of $10 million. These differences in the nominal tax rates were compounded by differences in the manner in which the two taxes were computed. The estate tax was assessed on the entire estate, including the part that eventually went to pay the estate tax, whereas the gift tax was assessed only on the gift itself. For example, a parent who gave a child $5 million had to pay a gift tax of $1.8 million, for a total outlay of $6.8 million. However, a parent who wished to bequeath a child $5 million by will had to leave an estate of $15 million in order to pay the estate tax of $10 million. In this particular case, the estate tax was five times the gift tax for the same intergenerational transfer of wealth. The advantages of transferring wealth through lifetime gifts rather than testamentary bequests were not lost on the corporate rich. Most wealthy individuals opted to transfer the bulk of their assets to their children long before they died.

The disparity between the tax rates on gifts and estates was eliminated by the Tax Reform Act of 1976. From that point on, the different gift and estate tax rates were unified into a single transfer tax rate. This legislation also set the new maximum marginal tax rate at 70 percent on gifts or estates in excess of $5 million. In effect, the gift tax was raised while the estate tax was lowered. These uniform transfer tax rates were reduced even further by the Economic Recovery Tax Act of 1981. As a result of this legislation, the maximum marginal tax rate will eventually be reduced to 55 percent on gifts and estates in excess of $5 million. Although there is no longer a discrepancy between the gift and estate taxes, there are still tax advantages to lifetime gifts as opposed to testamentary bequests. For example, a parent who gives a child a gift of $5 million must pay a gift tax of almost $2.5 million, for a total outlay of $7.5 million. Conversely, a parent who wishes to bequeath a child $5 million by will must leave an estate of $10 million in order to pay the estate tax of $5 million. Even with a unified tax rate, the estate taxes are twice the gift taxes for the same intergenerational transfer of wealth. Once again, the advantage of lifetime gifts over testamentary bequests results largely from differences in the way the gift and estate taxes are computed. It must be noted, however, that the gift tax is based on the cumulative amount of wealth transferred over time. In other words, there is no major tax advantage to transferring wealth in a series of small gifts rather than a single large gift.

There are other tax incentives for transferring wealth through a series of lifetime gifts. One incentive is the annual exclusion. For several decades the federal gift tax contained an *annual exclusion,* which permitted an individual to give as much as $3,000 a year to someone else without any gift tax liability. For example, a wealthy individual could give up to $3,000 each year to each of his or her children and grandchildren. A married couple could double the ante to $6,000 per child by declaring these gifts to be split gifts. Therefore, a wealthy couple could, over a period of twenty years, give a total of $120,000 to each of an unlimited number of heirs without paying any gift taxes. As a result of the Economic Recovery Tax Act of 1981, the annual exclusion was increased from $3,000 to $10,000. Consequently, a married couple can now give $20,000 a year to each of any number of heirs without incurring any gift tax liability. Over a period of twenty years, a wealthy couple could transfer a total of $400,000 to each of their children and grandchildren. The most appealing feature of the annual exclusion, for tax-avoidance purposes, is that there is no limit on the number of recipients. A husband and wife with four children and sixteen grandchildren could, over a period of twenty years, give their progeny a total of $8 million without paying any gift taxes whatsoever. If they were willing to extend their generosity to the spouses of their progeny, the transfer of wealth could be increased substantially.

It is difficult to determine precisely how much wealth is transferred by lifetime gifts as opposed to testamentary bequests. Unlike testamentary bequests, which become part of the probate record of an estate, gifts are not generally a matter of public record. Only rarely does the public get any indication of the assets transferred to heirs through lifetime gifts by the members of corporate rich families. One of those rare glimpses was provided by Nelson A. Rockefeller in his quest to become vice president. In his hearings before the House Judiciary Committee in 1974, he was forced to disclose his personal finances in unprecedented detail. For example, he disclosed that he and his wife had a net worth of $62 million. They were also the sole income beneficiaries of three trusts worth another $120 million. An examination of his tax returns for the ten years previous to 1974 indicates that Nelson Rockefeller regularly transferred assets to his children as well as a number of close associates. Indeed, he paid gift taxes in each of those years. His gift taxes during this ten-year period alone amounted to nearly $4 million. According to his own testimony, Nelson Rockefeller had given members of his family a total of $15 million by 1974. This may seem like a paltry amount. However, his children were already the income beneficiaries of trusts established for them by his father, John D. Rockefeller, Jr. In all, these trusts were worth at least $35 million by 1974. Nelson Rockefeller also knew that, upon his death, his children would automatically become the income beneficiaries of a trust created for him by his father that was then worth another $106 million.

Despite the existence of progressive transfer taxes, there are several financial incentives for transferring wealth to children through lifetime gifts. To begin with, there is the problem of income taxes. Even with the best tax advice, a wealthy individual with a large income must often devote much of it to the payment of income taxes. Once again, Nelson Rockefeller has provided the public with a glimpse into the tax problems of the corporate rich. In the decade preceding 1974, he earned just over $47 million, almost all of it from dividends or capital gains on stock held by him or by trusts for his benefit. During this same period, he paid a total of $22 million in city, county, state, and federal taxes, including almost $15 million in federal and state income taxes. Although the children of Nelson Rockefeller were each multimillionaires in their own right, their incomes paled in comparison to the income of their father. Consequently, they were probably in somewhat lower income-tax brackets than their father. By transferring income-producing assets, such as stocks and bonds, to his children, Nelson Rockefeller was able to reduce the income taxes paid by the family as a whole. This strategy is known as *income shifting* among tax experts. A member of the corporate rich can even transfer wealth to a minor child or grandchild by assigning the assets to a guardian or by placing them in a trust. Among the corporate rich, then, it is not unusual for even the very young to pay income taxes on the dividend income they receive from stock given to them by parents and grandparents.

There is one other advantage to the strategy of using lifetime gifts rather than testamentary bequests to transfer wealth from one generation to the next. This advantage is related to the issue of capital appreciation. Most of the wealth transferred through lifetime bequests is in the form of assets, such as real estate and stock, that typically appreciate over time. For example, the sum of $100 invested equally in a portfolio of all of the stocks listed on the New York Stock Exchange in 1925 would have been worth $6,157 fifty years later, if all of the dividends received had been reinvested each year. Even if all of the dividends had been spent instead of reinvested, the stocks in this portfolio would still have appreciated in value to $682 by 1975. Even after removing the effects of inflation during this period, this portfolio would have been worth $256. By giving their heirs stock during their lifetimes, the corporate rich are able to ensure that the future capital appreciation in this stock is removed from their estates. It is typical for the older members of a corporate rich family to give most of their common stocks, as well as much of their real estate, to their children while they live on the stable income provided by preferred stocks and bonds. For example, by the time he died in 1937, John D. Rockefeller had given his son stock in the various Standard Oil companies worth almost $250 million. His own estate, which amounted to only $26 million, was composed largely of government bonds.

Most of the corporate rich have used lifetime gifts in order to reduce their own income and estate taxes and to increase the amount of wealth transferred to their heirs. There is the example of Charles S. Mott, one of the earliest and largest stockholders in General Motors Corporation. In 1940, Mott placed slightly more than $5 million in General Motors stock in a trust for the benefit of his fourth wife and their children. It was estimated at the time that he paid at least $1.5 million in taxes on this gift. Of course, the General Motors stock in these trusts has appreciated greatly in value since that time. By the time he died in 1973, the General Motors stock placed in this trust for the benefit of his wife and children was worth $45 million. As the result of capital appreciation and stock splits, one share of General Motors stock, which was worth $53 in 1940, was equivalent to six shares of General Motors stock, each worth $75 in 1973. In other words, Charles Mott succeeded in reducing the size of his estate by almost $40 million by paying $1.5 million in gift taxes thirty-three years earlier. If he had held on to this stock and bequeathed it to his children in his will, the estate taxes on this $45 million in stock would have come to just over $33 million, leaving them less than $12 million.

Of course, Mott also established similar trusts for the benefit of his four children by a previous marriage. Altogether, Charles Mott used lifetime gifts to transfer a vast fortune to his children. The Mott fortune now consists of roughly $75 million in General Motors stock and at least $200 million in the stock of several other corporations, including United States Sugar Corporation.

Lifetime gifts sometimes prove to be very valuable, as was demonstrated by the Watson family. As one of the first presidents of International Business Machines, Thomas J. Watson managed to accumulate an enormous fortune in company stock. When he first joined the company in 1914, he was given the option to buy $33,550 worth of IBM stock, which amounted to less than 1 percent of the stock in the company. Over the next few decades, Watson increased his stake in the company by buying additional shares, most of which he gave to his wife and children. He was able to afford these stock purchases because of a unique bonus system at IBM, which made him one of the highest paid individuals in the country, even in the midst of the Great Depression. By 1937, the Watson family owned over 2 percent of IBM stock, worth a little more than $2 million. Even at this early point, most of the family fortune was held by his wife as guardian for their children. The growth of the Watson fortune was due largely to the spectacular appreciation of IBM stock. One share of IBM stock purchased in 1914 for $28 was equivalent, after nine stock splits and dividends, to 4.8 shares by 1937, each worth $132. In the years to come, the Watson family fortune grew steadily with the unprecedented appreciation of IBM stock. When Thomas J. Watson died in 1956, the Watson family owned a little less than 3 percent of IBM, worth roughly $69 million. The one share of IBM stock purchased in 1914 for $28 was now equivalent, after twenty-eight stock splits and dividends, to 36.7 shares by 1956, each worth $456. However, by the time he died, Watson had succeeded in transferring the bulk of his IBM stock to his children. He died with less than $4 million worth of IBM stock in his estate. In short, he had managed to transfer almost 95 percent of his fortune to his family during his lifetime.

Many of the wealthiest entrepreneurs of recent decades have succeeded in giving most of their fortunes to their children during their own lifetimes. These include Henry J. Kaiser of Kaiser Industries, James S. McDonnell, Jr., of McDonnell Douglas Corporation, Paul V. Galvin of Motorola Inc., and J. Willard Marriott of Marriott Corporation. Perhaps the most vocal advocate and avid practitioner of the strategy of lifetime giving to avoid estate taxes is Henry Crown. As the founder of Material Services Corporation, which he merged into General Dynamics Corporation in 1958 for $125 million in stock, Crown managed to amass a fortune in corporate stock and real estate worth over $600 million by 1980. The cornerstone of this fortune was a 16 percent stake in General Dynamics worth $342 million at the time. As the result of careful planning, most of the wealth amassed by Henry Crown was already held by other family members through a complex maze of trusts, partnerships, and holding companies. By 1980, Crown owned only about $3 million in General Dynamics stock. The rest was held by family members, at least twenty-four trusts for their benefit, and several family-controlled entities including Henry Crown and Company, a family partnership; Crown Fund, a private mutual fund; and Areljay Company, another family partnership. In other words, he had succeeded in giving over 99 percent of his General Dynamics stock to his family. At age seventy-nine, Henry Crown was not reticent about explaining his strategy for avoiding estate taxes. "My objective," he said, "is to make my net worth less at the end of any one year than it was at the beginning." In terms of tax avoidance, then, the goal of many wealthy individuals is to die poor.

SKIPPING GENERATIONS

Tax lawyers have developed a number of ingenious strategies over the years for reducing the gift and estate taxes of their wealthy clients. Perhaps the most notorious of these is a rather complicated but effective device known as a trust. Trusts, which originated in English common law, have been around for centuries. In general, a *trust* is simply an arrangement by which one person sets aside certain assets for the benefit of another person and appoints a trustee to carry out the terms of the trust agreement. The trustee can be an individual, such as a friend or relative, or an institution, such as a bank or trust company. In either case, the trustee assumes a fiduciary responsibility to manage the trust assets for the benefit of its beneficiaries. Trusts typically contain *spendthrift* provisions that are designed to prevent their beneficiaries from squandering their assets. As a result, they are the perfect means of providing financial security for minors, widows, and those individuals who are not competent to handle their own affairs. To this end, trust agreements usually specify how much income each beneficiary is to receive from the trust as well as when the trust is to be terminated and how its assets are then to be distributed. As a result of these characteristics, trusts are the perfect mechanism for perpetuating family dynasties. A wealthy entrepreneur can deposit the bulk of his fortune in a trust that provides his children as income beneficiaries with adequate incomes during their lifetime while the principal is preserved for his grandchildren as remaindermen. In this way, the family fortune, composed largely of stock in the family corporation, is kept intact for at least a couple of generations.

Any trust that distributes its income among one generation of beneficiaries while it conserves its principal for eventual distribution among the next generation of beneficiaries is known as a *generation-skipping trust.* The term derives from the fact that one generation is skipped in the sense that it does not receive any of the principal held by the trust, only the income produced by that principal. Although trusts of this type had been used for spendthrift purposes for decades, it was not until the passage of the first estate taxes in 1916 that lawyers and accountants began extolling the virtues of generation-skipping trusts as a means of tax avoidance. A trust can be created either by gift or by will. If it is created by gift, the creator of the trust must first pay the applicable gift tax. Similarly, if it is created by will, the estate of the creator of the trust must first pay the necessary estate tax. However, once such a trust has been created, its assets are not subject to either gift or estate taxes. Despite the fact that income beneficiaries receive all of the income produced by such a trust, its assets are not included in their estates for tax purposes. Moreover, when such a trust is finally dissolved, its principal is distributed among the remaindermen free of any gift or estate taxes. In this way, a family fortune can be protected from gift and estate taxes for at least one or two generations. The only limitation on the duration of such trusts is imposed by the *rule against perpetuities,* which declares that a trust must be dissolved after the death of the last income beneficiary who was alive at the time the trust was originally established.

One of the best-documented examples of the tax savings associated with generation-skipping trusts is provided by William du Pont, a major partner in the original E.I. du Pont de Nemours and Company. When he died in 1928, he left an estate assessed at $35 million. Because estate tax rates were relatively modest in 1928, the taxes on his estate were only about $6 million. In his will, William du Pont created a testamentary trust for the benefit of his descendants who received the bulk of his estate. According to the terms of this trust, his son, William du Pont, Jr., was to receive a lifetime interest in 60 percent of the income produced by the trust, and his daughter, Marion du Pont, was to receive a lifetime interest in the remaining 40 percent of the income. The trust agreement also specified that, upon the death of each child, his or her share of the principal was to be divided among their respective children. Of course, the assets held by the trust, comprising primarily Du Pont Company stock, appreciated in value over the next few decades. By the time William du Pont, Jr., died in 1965, the trust held assets worth $404 million. In accordance with the terms of the trust, 60 percent of the principal was distributed equally among his five children free of any gift or estate taxes. Moreover, because their aunt, Marion du Pont Scott, never had any children of her own, the children of William du Pont, Jr., also divided her 40 percent share of the trust assets when she died in 1983. If William du Pont had not put his fortune into trust, most of it would have gone to pay the taxes on the estates of his children. As it is, no gift or estate taxes will be paid on this fortune until the grandchildren of William du Pont begin to give or bequeath some of it to their own children and grandchildren.

Whenever a trust skips more than one generation, the resultant tax savings can be enormous. This is certainly the case with the trust established by Sarah Getty, the widow of the founder of the original Getty Oil Company. After the passage of more progressive estate taxes in 1934, J. Paul Getty convinced his mother to place most of her stockholdings in the family oil business into a generation-skipping trust. Because J. Paul Getty was her only heir, she named him as the sole trustee and primary income beneficiary of the trust. Moreover, because her son had provided her with four grandsons by then, she named them as income beneficiaries as well. Sarah Getty paid a small gift tax on this trust, which consisted of Getty Oil stock worth less than $4 million at the time. In the years that followed, of course, Getty Oil stock appreciated greatly in value. By the time J. Paul Getty died in 1976, the Getty Oil stock held by the Sarah Getty Trust was worth $1.5 billion. Because J. Paul Getty was only an income beneficiary of the trust, it was not included in his estate. Gordon Getty and his half-brother, J. Paul Getty, Jr., now share the trust income with the three daughters of their deceased half-brother, George F. Getty II. After the merger of Getty Oil and Texaco in 1984 and the payment of capital-gains taxes on the sale of its stock, the trust held government securities worth almost $3.2 billion. After the death of the last surviving grandson of Sarah Getty, the assets held by this trust will be distributed free of any taxes among her fifteen great-grandchildren. In this way, the bulk of the Getty family fortune will have escaped gift or estate taxes for at least two generations.

Many of the largest fortunes in America, including those of the Rockefellers, du Ponts, and Mellons, are held in a series of generation-skipping trusts. In most cases, each generation has its own trusts. John D. Rockefeller, Jr., for instance, not only established large trusts for each of his children but also a series of smaller trusts for each of his grandchildren as well. In this way, his grandchildren received independent incomes of their own. They did not have to wait until their parents died before they were able to enjoy the financial security associated with being a member of the Rockefeller family. Because of generation-skipping trusts, many of the more recent fortunes will escape estate taxes for generations to come. For example, almost all of the fortune accumulated by H. L. Hunt, the eccentric Texas oilman, was long ago placed in trusts at the insistence of his first wife, Lyda

Hunt. She knew all too well that her husband was an inveterate gambler, and she was determined to safeguard at least part of his fortune for their six children. H. L. Hunt created trusts for each of their children in 1935, and he eventually turned over to those trusts all of the stock in his Placid Oil Company as well as many of his most productive oil leases. When he died in 1974, the man whom J. Paul Getty once declared to be the richest single individual in the country left an estate initially assessed at only $55 million. As a master of tax avoidance himself, Getty should have known that Hunt too had long ago placed most of his wealth in generation-skipping trusts in order to avoid estate taxes.

Generation-skipping trusts eventually became so popular among the corporate rich that several major corporations are now controlled by these trusts. For example, all of the common stock of the Hearst Corporation, one of the largest media companies in the nation, is held by a trust created in 1954 by the will of William R. Hearst. Indeed, there are several companies, such as E.W. Scripps Company, S.C. Johnson and Company, and Adolph Coors Company, in which a majority of the voting stock is held by a single trust. In many cases, the bulk of the fortune of a corporate rich family is held in a series of such trusts. The children and grandchildren of John T. Dorrance, the founder of Campbell Soup Company, own stock in the company worth roughly $1.2 billion. Most of this stock is held by a series of trusts. Indeed, one trust alone holds over $650 million in Campbell Soup stock. Similarly, almost all of the Times Mirror stock owned by the descendants of Harry Chandler is held by two giant trusts. Either directly or indirectly through a family holding company, these trusts control over $1 billion in Times Mirror stock. Conversely, the stock held directly by members of the Chandler family is worth less than $30 million. Members of the corporate rich who placed the bulk of their fortunes in generation-skipping trusts include August A. Busch of Anheuser-Busch; Charles H. Deere of Deere & Company; Mahlon N. Kline of SmithKline Beckman; James H. McGraw of McGraw-Hill; Amory Houghton, Jr., of Corning Glass Works; Lucius P. Ordway of Minnesota Mining and Manufacturing; and Harvey S. Firestone of Firestone Tire & Rubber. In each case, these trusts held corporate stock that was eventually worth in excess of $200 million.

Over the years, the labyrinth of overlapping trusts within a corporate rich family can become incredibly complex. As a result, it is difficult to determine the exact wealth of an individual family member. There is the example of Edgar B. Stern, Jr., one of the sixteen grandchildren of Julius Rosenwald, an early president of Sears, Roebuck and Co. As one of the two members of the Rosenwald family on the board of directors of Sears in 1968, Edgar Stern disclosed that he controlled over $50 million in company stock. However, he and his wife owned less than $5 million of this stock outright. An additional $2 million of Sears stock was held through a partnership with their four children. The rest of the stock was held in a series of family trusts. To begin with, Edgar Stern was the trustee and an income beneficiary of two trusts created by his parents that held over $7 million in Sears stock. He was also a co-trustee of three other trusts, in which his children were one-third income beneficiaries, which held another $20 million in Sears stock. Finally, he was a co-trustee of yet two more trusts that held $16 million in Sears stock for still other members of the Rosenwald family. Indeed, the bulk of the Rosenwald fortune, which is now worth well over $400 million, is held by a complex maze of family trusts. Until the tax laws were changed, a few corporate rich families created multiple trusts for each family member as a means of reducing their income taxes. For example, the ten children of Frank D. Stranahan and Robert A. Stranahan, Jr., the two brothers who founded Champion Spark Plug, were the beneficiaries of over thirty trusts as early as 1937.

As a means of avoiding estate taxes, generation-skipping trusts eventually became too successful. They attracted the attention of politicians for a variety of reasons. To begin with, trusts of this type were denounced because they enabled corporate rich families to shelter most of their fortunes from estate taxes. Family trusts were also condemned because they served to concentrate the wealth of the family in a few hands and to immobilize their investment capital in stock of a single company. As a result of these objections, the Tax Reform Act of 1976 removed most of the tax advantages of generation-skipping trusts by creating a special generation-skipping transfer tax. In effect, a tax equivalent to the uniform transfer tax is now imposed on the principal of a trust upon the death of its income beneficiary. Thus, the law treats a trust fund as part of the estate of its income beneficiary. This one change in the tax law will force most corporate rich families to modify some of their tax-avoidance strategies. In any event, the generation-skipping transfer tax poses only a remote threat to most of the fortunes held by the corporate rich. The Tax Reform Act of 1976 contained a grandfather provision that exempted all existing trusts, as well as any created by will before 1982, from the generation-skipping transfer tax. The enormous generation-skipping trusts created earlier by the Rockefellers, Gettys, Mellons, Hunts, and other corporate rich families are not subject to the new generation-skipping transfer tax.

FRIENDLY HOLDING COMPANIES

Of all the techniques devised to avoid gift and estate taxes, none has proved more durable than the *family holding company.* In general, this term refers to any corporation that is owned almost entirely by the members of a corporate rich family and whose assets consist primarily of stock in other corporations. Of course, not all family-owned companies are holding companies. Some of the companies owned entirely by wealthy families are operating companies in the sense that they manufacture products for sale or provide services to customers. Holding companies, however, exist for the sole purpose of holding investments. Many of the oldest corporate rich families have maintained holding companies for decades. For example, much of the fortune held by the descendants of Henry Phipps, one of the major stockholders in Carnegie Steel before it was acquired by United States Steel, is still held through a family holding company, Bessemer Securities Company. Similarly, Miami Corporation has served as a holding company for the descendants of William Deering, one of the founders of International Harvester, for over half a century. Some of the newer corporate rich families have also entrusted the bulk of their fortunes to family holding companies. The most recent example of this pattern is the Walton family, which owns stock in Wal-Mart Stores with a market value of approximately $2.8 billion. Sam M. Walton, the founder of the company, owned only 3 percent of the stock in Wal-Mart outright. However, he and his family held another 38 percent of Wal-Mart stock through Walton Enterprises, a family holding company.

One of the advantages of holding companies is that they enable corporate rich families to control very large corporations by concentrating the dispersed stockholdings of individual family members into a single entity. Until recently, the largest and best-known holding company in American business history was Christiana Securities. This corporation was formed in 1915 by Pierre S. du Pont II and his associates as a vehicle for purchasing a large block of stock in E.I. du Pont de Nemours and Company. Although there were 11 stockholders in the original Christiana Securities Company, 4 members of the du Pont family owned roughly 75 percent of its stock. By virtue of the fact that it eventually held 28 percent of Du Pont stock, this holding company enabled Pierre du Pont and his relatives to exercise effective control of the giant chemical corporation for almost six decades. Over the years, many of the original stockholders sold some of their Christiana stock, and, as a result, the holding company was eventually converted into a public investment company with over 8,000 stockholders. Nevertheless, 75 percent of its stock remained in the hands of some 200 members of the du Pont family. Christiana Securities was finally merged into Du Pont in 1974 through an exchange of stock. According to the SEC, which approved the merger, "those who control Christiana think that Christiana has outlived its usefulness." Specifically, the du Ponts decided to liquidate their family holding company because they were no longer willing to abide the double taxation that occurred as a result of the fact that Christiana Securities had to pay taxes on the dividends it received from Du Pont.

In addition to their functions as control mechanisms, family holding companies also provide corporate rich families with substantial tax advantages. The major advantage stems from the valuation discount associated with closely held corporations. As the result of numerous court rulings, the Internal Revenue Service applies a discount to the stock of a closely held corporation in its estate tax valuations. In general, the *valuation discount* for stock in a closely held corporation ranges between 30 and 70 percent of its underlying net asset value. For example, a 10 percent share of the stock in a family holding company that, in turn, owns $100 million in marketable securities will not be valued at $10 million by the Internal Revenue Service. Depending on the circumstances, this block of stock will instead be valued at between $3 million and $7 million for estate tax purposes. This practice of discounting the underlying net asset value of stock in a closely held corporation is based on several considerations. To begin with, there is the issue of marketability. Because the stock of a closely held corporation is not normally traded on any exchange, prospective buyers may not be willing to pay its full net asset value. Indeed, some family holding companies place restrictions on the disposition of their stock. Moreover, buyers may discount the value of such stock whenever a majority of it is held by the members of a single wealthy family. The problem is compounded even more if this stock does not have full voting power. Of course, nonvoting stock is discounted more than voting stock.

Corporate rich families have long recognized the advantages, for gift and estate tax purposes, of family holding companies. Moreover, they have often manipulated the capital structures of their holding companies in order to exploit these tax advantages. For example, a corporate rich family may issue more than one class of stock in order to complicate the valuation process. The complexity of this problem is demonstrated by the estate valuation applied to the holding company controlled by the Blaustein family. Alvin Thalheimer was the husband of the late Fanny Blaustein Thalheimer, one of the three children of Louis Blaustein, the founder of a major oil retailing company. When Alvin Thalheimer died in 1965, the primary asset in his estate was a relatively small block of stock of American Trading and Petroleum Company, the Blaustein family holding company. The major asset of American Trading and Petroleum, in turn, was a large block of stock in Amoco, then worth almost $98 million. An additional $34 million in Amoco stock was held directly by various members of the Blaustein family. They had received this stock as the result of the merger of their oil retailing company into Amoco in 1954. American Trading and Petroleum also owned nearly 49 percent of Crown Central Petroleum Company, a relatively small gasoline-refining and marketing company. This stock was worth slightly less than $11 million at the time. In addition, the family holding company owned real estate, oil and gas properties, oil tankers, manufacturing companies, and other assets worth at least another $36 million. Altogether, the company owned assets worth in excess of $145 million in 1965. Indeed, the bulk of the Blaustein fortune was held by this holding company.

Although the assets of American Trading and Petroleum were easily identified, the capital structure of this holding company was so complex that it was difficult to determine the exact value of the shares of its stock. To begin with, the valuation process was confounded by the fact that American Trading and Petroleum had two different classes of common stock. As of 1965, it had 185,310 shares of Class A common stock and 541,630 shares of Class B common stock. The two classes of common stock received the same dividends, but the Class A common stock had sole voting power. To complicate matters even more, the company also had two classes of preferred stock. As of 1965, it had 116,496 shares of 5 percent Cumulative Class B First Preferred stock and 391,092 shares of 6 percent Cumulative Second Preferred stock. Both classes of preferred stock had a par value of $10 a share, but they paid different dividends. Finally, the valuation problem was compounded by the fact that each member of the Blaustein family owned a different proportion of each class of stock. Alvin Thalheimer, for example, owned 8.3 percent of the Class A common stock but only 5.3 percent of the Class B common stock. He also owned very small amounts of both classes of preferred stock. Because all of the stock in American Trading and Petroleum Company was owned by members of the Blaustein family or foundations controlled by them, it qualified for a valuation discount. Although the court determined that the common stock in this company held by Alvin

Thalheimer had a net asset value of $7.4 million in 1965, the court ruled that it had a fair market value for estate tax purposes of only $4.7 million. In short, this holding company reduced the taxes on his estate by at least 37 percent.

The use of family holding companies to reduce gift and estate taxes can sometimes reach absurd proportions. A case in point is the pyramid of holding companies in which Paulina du Pont Dean was a principal stockholder. As one of the thirty-four nieces and nephews of Pierre S. du Pont II, she was an heir to part of the du Pont fortune. In 1924, she was made the sole stockholder of a family holding company, Nemours Corporation, which was to be the repository for her share of the du Pont fortune. The primary asset of this holding company was stock in another du Pont family holding company, Delaware Realty and Investment Company. This holding company had been formed that same year by Pierre S. du Pont as a vehicle for transferring the bulk of his fortune to his brothers and sisters and their children. Although Delaware Realty and Investment held a large block of stock in E.I. du Pont de Nemours and Company outright, its major asset was stock in yet another du Pont family holding company, Christiana Securities. This holding company, which Pierre du Pont and his associates had created nine years earlier, held an even larger block of Du Pont stock. Whenever Du Pont paid a dividend, it passed first through Christiana Securities, then Delaware Realty and Investment, and finally Nemours Corporation before it reached Paulina Dean. In 1954, when Paulina Dean and her husband began placing shares of Nemours stock in trusts for their children, they were allowed a series of valuation discounts on the stock. Although Nemours Corporation had an underlying net asset value of $36 million in Du Pont stock, it was valued for gift tax purposes at only $23 million.

Family holding companies have other tax advantages besides those associated with valuation discounts. Specifically, family companies of any type are amenable to a tax-avoidance strategy known as *estate freezing*. In particular, closely held corporations are excellent vehicles for preferred stock recapitalization. The object of this maneuver is to freeze the value of the stock in a company held by one generation of family members while permitting the value of the stock held by members of the succeeding generations to appreciate over time. For example, a wealthy individual might turn over $10 million in investments to a family holding company in exchange for shares of preferred stock in that company with a par value of $10 million. At the same time, that person could distribute all of the common stock in this holding company to his or her children. At that point in time, this common stock might be almost worthless, for gift tax purposes, because most of the income received by the holding company on its investments must be devoted to paying the dividends on its preferred stock. However, as the investments held by the holding company appreciate in value, the common stock held by the children also appreciates in value. Moreover, because the dividends paid on preferred stock are fixed, any increase in the investment income of the holding company can be used to pay dividends on the common stock. In other words, the value of the preferred stock, held by the older generation, is frozen. The common stock in the holding company, held by the younger generation, appreciates over time with increases in the value of its investments and increases in its dividends. Finally, as members of the older generation pass away, the holding company can redeem their shares of preferred stock at their original par value.

The Phipps family was one of the first to employ the tactic of estate freezing on a large scale. Bessemer Securities was created in 1911 by Henry Phipps as a family holding company for his five children. He contributed $5 million at the outset to fund its investment portfolio, and his children later contributed smaller amounts. The capital structure of Bessemer Securities was designed in a way that enabled the Phipps children to freeze their estates. In 1938, the company had two classes of stock: 100,000 shares of preferred stock and 5,000 shares of common stock. Both classes of stock were initially distributed evenly among the five children of Henry Phipps. The adult children kept their 20,000 shares of preferred stock, which guaranteed them generous dividend incomes. However, they each distributed their 1,000 shares of common stock among their own children. Specifically, 4,500 shares of the 5,000 shares of common stock in Bessemer Securities were held in trust for the seventeen grandchildren of Henry

Phipps by 1938. All of these trusts were administered by Bessemer Trust Company, which, in turn, was controlled by the Phipps family. The entire 5,000 shares of Bessemer Securities common stock were initially worth only $500,000. Of course, the value of the corporate stock and real estate owned by Bessemer Securities has increased greatly over the years. Consequently, the value of its common stock has increased as well. The common stock in Bessemer Securities was worth approximately $40 million by 1932 and roughly $260 million by 1954. By 1982, Bessemer Securities had a net asset value of at least $550 million.

Family holding companies provide the corporate rich with several other tax advantages. One of these is the deferred payment of estate taxes. If at least 35 percent of the value of an estate is composed of stock in a closely held corporation, the taxes on that estate can be paid on the installment plan over a period of fifteen years. During the first five years, the estate has to pay only interest on these taxes. Over the next ten years, the estate must pay at least 10 percent of the total estate tax liability each year as well as interest on the unpaid balance. This deferred payment option enables family members to pay relatively large estate tax assessments without having to sell any of the assets of the family holding company. In addition, family holding companies can, under certain conditions, reduce the income taxes of the members of a corporate rich family. Because the corporate income tax is not progressive, family holding companies often have lower income-tax rates than their individual stockholders. For this reason, it may be to the advantage of a corporate rich family to have the family holding company retain at least part of its earnings for reinvestment. In this way, the family holding company can become a vehicle for accumulating additional capital. There are special taxes on the accumulated earnings of holding companies, but these taxes can be avoided through diversification. In particular, a holding company can use earnings derived from its investment portfolio to participate in real estate developments or acquire operating companies. For example, the Blaustein family holding company, American Trading and Petroleum, has purchased real estate developments in several cities as well as two small manufacturing companies.

The only major disadvantage of family holding companies is the problem of multiple taxation. Specifically, a holding company must pay corporate income taxes on its investment income. In the case of the Blaustein family, American Trading and Petroleum Company must pay taxes on the dividends it receives on its Amoco stock. Of course, the individual members of the Blaustein family must then pay taxes on their dividends from American Trading and Petroleum as well. Although multiple taxation does reduce the income available to family members, the situation is not all that onerous. To begin with, corporations have generally paid lower taxes than most wealthy individuals. Moreover, many of them invest in real estate in order to reduce their income taxes through the use of the depreciation allowance. In any event, the family holding company can be liquidated or merged into another company in exchange for cash or stock after it has served its purpose in terms of tax avoidance. In order to avoid capital-gains taxes, family members usually prefer to merge their holding company into another company in exchange for stock. For example, the du Ponts eventually merged Delaware Realty and Investment into Christiana Securities for Christiana stock and then merged Christiana Securities into E.I. du Pont de Nemours and Company for Du Pont stock. Similarly, Midland Investment Company, a holding company for the descendants of Joseph M. Hixon that held 12 percent of the stock of AMP Incorporated, was merged into AMP in 1981 for common stock worth roughly $300 million.

FAMILY FINANCES

A number of tax-avoidance strategies involve simple transactions between family members. One of the most important of these family transactions is the *marital deduction*. In general, this provision permits an individual to bequeath at least half of his or her estate to a surviving spouse free of any estate taxes. For many years the marital deduction was limited to one-half of an estate. However, this limitation on the size of the marital deduction was eliminated by the Economic Recovery Tax Act of 1981. This deduction was incorporated into the federal tax code because many states had community property laws that maintained that any property accumulated by a husband and wife in the course of their marriage belonged to them equally, even though the property might be held in just one of their names. A great many of the corporate rich have resorted to the marital deduction in order to reduce their estate taxes. For example, when Richard K. Mellon died in 1970, he left half of his $226 million estate to his wife and most of the rest to his Richard K. Mellon Foundation. As a result, his estate paid only nominal taxes. Many of the wealthiest men in America in recent years have used the marital deduction to leave at least half of their estates to their wives. These include H. L. Hunt of Hunt Oil Company, J. Seward Johnson of Johnson & Johnson, and John H. Whitney of Whitney Communications. In a few instances, these widows inherited enough stock in the family corporations to become powerful members of their boards of directors. For example, Joan B. Kroc, the widow of McDonald's Corporation founder Ray Kroc, became a director of that corporation after the death of her husband in 1984. Similarly, Jane R. Engelhard served as a director of Engelhard Minerals and Chemicals, the predecessor of both Phibro-Salomon Corporation and Engelhard Corporation, after the death of her husband, Charles A. Engelhard, in 1971.

There are many other types of family transactions that enable corporate rich families to avoid estate taxes. One tactic for transferring wealth between generations of family members involves private annuities. In general, an *annuity* is an arrangement in which an individual receives a guaranteed income, either for a specified period of time or for life, in return for paying a single premium. Most annuities are sold by life insurance companies. The amount of the premium is based on the life expectancy of the individual, the amount of the annuity, and the expected rate of return on the premium once it has been invested. In short, an annuity is a gamble. On the one hand, if an individual purchases an annuity but dies at a relatively early age, the insurance company makes money because it received more from the premium than it paid out in income. If that same individual lives to an advanced age, on the other hand, the insurance company loses money. In the case of a private annuity, no insurance company is involved; one family member agrees to pay an annuity to another family member in exchange for a suitable premium. For example, wealthy parents might purchase an annuity from their children by simply transferring certain assets to them as a premium in return for a guaranteed income for life. In order to avoid being considered a direct gift for tax purposes, the premium must be appropriate to the life expectancies of the parents, the amount of the annuity, and the normal rate of return on investments. This tactic has rather morbid implications because a private annuity is most effective, at least in terms of tax avoidance, if the parents die soon after transferring the property to their children.

One of the first and most famous examples of a private annuity involved Pierre S. du Pont II, the founder of much of the du Pont fortune. When Congress raised the gift and estate tax rates in 1924, Pierre du Pont became concerned about the threat that these taxes posed to his estate. Although he was childless, he was determined to pass on the bulk of his fortune to his siblings and their children. At one point, he carried $6 million in life insurance in order to take care of the taxes on his estate. But, as he grew older and his estate grew larger, these insurance premiums became prohibitively expensive. In order to reduce his estate without reducing his income, Pierre du Pont decided to transfer the bulk of his assets to a family holding company to be owned equally by each of his brothers and sisters or their children. In return, this holding company would pay him and his wife a substantial lifetime annuity. That same year, at the age of fifty-four, he turned over to this holding company, Delaware Realty and Investment, stock in Du Pont and Christiana Securities worth roughly $13 million in exchange for an annuity of $900,000 a year. In this particular case, the amount of the annuity was based on the amount of dividends paid on the stock transferred to the holding company rather than any exact actuarial computations. Although Pierre du Pont lived to be eighty-four years old and eventually received $27 million in annuity payments, his brothers and sisters and their children profited

181

even more from this arrangement. By the time Pierre du Pont died in 1954, the Du Pont and Christiana stock held by Delaware Realty and Investment was worth $858 million. Moreover, the holding company had received over $250 million in dividends from this stock during that period.

For many years, one of the most popular means of transferring wealth from one generation of family members to the next involved the use of *no-interest* loans. Using this strategy, parents would lend their children money at no interest so they could purchase an interest in the family corporation. One of the most famous cases involved the family of Henry Crown. The Crown family fortune, which is now worth nearly $1 billion, is held largely by a labyrinth of trusts and family partnerships. In 1967, one of these family partnerships, Areljay Company, owned by the sons of Henry Crown, lent a total of $18 million to twenty-four family trusts, many of them for the benefit of their respective children. In turn, these loans enabled those trusts to purchase an interest in another family partnership, Henry Crown and Company. In effect, the sons were helping their children buy property from their father. Moreover, the trusts were not required to pay any interest on these loans, even though the average interest rate was at least 5 percent at the time. In other words, one family partnership was deliberately forgoing roughly $1 million in interest each year in order to enable a series of family trusts to purchase an interest in another family partnership. The Crown Fund had a substantial stock portfolio, and the trusts were able to repay the loans from the income they received from stock dividends and capital gains. While the initial loan was being repaid, the value of the interest in the family partnership purchased by the trusts increased substantially. For example, one of the major assets of Henry Crown and Company in 1967 was General Dynamics stock worth no more than $13 million. Less than twenty years later, this same stock was worth over $69 million.

The Supreme Court recently ruled that loans at interest rates below the market interest rate are taxable as gifts. In order to avoid having their loans taxed as gifts, parents must charge their children a fair market interest on those loans. For example, if a wealthy parent makes an interest-free loan of $10 million to a child when the going interest rate is 10 percent, then that parent must pay a gift tax on the imputed gift of $1 million in interest. In some cases, the parent must take precautions to ensure that the loan principal is not considered as a gift by the Internal Revenue Service. Nelson B. Hunt, for one, has received an object lesson in the importance of distinguishing between loans and gifts. In 1979, Nelson Hunt and two of his brothers, Herbert and Lamar Hunt, began speculating in the silver market. They held silver and silver futures, contracts to deliver silver at a set price in the future, that were worth over $7 billion by early 1980. In order to share the anticipated profits with his family, Nelson B. Hunt lent some of his children large sums of money to speculate in the silver futures market. However, when the price of silver fell later that year, the Hunts were forced to borrow heavily to meet margin calls from their brokers. At one point, Nelson Hunt promised these brokers that he would personally guarantee the losses incurred by his children on their silver futures contracts. Before it was over, Nelson Hunt had lent his children and their spouses over $147 million. In his income-tax return for 1980, he declared these bad loans as capital losses that offset other capital gains. The Internal Revenue Service later filed suit against Nelson Hunt, demanding the payment of an additional $56 million in taxes, on the grounds that these loans were actually gifts.

Despite these problems and restrictions, parental loans to finance stock purchases can still provide family members with opportunities to profit from special situations. One example of such an opportunity involves the acquisition of Clark Oil Company, a relatively small oil refining and marketing company. In early 1980, Emory T. Clark, the seventy-six-year-old founder of the company, was approached by another firm interested in acquiring Clark Oil. At the time, Emory Clark owned 23 percent of the stock in the company, and his children and grandchildren owned directly or indirectly another 19 percent. Altogether, their combined stockholdings had a market value of approximately $116 million. He rejected the acquisition offer and, five months later, sold almost all of his stock to twenty-four trusts he had established for his children and grandchildren. These trusts bought his 23 percent stake in Clark Oil for approximately $64 million. Because

Emory Clark lent the trusts most of the money required to purchase this stock, it was pledged to him as collateral. Almost a year later, the Clark family let it be known that their company was indeed for sale. Within a month, it was announced that the Clarks would sell their 42 percent stake in Clark Oil to another company for approximately $203 million in cash and notes. Consequently, the family trusts were able to repay the $64 million they owed Emory Clark and keep the remaining $57 million in profits. As a result of these transactions, most of the profits received from the sale of the company went to the family trusts. Because this sale occurred one year after the trusts acquired the additional stock, the profits received the favorable tax treatment accorded long-term capital gains.

7

Practical
Philanthropy

There are literally thousands of private foundations in America. Unlike community foundations, which solicit contributions from the public, or company foundations, which derive all of their contributions from particular corporations, private foundations are independent entities created by wealthy individuals. Of course, the vast majority of all foundations are relatively small. Fewer than three hundred foundations had assets in excess of $25 million by 1982. Indeed, almost half of all foundation assets are held by the sixty largest foundations. Most philanthropic foundations were created and endowed by members of corporate rich families. In fact, a majority of them are still controlled, at least to some extent, by members of these same families. Each year these foundations donate hundreds of millions of dollars to nonprofit organizations and charitable causes of every description. The specific activities that they fund are as diverse as the individuals who created them. For example, some foundations serve to ameliorate the effects of social inequality by donating funds to local charities that provide various social services to the poor. Other foundations serve to maintain the present distribution of income and wealth by donating funds to private educational institutions that cater primarily to children from affluent families. As a matter of fact, a foundation can legally donate funds to virtually any tax-exempt organization. Aside from a few restrictions imposed by the Internal Revenue Service, foundations are not responsible to any public regulatory agency. Their initial goals are established by their donors, and their subsequent operations are determined solely by their boards of trustees.

Philanthropic foundations created by the corporate rich provide a partial justification for the concentration of wealth generated by the free-enterprise system. In this view, the great fortunes amassed by wealthy capitalist families serve important functions in American society. Specifically, the charitable foundations endowed by these families are essential to the maintenance of a nonprofit private sector that is not directly responsible to either big government or big business. These private foundations often fund nonprofit organizations that have been ignored by both government agencies and business corporations. As a result, foundations are essential to the continuation of many innovative social programs and cultural activities. But, if foundations are the creations of the capitalist economic system, they are also the creation of the taxes imposed by the democratic political system in the United States. Most of the large philanthropic foundations were created in order to protect at least part of the massive fortunes accumulated by the corporate rich from gift and estate taxes. Consequently, they enable wealthy capitalist families to avoid these taxes and perpetuate their control over corporations in which they are major stockholders. Philanthropic foundations serve other functions for the corporate rich as well. The members of wealthy capitalist families derive much goodwill from the public at large as a result of the charitable activities of their foundations. Last but not least, foundations often contribute to nonprofit organizations that advocate policies consistent with the economic and political interests of these families.

THE BIG DONORS

The first wealthy American to espouse and practice philanthropy on a grand scale was Andrew Carnegie. For the greater part of his life, Carnegie was the epitome of the avaricious capitalist concerned solely with the pursuit of profit. As the founder of Carnegie Steel, he was equally ruthless with both his workers and his competitors. Once he had accumulated his fortune, however, Carnegie decided that it was incumbent upon him to give it away. In 1901, he sold his company to the newly created United States Steel Corporation and received, as his share, $225 million in bonds. His devotion to philanthropy almost matched his zeal for business. By 1910, he had given away over $100 million to a variety of educational and philanthropic causes, including $43 million for the construction of hundreds of public libraries across the country. The following year, he used most of the rest of his fortune, $125 million to be exact, to create the Carnegie Corporation, the largest foundation in the United States at the time. Although Carnegie provided his wife and daughter with ample fortunes of their own, the vast bulk of his wealth went to charity during his own lifetime. Moreover, his motives appear to have been genuinely philanthropic inasmuch as there were no federal gift or estate taxes at the time. He explained his philosophy in a book titled *The Gospel of Wealth.* In this treatise, Carnegie denounced the inheritance of great wealth and declared that the rich had a moral obligation to provide for the poor. Although very few of the corporate rich subscribed wholeheartedly to his views concerning the moral obligations of great wealth, they were unable to ignore the example of his philanthropic activities.

Philanthropists may be motivated in part by a genuine concern for others, but they often have ulterior motives as well. To begin with, the creation of a foundation may be motivated by a desire to refurbish a tarnished family name. Many wealthy entrepreneurs, condemned by the general public for their predatory business practices, have sought to rehabilitate their reputations through large and public contributions to charitable organizations. This consideration may explain why John D. Rockefeller, once labeled by a prominent reform politician as "the greatest criminal of the age," became one of the most prodigious philanthropists in American history. Indeed, critics were especially skeptical about his motives for creating the Rockefeller Foundation in 1910. They felt that it was not purely coincidental that his initial gift of $50 million in Standard Oil stock to the new foundation was announced only a few days before company attorneys filed their briefs with the Supreme Court in the government suit to dissolve the Standard Oil trust. Indeed, Rockefeller seems to have taken more satisfaction from the favorable publicity generated by his philanthropies than the actual operations of the Rockefeller Foundation and his other charities. Similarly, the Annenberg family may have created the M. L. Annenberg Foundation and other charitable trusts at least in part to restore a measure of respectability to their family name. Moses L. Annenberg, the founder of Triangle Publications, had been convicted of income-tax evasion and sentenced to three years in prison in 1940.

Alternatively, a foundation may be created for the purpose of ensuring family control over a company. For example, the Ford family was forced to create the Ford Foundation primarily because Henry Ford had failed to take the necessary precautions to shield his fortune from estate taxes. If Henry and Edsel Ford had not given most of their stock to the foundation, their estates would have been forced to sell a majority of this stock to the public in order to pay estate taxes that might have reached $320 million. In such a case, the Ford family would have certainly lost its control over the company. The Fords later agreed to a financial reorganization in which they relinquished absolute control over Ford Motor Company in exchange for a larger equity position in the company. It appears that William R. Hearst created his William Randolph Hearst Foundation for much the same reason. In his will, he donated almost all of his common stock in the Hearst Corporation to the foundation, but he bequeathed all of his preferred stock, which held control of the corporation, to a trust for the benefit of his family.

Another primary motive for the establishment of philanthropic foundations is tax avoidance. Members of the corporate rich are encouraged to give at least part of their wealth to charity by the existence of progressive gift and estate taxes. Beginning with the passage of the first federal estate tax in 1916, it became increasingly difficult to transfer large fortunes in their entirety from one generation of family members to the next. As a result, charitable donations became the tax-avoidance strategy of last resort. Indeed, after the imposition of highly progressive gift and estate taxes in 1934, testamentary bequests to charity became the main alternative to the payment of almost confiscatory estate taxes on the assets held by the corporate rich at death. An estate does not pay any taxes on those assets bequeathed to charity. Consequently, many of the largest donations to charitable foundations have been testamentary bequests created by the wills of the corporate rich. In most cases, members of wealthy capitalist families have bequeathed to charity only those portions of their fortunes that they were unable or unwilling to transfer to their heirs through lifetime gifts. Those large estates that did not use the charitable deduction have been virtually consumed by taxes. For example, much of the estate of Howard R. Hughes, Jr., the reclusive billionaire, will eventually go to estate taxes. Although he had transferred all of his stock in Hughes Aircraft Company to the Howard Hughes Medical Institute during his lifetime, he left no valid will to dispose of his other assets, including Summa Corporation. As a result, his estate, which had an assessed value of $371 million in 1976, has paid $300 million in state and federal taxes.

In a few cases, large foundations have been created by wealthy individuals who simply had no heirs to inherit their fortunes. One example of this pattern is the A. P. Sloan Foundation. The creator of this foundation, Alfred P. Sloan, Jr., was one of the first presidents of General Motors Corporation. Indeed, he held that position for almost thirty-five years. In that capacity, Sloan became the object of public condemnation in 1937 as a result of his militant opposition to a strike by automobile workers. That same year, a congressional committee disclosed that Sloan and his wife had avoided nearly $2 million in income taxes through the use of a personal holding company. Amid this controversy, he gave $10 million to create the A. P. Sloan Foundation. Because Sloan and his wife never had any children, all of their wealth eventually went to charity. By the time he died in 1966, their foundation was worth $275 million. Similarly, John A. Hartford, one of the sons of the founder of the Great Atlantic & Pacific Tea Company, was without any heirs when he died in 1951. For that reason, he willed almost his entire fortune to the John A. Hartford Foundation. Six years later, his brother and business partner, George L. Hartford, bequeathed his entire estate to the foundation as well. Like his brother, George Hartford was a widower without any surviving children. As a result of these two bequests, the Hartford Foundation was worth $413 million by 1958. Several other wealthy individuals endowed major foundations because they had no children. These include, most notably, Archibald G. Bush, Herman Brown, Melvin J. Murdock, and Mabel Pew Myrin. In each case, a private foundation became the recipient of virtually the entire estate of its founder.

Large contributions to charity are much less common among those wealthy individuals with large families. One of the few philanthropists to give most of his fortune to charity rather than his family was Will K. Kellogg, one of the inventors of corn flakes cereal and the founder of Kellogg Company. Moreover, Kellogg was unusual in that he gave away most of his fortune while he was still alive. By 1930, his 60 percent stake in Kellogg Company was worth approximately $50 million. That same year, Kellogg announced that he was creating the W. K. Kellogg Foundation, a charity intended primarily to promote child welfare. Five years later, he turned over $35 million in Kellogg Company stock to the foundation. Although he served as a trustee, he resisted the temptation to run the foundation on a daily basis. By the time he died in 1951, Kellogg had transferred most of his wealth, consisting of Kellogg stock then worth almost $120 million, to a trust for the W. K. Kellogg Foundation. Despite the fact that he had a large family, three children and nine grandchildren, he gave them only a relatively small amount of Kellogg Company stock, most of it held by trusts. His decision to give almost all of his fortune to charity instead of his family may be due to the fact that Kellogg was unable to establish a tradition of family participation in the management of the company. One son did serve as an officer and director of Kellogg Company for several years, but he resigned after a series of disputes with his father. Later, a grandson also served as an officer and director of the company, but he too resigned after being demoted by his grandfather.

Only a few members of the corporate rich have given most of their wealth to charity during their own lifetimes. In general, lifetime philanthropists have been entrepreneurs who devoted almost as much attention to the activities of their philanthropies as they did to the operations of their corporations. One of these lifetime philanthropists was Sebastian S. Kresge, the founder of the predecessor of the present K mart Corporation. Kresge was a man of contradictory impulses. His first wife divorced him on grounds of "frugality and humiliation." In fact, he was so miserly that he quit playing golf because he could not stand to lose the balls. Nevertheless, when he was fifty-seven years old, Kresge decided to give most of his fortune to charity. By the time he died in 1966, at the age of ninety-nine, he had managed to give the bulk of his wealth to his Kresge Foundation. In his will, he left his last $2 million to the foundation as well. Altogether, the endowment of the Kresge Foundation, consisting primarily of K mart stock, was worth $172 million that same year. By comparison, his family was then probably worth no more than $50 million. Another lifetime philanthropist was Charles S. Mott, one of the early participants in General Motors. In 1963, he gave almost $129 million in General Motors stock to his Charles S. Mott Foundation. By the time he died in 1973, the foundation had assets of $321 million. Conversely, his wife and six children were probably worth only about $180 million that same year. Other successful entrepreneurs who became lifetime philanthropists and gave over half of their fortunes to charitable foundations include James B. Duke, William H. Danforth, Charles A. Dana, and Frank E. Gannett. In each case, these donors gave substantial amounts to their children as well.

TAXES AND CHARITY

In most cases, the practice of philanthropy is inextricably tied to the exigencies of tax avoidance. This relationship is evident from the fact that the vast majority of large contributions to philanthropic foundations are the result of testamentary bequests rather than lifetime gifts. Members of the corporate rich often bequeath their residual estates to family foundations simply to shield part of their fortunes from estate taxes. Indeed, some of the largest foundations created in recent years have been endowed primarily by testamentary bequests. The most recent example of a large testamentary bequest is that of John D. MacArthur, the founder of Bankers Life and Casualty Company. Perhaps because he was estranged from his two children for many years, MacArthur transferred very little of his massive fortune to them in the form of lifetime gifts. As a result, when he died in 1978, he was the sole owner of Bankers Life and Casualty. Despite the fact that he had not demonstrated much of an interest in philanthropy during his lifetime, he willed almost his entire estate, worth in the neighborhood of $1 billion, to the John D. and Catherine T. MacArthur Foundation. Other major philanthropists have usually made ample provisions for their children through lifetime gifts before bequeathing their estates to charity. For example, Robert W. Johnson, Jr., one of the two sons of the founder of Johnson & Johnson Company, gave less than $100 million to his Robert Wood Johnson Foundation during his lifetime. However, when he died in 1968, he bequeathed virtually his entire estate, worth almost $1 billion, to the foundation. By that time, he had already transferred Johnson & Johnson stock worth at least another $400 million to his two children.

Many large foundations were created from the residual estates of wealthy individuals who had already managed to transfer most of their fortunes to their heirs through lifetime gifts. In other words, the wealth bequeathed to charity by these individuals typically represented only a small portion of the total wealth held by their families. For example, when William M. Keck, the founder of Superior Oil Company, died in 1964, he owned stock in the company worth $121 million. In his will, he gave half of this stock to his William M. Keck

Foundation. Public accounts of this bequest generally failed to mention that he had previously given his four children Superior Oil stock worth $131 million at the time. Similarly, the Henry J. Kaiser Family Foundation was endowed almost entirely by testamentary bequests from the residual estates of various family members. Henry J. Kaiser, the founder of Kaiser Industries, was not an active philanthropist during his lifetime. However, he and his wife eventually bequeathed the bulk of their estates to the family foundation. The foundation also received a major bequest from the estate of one of their sons, Henry J. Kaiser, Jr. As a result, the foundation was the recipient of Kaiser Industries stock worth $210 million by 1968. Their other son, Edgar F. Kaiser, and his wife and children owned only about $103 million in Kaiser stock at that point. Other wealthy individuals who endowed large foundations through testamentary bequests, after successfully transferring most of their fortunes to their heirs through lifetime gifts, include Charles F. Kettering, Otto F. Haas, Sid W. Richardson, Richard K. Mellon, and J. Howard Pew. In each case, philanthropy was not a lifetime pursuit but rather a final act of tax avoidance.

The effect of estate taxes on philanthropy is also evident among corporate rich families that have not established large foundations. Some of the wealthiest families in the country have given only a small portion of their fortunes to charitable foundations. This blatant indifference to philanthropy can be attributed to the simple fact that these families have not been confronted with large estate taxes. Indeed, they have been extremely successful in avoiding estate taxes. For example, H. L. Hunt, the Texas oilman who was once proclaimed the richest man in America, left an estate initially assessed at less than $56 million. Moreover, instead of bequeathing his estate to charity, he left almost all of it to his second wife. However, the estate of H. L. Hunt was only a small part of the Hunt family fortune. He had already transferred most of his enormous wealth to his six children by his first wife decades earlier. In fact, they were able to pledge assets worth over $3 billion as collateral for a loan in 1980. Several other families with fortunes worth at least $500 million apiece have also avoided donating any significant portion of their fortunes to charity. They include the descendants of Samuel I. Newhouse, James Cox, John T. Dorrance,

Clarence Barron, Alice King Kleberg, Elbridge A. Stuart, and Samuel C. Johnson. In each case, the vast bulk of the family fortune has been passed from one generation to the next without incurring any substantial estate taxes through the use of generation-skipping trusts.

A few wealthy entrepreneurs, however, have failed to protect their fortunes from estate taxes. Consequently, they have been forced to resort to special arrangements involving contributions to charitable organizations in order to pass on at least part of their wealth to their children and grandchildren. One of the most interesting of these arrangements is the *charitable remainder trust,* in which family members are able to receive lifetime incomes from a trust whose assets are pledged to charity. Although the laws and regulations governing the different forms of charitable remainder trusts are complex, the essential logic of these arrangements is simple. The creator of the trust sets aside certain assets for distribution to a charity at some point in the distant future. In the interim, however, family members are entitled to receive all of the income produced by those assets. No taxes are paid either when the trust is created or when it is dissolved, because the ostensible purpose of the trust is charitable. The only taxes paid in such an arrangement are those on the incomes received by the family members. Of course, there are legal restrictions on the duration and operation of such a trust. For example, only those individuals who are alive at the time the trust is created can be named as lifetime income beneficiaries. In effect, this provision limits the duration of the trust to a couple of generations. Because each income beneficiary has only a lifetime interest in the trust, the total income eventually paid to all the income beneficiaries is determined by their longevity and the income produced by the assets held in the trust.

One of the largest charitable remainder trusts in existence was created in 1943 by the will of Libbie S. Moody, the wife of William L. Moody, Jr., a wealthy Texas financier. Because Texas is a community property state, her estate included half of their community property, which consisted of a bank, two newspapers, a chain of hotels, and several large ranches as well as most of the stock in American National Insurance Company, a major life insurance company. The 32 percent of American National Insurance stock held by the Libbie Shearn Moody Trust is currently worth in the neighborhood of $300 million. Under the terms of her will, the income provided by this trust was to be shared successively by three generations of family members. To begin with, her husband was entitled to all of the income from the trust during his lifetime. At his death, the income from the trust was to be shared equally by their children. In turn, at the death of these children, their share of the income from the trust was to be shared equally by their respective children for life. Only when each of the seven grandchildren has died is his or her share of the trust income to be paid to the two charities named in her will. Consequently, the trust itself will not be dissolved and its principal will not be distributed to these charities until after the death of her last surviving grandchild. In her will, Libbie Moody stipulated that three-quarters of her trust was to go to the Moody Foundation, created by her husband, and the remaining one-quarter to the First Methodist Church of Galveston, her favorite church.

By having his wife bequeath her estate to a charitable remainder trust, William L. Moody, Jr., was able to ensure family control over an extensive financial empire for several decades. Perhaps because he wished to retain absolute control over his corporation, Moody neglected to put the bulk of his fortune into generation-skipping trusts for his children and grandchildren. Although he did transfer some of his wealth to his children through lifetime gifts, he was still the majority stockholder in American National Insurance Company when his wife became terminally ill in 1943. Any attempt to have his wife bequeath her share of their community property to their children in her will would have created enormous estate tax liabilities. The payment of such taxes, in turn, would have necessitated the sale of much of her stock in American National, which would have seriously jeopardized his control over the company. In the end, the only way for the Moody family to avoid estate taxes and retain control over its financial empire was to place most of the fortune in the hands of charitable institutions controlled by family members. When he died in 1954, William L. Moody, Jr., left virtually all of his estate to the Moody Foundation as well. Of course, all the trustees of the Moody

Foundation were members of the Moody family. The Moody National Bank of Galveston, which was owned almost entirely by the Moody Foundation and the Libbie Shearn Moody Trust, was the sole trustee of the Libbie Shearn Moody Trust. Consequently, the four members of the Moody family who served as trustees of the foundation were able to control the trust, the bank, and the insurance company.

The financial and charitable complex created by the Moody family is a testament to the intricacies of the tax laws. Although family members own less than 5 percent of the stock in American National Insurance outright, they are still able to vote over 68 percent of its stock. As the result of changes in the tax laws concerning philanthropic foundations, the Moody Foundation will someday be forced to sell most of this stock. Nevertheless, the charitable remainder trust did enable the family to avoid gift and estate taxes on a substantial portion of the family fortune. Over the past three decades, four family members, including one of the children and three of the grandchildren of William L. Moody, Jr., have received over $66 million in income from the Libbie Shearn Moody Trust. Because the youngest of these grandchildren is not yet fifty years old, the trust itself may not be dissolved for several decades to come. The other children and grandchildren of William L. Moody, Jr., were not content with their guaranteed incomes; they sued the Moody Foundation for a larger share of the estate of their father. In 1957, they agreed to forfeit their lifetime interest in the income of the Libbie Shearn Moody Trust in return for a total of $12 million in cash. Although a charitable remainder trust eventually deprives a corporate rich family of much of its fortune, it can provide family members with incomes large enough to enable them to establish their own fortunes. For example, two of the grandsons of the founder of American National Insurance, Robert L. Moody and Shearn Moody, Jr., are now major stockholders and chief executive officers of their own insurance companies.

In terms of tax avoidance, the charitable remainder trust is usually the option of last resort. Trusts of this type are not very popular among the corporate rich because most of the family fortune eventually goes to charity. Consequently, most charitable remainder trusts are created by testamentary bequests simply as a means of disposing of residual estates. In other words, wealthy individuals typically have turned over to them only those assets that they failed to transfer to their heirs by other means. For example, the Howard Heinz Foundation, with assets of $101 million in 1983, was created by such a charitable remainder trust. Howard Heinz was the eldest son of Henry J. Heinz, the founder of H.J. Heinz Company. When he died in 1941, he still held almost 20 percent of the company stock. In his will, he bequeathed all of this stock to a charitable remainder trust with his wife as the lifetime income beneficiary. Over the next eleven years, his widow received over $4 million in income from this trust. Howard Heinz did not name his only son, Henry J. Heinz II, as an income beneficiary, perhaps because he already had given him roughly 17 percent of the stock in H.J. Heinz Company. Similarly, when Alfred I. du Pont died in 1935, he bequeathed most of his estate, worth over $39 million at the time, to a charitable remainder trust. According to his will, his wife was to be the primary lifetime income beneficiary of this trust. At the death of the last income beneficiary of this trust, its principal was to go to his Nemours Foundation. By the time his wife died thirty-five years later, she had received over $100 million in income from the trust.

Another arrangement that enables wealthy parents to pass on at least part of their wealth to their descendants is the *charitable lead trust*. In this case, assets are placed in a trust in order to provide a fixed income for the benefit of some charitable organization for a specified period of time. At the end of that time period, these trust assets revert to the remaindermen, typically the grandchildren of the donor, free of any gift or estate taxes. In order to qualify for this special tax treatment, charitable lead trusts must remain in effect for at least two to four decades, depending on the proportion of the initial trust assets paid out each year in income. For that reason, they are typically used to transfer assets that can be expected to appreciate in value over time, such as corporate stock, to distant descendants of the donor. One of the largest charitable lead trusts was established by James S. Abercrombie, the founder of Cameron Iron Works. In 1968, he established a charitable lead trust for the benefit of Texas Childrens Hospital. The trust received all of the stock in a family holding company, which, in turn, owned over 49 percent of the stock in Cameron Iron Works. This trust will remain in effect for forty years. In the year 2008, it will distribute its assets to the grandchildren of James S. Abercrombie. The Cameron Iron Works stock held indirectly by this trust, which was initially worth only about $90 million, is now worth over $230 million. Several other members of corporate rich families, such as J. Seward Johnson, whose father founded Johnson & Johnson Company, and James L. Knight, whose father founded the predecessor of Knight Ridder Corporation, have established charitable lead trusts for their grandchildren.

CHARITABLE HOLDING COMPANIES

One of the main advantages of philanthropic foundations is that they enable wealthy capitalist families to avoid estate taxes without relinquishing control over their family corporations. For example, when William R. Hearst died in 1956, he left an estate assessed at $59 million, most of it in Hearst Corporation common stock. In his will, he left all of his remaining stock in the company to his William Randolph Hearst Foundation. If he had not given this stock to charity, his estate would have been forced to sell most of it in order to pay estate taxes that, on an estate of this size, might have reached $45 million. But, because Hearst bequeathed the bulk of this stock to a family foundation, the Hearst Corporation was able to remain a private company owned entirely by the Hearst family and its two foundations. In short, although a corporate rich family loses the ownership of any stock it donates to a charitable foundation, it does not necessarily lose control of this stock. As long as family members are able to control a foundation, they are able to control the stock in its investment portfolio. As trustees of the foundation, they can use this stock to elect family members as directors of the corporation. They can also refuse to sell this stock to other companies seeking to gain control of the family corporation. In this sense, then, a philanthropic foundation, controlled by members of the donor family, can serve in effect as a charitable holding company.

Indeed, individuals who donate part of their fortunes to family foundations during their lifetimes are able to claim a deduction on their taxes without relinquishing control over those assets. Sebastian S. Kresge, for example, donated most of his substantial fortune in K mart stock to his Kresge Foundation during his own lifetime. At the same time, however, he maintained personal control over the foundation and, through it, the K mart Corporation. While he was alive, Kresge not only influenced the philanthropic activities of the foundation, he also refused to permit it to sell any of its K mart stock. A more recent example of this pattern is Leon Hess, the founder of Amerada Hess Corporation and the sole donor of the Hess Foundation. The endowment of the foundation consists almost entirely of Amerada Hess stock currently worth $70 million. Hess serves as both company chairman and foundation president. Conversely, the Richard King Mellon Foundation provides an example of indirect donor control. Although its donor, Richard K. Mellon, declined to serve as a trustee, the foundation was completely controlled by his family. During his lifetime, its board of trustees consisted of his wife, two of their children, and four of his financial advisers. Before his death in 1970, over 80 percent of the $208 million in assets held by the foundation consisted of stock in two Mellon family companies, Gulf Oil and General Reinsurance Corporation. In a similar manner, four of the children of Joseph N. Pew endowed the Pew Memorial Trust with $50 million in Sun Company stock in 1948. Eight years later, they formed the Glenmede Trust Company and named it the sole trustee of the family foundation. Their control over both the Pew Memorial Trust and Sun Company was indirect but virtually absolute.

As a general rule, a family can continue to control a foundation for several decades after the death of the original donor. For example, the Rockefeller Brothers Fund was endowed initially in 1951 with $58 million in stock from John D. Rockefeller, Jr. Over three decades later, members of the Rockefeller family still represent a clear majority among its trustees. At last count, over half the major foundations in America were controlled to some extent by members of their donor families. These include such major entities as the Smith Richardson Foundation, the W. M. Keck Foundation, the Edna McConnell Clark Foundation, the McKnight Foundation, the Hess Foundation, the William Penn Foundation, and the Timken Foundation. A family does not necessarily have to represent a majority on the board of trustees of a foundation in order to control it; it can maintain control by appointing friends, business associates, financial advisers, and officers of the family corporation as trustees. In other cases, whenever family members and their associates are a minority on the board of trustees, a family member may exercise effective control by serving as the chairman or president of the foundation. For example, although there are only two family members among the eight trustees of the Sarah Scaife Foundation, Richard M. Scaife, the son of the donor, serves as the chairman of the foundation. Family members serve either as the chairmen or presidents of several foundations in which a majority of the trustees are not members of the donor family. These include such major foundations as the Henry J. Kaiser Family Foundation, the Charles S. Mott Foundation, the Richard King Mellon Foundation, and the Henry Luce Foundation.

There are a number of exceptions to the pattern of family control among major foundations. The most obvious exceptions involve foundations created by individuals without any families. For example, the Alfred P. Sloan Foundation, the Vincent Astor Foundation, the Sherman Fairchild Foundation, the Brown Foundation, and the Bush Foundation were all established by individuals who were childless. By and large, the boards of trustees of these foundations were composed, at least initially, of friends, business associates, and distant relatives of the donor. Problems sometimes arise whenever a foundation becomes dominated by trustees with business ties to a corporation in which the foundation is a major stockholder. Under these circumstances, corporate officers who serve as trustees may consider the foundation to be a mechanism for protecting corporate management. For example, when John A. Hartford died in 1951, his will stipulated that the president of the Great Atlantic & Pacific Tea Company was to be named president of his John A. Hartford Foundation. In the years that followed, several officers or retired officers of the company served as trustees of the foundation as well. Because the foundation eventually owned 34 percent of the stock in the grocery store chain, management officials were able to exercise almost absolute control over the company. Largely as a result of the fact that its management occupied an unassailable position of power within the company, it gradually entered a prolonged period of declining sales and profits. The foundation, which refused to diversify its investment portfolio, saw the market value of its A&P stock decline from a high of $404 million in 1958 to a low of $41 million in 1978.

The other notable exceptions to the pattern of family control over foundations involve very large foundations. In general, the largest philanthropic foundations in America are not controlled by members of their donor families, even though they may have token representatives among the trustees. In most of these cases, donor families have gradually relinquished their control over large foundations because they became the subject of considerable public scrutiny. For example, there are no longer any members of the Rockefeller family among the trustees of the Rockefeller Foundation. In point of fact, the family maintained only token representation on the board of trustees after 1936. Along these same lines, there are no family representatives among the trustees of the W. K. Kellogg Foundation, the Carnegie Corporation, or the Robert Wood Johnson Foundation. In other cases, a family has only one token representative on the board of trustees of a large foundation. For example, only one member of the MacArthur family serves as a trustee of the giant John D. and Catherine T. MacArthur Foundation. Similarly, only one family member serves among the trustees of the Lilly Endowment, the Andrew W. Mellon Foundation, the Duke Endowment, and the Kresge Foundation. Until recently, there was one member of the Ford family among the dozen or so trustees of the Ford Foundation. However, the last family representative on the board of trustees, Henry Ford II, resigned in 1978 in protest over the activities of the foundation. In his letter of resignation, he decried the fact that the foundation failed to appreciate the virtues of the capitalist system that was responsible for its very existence.

The extent to which a philanthropic foundation serves as a charitable holding company for the donor family is usually evident from the composition of its investment portfolio. Foundations that serve as holding companies in order to maintain family control over a particular corporation typically have most of their assets invested in the stock of that corporation. Of course, most foundations receive their initial endowment in the form of stock in a family corporation. But a prudent investment strategy dictates that a foundation should diversify its investment portfolio by selling most of this donated stock and using the proceeds to buy a variety of stocks and bonds. However, a majority of the large charitable foundations have not diversified their portfolios to any great extent. As a result, these foundations remain, even after many years of operation, principal stockholders in the corporations founded by the donor family. One example of this pattern is the Pew Memorial Trust. The Pew family has maintained strict control over this foundation ever since its creation in 1948. Although no family members are associated directly with it, the Glenmede Trust Company, which is controlled by members of the Pew family, serves as the sole trustee of the foundation. As late as 1980, $602 million of the $890 million in foundation assets was still invested in Sun Company stock. The stock held by the Pew Memorial Trust represented 20 percent of the outstanding stock in Sun Company. The stock held by the foundation, in combination with the Sun Company stock owned by members of the Pew family and other family foundations of which the Glenmede Trust Company is the sole trustee, ensures their almost absolute control over the company.

Many other family foundations have also resisted diversifying their investment portfolios. As a result, these foundations are often the largest single stockholders in family corporations. In 1962, the House Select Committee on Small Business issued the first of a series of investigative reports on tax-exempt foundations. This report listed over one hundred foundations that held more than 10 percent of at least one class of stock in any company. Major companies identified as being subject to at least some degree of foundation control included such major corporations as the Great Atlantic & Pacific Tea Company, Kaiser Industries, Eli Lilly and Company, Kellogg Company,

Duke Power, Ralston Purina, American National Insurance, and Sun Company. In response to these and other studies of foundation activities, Congress incorporated into the Tax Reform Act of 1969 a number of provisions designed to regulate foundations. Specifically, the rules promulgated by the Internal Revenue Service under this legislation limit the amount of stock that any foundation can hold in any business corporation. In general, the stockholdings of a foundation in combination with the stockholdings of the donor family cannot exceed 20 percent of the stock in a corporation. For example, if a family owns 10 percent of the stock in a corporation, a foundation endowed by members of that family may not own more than another 10 percent of that stock. Any foundation that violates these regulations must pay a special tax on its excess stockholdings in the family corporation. There are, of course, a number of exceptions to these regulations. In any event, the Internal Revenue Service gave most foundations at least two decades to achieve compliance with these limitations.

The regulations imposed by the Internal Revenue Service on the amount of stock that a foundation may own in any corporation have not prevented many foundations from continuing to serve as charitable holding companies. For example, the use of multiple family foundations has enabled the Pew family to maintain its control over Sun Company. As late as 1980, the two Pews on its board of directors were able to force the resignation of the chairman of the company after a dispute over corporate strategy. Although family members probably owned no more than 6 percent of the stock in Sun Company at the time, four ostensibly separate family foundations owned at least another 26 percent of the company stock. In any case, it is usually possible to exercise almost absolute control over a very large corporation with much less than 20 percent of its stock. For example, the Andrew W. Mellon Foundation and ten other smaller foundations endowed by members of the Mellon family owned only 6 percent of the stock in Gulf Oil in 1976. At the same time, various members of the Mellon family and trusts for their benefit probably held another 12 percent of the stock in the company. Although the family together with its foundations owned less than 18 percent of the stock in Gulf Oil by 1976, their combined stockholdings were sufficient to ensure effective family control over the company. For example, after the company issued a report that revealed that senior management officials had diverted corporate funds for illegal political contributions, the two representatives of the Mellon family on the board of directors demanded a change of management. Four senior officers, including the chairman, resigned under duress.

In general, family foundations serve as charitable holding companies only as long as the donor family maintains control over the family corporation. Over time, most corporate rich families eventually begin to relinquish their control over these corporations. Once that process has begun, the foundations controlled by these families may begin to diversify their investment portfolios. Even if the family does permit the foundation to dispose of the bulk of its stock in the family corporation, it may maintain control of the foundation for other reasons. To begin with, a corporate rich family may derive a great deal of power and status from the activities of its foundation. For example, the Rockefeller family no longer controls any of the former Standard Oil companies. Even the Rockefeller Brothers Fund, which was endowed initially with stock in these companies, has almost completely diversified its portfolio. As a result, the foundation no longer qualifies as a charitable holding company. Nevertheless, the Rockefeller Brothers Fund is still very much a family foundation. At last count, ten of its fifteen trustees were members of the Rockefeller family. Despite the fact that it is one of the largest foundations in the nation, the Rockefeller Brothers Fund devotes most of its funds to organizations based in New York City. The largely local focus of this foundation may be related to the fact that much of the Rockefeller fortune consists of New York City real estate owned by the family holding company, Rockefeller Group Inc. Also, those members of the Rockefeller family who still live in or near New York City undoubtedly derive considerable power and prestige from the activities of the Rockefeller Brothers Fund.

PET PROJECTS

Wealthy individuals who endow foundations have the prerogative of determining the philanthropic purposes of those foundations. Consequently, they can finance such diverse charitable causes as medical research, art museums, conservation programs, evangelical crusades, private colleges, social welfare services, or public policy research. In point of fact, there are virtually no legal restrictions on the power of philanthropists to determine which organizations may receive money from their foundations so long as the recipients qualify as nonprofit organizations. Lifetime philanthropists, of course, can direct the activities of their foundations while they are alive by serving as officers and trustees of their own foundations. Moreover, philanthropists can influence the activities of a foundation, even after they have passed away, by appointing family members, close friends, and business associates as officers and trustees of their foundations. For example, the Robert Wood Johnson Foundation is unique among very large foundations inasmuch as it devotes virtually all of its substantial income to a single field: medical education and health services development. It was given this particular philanthropic mission by Robert W. Johnson, Jr., one of the sons of the founder of Johnson & Johnson. He not only directed the foundation into this field during his lifetime by serving as one of its trustees but ensured the continuation of that focus after his death by appointing several physicians and officers of the company as trustees of the foundation as well. Johnson & Johnson, in which members of the Johnson family are still major stockholders, undoubtedly derives a great deal of goodwill within the medical community from the activities of this foundation.

Although most foundations award their grants to charitable organizations on the basis of fairly objective criteria, donor families frequently give preferential treatment to projects in which they have a special interest. For example, the descendants of John Pitcairn, one of the founders of PPG Industries, have used their family foundations to support the activities of a small religious sect, the General Church of New Jerusalem. John Pitcairn was one of the founders of this church in the United States, and three relatively small foundations endowed by his sons now devote almost all of their income to the Academy of the New Church in Bryn Athyn, Pennsylvania. In 1980, one of these foundations donated over $8 million in stock and art that it had received from the estate of Mildred G. Pitcairn to the Academy of the New Church. Other members of the corporate rich have used family foundations to support their favorite educational institutions. For example, Peddie School, a small and largely undistinguished preparatory school in Hightstown, New Jersey, has received several large grants from the Annenberg Fund. In 1979 alone, it received over $1 million from the foundation. It is hardly coincidental that Walter Annenberg, the president of the Annenberg Fund, attended Peddie School and serves as one of its trustees. Similarly, the F. M. Kirby Foundation has given several relatively large grants to small Lafayette College and two preparatory schools, Lawrenceville School and Morristown School. These schools are fortunate to count Allan P. Kirby, Jr., and Fred M. Kirby II among their graduates. They and their two sisters are the sole trustees of the F. M. Kirby Foundation, which is named after their grandfather, one of the original stockholders in F.W. Woolworth Company.

Foundations are obviously important to corporate rich families for reasons that go beyond their role as charitable holding companies. To begin with, family control of a foundation enables members of the family to extend their power and prestige beyond the economic sphere and into the realm of civic affairs. Those family members who serve as foundation trustees are able to choose which nonprofit organizations are to receive financial support from the foundation. Of course, foundations that are controlled by their donor families rarely give grants to charitable organizations that even remotely challenge the interests of these families. To the contrary, foundation grants generally go to those organizations that either serve the interests of these families in some way or at least enhance their standing within the local community. In this sense, one of the most obvious functions of a family foundation is to serve as a charitable public relations firm for the donor family and its business interests. The members of a wealthy capitalist family are the beneficiaries of the often considerable goodwill generated within a community by foundation grants to local charities. Indeed, even a small foundation can have a tremendous impact at the local level. For example, the Timken Foundation has restricted most of its grants to the Canton, Ohio, area. By 1981, it had donated over $5 million to the building fund of the Timken Mercy Medical Center. This city is the headquarters of the Timken Company as well as the home of many of the descendants of its founder, Henry H. Timken. Family members control both the Timken Foundation and the Timken Company. In short, the Timken Foundation has served to reinforce the power and prestige of the Timken family within the local community.

Most foundations, especially the smaller ones, have chosen to limit their philanthropic activities primarily to their local communities. Even a few of the largest foundations have restricted most of their grants to a single community. One example of this pattern of local concentration by a large foundation is the William Penn Foundation. This foundation was endowed by Otto Haas, one of the founders of Rohm and Haas Company, and is still largely controlled by his two sons. Because the company, the foundation, and the founding family are all based in Philadelphia, the foundation restricts its grants almost exclusively to local schools and charities. The same is true of the McKnight Foundation, which was endowed by William L. McKnight, one of the founders of Minnesota Mining and Manufacturing Company, and which concentrates primarily on charities in the Minneapolis area. There are many other examples of large foundations that are controlled by donor families and that devote most of their grant funds to local charities. These foundations include the William and Flora Hewitt Foundation in the San Francisco area, the McDonnell Foundation in the St. Louis area, and the Howard Heinz Endowment in the Pittsburgh area. Even if a foundation does distribute most of its grant funds to nonprofit organizations across the nation, it may devote a disproportionate amount of its resources to local charities. For example, the Charles Stewart Mott Foundation, which still has several members of the Mott family as trustees, continues to provide considerable financial support to charities in Flint, Michigan. Similarly, both the Richard K. Mellon Foundation and the Sarah Scaife Foundation, controlled by members of the Mellon family, still devote a significant portion of their grant funds to charitable organizations in and around Pittsburgh.

Foundations also enable members of the corporate rich to influence public policy. Because they are tax-exempt charitable organizations, foundations are prohibited from lobbying for specific pieces of legislation. However, they can fund research on the feasibility of particular public policies. One of the most established and influential public policy-research institutions in America is the Council on Foreign Relations. Although it now derives the bulk of its funds from individual and corporate donations, the Council on Foreign Relations once relied on a few large foundations, including the Rockefeller Foundation, the Carnegie Corporation, and the Ford Foundation, for a large portion of its funds. These same foundations also provided funds to other influential public policy-research institutions such as the Brookings Institution and the Committee for Economic Development. In recent years, however, a number of newer foundations, including the Smith Richardson Foundation, the Sarah Scaife Foundation, the John M. Olin Foundation, and the J. Howard Pew Freedom Trust, have become involved in the formation of public policy. Furthermore, these foundations have funded organizations and groups that advocate blatantly conservative and neoconservative policies. Indeed, these foundations have been instrumental in the formation or renovation of several public policy-research institutions such as the American Enterprise Institute for Public Policy Research; the Hoover Institution on War, Peace, and Revolution; the Heritage Foundation; and the Center for Strategic and International Studies. In the past few years, these public policy-research institutions have succeeded in influencing many of the policies of the Reagan administration.

In general, those philanthropic foundations that are still controlled by their donor families have acted as a conservative force in American politics. Although most of these foundations have contributed to the public welfare through their support of local charities, they have only rarely funded organizations advocating fundamental social change. In his seminal study *The Big Foundations,* Waldemar A. Nielsen concluded that "the boards of the large foundations make up a partial political spectrum ranging from liberal-conservative to ultraconservative." Indeed, there are only a handful of foundations that have funded nonprofit organizations advocating progressive causes. Perhaps the most progressive of all family foundations is the Stern Fund, endowed primarily by Edith Rosenwald Stern, the daughter of Julius Rosenwald, an early president of Sears, Roebuck and Co. In recent years, the Stern Fund has given grants to groups involved with such controversial political issues as nuclear disarmament, abortion rights, campaign reform, and civil rights. However, the Stern Fund is relatively small, with assets of less than $2 million. There are a few other foundations that fund slightly less progressive but decidedly liberal causes. These include the New World Foundation, endowed by Anita McCormick Blaine, and the Field Foundation, endowed by Marshall Field III. Both of these foundations were founded by scions of wealthy capitalist families who had a personal commitment to the issues of social justice and civil rights. However, these foundations are philanthropic dwarfs in comparison to those giant foundations that support conservative and ultraconservative causes.

DEALING WITH CHARITY

Charitable foundations that have remained under the control of their donors have, on occasion, engaged in questionable financial transactions. One of the most questionable transactions between a donor and a foundation involved Howard R. Hughes, Jr., and his Howard Hughes Medical Institute. Hughes was for many years the sole proprietor of Hughes Tool Company, a highly profitable oil drill bit manufacturer founded by his father. In 1953, he decided to create a charity as a means of reducing his income taxes. Hughes started by giving all the stock in a newly formed Hughes Aircraft Company to his newly created Howard Hughes Medical Institute. At that point, however, the only assets of Hughes Aircraft were the patents, trademarks, and goodwill formerly held by the aircraft division of Hughes Tool Company. Next, he sold other assets of the aircraft division, including inventories and receivables, to his medical institute for $74 million. As partial payment, the medical institute assumed the $56 million in liabilities of the aircraft division. In short, Howard Hughes had created a charity that began operation by owing him $18 million. Moreover, the assets purchased by the medical institute did not include the land and buildings formerly used by the aircraft division. The medical institute had to lease these facilities from Hughes Tool. In the first two decades of its existence, the medical institute received $56 million in income from Hughes Aircraft Company. During this same period, however, the medical institute paid $30 million in principal, interest, and lease payments to Hughes Tool. Howard Hughes, the sole proprietor of Hughes Tool, served as sole trustee of the Howard Hughes Medical Institute as well as the president of Hughes Aircraft Company during much of that period.

As a result of a number of such flagrant abuses, Congress included prohibitions against "self-dealing" between charitable foundations and their donor families in the Tax Reform Act of 1969. Despite these regulations, foundations can still assist corporate rich families in avoiding estate taxes and preserving their control over family corporations. For example, foundations can serve as temporary repositories for large blocks of stock in family corporations. A major stockholder in a family corporation can simply donate his or her stock to a family foundation until the family corporation is able to repurchase it from the foundation. This strategy avoids the problem of selling a controlling block of company stock to the public in order to pay taxes, because lifetime donations or testamentary bequests to charitable foundations are not subject to gift or estate taxes. Moreover, to the extent that members of the donor family serve as trustees of the foundation, the stock owned by the foundation remains under family control. Although the law prohibits family members from purchasing stock held by a family foundation, the family may direct the family corporation to repurchase all or most of its stock from the foundation. The donor family still benefits, albeit indirectly, from such a transaction. Corporations that buy back the stock held by some of their stockholders simply increase the proportion of the outstanding stock held by each of their remaining stockholders. Consequently, whenever a family corporation repurchases a large block of its stock from a foundation, members of the founding family often wind up with a larger equity position in the corporation without having to spend any of their own money.

The Olin Corporation was one of the first companies to repurchase its stock from a family foundation. This chemical company was founded by Franklin W. Olin, who resigned as its chairman in 1944. That same year, at the age of eighty-four, he decided to donate the bulk of his stock in the company to his Olin Foundation. Consequently, the foundation became the largest single stockholder in the corporation, with roughly 37 percent of its common stock. The only other major stockholders in the firm were John M. Olin and Spencer T. Olin, the two sons of the founder, who held another 32 percent of the Olin stock. Six years later, they decided to have the Olin Corporation repurchase its stock from the Olin Foundation. The sons wanted the company to buy back this stock for two reasons. To begin with, this purchase would eliminate the foundation as a major stockholder. Because their father was ninety years old and had not appointed any other family members as trustees of his foundation, this block of stock represented a potential threat to their control of the company. In addition, by retiring over a third of the outstanding stock in the corporation, this transaction would increase the proportion of Olin stock held by other members of the Olin family. In all, it cost the Olin Corporation about $50 million to buy back the stock held by the Olin Foundation. However, as a result of this reduction in the outstanding stock of the company, the Olin stock held by John and Spencer Olin and their children came to represent approximately 51 percent of the total. In other words, the corporation paid $50 million to reduce its outstanding stock and, not coincidentally, enhance the control exercised by the two sons of the founder.

Perhaps the most lucrative financial transaction on record between a corporation and foundations controlled by a corporate rich family involves the Hearsts. William R. Hearst, the only son of a wealthy mining speculator, was the owner of a major metropolitan newspaper before he was twenty-five years old. Over the next six decades, he created one of the largest media companies in the country. Although all five of his sons worked for the Hearst Corporation in various capacities, Hearst never relinquished his absolute control over the company. He also neglected to transfer much of his wealth to his sons during his lifetime. Indeed, he did not even prepare a will to dispose of his vast fortune until 1947, when he was already eighty-four years old. However, the will itself was a masterpiece of estate tax avoidance. When he died four years later, Hearst left an estate appraised at $59 million, most of it in Hearst Corporation stock. Specifically, the estate held almost 67 percent of the common stock in the company with an appraised value of nearly $44 million. This stock, which did not have any voting rights, was bequeathed to the William Randolph Hearst Foundation. The remaining 33 percent of the nonvoting common stock had been previously donated to a separate charitable entity, the Hearst Foundation. The estate also held 52 percent of the preferred stock in the company with a stipulated value of $8 million. Unlike the common stock left to the foundation, the preferred stock did have voting rights. In his will, Hearst bequeathed most of this preferred stock to his wife. His five sons were named in the will as the income beneficiaries of a trust that held less than $3 million in preferred stock.

The will of William R. Hearst created a bizarre relationship among the Hearst family, the two family foundations, and the Hearst Corporation. On the one hand, Millicent Hearst and her five sons received only modest incomes from the preferred stock held in trust for them. Indeed, the preferred stock held in trust for the benefit of his five sons paid each of them only $30,000 per year. Moreover, because the dividend on this preferred stock was fixed, their trust income did not increase over time. In this way, William R. Hearst ensured that his sons would have to work for the family corporation in order to receive adequate incomes. On the other hand, the stock held in trust for the family was the only Hearst stock with voting rights. Although the common stock held by the two family foundations did entitle them to the bulk of the dividend income paid by the corporation, this stock did not have any voting rights. In this situation, the ultimate power rested with the trustees of the family trusts that held the voting stock in the company. Perhaps because he did not entirely trust the business acumen of his own sons, Hearst had deliberately appointed several Hearst Corporation officers to serve with his sons as trustees of these trusts. For two decades after the death of its founder, the corporation was largely controlled by managers who were not family members. However, family members were eventually able to win enough allies among the other trustees to regain effective control of their trusts and the company. In 1973, the family succeeded in forcing the resignation of the company president appointed by William R. Hearst three decades earlier. At the same time, family lawyers began exploring means of increasing the share of the company profits distributed to family members.

The financial reorganization of the Hearst Corporation was completed in 1975. Specifically, the family decided to have the Hearst Corporation repurchase all of its nonvoting common stock from the family foundations and then convert all of the voting preferred stock held by the family trusts into voting common stock. In point of fact, the company had quietly begun preparing for this transaction years earlier. For example, the Hearst Corporation had paid only meager dividends on the common stock held by the foundations. Instead, it had used retained earnings to eliminate its debt and to build up its publishing and broadcasting properties. The Hearst Foundation and the William Randolph Hearst Foundation, which were both controlled by family members and officers of the Hearst Corporation, readily agreed to the transaction. The only matter to be negotiated was the price for the common stock. At this point, the attorneys general of the states of California and New York were brought into the negotiations, because the two family foundations were incorporated in their respective states. They originally appraised the value of the Hearst common stock held by the two foundations at $205 million. However, lawyers for the Hearst family claimed that this stock was worth no more than $50 million, because it had no voting rights and was not readily marketable. After lengthy negotiations, the attorneys general settled on $135 million as a fair price for all of the common stock held by the foundations. Because it had no debt and owned a large number of profitable publishing and broadcasting properties, the

Hearst Corporation had no difficulty in financing the purchase of its common stock.

When the Hearsts became the sole owners of the Hearst Corporation, they also became one of the richest families in the country. Moreover, their rise to the highest echelons of the corporate rich was financed entirely by the Hearst Corporation. The family had simply traded preferred stock worth roughly $5 million for common stock that would soon be worth at least $500 million. After all, Hearst Corporation owned, among other things, twelve daily metropolitan newspapers, thirteen national magazines, a major book publisher, three metropolitan television stations, and seven radio stations. Indeed, the president of Hearst Corporation intimated that its revenues were roughly $590 million by 1977. On the basis of the stock valuations enjoyed by other media companies of comparable size and profitability, Hearst Corporation was probably worth at least $500 million and perhaps as much as $1 billion that year. As a result of this financial reorganization, the annual income received by the Hearst family from the stock held in trust has increased dramatically. By 1981, the sons and grandchildren of William R. Hearst were sharing almost $10 million in dividend income each year. Moreover, this common stock remains protected from any immediate estate taxes because all of it is held by the testamentary trust created by the will of William R. Hearst. The five Hearst sons were income beneficiaries of this trust, but the trust itself will not be dissolved until the death of the last descendant of William R. Hearst who was alive when the trust was created in 1951. In short, it will be several decades before this trust is dissolved and its Hearst stock is distributed to the grandchildren and great-grandchildren of the founder.

8

Making
It
Big

Entrepreneurs are essential to the efficient operation of the free-enterprise system. They create new firms that provide consumers with products and services that are either better or cheaper than those that are already available. In the process, they also create new jobs. However, entrepreneurs are not motivated to invest all of their savings and devote most of their lives to a business by any sense of altruism. To the contrary, they are motivated largely by the prospect of becoming rich. Even the most ardent advocates of the free-enterprise system understand the importance of greed. Although it is not generally considered an admirable motive in most social situations, greed is exalted as a motive in the realm of business. Economic theory maintains that individuals require incentives in order to take risks and work hard. In this view, entrepreneurs must be offered the prospect of becoming wealthy before they can be expected to invest their money and effort in establishing and operating a new business. As a result, wealth is typically considered the hallmark of success in a capitalist society. The contribution of an entrepreneur to the economic welfare of the nation is often measured by the magnitude of his fortune.

Indeed, material success in the form of tangible wealth is often interpreted as a sign of moral superiority by those wealthy individuals who seek justification for their fortunes.

The folklore of capitalism is resplendent with epic accounts of ordinary individuals who struggled against overwhelming odds to achieve success in business. The main purpose of such "rags to riches" tales is to demonstrate that anyone can succeed in America if he or she is innovative and industrious enough. Although these anecdotal accounts serve a certain ideological function, they fail to provide an adequate description of the origins of most large fortunes. Because wealthy entrepreneurs often seek to justify their newfound wealth, their own accounts of their business experiences are not always accurate. Moreover, different families have had very different relationships with their family corporations. Some entrepreneurs founded their firms on their own; others required the assistance of partners and other investors. Similarly, each of these firms grew from a small company into a large corporation as the result of different economic conditions and management strategies. A few of these companies grew rapidly, whereas others required several decades to become major corporations. At one level, then, each corporate rich family is unique in terms of its relationship to a particular firm. Nevertheless, corporate rich families demonstrate certain common patterns in the accumulation of their wealth. Indeed, wealthy entrepreneurs and their heirs often adopt very similar strategies for accumulating and enhancing their fortunes.

MYTHOLOGY OF WEALTH

The accumulation of wealth is a much neglected topic in economics. Traditional economic doctrine steadfastly maintains that wealth is created by a long and slow process of savings. Of course, a diligent savings program will eventually yield a modest accumulation of wealth. However, it is impossible for one individual to amass a fortune comparable to those possessed by the corporate rich by savings alone. One of the few economic theories that even attempts to explain the accumulation of great wealth is provided by Lester Thurow in his classic study *Generating Inequality*. Specifically, Thurow argues that most large fortunes are examples of *instant wealth* resulting from the valuations assigned to highly profitable corporations by the stock market. Some corporations are more profitable than others and, consequently, are assigned a more generous capitalization by the stock market. Investors are willing to pay a premium price for stock in corporations that are highly profitable for several reasons. First and foremost, highly profitable corporations can use their surplus earnings to pay more generous dividends to their stockholders. Alternatively, these corporations can retain part of their surplus earnings in order to finance growth either by investing in new plants and equipment or by acquiring other corporations. Those individuals who were early investors in such highly profitable companies are likely to become very wealthy from the appreciation in the market value of their stock. As Thurow observes, "to become very rich one must generate or select a situation in which an above-average rate of return is about to be capitalized."

Although the fortunes of the corporate rich are usually based on the market valuations assigned to their stockholdings in family corporations, these fortunes are only rarely instantaneous. Indeed, the notion of instant wealth best describes the *capitalization* process that occurs whenever a private company goes public by selling stock to the public for the first time. Edwin C. Whitehead provides an example of an entrepreneur who achieved instant wealth in the stock market as a result of this capitalization process. Whitehead and his father founded Technicon Corporation, a laboratory-supply company, in 1939. Their company became highly profitable in 1957 after it began marketing an automated blood analyzer for use in hospitals. By the time his father died in 1968, Whitehead was already wealthy, because he owned virtually all of the stock in a corporation that had assets of $49 million. However, as long as Technicon was a private corporation, his actual wealth was a matter of speculation. In 1969, Technicon sold 5 percent of its stock to the public for $40 million. Although Whitehead received only $20 million in cash from the sale of some of his Technicon stock, this stock offering made him one of the wealthiest individuals in the nation. On the basis of the market price at the time, the 92 percent of Technicon stock that he kept was worth over $800 million. Over the next several years, his fortune rose to a high of $1 billion and fell to a low of $150 million with fluctuations in the market price of Technicon stock. Technicon was finally acquired by Revlon in 1979. In exchange for their Technicon stock, Whitehead and his family received a large block of Revlon preferred stock, which was later redeemed for $285 million in cash.

Most of the massive fortunes held by corporate rich families have taken one or more generations to reach their zenith. These fortunes were often created by entrepreneurs who became extremely wealthy only later in their lives. Of course, there are a few cases of entrepreneurs who became rich after only a few years in business. The best example of truly instant wealth is provided by Apple Computer Inc. Two computer geniuses, Steven P. Jobs and Stephen G. Wozniak, designed and produced their first microcomputer in 1976. A year later, they convinced A. C. Markkula, Jr., to invest in their company. The three founders incorporated Apple Computer in 1977. By the time the company went public only three years later, their 37 percent of Apple stock was worth a total of $630 million. Nevertheless, most entrepreneurs have not enjoyed great wealth until after they had been active in business for at least a couple of decades. In fact, fortunes based on stockholdings in family corporations often continue to increase in value long after the entrepreneurs who founded them have passed away. For example, Robert W. Johnson, one of the founders of Johnson & Johnson, was only modestly wealthy when he died in 1910. His entire estate, which included all of the stock in the company, was worth only $3 million at the time. By the time the company went public in 1944, this same Johnson & Johnson stock was worth $30 million. By 1961, the 55 percent of Johnson & Johnson stock held by the two sons of Robert W. Johnson and their eight children was worth $150 million. Only ten years later, the 34 percent of the stock in Johnson & Johnson still owned by the descendants of the founder and foundations created by them was worth over $2.2 billion.

The growth of large fortunes is inextricably linked to the growth of large corporations. All of the large corporations in existence today were once small companies. At one time, most of them were engaged in vigorous competition with many small companies within the same industry. Over time, however, industries usually become more concentrated as unsuccessful companies go bankrupt or are acquired by more successful companies. As a result, it is typical for an industry to become dominated by a few large corporations within a matter of decades. Once an industry has become concentrated, the competition among the remaining corporations usually becomes less intense as each of them seeks to gain market share through advertising campaigns rather than direct price competition. This gradual reduction in the level of price competition within an industry allows the surviving corporations to earn relatively high rates of return on their investments. For example, General Motors has earned generous profits for most of the last half century. In this view, major corporations are the survivors of a constant process of economic elimination. This process of consolidation is virtually complete in most mature industries. Many of the basic industries, such as steel, automobiles, tobacco, food, and chemicals, were consolidated in the early part of this century. Of course, this process did not occur until later in such newer industries as aircraft, drugs, and electronics. In recent years, established industries that had remained geographically fragmented, such as the media, financial services, and retailing, have also become increasingly consolidated.

The fortunes amassed by most corporate rich families are the result of their initial stockholdings in corporations that were early entrants into fields that became growth industries. New industries give rise to new firms. As these companies grow into major corporations, they create new family fortunes. Many of the largest fortunes that have emerged in recent decades have arisen mainly out of relatively new industries, such as drugs and electronics. The Galvin family of Motorola Inc. provides an example of a fortune derived from early involvement in an emergent growth industry. Paul V. Galvin and his brother, Joseph Galvin, founded the predecessor of Motorola in 1928 with a total investment of $1,315. The company prospered because it was, for many years, the sole supplier of car radios to the burgeoning automobile industry. Motorola later expanded its operations by supplying electronic components to other manufacturers. It also developed two-way radios for the military. By 1952, the 31 percent of Motorola held by various members of the Galvin family was worth $21 million. The company has been highly profitable during most of the past few decades. Moreover, it has retained most of these profits in order to finance its entry into new markets. In the years that followed, the company entered a number of growing markets within the electronics industry. Although it eventually abandoned the production of television sets, Motorola succeeded in becoming the leading manufacturer of semiconductor devices and mobile communications systems. The Galvin family, which still retains close to 12 percent of the stock in Motorola, is now worth well over $550 million.

The accumulation of a large family fortune does not always depend on the growth of an entirely new industry. In some cases, a family can amass a fortune simply because of its stockholdings in a corporation that has been able to increase its share of an important market. For example, the Busch family fortune grew apace with the emergence of Anheuser-Busch, the family brewing company, as the major producer of beer in the country. The company grew despite the fact that it was not in a growth industry. When Anheuser-Busch was incorporated in 1875, it was only one of several hundred breweries in America, each supplying a local market. However, the beer industry eventually entered a period of consolidation. Many local breweries closed because they could not match the economies of scale enjoyed by the major brewing companies. Anheuser-Busch was one of the first brewing companies to establish a national distribution system for its products. It also invested heavily in national advertising to promote its brands. As late as 1952, Anheuser-Busch produced only about 7 percent of all beer sold in the United States. The entire corporation had a market value of slightly less than $100 million. Consequently, the 50 percent of Anheuser-Busch Companies stock held by the children and grandchildren of Adolphus Busch, the founder of the company, was worth only about $50 million. In the last three decades, however, Anheuser-Busch has increased its dominance within the brewing industry. At present, it produces 37 percent of all the beer sold in the United States. The company now has a market value of $5.6 billion. The Busch family, which still owns about 20 percent of Anheuser-Busch stock, is now worth at least $1.1 billion.

Contrary to popular opinion, inventors of new products rarely achieve great wealth. Most of the inventors who achieved great wealth did so only by founding their own companies. In short, they were successful entrepreneurs as well as successful inventors. One of the first inventors to achieve great wealth in this manner was Cyrus McCormick, who assisted his father in developing the mechanical reaper. He and his brothers eventually formed the McCormick Harvester Machine Company to manufacture and sell their reapers. Later, the McCormicks became the principal stockholders in International Harvester. Similarly, Charles Kettering patented a number of important automotive inventions, such as the self-starter, but he was also an astute businessman. The company he founded, Dayton Engineering Laboratories Company, was later merged into General Motors. As a result, Kettering received General Motors stock that was worth over $200 million by the time he died in 1955. A more recent example of an inventor who became a successful entrepreneur is Edwin Land. He founded Polaroid Corporation in 1937 in order to produce polarizing filters by using a process that he had developed. Ten years later, he introduced the instant photography system. By 1978, the 12 percent of Polaroid stock held by Edwin Land and his family had a market value of over $330 million. Other inventors who have formed their own companies include Gordon E. Moore of Intel and An Wang of Wang Laboratories. Both men were scientists who contributed to important technological innovations in the electronics industry, but they both owe their substantial fortunes to the fact that they left positions with major corporations in order to found their own companies.

Although most large fortunes have been created by successful entrepreneurs who were concerned primarily with the actual operations of their companies, more than a few fortunes have been amassed by financiers. In general, financiers concentrate on manipulating the finances of corporations rather than managing their operations. Typically, financiers accumulate wealth by increasing their equity positions in corporations. Alternatively, they accumulate wealth by having the corporations they control acquire other corporations using debt. In either case, financiers typically demonstrate very little interest in the actual operations of their corporations. The distinction between entrepreneurs and financiers is sometimes ambiguous. Henry Ford, for example, was an entrepreneur who was intimately involved with operations of Ford Motor Company. He introduced a series of innovations that enabled his factories to produce reliable and affordable automobiles. Henry Ford also proved himself to be an astute financier. When he founded Ford Motor Company in 1902, he relied on several investors to provide the company with the necessary capital. Consequently, he initially owned only 25 percent of the stock in his own company. Two years later, he gained majority control of the company by buying out several of his initial investors. Fourteen years later, he and his family borrowed $104 million from a consortium of banks to buy out the remaining investors. As a result, Ford Motor Company became a private company owned entirely by the Ford family. In short, Henry Ford, the legendary entrepreneur, was enough of a financier to engineer the first major "leveraged buyout" by management.

LONG HAULS

Many of the largest fortunes in America are old in the sense that they stem from companies that were founded many decades ago. As a result, established corporate rich families such as the Wimans of Deere & Company, the Dows of Dow Chemical, and the Danforths of Ralston Purina have enjoyed the advantages of great wealth for at least three generations. Even those fortunes that have increased greatly in value in recent years often have venerable histories. The Houghton family of Corning Glass Works is fairly typical of families that have been major stockholders for many decades in companies that eventually became large corporations. Although family members have sold some of their stock in Corning Glass Works in recent years, most of their fortune still comprises stock in the family corporation. The original Corning Glass Works was a family partnership until Amory Houghton, Jr., incorporated it in 1875. The company grew rapidly after it became the first producer of bulbs for incandescent lights. Many years later, it became the major producer of picture tubes for television sets. By the time the company first went public in 1945, the 66 percent of Corning Glass stock owned by the grandchildren of the founder was worth $58 million. Over the next decade, the Houghtons sold almost $38 million in Corning Glass stock. However, they kept roughly 36 percent of the stock in the company, worth $115 million by 1955. Only recently has Corning Glass issued additional stock in order to finance acquisitions. Consequently, the Houghtons now own only about 13 percent of the stock in the company worth $340 million. Altogether, the Houghton family is worth in the neighborhood of $450 million.

The wealthiest of the established corporate rich families were able to amass large fortunes because the companies in which they were major stockholders were able to expand into large corporations without greatly diluting the equity positions of their initial stockholders. Of course, not all companies grow into large corporations, and even fewer are able to finance such growth without issuing additional stock. Only highly profitable companies are able to finance their expansion through retained earnings. In many cases, these corporations were profitable because they dominated a particular market. In addition, these corporations typically operated in industries that did not require extensive outlays of capital. For example, the Donnelley family has been the principal stockholder in R.R. Donnelley & Sons, a major commercial printing company, since it was founded in 1871. The company thrived almost from the outset because it established itself as the largest printer of mail-order catalogs in the country. Later, it pioneered the printing of regional editions of national magazines. The company was able to finance most of its initial growth from retained earnings without the necessity of issuing additional stock to the public. By 1963, the children and grandchildren of Thomas E. Donnelley, the son of the founder who eventually gained control of the company, owned over 40 percent of R.R. Donnelley stock, worth nearly $100 million. In the past couple of decades, family members have sold roughly half of their stock in the company. As a result, the Donnelleys now own only 21 percent of the stock in the company. However, this stock is currently worth over $490 million.

Many of the oldest and wealthiest of all corporate rich families are those whose companies have not yet gone public. The Hearsts of Hearst Corporation, the MacMillans of Cargill Corporation, and the Johnsons of S. C. Johnson and Sons are still majority stockholders of private corporations that were founded many decades ago. Indeed, private corporations offer a variety of advantages over public corporations in terms of safeguarding the wealth of their founding families. Other corporate rich families are major stockholders in companies that grew into large corporations before they finally went public. For example, the Dorrance family has been one of the wealthiest families in the nation for at least the last half century. John T. Dorrance joined the Campbell Soup Company in 1897. When he died in 1930, he owned virtually all of the stock in the company, worth approximately $150 million. In accordance with his will, all of this stock was placed in a series of generation-skipping trusts for the benefit of his wife and five children. Campbell Soup did not go public until 1954, when these trusts sold 13 percent of the stock in the company for $48 million. By then, the remaining Campbell Soup stock held by the family trust was worth at least another $325 million. These trusts sold another $50 million in Campbell Soup stock to the public six years later. Although much of the Campbell Soup stock once held by the family trusts has been distributed to the ten grandchildren of the founder in recent years, they have sold very little of their stock in the company. Indeed, members of the Dorrance family still own almost 60 percent of Campbell Soup stock, worth well over $1 billion.

In a few other cases, descendants of a founder have remained major stockholders in the family corporation even though they have sold large portions of their stock. This is often the case with companies that were once almost entirely owned by the founding family. For example, the descendants of Henry J. Heinz are still major stockholders in H.J. Heinz Company, the family food-processing firm founded in 1876. When the company went public in 1946, the children and grandchildren of the founder owned over 72 percent of H.J. Heinz stock, worth nearly $40 million. Since that time, however, various members of the Heinz family have sold much of their stock in the company. Consequently, the grandchildren and great-grandchildren of the founder probably still own only about 16 percent of the outstanding stock in H.J. Heinz. Nevertheless, this stock, which is now worth over $650 million, continues to represent the bulk of the Heinz family fortune. There is also the case of The Upjohn Company, which was founded in 1886 but which did not go public until 1958. At that point, the children and grandchildren of William E. Upjohn, the founder of the company, owned 68 percent of the stock in Upjohn Company worth about $430 million. Over the next six years, the Upjohns sold just over $200 million in Upjohn stock. They kept 43 percent of the stock in the company, worth over $300 million by 1964. Currently, the family probably owns about 30 percent of the stock in Upjohn Company. Due to the tremendous growth of the company in recent years, the remaining Upjohn stock held by the founding family is worth close to $1.3 billion.

Those families that have held large blocks of stock in major corporations for several decades have sometimes augmented their fortunes with the dividend income they receive from this stock. For example, members of the Dorrance family have received extremely large incomes from the dividends paid on their Campbell Soup stock. Over the past three decades alone, the heirs of John T. Dorrance have received over $800 million in dividends on their Campbell Soup stock. During much of this period, this income was shared by the widow and five children of the founder. Most of it is now shared by his ten grandchildren. John T. Dorrance, Jr., the last surviving child of the founder, currently receives over $24 million a year in income from the Campbell Soup stock held in his trust. Other established corporate rich families have received smaller but still substantial dividend income from their stock in family corporations. Altogether, the Upjohn family, for example, has received a total of $250 million in dividends on its stock in Upjohn Company in just the last two decades. Similarly, both the Houghton family of Corning Glass Works and the Donnelley

225

family of R.R. Donnelley & Sons have received approximately $100 million in dividends from their family corporations over the last two decades. The ability of a particular corporate rich family to accumulate additional wealth from their dividend income depends primarily upon the number of individuals within the family who rely on these dividends for their income. Nevertheless, it seems that most of these families are able to accumulate additional wealth from their dividend income for at least the first two or three generations.

In a few cases, entrepreneurs have sold most of their stock in the companies they founded before they became major corporations. As a result, they did not amass large fortunes from their initial stockholdings. Erle P. Halliburton, for example, sold most of his stock in Halliburton Corporation while it was still a comparatively small corporation. Halliburton founded his oil well cementing company with only $1,500 in capital in 1919. Three decades later, Halliburton Corporation was one of the leading oil-services companies in the nation. At that point, Halliburton and his wife decided to sell most of their 54 percent stake in the company. In 1948, they sold 49 percent of the stock in Halliburton to the public for $14 million. The reasons for this sale were never announced. Halliburton was an active oilman, and he may have used some of the proceeds from this sale of stock to finance additional exploration activities. Nevertheless, he continued to serve as chairman of Halliburton Corporation for several years. As a result of this sale, however, the Halliburton family missed the opportunity to become even richer from the appreciation in the market value of their Halliburton stock. After two stock dividends and three stock splits, the Halliburton stock that the family sold in 1948 would be worth over $580 million today. Moreover, this same stock would have paid a total of $295 million in dividends during this period. The Halliburtons could probably have maintained control of the corporation as well, because that same stock would currently represent 18 percent of the outstanding stock in Halliburton. At most, the Halliburton stock actually retained by the family is now worth about $55 million.

Corporate rich families do not always become wealthier over time simply from holding on to their stock in family corporations. In a few instances, families have lost much of their fortunes as the result of the mismanagement of these corporations. The Friedland family, for example, saw its fortune rise and fall with the performance of their family corporation, Food Fair Stores. Samuel Friedland and his brother, George Friedland, opened their first supermarket in 1933. Within a few years, they were joined by their brother-in-law. Over the next two decades, the Friedlands built Food Fair Stores into one of the largest supermarket chains in the country. Beginning in 1953, the Friedland brothers began to withdraw from the active management of the company. Sam Friedland moved to Florida, where he invested in a number of real estate developments. However, the founders continued to serve as directors of Food Fair while two sons of Sam Friedland assumed senior management positions. After all, the family still owned over 30 percent of the stock in the company. At its high point in 1961, the Food Fair stock held by the Friedland family was worth almost $100 million. However, company profits soon began a prolonged decline as the result of an unsuccessful expansion program. As profits fell, so did the value of Food Fair stock. By 1978, members of the Friedland family still held over 25 percent of the stock in the company. However, the value of their Food Fair stock had declined to less than $10 million. Three years later, the company filed for bankruptcy. The Friedlands were not reduced to poverty by this debacle, but their fortune was severely depleted.

NEWCOMERS

A few very successful entrepreneurs have managed to amass substantial fortunes in the course of a single generation. Indeed, some of the largest fortunes in America were accumulated in the past few decades. These fortunes were created by family corporations that have been able to finance their growth largely from retained earnings. Only highly profitable companies are able to generate enough retained earnings to finance rapid expansion. In fact, the need to maximize retained earnings leads many growth firms, especially those with large capital requirements, to pay little or nothing in the way of dividends to stockholders, at least during their formative years. For example, relatively new electronics companies such as Intel and Digital Equipment, which must invest heavily in research and development, do not pay any dividends at all, and others such as Hewlett-Packard and Tektronix devote only a comparatively small portion of their earnings to dividends. By and large, most new fortunes stem from initial family stockholdings in highly profitable corporations that have established important niches in growth industries. Several of the largest of these new fortunes are associated with companies in such growth industries as electronics and financial services. Other new fortunes are associated with corporations that are engaged in activities such as specialty retailing that do not require massive capital investments.

One of the most significant growth industries in recent years has been the electronics industry. Many of the largest electronics corporations of today were very small firms only a few decades ago. As a rule, these firms have been profitable enough to finance most of their own expansion. One of the oldest electronics companies, Hewlett-Packard Corporation, was founded in 1939 as a small electronics instruments firm by William R. Hewlett and David Packard. After they took their company public in 1958, their 88 percent of Hewlett-Packard stock was worth $43 million. Today, Hewlett-Packard Corporation is a major manufacturer of electronic equipment and computers. The two founders still own 30 percent of Hewlett-Packard stock, worth over $2.3 billion. They were able to maintain their equity position in the company because it was able to finance its initial growth from retained earnings. The founders of another early electronics company, Texas Instruments, were also able to avoid much dilution of their equity positions. Texas Instruments was founded in 1930 as a geophysical exploration firm. When the company first went public in 1953, its three principal founders, Eugene McDermott, J. Erik Jonsson, and Cecil H. Green, owned 53 percent of the company, worth almost $8 million. Texas Instruments went on to become a major producer of electronic components. By 1968, the three founders had sold over half of the stock in the company. However, the 17 percent of Texas Instruments stock still held by the three founders was worth as much as $210 million. Although they have since sold the bulk of their stock in the company, their combined fortunes are now probably worth at least $300 million.

Entrepreneurs who have entered the electronics industry in recent years have usually confronted substantial financial obstacles. It now requires large amounts of capital to develop and produce sophisticated electronic devices. Indeed, new companies often must issue large blocks of stock to venture capitalists in order to finance their initial operations. Consequently, new entrepreneurs are often forced to reduce their equity positions in their own companies. For example, Robert N. Noyce and Gordon E. Moore were research scientists working for Fairchild Semiconductor when they decided to start their own company, Intel Corporation. Although they had each accumulated about $1 million in Fairchild Semiconductor stock, they soon discovered that they would need additional capital to finance the development of their first microprocessor. In order to raise the necessary capital, Intel issued $2.5 million worth of convertible debentures to a group of investors. Once the company became profitable, these investors converted their debentures into shares of Intel common stock. The company later issued another $9 million worth of stock as well. As a result of this initial dilution of their equity positions, Noyce and Moore owned only 28 percent of Intel stock, worth nearly $18 million after the company went public in 1971. Intel is now a leading manufacturer of microprocessors. With the exception of a recent investment by another corporation, Intel has not had to issue any more stock to meet its capital requirements. However, Noyce was forced to part with half of his Intel stock in 1975 as the result of a divorce settlement. At this point, the two founders own about 8 percent of Intel stock, worth over $300 million.

Any firm can become a growth company as long as it has a large and unexploited market for its product or service. Moreover, the founder of such a company can become rich as long as his company is profitable enough to finance this expansion. One growth industry that requires only a minimal investment of capital has been specialty retailing. One of the pioneer specialty retailers was Ray Kroc. While selling milk-shake machines in 1954, Kroc stumbled upon McDonald's, a couple of small but popular drive-in restaurants in California. The restaurants offered only a limited menu, but the food was cheap and the service was fast. Most important, both restaurants generated a tremendous volume of sales. Although he was fifty-two years old and had virtually no capital of his own, Kroc convinced the owners to let him franchise other McDonald's restaurants. Later, he began leasing the restaurant buildings to the franchise operators as well. In 1961, Kroc borrowed $2.7 million to buy out the original owners. When the company went public four years later, he owned 53 percent of McDonald's stock, worth almost $18 million. Because McDonald's owned the leases as well as the franchises to its restaurants, Kroc was able to enforce standardized operating procedures that kept costs to a minimum. These procedures also ensured that the food and service were of uniform quality across the nation. McDonald's charged each restaurant operator a substantial franchise fee, which included rent for the building. In return, the parent company spent heavily on advertising. Even after selling over $100 million in company stock, Kroc still owned 11 percent of McDonald's stock, worth $480 million by the time he died in 1984.

The retailing formula based on low prices and high sales volume developed by Ray Kroc has been applied with equal success in a different context by Sam Walton. After operating several franchise variety stores, Walton decided to enter the discount retailing business. Discount stores were already very successful in large cities, and Walton realized that he could not compete with the large discount chains in those markets. However, he felt that he could succeed by operating smaller discount stores in smaller cities. Walton opened his first Wal-Mart store in 1962. Eight years later, he took the company public in order to raise enough capital to build a regional distribution center to service his chain of 30 Wal-Mart stores. At that point, he and his family owned 68 percent of Wal-Mart stock, worth about $17 million. Walton continued opening new stores in small cities. Wal-Mart stores have been able to generate more revenues than other discount stores of comparable size because they offer lower prices than their competitors. Moreover, the company has been able to maintain this price advantage because of its highly efficient distribution system. By 1982, there were over 500 Wal-Mart stores, each of them linked by a fleet of company trucks to one of several highly automated distribution centers. More recently, Wal-Mart has established Sam's Warehouse Clubs, a chain of large wholesale stores located in large metropolitan areas. Walton, his four children, and his brother, James L. Walton, still own almost 41 percent of the stock in Wal-Mart Stores, now worth $2.8 billion.

Another business that does not always require a huge investment of capital is oil and gas exploration. Although it has become increasingly expensive to drill for oil and gas, independent drillers are often able to form drilling partnerships with wealthy investors in order to finance the completion of an exploratory well in an area abandoned or ignored by the large oil companies. Occasionally, these wildcat wells produce enough oil and gas to make both the driller and the investors rich. One of the most recent examples of this pattern is George Mitchell, the principal founder of Mitchell Energy and Development Corporation. George Mitchell and his brother, Johnny Mitchell, began exploring for oil together in 1946. In order to finance their geological surveys and drilling operations, they formed a series of partnerships with wealthy investors. The Mitchells got lucky in 1952 when they bought a promising gas well and leases on the surrounding acreage on a ranch north of Fort Worth for $55,000. They drilled another well and discovered more gas. They bought leases to adjoining acreage and continued drilling. Only 2 of the first 85 wells drilled on the acreage were dry, and the field eventually proved to be one of the largest gas fields in Texas. George Mitchell gradually bought out all of his partners, except his brother, and formed his own independent oil and gas company, Mitchell Energy and Development. After he took his company public in 1972, his 71 percent of Mitchell Energy stock was worth $42 million. During this period, the company also developed Woodlands, a highly successful 23,000-acre planned community near Houston. George Mitchell still owns 62 percent of the stock in his company, worth $520 million.

WHEELERS AND DEALERS

Several entrepreneurs have amassed large fortunes by becoming financiers. One of the most successful of these entrepreneurs-as-financiers was J. Paul Getty. He took charge of a small oil company founded by his father, George F. Getty, and built it into a major oil company, not by discovering more oil, but by buying stock in other oil companies. As one associate put it, "Paul was obsessed by the idea that he could get oil reserves cheaper by stock purchases than by developing fields." Soon after his father died in 1930, Getty had the family oil company, George F. Getty Inc., borrow money to buy shares in a much larger oil company, Pacific Western Oil Company, whose stock was selling at a discount from its asset value. After a series of stock purchases, he gained majority control of Pacific Western in 1931. Encouraged by the ease of this conquest and the continuing depression in oil stocks, Getty quickly turned his attention to an even larger oil company, Tidewater Oil Company. In order to finance this acquisition foray, he had Getty Oil sell its most valuable oil leases for $4.5 million in cash. By the end of 1933, Getty Oil and its affiliate, Pacific Western, had accumulated 8 percent of the stock in Tidewater Oil. Only then did Paul Getty discover that Tidewater Oil was, in fact, controlled by the predecessor of Exxon, the behemoth of the oil industry. He offered to buy the Tidewater shares held by Exxon but was rebuffed. When Getty threatened suit on antitrust grounds, Exxon retaliated by turning over its Tidewater stock to a newly created holding company, Mission Corporation, whose stock it then distributed to its own shareholders.

J. Paul Getty once described his principal qualities as a businessman simply as "determination, persistence, and mulish stubbornness." Undeterred by the transfer of this large block of Tidewater stock to Mission Corporation, he simply had Pacific Western buy Mission stock as well as Tidewater stock. After three more years of continual stock purchases and occasional legal skirmishes, Getty finally gained minority control over Mission Corporation in 1937. It was during this period that Getty discovered that Mission Corporation also controlled another sizable oil company, Skelly Oil Company.

In the span of seven years, Getty had amassed the beginnings of an oil empire, albeit one based largely on minority stockholdings. Because he owned 43 percent of the stock in George F. Getty Inc. and was the sole trustee of a family trust that held the remaining 57 percent, Getty exercised complete control over the family holding company. Also, George F. Getty Inc. owned almost 68 percent of Pacific Western Oil, which, in turn, owned over 46 percent of Mission Corporation. Together, Getty Oil, Pacific Western, and Mission owned over 23 percent of Tidewater. Mission Corporation also owned over 56 percent of Skelly Oil. The various pieces that eventually formed Getty Oil Company were in place. Having gained control of these oil companies, Getty next began a long process of consolidating these disparate companies into a single giant corporation. One by one, he had each oil company use part of its income, including dividend income that it received on its stockholdings in other Getty Oil companies, to buy additional stock in those companies. In this way, each oil company was slowly but surely financing its own acquisition.

To begin with, Getty had George F. Getty Inc. use the dividends it received from Pacific Western to buy more Pacific Western stock. By 1946, the Getty family holding company owned 80 percent of the stock in Pacific Western. Later that same year, George F. Getty Inc. was merged into Pacific Western, and the Getty family wound up with 85 percent of the stock in the combined corporation, worth about $40 million. Next, Getty had Pacific Western and Mission Corporation use the dividends they received from Tidewater Oil and Skelly Oil to purchase more Tidewater and Skelly stock. It was not until 1951 that Pacific Western gained majority control of Tidewater. Three years later, Getty decided to expedite the consolidation of his oil empire by having Tidewater repurchase 19 percent of its common stock. Public stockholders were willing to exchange their common stock in Tidewater for preferred stock because the common stock was not paying any dividends at the time. It was during that period that Pacific Western Oil Company was renamed Getty Oil Company. By 1967, Getty Oil and its affiliates owned 72 percent of the stock in Tidewater Oil. That same year, Tidewater was finally merged into the much smaller Getty Oil. As a result of this merger, the stockholdings of the Getty family in the combined company were reduced to 62 percent. By 1976, Getty Oil and its affiliates had acquired 72 percent of the outstanding Skelly Oil stock. Only then was it too merged into Getty Oil. As a result of this last merger, the Getty family stake in Getty Oil was reduced to 58 percent. It had taken over four decades to build Getty Oil into a major oil company, but, by the time he died in 1976, Paul Getty and his family owned Getty Oil stock worth at least $2 billion.

The advantages of corporate control in terms of manipulating the value of the stock in a corporation are evident in the case of Teledyne. This company was founded in 1960 by Henry Singleton and George Kozmetsky, each of whom contributed $225,000 in equity. In 1962, Teledyne acquired another company in exchange for shares of its common stock. Over the next seven years, Teledyne acquired another 90 companies. Almost all of these companies were acquired through the issuance of additional Teledyne common stock. After a decade of acquisitions and mergers, Henry Singleton had transformed Teledyne from a small company into a giant conglomerate. However, the issuance of all this additional Teledyne stock had severely diluted his equity position in the company. In 1962, Singleton had owned roughly 24 percent of the common stock in Teledyne, worth $5 million. By 1972, his Teledyne stock, which was then worth $12 million, represented only about 2 percent of the outstanding stock in the company. In 1972, Singleton decided it was time for Teledyne to begin repurchasing large portions of its common stock from the public. Over the next four years, Teledyne paid over $470 million for shares of its common stock. By reducing the amount of outstanding Teledyne stock, Singleton increased his equity position in the company from 2 percent to 5 percent. At that point, his Teledyne stock was worth $27 million. In 1980, Teledyne offered to repurchase more of its common stock from the public. This tender offer cost the company $480 million. By the end of 1980, Singleton owned over 7 percent of the stock in Teledyne, worth $160 million. Obviously, these transactions have had the cumulative effect of increasing the wealth of Henry Singleton.

Unlike most corporations, Teledyne has been able to spend a

large portion of its cash flow on repurchasing its own stock, largely because it has never paid a cash dividend. Although he had managed to increase his wealth by about $148 million in just eight years, Henry Singleton was not finished. In 1984, Teledyne announced yet another tender offer for a large portion of its common stock. This time the company paid over $1.7 billion to repurchase over 42 percent of its remaining outstanding stock. Over a period of twelve years, then, Teledyne has spent a total of $2.7 billion in corporate funds repurchasing its own stock. During this same period, as the amount of Teledyne stock outstanding has plummeted, the equity position of the founder in the company has increased from 2 percent to over 14 percent. Of course, he did not actually buy any more Teledyne stock, but simply held on to what he already had. Last but not least, the value of his stock in Teledyne has increased from $12 million to over $490 million since 1972. If Teledyne had not repurchased any of its shares during this period, Singleton would still own 2 percent of the total outstanding stock in the company. However, this stock would be worth only about $70 million. In this case, the fact that Singleton has been able to exercise control over Teledyne and manipulate its financial structure has added over $420 million to his fortune. Of course, other Teledyne stockholders were not forced to sell their shares back to the company. However, Singleton gave them every incentive to do so by refusing to pay any cash dividends. He could ignore the issue of cash dividends because he drew a large salary from the company for serving as its chairman.

DEBTS FOR SUCCESS

Some financiers have used copious amounts of debt to amass their fortunes. Specifically, they have acquired companies by using borrowed funds and have later repaid those loans either from the cash flow generated by those companies or from the sale of some of the assets of those companies. Using this technique, they have been able to accumulate large fortunes relatively quickly. Few entrepreneurs have used debt as extensively or as successfully as Kirk Kerkorian. He got his start in business by buying surplus transport airplanes from the military, renovating them, and selling them to commercial airlines at a substantial profit. Later, he began chartering these airplanes to the military as well as occasional tourist groups. In 1962, he sold his charter airline, Trans International Airlines, to Studebaker Corporation. Kerkorian eventually received over $2.7 million in Studebaker common stock, which he quickly sold. Two years later, he repurchased Trans International from Studebaker for $2.5 million. Instead of using his own money for this purchase, Kerkorian borrowed the entire amount from Bank of America. In 1965, he took Trans International public and sold just enough stock in the company to repay the bank loan. He kept 66 percent of the stock in Trans International, worth over $7 million. Three years later, Kerkorian sold Trans International again, this time to Transamerica Corporation, a large financial services corporation. He received $85 million in Transamerica common stock for his remaining 58 percent interest in Trans International. Even before he sold out to Transamerica, Kerkorian was preparing other deals.

Two years after he took his charter airline company public, Kerkorian had sold a small block of his Trans International stock in order to enter the gambling business. In 1967, he paid $12 million for the Flamingo Hotel, one of the oldest casinos in Las Vegas. About the same time, he borrowed $30 million from a local bank to begin construction on an even larger casino, the International Hotel. In order to raise the capital needed to complete this project, Kerkorian transferred his interests in both casinos to a new company, International Leisure Corporation. He then sold 15 percent of the stock in this company to the public for a total of $24 million. Two years later, he borrowed $72 million from two European investment banks to purchase stock in Metro-Goldwyn-Mayer, a major film company. Altogether, he paid $84 million for almost 40 percent of the outstanding stock in MGM. In 1971, however, the stock that Kerkorian had pledged as collateral for his loans declined in value, and he was forced to sell the remainder of his stock in International Leisure in order to reduce his indebtedness. Altogether, Hilton Hotels paid him $48 million for his 83 percent stake in International Leisure. He used the proceeds and a $25 million loan from Bank of America to repay the $72 million he had borrowed to purchase his MGM stock. That same year, Kerkorian announced that MGM would enter the gambling business by buying an old casino in Las Vegas, the Bonanza, and building a new casino, the MGM Grand Hotel. He subsequently split MGM into two companies: a film company, MGM Films, and a casino company, MGM Grand Hotels. By 1980, Kerkorian owned roughly 47 percent of the stock in two companies, worth a total of roughly $300 million.

In 1981, MGM Films agreed to acquire another film company, United Artists, from Transamerica Corporation for $380 million. In order to finance this acquisition, MGM was forced to issue additional stock. Kerkorian, in turn, was forced to buy more MGM stock in order to maintain his equity position in the company. Altogether, he bought $110 million of MGM stock, raising his stake to over 54 percent. Because he did not have that much cash on hand, Kerkorian borrowed $100 million from the Bank of America and pledged his initial MGM Films stock as collateral. The two film companies were then merged to form MGM/UA Entertainment. Kerkorian also consolidated his control over MGM Grand Hotels during this period. In 1984, the company exchanged $186 million in preferred stock for 28 percent of its common stock. As a result of this exchange offer, Kerkorian was left with over 69 percent of the common stock in the company. The following year, he agreed to sell MGM Grand Hotels to Bally Manufacturing for $440 million. Kerkorian received $286 million in cash for his stock in MGM Grand Hotels, more than enough to pay off all of his loans. Later that same year, he agreed to sell MGM/UA Entertainment to Turner Broadcasting System for $1.5 billion. He used $470 million of the roughly $750 million he received for his 50 percent stake in MGM/UA Entertainment to repurchase its United Artists subsidiary. After selling some United Artists stock to the public, he wound up with 80 percent of the stock in the company. The United Artists stock and other assets held by Tracinda, the Kerkorian family holding company, are currently worth well over $600 million.

Some entrepreneurs accumulate wealth by using debt issued by companies they control to acquire other companies. One example of this pattern involves the Tisch brothers. Laurence and Preston Tisch took over a resort hotel owned by their parents and built it into a small hotel chain. In 1958, they had Tisch Hotels buy stock in Loews Theatres, a venerable theater chain that owned valuable real estate in many large cities. Within two years, they had accumulated over 18 percent of the stock in the company, and Laurence Tisch was elected chairman. Once they had gained control of Loews, the Tisches closed many old theaters located in downtown areas and leased the land to other businesses. By 1964, Tisch Hotels had amassed 23 percent of the outstanding stock in Loews at a cost of nearly $9 million. About the same time, the Tisches had Loews start buying back shares of its common stock from the public. Over the next four years, Loews Theatres spent over $14 million to repurchase more than 28 percent of its stock. As a result of these stock repurchases, the Loews stock owned by Tisch Hotels eventually represented 32 percent of the outstanding stock in the company, worth $210 million by 1968. That same year, the Tisch brothers decided to acquire Lorillard Corporation, a large tobacco and food company. They financed the acquisition by using debt in the form of debentures issued by Loews. In all, Loews issued $450 million in debentures and warrants to acquire Lorillard. Because no shares of Loews common stock were issued in the acquisition, the Tisch brothers were not forced to dilute their equity in the company. Their family holding company, Tisch Hotels, still owned 32 percent of the stock in Loews Corporation.

In 1975, the Tisch brothers decided to acquire a controlling interest in CNA Financial, a large financial holding company. Loews paid approximately $100 million in cash for 57 percent of the outstanding stock in CNA. This acquisition was financed largely by loans from a group of banks. Over the next four years, Loews spent another $230 million purchasing additional CNA shares. It eventually bought

83 percent of the stock in CNA Financial. However, the rapid expansion of Loews had created one problem. In 1969, as an incentive to induce Lorillard stockholders to exchange their common stock for debentures, Loews had also issued warrants that allowed them to purchase Loews common stock at a fixed price anytime during the next decade. As the market value of Loews stock increased, the company faced the prospect of issuing an additional $258 million in common stock. The issuance of this much new stock would reduce the equity position of the Tisch brothers in Loews Corporation from 32 percent to only 22 percent. In order to avoid any dilution of their equity position, the Tisches had Loews begin repurchasing its warrants and much of its common stock from the public. Between 1973 and 1984, Loews spent $386 million to repurchase enough stock and warrants to reduce its potential outstanding stock by 48 percent. As a result, the equity position of the Tisch brothers in Loews Corporation increased from 32 percent to 45 percent by 1985. This drastic reduction in the amount of common stock outstanding also increased the value of the stock held by the Tisch brothers. That year, they announced that they were selling $160 million of their Loews stock. Their remaining 36 percent of the stock in the company is now worth $1.4 billion.

IN PURSUIT OF PRIVACY

Sometimes an entrepreneur employs *recapitalization* as part of a larger strategy to take a company private. This strategy requires an entrepreneur to induce the public stockholders in a corporation to exchange their common stock for preferred stock or debentures issued by the same corporation. Of course, any reduction in the amount of outstanding common stock in a corporation increases the equity positions of the remaining stockholders. One example of this strategy involves American Financial Corporation, a large insurance and financial services company assembled over the past three decades by Carl H.

Lindner and his two brothers, Robert and Richard Lindner. The Lindner brothers started in business with a family dairy store in Cincinnati. In 1940, Carl Lindner expanded the store into a chain of retail dairy stores. Several years later, he convinced his brothers that they should enter the banking business. In 1959, the Lindners went into debt in order to acquire three small Cincinnati savings and loan associations, which they later merged to form one of the largest savings and loan institutions in Ohio. American Financial Corporation, their financial holding company, went public two years later. By then, the three Lindner brothers owned 46 percent of the stock in the company. Over the next several years, their company acquired a number of smaller companies. However, American Financial did not become a major financial services company until 1972, when it acquired National General Corporation, a conglomerate that owned Great America Insurance Company, a large casualty insurance company.

American Financial financed almost all of its acquisitions, including its acquisition of National General, by issuing additional shares of its common stock. Consequently, these acquisitions diluted the equity positions of Carl and Robert Lindner, the two brothers who remained with the company after the departure of Richard Lindner. By 1973, they owned less than 25 percent of the outstanding common stock in American Financial. In order to strengthen their control over the company and enhance the value of their stock, they initiated a series of exchange offers designed to reduce the amount of common stock held by the public. Between 1974 and 1978, American Financial conducted five exchange offers in which stockholders were offered either debentures or preferred stock for their common stock. During this five-year period, American Financial repurchased over 58 percent of its common stock. In exchange for this common stock, the company issued over $58 million in preferred stock and $86 million in debentures. As a result of this recapitalization program, the proportion of American Financial common stock held by Carl and Robert Lindner and their families almost doubled. By 1979, they owned over 48 percent of the outstanding common stock in American Financial, worth $44 million. Of course, they had not purchased any additional shares of common stock during this period. Indeed, they had even sold some of their American Financial stock. The increase in their equity positions was achieved solely by the reduction in the number of common shares outstanding.

In 1979, Carl Lindner decided that the Lindner family should take their financial services company private by buying out its public stockholders. He proposed to accomplish this by having American Financial exchange debentures and preferred stock for the common stock not held by members of the Lindner family. However, this attempt to take the company private was called off after an investment banking firm retained by American Financial concluded that the value of the debentures and preferred stock being offered to the public stockholders in exchange for their common stock was inadequate. Carl Lindner was so furious about this turn of events that he fired the investment banking firm and called off the acquisition. Two years later, American Financial offered once again to repurchase all of its common stock from the public in exchange for cash or preferred stock. The value of the debentures and preferred stock offered to the public stockholders was increased somewhat, and the new investment banking firm hired by American Financial concluded that the offer was adequate. As a result, Carl Lindner, his wife and children, and three of his nephews became the sole owners of the common stock of American Financial. This diversified financial corporation now has over $6 billion in assets. However, the company is also deeply in debt and must still devote much of its income to paying interest and dividend payments on the debentures and preferred stock issued to its former public stockholders. Despite its heavy debt load, American Financial Corporation is probably worth at least $300 million.

A more convoluted but equally successful example of this strategy for accumulating wealth involves the Steinberg family and Reliance Financial Group. Saul Steinberg became an entrepreneur two years after he graduated from college. In 1961, he borrowed $100,000 from his father, Julius Steinberg, and his uncle, Mayer Steinberg, to found Leasco, a computer leasing firm. By the time the company went public four years later, it had assets of over $5 million. At that point, Saul

Steinberg, along with his father and his uncle, owned roughly 40 percent of Leasco stock, worth $20 million. Leasco was highly profitable from the outset because it leased computers at lower costs than its competitors. Steinberg was able to lease his computers at discount prices because he required his customers to sign long-term leases that could not be canceled. He then used these long-term leases as collateral for loans to purchase additional computers. In 1968, Saul Steinberg decided to expand his operations into the field of financial services by having Leasco acquire Reliance Insurance Company, a major insurance company. Because it was much smaller than the company it was acquiring, Leasco did not have nearly enough cash to purchase Reliance Insurance outright. Instead, the acquisition was financed entirely with newly issued Leasco preferred stock. Reliance stockholders received preferred stock and warrants in exchange for their Reliance Insurance common stock. They were induced to accept the offer by the fact that the preferred stock issued by Leasco paid a higher dividend than the Reliance Insurance common stock. In all, Leasco issued over $292 million in preferred stock to former Reliance Insurance stockholders.

In 1973, Leasco changed its name to Reliance Group. That same year, Saul Steinberg took the first steps to recapitalize Reliance Group by having the company repurchase some of its common stock. In two separate tender offers, Reliance Group exchanged debentures for common stock. The company also purchased large amounts of its common stock for cash on the open market. Over a two-year period, Reliance Group repurchased 46 percent of its outstanding common stock. The company had to issue approximately $67 million in debentures in order to finance the bulk of these repurchases. After a brief hiatus, Reliance began buying more of its common stock on the open market in 1978. During that year alone, the company spent $150 million in cash repurchasing its common stock. By then, Saul Steinberg and his father, the only members of the family serving as directors of the company at the time, owned slightly more than 15 percent of the common stock in Reliance Group. The following year, Reliance Group divested itself of its computer leasing operations by distributing Leasco stock to Reliance Group stockholders. Consequently, the Steinbergs, who were the principal stockholders in Reliance Group, became the principal stockholders in Leasco. That same year, Saul Steinberg spent $9 million buying additional Leasco stock. The Steinbergs soon owned 51 percent of the stock in Leasco. During this period, Reliance Group began repurchasing more of its own common stock. In 1979, it sold a major subsidiary for cash and used $98 million of the proceeds to repurchase more of its own common stock. The following year, Leasco issued $100 million in debentures in order to finance the purchase of additional Reliance Group common stock.

By 1981, Leasco had acquired 25 percent of the common stock in Reliance Group. Saul Steinberg was now ready to take Reliance Group private. Although the Steinbergs still owned only about 15 percent of Reliance Group common stock outright, they controlled the 25 percent of Reliance Group common stock held by Leasco. Later that year, Saul Steinberg and other members of the Steinberg family offered to buy the 60 percent of Reliance Group common stock still held by the public for a total of $530 million. The public stockholders in Reliance Group were offered a choice of either cash and preferred stock or cash and debentures for their Reliance Group common stock. The public stockholders in Leasco were offered a similar choice. As a result, only $96 million of the $530 million purchase price was paid in cash. The remainder comprised preferred stock and debentures issued by a new holding company, Reliance Group Holdings. Indeed, cash was in such short supply that the Steinbergs admitted that they might be forced to sell some of the real estate held by Reliance Group in order to finance the acquisition. Saul Steinberg and other members of the Steinberg family now own all of the common stock in Reliance Group Holdings, a diversified financial corporation with assets of over $5 billion. In all, the Steinbergs invested less than $10 million of their own money in the company. Given enough time, the company will probably be able to redeem all of the debentures and preferred stock issued to finance its own acquisition. Although it is still burdened with debt, Reliance Group Holdings is probably worth about $300 million.

The most lucrative example of recapitalization as a prelude to going private involves John W. Kluge and Metromedia Inc. Kluge was a successful entrepreneur who had amassed a small fortune in the food distribution business before he became involved with Metromedia. In 1958, Kluge decided to purchase a substantial block of stock in a small and struggling broadcasting company. He became chairman of the company the next year and later changed its name to Metromedia. By 1964, Kluge owned almost 10 percent of the common stock in the company, worth about $8 million. Over the next several years, Metromedia went into debt in order to acquire several other radio and television stations in major markets. It also acquired a large outdoor advertising company that owned over a thousand billboards across the nation. In 1977, Kluge decided that Metromedia should repurchase some of its stock. During the next two years, the company spent $23 million in cash and issued $70 million in debentures to repurchase over 31 percent of its common stock. After these repurchases, the Metromedia stock held by Kluge represented 16 percent of the stock in the company. At that point, this stock was worth $51 million. By 1982, Metromedia had become a major broadcasting corporation with seven television stations in such major markets as New York, Los Angeles, and Boston. It also operated fourteen radio stations. That same year, Metromedia spent another $200 million in cash to repurchase more of its common stock. As a result, Kluge finally wound up with 26 percent of the stock in the company, worth $158 million.

In 1983, John Kluge announced plans to take Metromedia private. In a complex financial restructuring, a new holding company was formed to purchase all of the stock in Metromedia. This holding company, in turn, borrowed $1.3 billion from a consortium of banks. In exchange for their common stock, stockholders in Metromedia received a total of $725 million in cash and debentures issued by the new holding company worth roughly another $625 million. Even Kluge received $114 million in cash and debentures in exchange for a portion of his Metromedia stock. However, he exchanged his remaining Metromedia stock for over 75 percent of the common stock in the new company. The following year, the new Metromedia formed a subsidiary, consisting of its television stations. This subsidiary then issued $1.3 billion in debentures in order to retire the bank loans to the parent company. In 1985, Metromedia agreed to sell its television station subsidiary for about $2 billion. According to this agreement,

Metromedia will be relieved of the $1.3 billion in debentures issued by its television subsidiary and will receive $650 million in cash. Metromedia was left with its fourteen radio stations, its outdoor advertising subsidiary, and a telecommunications operation. According to one estimate, the remaining company is worth about $1.4 billion. The 75 percent of the company held by Kluge is probably worth approximately $1.5 billion. In short, an aggressive recapitalization program enabled John Kluge to increase the value of his initial investment in Metromedia from slightly more than $8 million to roughly $1.5 billion in a little over two decades.

9

Life-Styles
of the
Rich

For most people, including most of the corporate rich, wealth is not a goal in itself. Wealth is important to members of the corporate rich primarily because it provides them with the personal autonomy that comes with financial security. It is also important because it enables them to enjoy some of the minor luxuries, such as spacious homes and extended vacations, that contribute to the quality of their lives. Consequently, the members of corporate rich families are different from the members of less affluent families, not simply because they possess more wealth, but because this wealth enables them to pursue very different life-styles. Some of the differences between the life-styles of the very rich and those of the merely affluent are obvious. In purely material terms, the rich live better than everyone else. Wealthy individuals generally own large homes located in exclusive neighborhoods. Moreover, these homes typically contain fine furniture and original works of art. Those who are rich are also able to eat in the best restaurants and shop in the best stores. When they are sick, they are able to afford the very best medical care. As a rule, they also send their children to the most exclusive private schools. Those members of the corporate rich who have particularly large fortunes are likely to indulge in various esoteric pursuits ranging from art collecting to breeding and racing thoroughbred horses. Most of these activities are beyond the financial resources of the average American. Although a few affluent individuals are able to engage, to a limited extent, in some of these activities, they are rarely able to pursue all of the activities that are part and parcel of the life-styles of the very rich.

Even though they enjoy a comparatively high standard of living, most wealthy individuals are not really extravagant. Contrary to popular opinion, they do not engage in ostentatious displays of their wealth. In point of fact, most of the very rich are rather conservative about their personal finances. The corporate rich are acutely aware of the fact that their status in society is based solely on the fact that they possess great wealth. Consequently, they are almost obsessed with the problem of conserving their capital. Indeed, because much of the wealth owned by members of the corporate rich is held in trusts, many of them must be content with subsisting on the income provided by their trusts. Nevertheless, there is considerable evidence that the corporate rich are willing and able to spend large sums of money on certain items. For example, most scions of corporate rich families own very expensive homes. Moreover, some of the wealthiest members of these families have purchased incredibly expensive works of art. Others have purchased expensive thoroughbred horses. At first glance, these lavish expenditures seem both superfluous and idiosyncratic. They appear to confirm the stereotype of the eccentric millionaire. However, the patterns of consumption displayed by the corporate rich are neither arbitrary nor capricious. In fact, the members of different wealthy families often indulge in common pursuits. These common patterns of consumption indicate that the corporate rich possess relatively distinct and identifiable life-styles. Although there is considerable variation among individuals, these life-styles are clearly influenced by a number of social and financial considerations.

STATUS INVESTMENTS

The life-styles of the very rich were first examined in detail by Thorstein Veblen in his classic study *The Theory of the Leisure Class.* According to Veblen, the members of the "leisure class" engaged in "conspicuous consumption" in order to gain social status by demonstrating the extent of their wealth to others. For that reason, they purchased various luxury items, such as expensive jewelry and furs, and displayed them as ostentatiously as possible. Indeed, the ultimate form of conspicuous consumption was the purchase of an object that was both expensive and useless. Only by such ostentatious expenditures could the very rich demonstrate the superfluousness of their wealth. Very few members of the corporate rich engage in this type of conspicuous consumption today. To begin with, the corporate rich have little interest in provoking the envy and enmity of those who are less fortunate by such ostentatious displays of their wealth. In point of fact, ostentatious behavior of this sort is generally considered vulgar by the members of those socially prominent families that comprise the upper class in America. As a result, the children of wealthy entrepreneurs are prone to emulate the more conservative life-styles of the more established members of the upper class. Many of their expenditures are intended primarily to ensure their status within the upper class. Consequently, the ideal expenditure is one that represents a sound financial investment and that simultaneously enhances the social status and political influence of the family. In this sense, many of the major expenditures of the corporate rich are essentially status investments.

Education provides an example of such an expenditure. The members of corporate rich families usually provide their children with private educations. Their investment in education involves both tuition and room and board at exclusive preparatory schools and again at elite private colleges and universities. In fact, the total cost of tuition and room and board for several years of private education can be substantial. For individuals from merely affluent families, the cost of a private education is an investment in the economic future of their children. They expect their children to benefit financially from this investment. In this view, graduation from an exclusive prep school increases the likelihood that a son or daughter will be admitted to an elite private university. Similarly, graduation from an elite private university increases the likelihood that the son or daughter will obtain a lucrative managerial position or gain admittance to a prestigious professional school. The motives of the corporate rich are different. Ordinarily, the children and grandchildren of a wealthy entrepreneur do not have to worry about pursuing careers in business or the professions. Indeed, most of them are able to subsist quite nicely on the dividend income they receive from their stock in the family corporation. Moreover, any male heirs who desire a career in business can usually obtain a managerial position in the family corporation. Given these circumstances, private educations may seem totally superfluous for the scions of corporate rich families. However, the decision to invest in the cost of attendance at prep schools and elite private universities is often based on social rather than economic considerations.

For the members of corporate rich families, the cost of a private education is an investment in the social future of their children. As a matter of fact, it represents an investment in the social future of the entire family. The members of these wealthy families benefit in several ways from sending their children to exclusive prep schools and universities. To begin with, attendance at prep schools and private elite universities provides the children and grandchildren of wealthy entrepreneurs with the cultural capital required for admittance into the most exclusive social circles of the upper class. One of the latent functions of prep schools, in particular, is to inculcate their students with the mannerisms, speech patterns, and dress codes of the upper class. Attendance at prep schools and private elite universities also provides the children and grandchildren of these wealthy entrepreneurs with valuable social capital. Because these schools are all relatively small, the scions of corporate rich families are able to meet and form friendships with the scions of other wealthy and socially prominent families. As one observer of these schools has observed, "they were places where children of both old and new wealth mingled." Indeed, the very fact that members of a corporate rich family have attended exclusive prep schools and elite private universities confers a measure of social status on the entire family. In some cases, several generations of family members have attended the same prep schools and elite private colleges and universities. Individual affiliations with these prestigious educational institutions eventually become incorporated into the symbolic estate of the entire family.

For precisely these reasons, many wealthy entrepreneurs have insisted that their children and grandchildren receive private educations. John D. Rockefeller, for example, had only a rudimentary education. Nevertheless, his son attended prep schools and eventually graduated from Brown University. His five grandsons also attended prep schools before going on to such elite private colleges and universities as Princeton, Yale, and Dartmouth. Similarly, Henry Ford had very little formal education. His son, Edsel Ford, attended a prep school. However, he did not go on to college. Instead, Edsel Ford became an officer and director of Ford Motor Company when he was only twenty-one years old. However, the three grandsons of Henry Ford did attend prep schools before going on to either Yale or Princeton. A very similar pattern obtains in most other corporate rich families. In some ways, attendance at an elite private university is at least as important as graduation. After all, a college degree is usually of only limited importance to the scion of a corporate rich family. As a result, more than a few of the descendants of wealthy entrepreneurs have failed to graduate from college. For example, Winthrop Rockefeller and Henry Ford II both dropped out of Yale, and Benson Ford dropped out of Princeton. It is possible, of course, that these scions of corporate rich families were at an academic disadvantage at these schools. Both prep schools and private colleges and universities depend heavily on contributions from their alumni for their financial survival. Consequently, an admissions officer may find it difficult to reject a marginal applicant from a wealthy family that might someday be induced to contribute generously to the school.

The costs of providing private educations for their children are relatively small expenditures for most members of the corporate rich. However, the distinctive patterns of consumption common to corporate rich families indicate that major expenditures by the members of these families are also governed by both social and financial imperatives. Despite the fact that they often possess substantial fortunes that provide them with generous incomes, even the wealthiest members of the corporate rich do not pursue lives of unabashed luxury. Indeed, the members of established corporate rich families are likely to denigrate the ostentatious displays of wealth by others as the déclassé actions of the nouveau riche. Most of the major expenditures by wealthy entrepreneurs and their descendants are based on a series of financial and social considerations. To begin with, most major purchases are not cases of consumption, despite the fact that the object purchased may provide the purchaser with some immediate gratification. To the contrary, these purchases are usually investments in disguise inasmuch as they provide the purchaser with the opportunity for capital appreciation. Moreover, these major purchases are typically status investments inasmuch as they enhance the status of the purchaser within the upper class. In a few cases, these purchases also enhance the social status and political influence of the purchaser within the local community. The inclination of the corporate rich to indulge in such apparent extravagances as mansions, cattle ranches, paintings, rare coins, thoroughbred horses, and even professional sports teams becomes intelligible only if these purchases are viewed as status investments.

NO PLACES LIKE HOME

One of the most common status investments of the corporate rich is housing. Residential real estate has usually been a good investment in terms of both capital appreciation and tax benefits. Of course, the homes of the corporate rich are generally much larger and more expensive than ordinary homes. Indeed, many of these homes are so large that they can only be described as mansions. They are often designed by architects to satisfy the particular whims of their owners. For example, homes owned by members of the corporate rich often contain very large dining rooms and living rooms that are suitable for entertaining. Moreover, they are typically built on spacious landscaped lots in exclusive residential neighborhoods. Until relatively recently, it was common for wealthy entrepreneurs and their children to build homes that were conscious replicas of the country estates of the European aristocracy. The du Ponts, for example, were one of the first corporate rich families in America. During the early part of this century, several of the wealthiest members of this family built large mansions that served as monuments to their newfound wealth and status. As a result, the country north of Wilmington, Delaware, became dotted with a series of large mansions situated on spacious estates. The owners of these estates gave them vaguely aristocratic names such as Granogue, Winterthur, Guyencourt, Chevannes, St. Armour, Nemours, and Bellevue. The largest and most lavish of these was Longwood, the estate of Pierre S. du Pont II, once the wealthiest member of the du Pont family. Longwood consists of a 200-room mansion situated among 1,000 acres of manicured gardens.

Other corporate rich families of that period adopted similar tastes in residences. When John D. Rockefeller moved from Cleveland to New York City, he bought a massive town house. A few years later, he purchased a summer home overlooking the Hudson River valley near Pocantico, New York. It was there that he built Kykuit, his fifty-room granite mansion. He and his son, John D. Rockefeller, Jr., bought land adjoining this property until the Pocantico estate encompassed 4,100 acres of fields and forests. Pocantico was eventually transformed into a lavish family compound for the private enjoyment of successive generations of Rockefellers. The estate has its own eighteen-hole golf course and miles of bridlepaths that meander through the forest. However, the most popular building among the Rockefeller grandchildren and great-grandchildren was a two-story gymnasium complete with an indoor swimming pool, indoor tennis and basketball courts, bowling alleys, and billiard room. After John D. Rockefeller passed away, his son moved into Kykuit. Most of his children, in turn, built separate homes on the estate. Another family of comparable wealth, the Mellons, lived in similar fashion near Pittsburgh. Andrew W. Mellon, for example, bought a large mansion on the edge of the city and enlarged it by adding tennis courts, two bowling alleys, and a huge indoor swimming pool. He later gave the house to his son, Paul Mellon. However, Paul Mellon eventually abandoned Pittsburgh for his horse-breeding farm in Virginia. Most of the other members of the Mellon family, the children and grandchildren of Richard B. Mellon, built spacious homes on Rolling Rock Farms, a 12,000-acre estate in the Ligonier Valley outside Pittsburgh.

The desire of the corporate rich to live life on a baronial scale probably reached its inevitable climax with San Simeon, the opulent castle built by William R. Hearst. San Simeon was a working ranch along the coast of California north of San Luis Obispo when it was purchased by George Hearst in 1865. Both George Hearst and his only son, William Hearst, added to the ranch until it encompassed 239,000 acres. In 1919, William Hearst decided to build a castle on an isolated mountaintop overlooking the ranch and the ocean. Although he intended it as a retreat where he could entertain his many friends and acquaintances, the castle also served as a museum for the many antiques and art objects that Hearst had purchased from castles and cathedrals across Europe. Hearst would sometimes invite a hundred guests at a time to spend several days at the ranch. He even built a large zoo on the property for the amusement of his guests. Craftsmen worked continually on the castle for over three decades. In all, the castle and guesthouses cost Hearst roughly $30 million. After William Hearst died in 1951, his five sons and their families continued to use the castle for vacations. However, the castle was so large that even his children could not afford to maintain it as a vacation home. Finally, the Hearst Corporation, which owned the property, tried to sell it. Unable to find any buyers, the company offered to donate the castle to the University of California, but the university declined the gift because of its enormous maintenance costs. After much negotiation, the state of California reluctantly agreed to accept the castle and the surrounding grounds as a state park in 1957. It is now a profitable tourist attraction.

Today, the homes of the corporate rich are generally less massive and ostentatious than those built earlier in the century by the du Ponts, Rockefellers, and Mellons. Indeed, most of the huge mansions built decades ago are simply too large to be maintained as single-family residences. Many of them have been either sold to institutions or simply converted into museums. For example, when Pierre S. du Pont died in 1954, he left $80 million to his Longwood Foundation in order to maintain and operate his Longwood estate as a public museum and garden. Similarly, Paul Mellon later donated the massive mansion in Pittsburgh given to him by his father to a nearby college, which converted it into a somewhat luxurious dormitory. Last but not least, the great-grandchildren of John D. Rockefeller recently decided that they did not want to inherit the Pocantico estate from their parents, because most of them had no desire to own homes there. They also rejected plans to despoil the estate by converting it into a massive residential real estate development. The great-grandchildren of John D. Rockefeller finally convinced their parents that they should each bequeath their share of the estate to the state of New York. Pocantico will eventually become a state park. Only a few of the wealthiest members of the corporate rich still attempt to live in manorial splendor. In 1972, J. Seward Johnson, one of the sons of the founder of Johnson & Johnson, began construction on a lavish 140-acre estate near Princeton, New Jersey. Although he already had several homes, his new wife insisted that they build a new and more lavish mansion. The mansion and nearby buildings, which contain a total of forty rooms, reportedly cost $21 million.

By and large, however, the corporate rich of today live in homes that are comparatively modest. Indeed, most of the grandchildren and great-grandchildren of wealthy entrepreneurs live in homes that are much less opulent than those occupied by those entrepreneurs and their children. For example, only a few of the great-grandchildren of John D. Rockefeller live in houses large enough to be called mansions. Instead, most of them live in spacious houses or apartments that are no different from those occupied by many affluent doctors, lawyers, and managers. The major exception is John D. Rockefeller IV, who purchased a large mansion on 15 acres in Washington for $6 million after he was elected to the Senate in 1984. Similarly, most of the younger members of the Mellon and du Pont families live in homes that are less than mansions. There are many reasons for this change in residential styles. Large mansions are very expensive to maintain and usually require a large staff of servants. These mansions and their large domestic staffs were suited to a style of entertaining that is no longer fashionable. For example, it is no longer common, even among the corporate rich, to entertain a large group of guests for a weekend. Today, even the wealthiest members of the corporate rich live relatively modestly. Gordon Getty, for example, lives much more modestly than his father. J. Paul Getty lived in a huge palace, Sutton Place, in England, attended by a large number of servants. Gordon Getty lives in a small mansion in San Francisco with only a small domestic staff. Although his house has a large enclosed courtyard for entertaining guests at dinner parties, it does not have a large number of bedrooms.

One of the most important advantages of wealth is the ability to live anywhere and everywhere. It is not uncommon for members of the corporate rich to have at least two homes, one more or less permanent home and a vacation home. In fact, the wealthiest of the corporate rich usually have several homes. Wealthy individuals often own vacation homes in Florida or southern California that they use only during the coldest months of winter. Conversely, many of these same individuals also own vacation homes in Maine and Canada that they use only during the summer months. It is possible to gain a fairly precise idea of the housing situation of some of the members of the corporate rich from the appraised value of their homes as stated in their estate tax returns. For example, Charles W. Engelhard, the son of the founder of Engelhard Minerals, had five different residences when he died in 1971. His primary residence, situated on his Cragwood estate outside Far Hills, New Jersey, was appraised at $460,000. Camp Chaleur, a summer lodge on the Grand Cascapedia River in Quebec, was appraised at $305,000. His winter home in Boca Grande, Florida, was appraised at $269,000. Engelhard also maintained a relatively modest residence, appraised at $178,000, near Aiken, South Carolina, in connection with his horse-breeding and racing operations. Last but not least, he owned a small estate in Austria that was appraised at $225,000. Although Engelhard was one of the wealthiest members of the corporate rich at the time, his residences were not especially opulent. Even at that point in time, many members of the corporate rich owned homes that were larger or more expensive.

The vacation homes of the corporate rich are frequently located in very exclusive resort areas. Perhaps the most popular of all the winter resort areas is Palm Beach, Florida. Many wealthy individuals own residences in Palm Beach or in such nearby communities as Hobe Sound and Delray Beach. Palm Beach itself is a fourteen-mile-long island connected to the mainland by three bridges. Among its residents are the scions of several corporate rich families, including Willis H. du Pont, Henry Ford II, and Ogden M. Phipps. Several wealthy entrepreneurs, such as Max M. Fisher and Estee Lauder, also own homes there. Because even comparatively modest beachfront homes routinely cost as much as $3 million, Palm Beach may well be the most exclusive community in the entire country. Other members of the corporate rich prefer to spend their winters in Palm Springs, California. Many wealthy individuals own residences in Palm Springs or in the surrounding communities of Rancho Mirage, or Indian Springs, Nevada. The residents of the area include such scions of corporate rich families as Leonard K. Firestone, Amory Houghton, and James Kemper. Wealthy entrepreneurs, such as Robert McCulloch and Allen E. Paulson, also own homes there. The most palatial residence in the area is owned by Walter Annenberg, who transformed 240 acres of desert near Rancho Mirage into a plush estate complete with its own golf course. In recent years, his estate has served as an unofficial retreat for several Republican presidents. Other resort communities in which members of the corporate rich maintain winter homes include Naples, Florida; Santa Barbara, California; Sea Island, Georgia; Lyford Cay in the Bahamas; and Antigua in the British West Indies.

The corporate rich also own summer residences. In earlier decades, many wealthy families had summer homes Newport, Rhode Island. This community became a popular summer resort among the corporate rich because of its proximity to New York City. With the development of aviation, however, wealthy individuals began to seek out more remote resort locations for their summer residences. One of the most secluded of these communities is Mount Desert Island in

Maine. The scions of several corporate rich families, including Benson Ford, John D. Rockefeller, Jr., and Roger Milliken, built summer homes on the island. Sailing is a popular pastime among the corporate rich who own summer homes in coastal resorts from Maine to Maryland. Similarly, boating is a popular pastime among the corporate rich who spend their summers in the lake country of Canada. For example, the scions of several corporate rich families, including J. Irwin Miller and Henry Hillman, own summer homes on Lake Muskoka in Ontario, Canada. Other corporate rich families own working cattle ranches that they use as summer homes. Malcolm Forbes, for example, the son of the founder of *Forbes* magazine, owns a 20-square-mile ranch in Montana near Yellowstone National Park. A great many wealthy entrepreneurs and their descendants own cattle ranches, including Robert O. Anderson, John Dorrance III, Payne Payson Middleton, and Peter Widener, Jr. Even Nelson A. Rockefeller, a confirmed urbanite, owned a large ranch in Texas. Wealthy individuals often buy cattle ranches because they are able to deduct the costs of operating the ranch from their incomes. In short, ranches provide their owners with secluded summer homes as well as substantial tax benefits.

COLLECTORS

One of the most popular forms of status investment among the corporate rich involves collecting art and other rare objects. Perhaps the most eclectic collector among the corporate rich was Josiah K. Lilly, Jr., a grandson of the founder of Eli Lilly and Company. By the time he died in 1966, Josiah Lilly had assembled a small but respectable art collection that included paintings by such artists as Gainsborough, Reynolds, and Goya. These paintings were later sold to the Indianapolis Museum of Art for $1.6 million. Although his art collection was relatively modest, his other collections were not. To begin with, he amassed a collection of over 6,000 rare gold coins, which was later appraised at almost $24 million. His heirs agreed to donate these coins to the Smithsonian Institution in return for a reduction in the taxes on his estate. Congress quickly passed a special law that allowed his estate a credit of $5.5 million on its federal estate taxes. Lilly also collected 77,000 rare postage stamps. These stamps were later sold at auction for a total of $2.7 million. In addition, Lilly owned over 1,000 rare books when he died, even though he had disposed of most of his rare book collection several years earlier by presenting Indiana University with over 20,000 first editions of American and European books. He also assembled a large collection of antique swords, pistols, guns, and cannons. Last but not least, he collected over 3,700 miniature soldiers. This unique collection contained replicas in miniature of the uniforms, colors, and weapons of every regiment in the United States Army up to the present century.

Although the corporate rich have collected everything from jewelry to antique cars, most of them have collected art. Indeed, some of the greatest collections of art in America have been assembled by wealthy entrepreneurs and their descendants. Scions of corporate rich families who have become major art collectors over the past few decades include Paul Mellon, Nelson A. Rockefeller, John H. Whitney, and Walter H. Annenberg. Several wealthy entrepreneurs, such as Norton Simon, Armand Hammer, and Daniel J. Terra, have also established themselves as major art collectors. In many cases, these wealthy individuals have been encouraged and assisted by their spouses. For example, Paul Mellon was encouraged to become a major art collector by his second wife. Similarly, J. Seward Johnson, a son of the founder of Johnson & Johnson, had no interest in art until he married his third wife. Wealthy individuals collect art for different reasons. Few of them are authentic connoisseurs capable of evaluating the aesthetic and historical value of a particular work of art. To the contrary, most of the corporate rich purchase art for its extrinsic value. To begin with, they may purchase works by famous artists simply to gain public recognition as art collectors. Indeed, wealthy entrepreneurs often accumulate expensive, if not distinguished, art collections in order to establish their cultural credentials for membership in the exclusive social circles of the upper class. In addition, art collectors among the corporate rich may have financial reasons for buying works by artists with established reputations. They often consider art as simply another financial investment.

Perhaps the most ardent and astute art collector among the corporate rich is Paul Mellon. As the son of Andrew Mellon, the ubiquitous Pittsburgh financier, Paul Mellon has long been one of the richest men in America. To some extent, collecting art runs in his family. Although his father was not a connoisseur, he did spend $32 million assembling an impressive collection of Old Masters. In 1930, Andrew Mellon managed to purchase 21 paintings, including masterpieces by Van Dyck, Raphael, and Titian, from the Soviet government for $6.5 million. In 1937, he donated his collection to the United States government. To house it, Andrew Mellon contributed $16 million for the construction of a National Gallery of Art in Washington, D.C. Despite the example set by his father, Paul Mellon did not begin collecting art in earnest until he married his second wife in 1948. With her encouragement, he gradually amassed the largest and finest collection of French impressionist and postimpressionist paintings in private hands. His collection contains several important works by such artists as Cézanne, Renoir, Manet, and Picasso. In 1961, Paul Mellon also began collecting the works of such renowned British painters as Constable, Hogarth, and Turner. Over the next few years, he amassed the largest collection of British art outside England. In 1967, he donated his entire collection of British art, which then consisted of 1,000 paintings, 3,000 drawings, and 4,000 rare books worth $35 million, to Yale University. He also contributed $10 million to the university for the construction of a Center for British Art. Although he has lent some of them to several museums, he has not yet parted with most of his impressionist and postimpressionist paintings.

Several other entrepreneurs and their descendants have amassed large and valuable art collections. One of the most aggressive of these wealthy collectors is Norton Simon. Although he is now known primarily as an art collector, Simon made his first fortune as an entrepreneur. In 1931, he invested $7,000 in a bankrupt orange juice bottling company. Through a series of acquisitions and mergers, he transformed his small company into a large corporation engaged in such diverse activities as food processing and magazine publishing. Simon began his career as an art collector in 1954 with the purchase of three impressionist paintings. When he resigned as chairman of Norton Simon Inc. in 1969, he and his children owned at least 8 percent of the stock in the company, worth over $40 million. By that time, his personal art collection was worth about $35 million. In 1975, Simon offered to pay off the debts accumulated by the Pasadena Museum of Modern Art, a private nonprofit museum built on public land by a group of wealthy donors. He soon gained control of its board of trustees; installed his wife, the actress Jennifer Jones, as its chairman; and changed the name of the museum to the Norton Simon Museum. Although he has lent much of his collection to the museum for display, he has not yet donated much of it to the museum. Simon has also managed to turn art collecting into a philanthropic activity. Some of the works of art that he has added to his collection in recent years are actually owned by the Norton Simon Foundation. By 1980, he and his foundation had spent over $100 million for an art collection that was then worth an estimated $400 million.

In general, art has been a good investment over the years. Most of the art collections amassed by the corporate rich have appreciated greatly in value. Henry Ford II never aspired to be a major art collector, but he nevertheless managed to accumulate a respectable collection of impressionist paintings. When he divorced his second wife in 1980, he sold ten paintings, including works by Cézanne, Gauguin, Degas, and Van Gogh, to raise cash for the divorce settlement. These paintings were auctioned off in a single night for a total of $18.3 million. They brought several times what he had paid for them only a couple of decades earlier. For example, one of the paintings, a Van Gogh that he had purchased at auction for $200,000 in 1958, sold for $5.2 million. Three years later, Paul Mellon auctioned off forty works of art, a small portion of his collection, for a total of $12.1 million. One painting, a Manet, sold for $3.96 million. He had purchased it at auction in 1958 for $249,000. Art has been an especially profitable investment for those who started early. Geraldine Keen, in her classic study *Money and Art,* studied the multiplication in prices paid at auction for works of art by various artists between 1951 and 1969. She found, for example, that paintings by modern artists such as Picasso, Bonnard, and Utrillo had multiplied in price 37 times during this period. In purely financial terms, the best performer was Chagall, whose paintings sold in 1969 for roughly 50 times what they had cost in 1951. Even paintings by such Old Masters as Rembrandt, Botticelli, and Brueghel, which have been relatively expensive for a long time, had multiplied in price 7 times during this eighteen-year period.

With the escalation of art prices in recent years, many of the established art collectors among the corporate rich have sold more art than they have collected. In particular, some of the collectors who bought much of their art before prices reached their current astronomical levels have sold part of their collections. Norton Simon, for example, has sold some of his early acquisitions in order to finance purchases of other works of art. Between 1971 and 1973, he sold 122 paintings, drawings, and sculptures for a total of $13 million. He used part of the proceeds when he recently paid $4.5 million for an Old Master. At the same time, other members of the corporate rich have decided to start their own collections, even at current price levels. By and large, the corporate rich who have purchased major works in recent years are those who have just become art collectors. For example, Barbara Johnson, the widow of J. Seward Johnson, recently paid $4.8 million for a painting by Raphael. In fact, most of the new collectors are successful entrepreneurs who have just recently amassed enough wealth to indulge in such expensive pursuits. In 1982, Daniel J. Terra, the founder of Terra Chemicals, paid $3.2 million for a painting by Morse. Similarly, Wendell Cherry, one of the founders of Humana Inc., the hospital management company, recently paid $5.3 million for a painting by Picasso. Other successful entrepreneurs who have purchased expensive works of art in order to establish their credentials as art collectors include Saul Steinberg, the founder of Reliance Financial Corporation, and Meshulam Riklis, the founder of Rapid American Corporation.

Almost all of the most valuable art in America is owned by either public museums or wealthy individuals. Indeed, many of the paintings, drawings, and sculptures owned by public museums were

261

donated to them by the members of corporate rich families. Other works of art on display in these museums are often on loan from these same collectors. The Metropolitan Museum of Art in New York, for example, owes much of its collection to donations and bequests from such scions of wealthy capitalist families as John D. Rockefeller, Jr., Robert Lehman, and Henry O. Havemeyer. Similarly, the National Gallery of Art in Washington, D.C., has received major donations and bequests from Andrew W. Mellon, Ailsa Mellon Bruce, Lessing J. Rosenwald, and Peter A. B. Widener. Although museums often receive works of art as the result of bequests from the estates of wealthy collectors, these same collectors sometimes donate works of art to museums during their lifetime. In fact, a wealthy art collector can succeed in protecting a substantial portion of his or her income from federal income taxes by donating a work of art, particularly one that has appreciated greatly in value, to a museum. Specifically, an individual who donates a piece of art to a museum can claim a charitable deduction equal to its appraised value. Museums, in return, have usually been more than willing to provide the donor with a generous appraisal of the value of the donated work in order to increase the amount of the charitable deduction. The Internal Revenue Service has recently concluded that most of the art donated to museums was overvalued by museum appraisers. Conversely, works of art bequeathed to museums are often undervalued in order to reduce the taxes on those estates.

One of the best known art collectors in recent decades was J. Paul Getty. Like most other wealthy art collectors, he had several motives for collecting art. According to one biographer, Getty became an art collector initially because "it was a way to satisfy his ambitions for social recognition as a man of culture." Having accumulated an impressive collection, he soon discovered that he could reduce his income taxes by donating to a museum some of the pieces that had appreciated in value. As early as 1948, Getty donated some of his art to the Los Angeles County Museum. After a few years, however, he began donating pieces to his own museum, which he had established at his home in Malibu, California. In this way, Getty was able to use the deduction for charitable contributions to shelter most of his enormous income from taxes. In 1975, for example, Getty managed to shelter most of his $14.8 million in income from taxes by donating works of art and securities worth $9.7 million to the J. Paul Getty Museum. On more than one occasion, the Internal Revenue Service challenged his charitable deductions on the grounds that the appraisals of the donated pieces were inflated. The collection at the J. Paul Getty Museum eventually became so large that he was forced to contribute $17 million for the construction of a new building. This new museum was not completed until 1974, two years before he died. In his will, Getty left almost all of his personal fortune, over $661 million in Getty Oil stock, in a trust for the benefit of the museum. The museum also received the remainder of his substantial art collection. With its massive endowment, the J. Paul Getty Museum now serves as an enduring memorial to its founder.

THE SPORT OF KINGS

The corporate rich have always been prominent figures in the world of thoroughbred horse racing. The owners of racing champions have included members of such established corporate rich families as the du Ponts, Whitneys, Mellons, and Phippses. In recent years, several wealthy entrepreneurs, including Allen E. Paulson and Jack K. Cooke, have also become involved in horse racing. Members of the corporate rich derive a number of benefits from breeding and racing horses. To begin with, it is an activity that gains newly rich entrepreneurs and their families immediate status among the more established families of the upper class. Horse racing was originally the almost exclusive domain of the European aristocracy. Even today, the queen of England maintains an impressive racing stable. In America, the Kentucky Derby and other important races are major social events that attract many members of the upper class. Major horse auctions, such as those held in Keeneland, Kentucky, and Saratoga Springs, New York, are also important social events. During these sales, the owners of nearby racing stables often host lavish parties for other members of the racing set. Moreover, there are financial benefits to be derived from breeding and racing horses. The owners of racing stables enjoy certain tax advantages because horses, like other forms of property, are subject to both depreciation and capital gains. Specifically, they are able to depreciate the cost of a horse over a period of five years, even though it may have a long future as a stud or broodmare. Last but certainly not least, horse racing can be highly profitable. Many horses earn small fortunes during their racing careers and then go on to earn even larger fortunes as studs or broodmares.

In the early part of this century, many of the most successful racing stables were owned by the scions of wealthy families. During this period, horses bred and raced by Harry P. Whitney and August Belmont II, both of whom were heirs to large fortunes, won several major stakes races. Several other scions of newly rich families have become involved in horse racing since then. Stephen C. Clark, Jr., and F. Ambrose Clark, whose great-grandfather was a founder of Singer Company, both owned champion horses. Similarly, Robert J. Kleberg, Jr., the son of Alice King Kleberg, bred and raced successful horses on behalf of the King Ranch. More recently, stable owners have included such scions of wealthy families as Howard B. Keck, whose father founded Superior Oil; Forrest E. Mars, whose father founded Mars Inc.; and John M. Olin, whose father founded Olin Chemical. Sometimes more than one generation of family members has become involved in racing as children inherited racing stables from their parents. One of the most successful racing stables in the country is Greentree Stables, which has been owned by various members of the Whitney family for several decades. The founder of Greentree Stables was Helen H. Whitney, the wife of Payne Whitney, who inherited a large fortune from his uncle, Oliver Payne, one of the early partners of John D. Rockefeller. Horses bred and raced by Helen Whitney won the Kentucky Derby twice: Twenty Grand in 1931 and Shut Out in 1942. She later gave the stable to her children, John H. Whitney and Joan Whitney Payson. Although their horses never won the Kentucky Derby, one of them, Capot, did win both the Belmont Stakes and the Preakness Stakes in 1949. More recently, another of their horses, Stage Door Johnny, won the Belmont Stakes in 1968.

In at least one instance, a corporate rich family has developed into a racing dynasty spanning several generations. The case in point involves the Phipps family, comprising the various descendants of Henry Phipps, a partner of Andrew Carnegie. The first racing enthusiast in the Phipps family was Gladys M. Phipps, the wife of Henry C. Phipps, one of the sons of Henry Phipps. She founded Wheatley Stables, a highly successful horse-breeding and racing operation. Her most successful colt was Bold Ruler, who won the Preakness in 1957. Helen Phipps also owned several other champion horses, including High Voltage, Castle Forbes, Queen Empress, and Successor. Her son, Ogden Phipps, and her daughter, Barbara Phipps Janney, both became involved in horse racing. Barbara Phipps Janney owned Ruffian, a champion filly. Ogden Phipps owned several champion horses, including Buckpasser, Numbered Account, and Queen of the Stage. His son, Ogden M. Phipps, and his daughter, Cynthia Phipps, also owned successful racehorses. Cynthia Phipps owned Christmas Past, a champion filly. Other members of the Phipps family have owned racehorses as well. Michael G. Phipps, a cousin of Ogden Phipps, owned several racehorses. Another cousin, Raymond R. Guest, owned several horses, including Reindeer, who won important stakes races in Europe. His daughter, Virginia Guest, was the breeder and owner of Life's Illusion, a champion steeplechaser. In addition, his sister, Diana Guest de la Valdene, raced horses in Europe. In all, at least eight members of the Phipps family, spanning three generations, have been active in horse racing.

Racehorses that have good bloodlines often earn a great deal of money for their owners by winning purses. Members of the corporate rich, who have enough money to purchase the most promising foals, are more likely to own winning hourses. One of the most successful racehorses of all time was Round Table, owned by Travis M. Kerr, one of the founders of Kerr-McGee Corporation. Between 1956 and 1959, Round Table earned over $1.7 million in purses. Ogden Phipps has also earned a lot of money from racing horses. His most famous horse, Bold Ruler, won $764,000 in purses between 1956 and 1958. Another of his horses, Buckpasser, earned over $1.4 million in purses between 1965 and 1967. William L. McKnight, a founder of Minnesota Mining and Manufacturing Company, is the breeder and principal owner of Dr. Fager, who earned just over $1 million in purses between 1966 and 1968. As a general rule, successful stallions and broodmares are usually retired after two or three seasons. However, a very successful colt with valuable syndication prospects may be retired to stud after only one season in order to avoid injury. Geldings, which have no breeding potential, are often raced for several years. One of the most famous geldings of all time, Forego, was owned by Martha Farish Gerry. Her pedigree was almost as impressive as that of her horse. She was a daughter of William S. Farish, a famous Texas oilman who helped found Humble Oil and Refining Company, which was later merged into Exxon, and the wife of Edward H. Gerry, whose grandfather, Edward Harriman, once controlled the Union Pacific Railroad. Forego was raced for four seasons and eventually won $1.9 million in purses between 1974 and 1977.

Perhaps the most successful racing stable operated by the scion of a wealthy family is Rokeby Stables, which is owned by Paul Mellon. His horses have won important stakes races in the United States and Europe. Two Rokeby colts have won the prestigious Belmont Stakes: Quadrangle in 1964 and Arts and Letters in 1969. From 1964 to 1972, these two horses along with two others, Fort Marcy and Mill Reef, earned over $3 million in purses for Rokeby Stables. However, the money that a racehorse can earn for its owner from racing is often incidental to the money that it can earn from breeding. In this regard, stallions are generally more valuable than fillies. A filly with a successful racing career can be retired as a broodmare, but she can be bred only once a year. A successful stallion that has been retired to stud can be bred with as many as forty broodmares each year. In order to capitalize on this potential, highly successful racehorses are usually syndicated by their owners after only one racing season. When a stallion is *syndicated,* his owner sells shares to other horse breeders. Each share entitles its owner to breed one mare with the stallion every year. Because a stallion can remain in stud service for a decade or more, the owner of one share can expect to get several foals out of the stallion. One of the first horses to be syndicated for a small fortune was Buckpasser, owned by Ogden Phipps. After three successful racing seasons, Buckpasser was syndicated in 1967 for $4.8 million.

The finances of syndication are evident in the case of Nijinsky II, a stallion owned by Charles W. Engelhard, the son of the founder of Engelhard Minerals. Engelhard bought the colt as a yearling for $84,000 in 1968. Although Nijinsky II was unproven at the time, his pedigree was promising. His sire, Northern Dancer, had won both the Kentucky Derby and the Preakness four years earlier. Indeed, Northern Dancer was already on his way to becoming one of the most successful sires in the history of racing. Nijinsky II never raced in America. In fact, he had raced only ten times before he was syndicated. However, his syndication value was enhanced by the fact that he was unbeaten in those races. Charles Engelhard syndicated Nijinsky II in 1970. The syndicate issued 32 shares. Of course, each share entitled its owner to breed one mare a year with Nijinsky II. Several wealthy horse breeders, including Paul Mellon, John H. Whitney, Ogden M. Phipps, William L. McKnight, and Robert J. Kleberg, Jr., bought shares in the syndicate. Altogether, Engelhard sold 22 shares at $170,000 each for a total of $3.7 million. In addition, Engelhard kept 10 shares, worth another $1.7 million, for himself. Charles Engelhard died in 1971 before Nijinsky II proved himself as a sire. Although his widow, Jane Engelhard, continued to race horses for several years, she gradually reduced the size of her stable. In 1978, she sold the last of her horses to Paul Mellon. Later that same year, she sold her stallion shares at an auction. At that point, the 10 shares in Nijinsky II that Charles Engelhard kept for himself were worth $3.4 million.

The owners of racing stables can also turn a substantial profit from their breeding operations. Perhaps the most extensive horse-breeding operation owned by one individual is Bluegrass Farms, established by N. Bunker Hunt, one of the sons of H. L. Hunt, the founder of Placid Oil Company. Although Bunker Hunt races most of his horses in Europe, his breeding operations are based in Kentucky. For many years, he was known mainly as a buyer of horses who often paid high prices for promising yearlings. His most successful purchase was Vaguely Noble. His half-interest in the colt cost him $171,360 in 1967. Vaguely Noble earned $366,646 in Europe before he was retired to stud in Kentucky. He was syndicated in 1969 for $5 million. One of the first foals that Vaguely Noble sired for Hunt was Dahlia, who became one of the most successful fillies of all time. She eventually won $1.5 million in purses. In 1973, Hunt bred another successful horse, Youth, who won $687,224 in two years. Because he owned shares in a number of successful stallions, Bunker Hunt was soon in a position to sell promising foals to others. In 1978, he sold 18 yearlings at the Keeneland Yearling Sale for $4.9 million. However, he was accused by other horse breeders of inflating the prices paid for his yearlings by providing various forms of financial assistance to several associates who purchased his yearlings. Rather than comply with new disclosure requirements imposed by the Keeneland Association, Hunt held his own Bluegrass Yearling Sale the following year. At that sale, he sold 69 yearlings for over $12 million. In 1985, he sold his remaining interest in Estrapade, his leading foal, for $3.6 million. At present, Bluegrass Farms has over 200 broodmares on 8,000 acres in nine counties in Kentucky.

Although most of the corporate rich have been attracted to horse racing because of its tax advantages, a few have actually augmented their fortunes by breeding and racing horses. For example, Catoctin Stud, a 2,000-acre broodmare and yearling farm near Waterford, Virginia, has enriched the fortunes of its owners, Bertram and Diana Johnson Firestone. The principal investor in this operation is Diana Firestone, a granddaughter of the founder of Johnson & Johnson. She and her five brothers and sisters were the beneficiaries of a series of trusts established by their father, J. Seward Johnson, comprising stock in Johnson & Johnson. Her trust fund alone was worth roughly $70 million by the time she met and married her second husband in 1974. She and her new husband, Bertram Firestone, had both been involved in horse racing on a small scale for a number of years. However, soon after their marriage, they greatly expanded their racing and breeding operations. Diana Firestone requested and received over $3 million from her trust to renovate Catoctin Stud. It is now one of the most successful racing stables in the country. At present, the Firestones own about 120 horses, including broodmares and yearlings. About half of their horses are bred and trained at either Gilltown Stud or Sallymount Stud, two stables they own in Ireland. They now race horses in both Europe and the United States. Their best-known horse, Genuine Risk, won the Kentucky Derby in 1980. They bought the filly as a yearling in 1978 for $32,000. Over the next two years, Genuine Risk earned $646,587. Their racing stable has been a highly profitable venture for the Firestones. In 1984, Bertram Firestone and his wife were worth over $100 million, not including some $70 million still left in her trust.

Some of the individuals who have become involved in horse racing in recent years are entrepreneurs who have a lot of cash to invest as a result of selling their companies to larger corporations. These newcomers to horse racing have approached it as a commercial venture. One of the newest entrants into the horse racing business is Allen E. Paulson, the founder of Gulfstream Aerospace, a leading manufacturer of corporate jet airplanes. He first became a major racehorse owner in 1985, after he sold his 71 percent stake in his corporate jet airplane company to Chrysler for $452 million. That same year, Paulson attended three major auctions, where he paid a total of almost $16 million for 45 yearlings. Altogether he has about 175 horses. Many of them are in training at Brookside Farms, a new racing stable and breeding farm that Paulson built in Kentucky. Another newcomer to horse racing is Jack Kent Cooke, who sold his 11 percent stake in Teleprompter, a major cable television company, to Westinghouse Electric in 1980 for $80 million. Although he is new to horse racing, he is not new to professional sports. He has owned, at one time or another, two hockey teams, the Toronto Maple Leafs and the Los Angeles Kings, and a basketball team, the Los Angeles Lakers. He now owns the Washington Redskins football team as well as the Chrysler Building in New York. In 1984, Cooke bought Elmendorf Farms, one of the most famous racing stables in the country, for $43 million. The purchase included the 503-acre racing stable in Kentucky, 325 racing and breeding horses, and shares in a number of syndicated stallions.

TEAM SPORTS

Of all the status investments of the corporate rich, perhaps the most conspicuous is their involvement in professional sports. Many of the professional football, baseball, and basketball teams in the nation are owned by wealthy entrepreneurs and their heirs. In recent years, the owners of major sports franchises have included such disparate individuals as Joan Whitney Payson, the scion of an old and established upper-class family, and Ray Kroc, the brash entrepreneur who founded McDonald's Corporation. By all accounts, Joan Payson was just as involved in the performance of her New York Mets as Ray Kroc was with the performance of his San Diego Padres. Wealthy individuals have a variety of reasons for owning professional sports franchises. Ewing Kauffman, the founder of Marion Laboratories Inc., once testified in court about his motives for establishing the Kansas City Royals baseball franchise. The reasons he gave ranged from the altruistic to the pecuniary. First, he stated that he wanted to bring major-league baseball back to his hometown of Kansas City. Next, he averred that he sought the enjoyment and prestige of being the owner of a major-league baseball team. Last but certainly not least, he admitted that he felt that the team might eventually become profitable. He was eventually able to achieve all of these goals. After years of relative obscurity, he gained national recognition in 1985 when his Kansas City Royals won the World Series. The franchise, which cost him a little over $5 million in 1968, also proved to be a good investment. In 1985, he agreed to sell the Kansas City Royals to another investor for $22 million.

Professional sports franchises earn money from several sources. The first and most obvious source of revenue is ticket sales. In 1984, 10 million fans attended 943 professional basketball games, 14 million fans attended 224 professional football games, and over 44 million fans attended 2,106 major-league baseball games. Attendance at games is important to sport franchises because the home team usually receives income from the concessions as well as the sale of tickets. In addition, several professional football franchises receive income from the rental of special suites in their stadiums. In recent years, however, most professional sports teams have come to rely on radio and television broadcasts for roughly half of their revenues. The National Football League, for example, receives over $500 million a year from the three major television networks for the broadcast rights to its games. Because this money is divided equally among the 28 teams in the league, each team receives $15 million a year. Similarly, major-league baseball receives over $200 million a year from two television networks. Consequently, the 26 major-league teams each receive an average of $7.5 million each season. The National Basketball Association currently receives $31 million a year from one television network and a national cable television station. These contracts provide each of the 23 teams in the National Basketball Association with just over $1 million each season. Some teams receive additional revenue from local television and radio broadcast rights. Although many of the less successful sports franchises have lost money over the years, the vast majority of them are now profitable as the result of revenues from radio and television broadcasts.

As a rule, professional sports teams play in publicly owned stadiums and coliseums. In order to maximize their profits, team owners attempt to minimize the rents they pay for these facilities. Indeed, teams are often in a position to extract favorable leases on these stadiums and coliseums. If city officials demand too much rent, the owners of these franchises can simply threaten to relocate the team to another city or to a nearby suburb. Consequently, team owners sometimes become embroiled in public disputes with local officials. For example, Leon Hess, the founder of Amerada Hess and the owner of the New York Jets football team, became involved in a controversy with the mayor of New York City over the facilities at Shea Stadium in 1983. After city officials refused his request to renovate the stadium, Hess announced that he was moving the New York Jets to a newer stadium in nearby New Jersey. In fact, the New York Jets agreed to share the Meadowlands Stadium with the New York Giants football team, which had moved there from New York City several years earlier. The following year, New York City officials agreed to spend $25 million to renovate Shea Stadium in order to keep the New York Mets baseball team as tenants. A similar controversy led the Dallas

Cowboys to abandon the Cotton Bowl in Dallas. They eventually moved to Texas Stadium, a newly constructed facility located in the nearby suburb of Irving. In a few celebrated instances, team owners have moved teams from one major city to another. One sports entrepreneur, Robert E. Short, was responsible for moving the Lakers basketball team from Minneapolis to Los Angeles and for transforming the Washington Senators baseball team into the Texas Rangers.

Professional sports teams have typically been profitable investments for the corporate rich. Although these teams have not always produced much income for their owners, they have usually provided them with substantial capital gains. For example, the Dallas Cowboys proved to be a very profitable investment for the Murchison family. Clint Murchison was a wealthy Texas oilman who later became a major stockholder in a number of small oil companies and insurance companies. By the time he died in 1969, he had transferred the bulk of his wealth to Murchison Brothers, a partnership owned by his two sons, Clint W. Murchison, Jr., and John D. Murchison. Clint Murchison, Jr., a former college football player, tried unsuccessfully for several years to buy one of the existing National Football League teams. He then managed to persuade several team owners that the league should add two expansion teams. He even went so far as to purchase the rights to the Washington Redskins fight song in order to convince the owner of that franchise to vote in favor of the expansion. In 1960, the Murchison brothers and a business associate paid $600,000 for the Dallas Cowboys franchise. In return, the new team received an assortment of marginal players from the other teams in the league. Not surprisingly, the Dallas Cowboys were not an immediate athletic or financial success. The team lost money during its first five years. However, it has been profitable for the last two decades. Indeed, the team has earned as much as $3 million annually in recent years. John Murchison died in 1979, and Clint Murchison, Jr., became ill a few years later. In 1984, the Murchison family sold the Dallas Cowboys to a group of local investors for roughly $60 million.

Several corporate rich families have become even wealthier as a result of their purchases of professional sports teams. Of course, those families that bought teams several decades ago, before the advent of television, have seen their investments appreciate the most. For example, William Wrigley, Jr., the founder of the chewing gum company of the same name, purchased majority control of the Chicago Cubs baseball team for a few thousand dollars in 1921. He and his son, Philip K. Wrigley, were majority owners of the team for six decades. In 1981, William Wrigley III, the grandson of the founder, sold the 81 percent of the stock in the Chicago Cubs franchise held by the Wrigley family for over $16 million. That same year, Robert R. M. Carpenter III, whose grandmother was a sister of Pierre S. du Pont II and a major stockholder in E.I. du Pont de Nemours and Company, sold the Philadelphia Phillies baseball team for $30 million. His father, Robert R. M. Carpenter, Jr., had purchased the team in 1943 for about $500,000. More recently, Joan Payson bought the expansion franchise for the New York Mets in 1960 for less than $4 million. She died in 1975, and five years later her husband and three daughters sold their stock in the team for just over $18 million. Other members of the corporate rich have retained ownership of their teams. William C. Ford, a grandson of Henry Ford, bought the Detroit Lions football team in 1964 for $6 million. According to a recent estimate, the team is now worth at least $66 million. Similarly, Leon Hess, the founder of Amerada Hess, has spent roughly $15 million over the past two decades to become the sole owner of the New York Jets football team. The team is now worth an estimated $90 million.

In addition to being profitable investments, professional sports teams also provide their wealthy owners with certain tax benefits. In most businesses, the salaries paid to employees are considered simply as an expense. Professional sports teams, however, have been permitted to treat their contracts with their players as investments that depreciate in value over time. Because most sports franchises are operated as partnerships or small-business corporations, owners are able to use their share of this depreciation allowance to protect income generated by other investments from income taxes. In 1974, for example, the National Football League awarded the Seattle Seahawks franchise to a group of Seattle investors led by seven members of the Nordstrom family, the principal stockholders in a chain of retail clothing stores. The Nordstroms and their associates paid the National Football League $16 million for this franchise. Although it was clearly a franchise fee, a large portion of this $16 million was officially considered an investment in player contracts because the Seahawks were entitled to draft thirty-nine marginal players from the other teams in the league. As a result, the Nordstroms and their associates were able to depreciate much of this initial $16 million investment from their individual income taxes over the next five years. In recent years, the owners of both baseball teams and basketball teams have asked their players to limit the salary demands on the grounds that most of these teams were losing money. Independent accountants later concluded that these losses were attributable, in large part, to allowances for the depreciation of player contracts.

Recent court decisions have reduced the proportion of the cost of a franchise that owners can attribute to player contracts. Nevertheless, the combination of immediate tax benefits and long-term prospects for capital appreciation has induced several wealthy entrepreneurs and their heirs to invest in professional sports teams in the last few years. For example, Harrell E. Chiles, the founder of Western Company of North America, an oil-field services company, bought the Texas Rangers baseball team in 1980. Edgar F. Kaiser, the son of the founder of Kaiser Industries, purchased the Denver Broncos football team the following year. However, they both sold their interests in these teams a few years later. In 1980, three members of the Haas family, the principal stockholders in Levi Strauss and Company, paid almost $13 million for the Oakland A's baseball team, even though it was the least successful baseball franchise in the country. More recently, Thomas S. Monaghan, the founder and owner of the Domino's Pizza chain, paid an estimated $43 million for the more successful Detroit Tigers baseball team. Another wealthy entrepreneur, Robert E. Turner, known to the public as "Ted," bought two sports teams with the intention of integrating them into his other business operations. In 1976, Turner paid an estimated $12 million for the Atlanta Braves baseball team. The following year, he paid $4 million for a controlling interest in the Atlanta Hawks basketball team. Not coincidentally, Turner is the owner of Turner Broadcasting System, the largest cable television station in the nation. Of course, these teams have since provided Turner Broadcasting System with free sports programs.

A few entrepreneurs owe most of their fortunes to their investments in sports teams. Jack Kent Cooke became wealthy working for a Canadian publishing and broadcasting magnate. In 1961, Cooke moved to California to retire. Two years later, he invested in a small cable television company, which became the predecessor of Teleprompter Corporation. He also bought a 25 percent interest in the Washington Redskins football team that same year. In 1965, Cooke paid just over $5 million for the Los Angeles Lakers basketball team. The following year, he purchased the expansion franchise for the Los Angeles Kings hockey team from the National Hockey League. He then decided to build his own coliseum near Los Angeles to house these two teams. Altogether, he spent over $16 million to build the Forum, a huge coliseum that hosts rock concerts and expositions as well as professional hockey and basketball games. During this period, Cooke became involved in other professional sports as well. In 1971, for example, he put up $5 million to underwrite the world championship heavyweight fight between Muhammed Ali and Joe Frazier. After an acrimonious and expensive divorce from his first wife, Cooke decided to sell all of his California properties in 1979. He received a total of $67 million for the Los Angeles Lakers, the Los Angeles Kings, the Forum, and his 13,300-acre ranch. Once he had sold his professional basketball and hockey teams, Jack Cooke increased his involvement in professional football. In the last few years, he has spent well over $10 million buying out all the other owners of the Washington Redskins. He has also expressed an interest in bringing a major-league baseball team back to Washington.

Of all the members of the corporate rich who have become involved in professional sports, none can match Lamar Hunt for sheer audacity. As the youngest son of H. L. Hunt, Lamar Hunt had the resources to take large risks in the field of professional sports. In 1959, at the age of twenty-six, he tried unsuccessfully to buy a National

Football League team. Later that same year, he and several other wealthy sports enthusiasts, including Barron Hilton, the son of hotelier Conrad Hilton, organized the American Football League. The new league started with only six teams, all of which lost money. Lamar Hunt formed a football team, which he called the Texans and which played its first games in Dallas. However, the National Football League retaliated by selling a franchise in Dallas to the Murchison family. Hunt then moved his team to Kansas City, where he was able to lease a stadium on favorable terms, and the Dallas Texans became the Kansas City Chiefs. The future of the American Football League was not secure until it signed a $36 million television contract with the National Broadcasting Company in 1963. Hunt was later a key participant in the merger of the American Football League and the National Football League in 1966. Three years later, his Kansas City Chiefs won the Superbowl. According to a recent estimate, his Kansas City Chiefs franchise is worth about $50 million. Hunt is also one of the owners of the Chicago Bulls of the National Basketball Association. At one point, Hunt even tried to create a monopoly in the field of professional tennis with the creation of World Championship Tennis. As a result, he almost inadvertently transformed tennis into a major professional sport.

10

Power
and
Privilege

It is usually assumed that the wealthy are also powerful. To begin with, it is not unusual for the members of corporate rich families to exercise some degree of control over those corporations in which they are major stockholders. Indeed, family members often serve as officers and directors of those corporations. As a result, they exercise considerable economic power. However, economic power is not the same as political power. Despite a few notable exceptions, only a few scions of corporate rich families have ever been elected or appointed to political office. Nevertheless, economic power can be translated into certain forms of political power. For example, the members of wealthy capitalist families are typically among the major contributors to political campaigns. Of course, campaign contributions, even substantial ones, do not permit contributors to dictate the actions of elected officials. After all, most candidates for political office receive contributions, both large and small, from many individuals and organizations. As a general rule, however, elected officials who plan to seek reelection at some point generally try to avoid antagonizing those who have contributed or might someday contribute generously to their campaigns. In fact, candidates who seek large campaign contributions from the members of corporate rich families must typically demonstrate that their political goals and beliefs are consistent with the economic interests of those families and their corporations. In this way, the members of these families are able to influence the selection of candidates for political office.

The corporate rich are powerful, but they are not omnipotent. There are definite limits to their power. After all, there are many examples of government actions that have not been entirely consistent with the economic interests of wealthy capitalist families and their corporations. The existence of formally progressive transfer taxes, for example, confirms that the corporate rich have been unable to prevent the passage of legislation that is clearly inimical to their interests. In this particular case, widespread popular sentiment in favor of the redistribution of wealth through the imposition of progressive taxes has simply overwhelmed the ability of the corporate rich to influence legislation. Although they have been unable to prevent the passage of progressive transfer taxes, the corporate rich have been able to introduce changes into these tax laws that have mitigated the effects of these taxes. Wealthy entrepreneurs and their descendants derive much of their political power from their campaign contributions, but they are able to influence the formation of public opinion and public policy in others ways as well. In fact, the corporate rich derive much of their political power from their control over major corporations and foundations. The ability of corporate rich families to control the major media corporations in America enables them to wield a subtle but pervasive influence on public opinion. Similarly, the ability of corporate rich families to control major foundations that, in turn, provide grants to policy-research institutions enables them to influence the formulation of public policy.

DEEP POCKETS

The relationship between wealth and power is especially apparent in the case of political campaign contributions. Corporate rich families are able to exert considerable political influence by virtue of the fact that they are usually among the largest contributors to political campaigns. Although a large contribution does not guarantee that a politician will invariably serve the interests of a particular contributor, such a contribution usually does ensure a contributor immediate access to that politician. For example, W. Clement Stone, the founder of Combined American Insurance Company and a major contributor to the Republican party in both 1968 and 1972, once claimed that he talked with President Nixon over the telephone about once a month. In a few cases, major contributors have actually sought specific forms of administrative or legislative relief in return for their contributions. In any event, campaign contributions are an important part of the candidate-selection process because candidates are not likely to win their elections unless they can raise sufficient campaign contributions. As a rule, individuals contribute money only to those candidates who share their political views. The members of corporate rich families typically contribute to candidates who share their opposition to government regulations that benefit either workers or consumers at the expense of corporate profits. Moreover, they are especially supportive of candidates who promise to reduce those taxes levied on wealthy capitalist families and their corporations. As one observer puts it, "a candidate is an extension of the political views of those from whom he receives money."

The dependence of politicians on the members of corporate rich families for campaign contributions has a long and somewhat ignoble history in American politics. One of the first researchers to examine the relationship between wealthy contributors and elected officials was Ferdinand Lundberg. In his classic study *America's Sixty Families,* Lundberg concluded unequivocally that "it is an established fact that vast sums about which the general public seldom hears are used to prostitute virtually all elections." One of the first public investigations of political campaign contributions was conducted in 1912 by the

279

Senate Privileges and Elections Committee. This investigation revealed that both political parties relied heavily on large contributions from major corporations and members of their founding families. In 1904, for example, the Republican National Committee received large contributions from such wealthy individuals as Edward H. Harriman, Mark A. Hanna, Henry C. Frick, T. Coleman du Pont, and Charles W. Post. The presidential nominee of the Republican party that year was Theodore Roosevelt. Although he publicly denounced the immorality of great wealth and the power of big business, President Roosevelt failed to mount any serious challenges to the privileges of the corporate rich or the power of the large corporations. Indeed, the actions that he initiated against a few corporations often served to obviate more radical challenges to the economic interests of the majority of corporate rich families and their corporations.

In recent years, the enactment and enforcement of more stringent federal campaign disclosure laws have revealed the full extent of contributions by members of corporate rich families to both presidential and congressional campaigns. Using information from a variety of sources, Herbert Alexander, a noted political scientist, has identified the major contributors to every presidential election since 1960. In each of these elections, a significant proportion of all the money raised for political campaigns at the national level was contributed by a few hundred wealthy contributors. In 1960, for example, there were 95 individuals who contributed $10,000 or more to the major political parties and their candidates. These contributions accounted for just over 16 percent of the $9.5 million raised from all individuals by these parties and their candidates. By 1968, there were 424 individuals who contributed $10,000 or more to the major political parties and their candidates. In that year, contributions from these 424 contributors accounted for over 40 percent of the $29 million raised from all individuals by the major political parties and their candidates. In each of these elections, most of the large contributors were members of corporate rich families. Between 1960 and 1968, for example, 75 individuals who were members of either the Rockefeller, du Pont, or Mellon family contributed a total of $2.7 million to political campaigns at the national level. However, this total includes at least $1.5

million contributed to the unsuccessful presidential campaigns of Nelson Rockefeller by other members of the Rockefeller family between 1960 and 1968.

The campaign contributions of the corporate rich to presidential campaigns have followed a consistent pattern over the past several decades. By and large, the members of wealthy capitalist families have directed the bulk of their contributions to the Republican party and its candidates. As a result of this largesse, Republican candidates have been better financed than their Democratic opponents. Although the corporate rich have contributed the vast bulk of their campaign funds to the Republican party in most presidential elections, they have not neglected the Democratic party entirely. As a rule, many of the wealthy contributors to the Democratic party over the years have been either Jews, Catholics, or Southerners. Of course, members of these groups have traditionally been Democrats. Moreover, even wealthy Jews, Catholics, and Southerners have often been excluded from elite positions by Protestant Northerners from established upper-class families. Moreover, incumbent presidents, even those who are Democrats, often receive generous campaign contributions from members of the corporate rich. For example, when President Roosevelt ran for reelection for the first time in 1936, he received large contributions from such scions of corporate rich families as Doris Duke Cromwell, Marjorie Post Davies, Joseph Medill Patterson, W. Averell Harriman, and Augustus A. Busch, Jr. Of course, his Republican opponent received substantially larger campaign contributions from several members of the Rockefeller, du Pont, Mellon, and Pew families. In many cases, those wealthy individuals who contributed to the Democratic party and its candidates were considered mavericks even by members of their own family.

The ability of corporate rich families to influence political campaigns by means of their contributions to particular candidates and parties may have reached its peak in the presidential election of 1972. The presidential campaign that year, between Richard M. Nixon and George F. McGovern, was very expensive, and the corporate rich responded to the challenge with their customary largesse. In all, the 1,254 largest contributors that year gave $51.3 million to the major presidential candidates and their parties. Moreover, 284 individuals lent a total of $11.8 million to these campaigns. The Republican party and its candidate, who was also the incumbent president, collected far more from wealthy entrepreneurs and their families than the Democratic party and its candidate, who proposed more progressive gift and estate taxes. For example, the top 20 contributors to the Nixon campaign gave a total of just over $8 million. Much of this money went directly to the Committee to Re-Elect the President. Conversely, the top 20 contributors to the McGovern campaign gave a total of less than $3 million. Almost all of the largest contributors to the Nixon campaign, as well as many of the largest contributors to the McGovern campaign, were members of corporate rich families. Major contributors to the Nixon campaign included such wealthy entrepreneurs as W. Clement Stone, Daniel Terra, and Ray Kroc, as well as such scions of corporate rich families as Richard M. Scaife, Arthur K. Watson, and Walter Annenberg. Among the major contributors to the McGovern campaign were several liberal members of the corporate rich, including Stewart R. Mott, Max Palevsky, and Anne Labouisse Peretz.

Many of the activities associated with the Watergate scandal, which eventually led to the resignation of President Nixon, were financed with illegal or misappropriated campaign contributions. In 1974, as a result of the disclosure of these financial abuses, Congress passed several amendments to the Federal Election Campaign Act. These and subsequent amendments established limits on the amount of money that individuals could contribute to any candidate for federal office. Specifically, these reforms prohibited individuals from contributing more than $1,000 to a candidate for each primary, runoff, or general election. Moreover, individuals were prohibited from contributing more than $5,000 to any political action committee or more than $20,000 to the national committee of any political party. In general, these reforms set an annual limit of $25,000 on individual contributions to candidates for federal office. However, because these limits apply to individuals, it is possible for a married couple to double these amounts. The Federal Election Campaign Act also limits the campaign expenditures of the candidates for federal office, including congressional candidates, and provides for some public financing of federal elections. These campaign-financing reforms have served to reduce the importance of large contributors to presidential and congressional campaigns. Nevertheless, wealthy contributors are still important, particularly in primary elections. For example, presidential candidates cannot continue to receive public funds unless they receive a sufficient proportion of the votes cast in the state primaries.

Even the Federal Election Campaign Act has failed to sever the tie between wealth and power entirely. For example, as the result of recent court decisions, individuals are free to pay for advertisements on behalf of a candidate. The Supreme Court concluded that any limitations on individual expenditures advocating the election of a candidate represent an infringement of the constitutional right of free speech. Consequently, an individual is free to make independent expenditures on advertisements on behalf of a candidate as long as those expenditures are not coordinated with the candidate or any of his or her committees. One of the first major campaign contributors to exploit this ruling was Stewart R. Mott. One of the children of Charles S. Mott, a principal stockholder in General Motors, Stewart Mott has contributed generously to a number of moderate or liberal presidential candidates in recent years. Faced with the limitations on campaign contributions imposed by the Federal Election Campaign Act, Mott decided to use independent expenditures to influence the 1980 election. To begin with, he spent $90,000 on advertisements advocating the nomination of John Anderson, a moderate, as the presidential candidate of the Republican party. Later, he established his own direct-mail company, Mott Enterprises, which extended John Anderson, by then an independent presidential candidate, a $500,000 line of credit for direct-mail solicitations. As Mott later boasted, "I've figured out how to be a fat cat again." Another gap in the Federal Election Campaign Act involves political campaigns by the members of wealthy families. Under the present law, there is no limit to the amount individuals can spend on their own political campaigns.

No family in American history has spent as much on politics as the Rockefeller family. The first member of the family to run for elected office was Nelson A. Rockefeller. In 1958, he defeated the incumbent governor of New York, W. Averell Harriman, who was also a scion of a corporate rich family. They both spent so much money on the campaign that newspapers referred to it as "the millionaires' sweepstakes." In all, he was elected governor of New York for four successive terms, longer than any other governor. He never hesitated to use his own money or money from other family members to finance his campaigns. Between 1958 and 1972, Nelson Rockefeller spent a total of $3 million of his own money on his four gubernatorial and three presidential campaigns. His family contributed another $14 million during that same period. It is not known how much his brother, Winthrop Rockefeller, spent on his four gubernatorial campaigns in the state of Arkansas. It may have been as much as $10 million. The biggest spender of them all, however, is undoubtedly John D. Rockefeller IV, the nephew of Nelson and Winthrop Rockefeller. After serving four years in the West Virginia state legislature, Jay Rockefeller decided to run for governor in 1970. He lost the election, but four years later he ran again. This time he spent over $11 million of his own money on the campaign and won. No one had ever spent so much money on a gubernatorial campaign in a state the size of West Virginia. In 1984, Jay Rockefeller decided to run for the Senate. He spent $12 million of his own money on the campaign and won. In all, Jay Rockefeller has spent well over $25 million of his own money on his political campaigns.

In the past, only a few scions of corporate rich families have sought political office. There is the example of James M. Cox, the newspaper publisher and founder of Cox Enterprises, who served as governor of Ohio before he became the presidential candidate of the Democratic party in 1920. However, as political campaigns have become increasingly expensive, candidates who are wealthy enough to finance their own primary campaigns have enjoyed a distinct advantage over their opponents. Scions of wealthy families have generally sought the prestige and security of the Senate. For example, H. John Heinz III, whose great-grandfather founded the H.J. Heinz Company, was elected to the Senate from Pennsylvania in 1976. In all, he spent $2.6 million of his own money during the campaign. That same year,

John C. Danforth, whose grandfather founded Ralston Purina, was elected to the Senate from Missouri. Although wealth typically provides a candidate with a distinct advantage, it is not always a decisive advantage. In 1982, Mark Dayton, a great-grandson of the founder of the Dayton Hudson Company, spent $6.7 million of his own money on his unsuccessful campaign for the Senate from Minnesota. During the campaign, Dayton referred to his wealth as his "original sin." However, eight other members of the Dayton family, who were apparently unrepentant about their wealth, contributed to his opponent. Other members of corporate rich families have pursued governorships. Pierre S. du Pont IV, whose family still controls E.I. du Pont de Nemours and Company, served as governor of Delaware for eight years. More recently, Lewis E. Lehrman, whose father founded Rite-Aid Corporation, spent $6 million of his own money on an unsuccessful campaign for governor of New York.

MEDIA POWER

The corporate rich exert a subtle but pervasive influence on the political agenda of the nation by their control over the news media. Over half of the newspapers in America, particularly those in major metropolitan areas, are owned by major media corporations. These same corporations also own most of the radio and television stations in the major metropolitan markets. Last but not least, most of the magazines and books sold in the country are published by these same corporations. Publishing and broadcasting have always been business enterprises. However, it is only in the last few decades that the ownership and control of these media have become concentrated in the hands of a few large corporations. Many of the major media corporations, such as The New York Times Company, The Washington Post Company, The Times Mirror Company, and the Tribune Company, had their origins as newspapers that served a single major city. These corporations now publish newspapers and operate radio and television stations in cities across the nation. Because media corporations have generally been able to finance their growth through retained earnings, they have been able to avoid diluting, to any great extent, the stock-holdings of their founding families. As a result, most of the large media corporations in America are subject to some form of family control. Indeed, several corporate rich families, such as the Hearsts, Scrippses, Pultizers, Coxes, and Newhouses, own virtually all of the stock in major media corporations. In other cases, corporate rich families, such as the Grahams, Sulzbergers, Chandlers, Medills, Knights, and Gannetts, are major stockholders in publicly owned media corporations.

The influence that the members of corporate rich families exert on the political affairs at the local, state, and national levels, through their control of major media corporations, is at once subtle but pervasive. Although newspapers cannot always determine the outcome of an election, even at the local level, they are able to influence public opinion about the various candidates for political office. To begin with, many newspapers publish formal endorsements of candidates for public office. However, the editorial endorsement of a newspaper can be less important than its news coverage. Newspapers can influence public opinion by the extent and nature of the coverage they provide to various candidates. Similarly, newspapers cannot determine the exact content of legislation, but they can influence public opinion about the urgency and necessity of any legislation. As a result of this pervasive political influence exercised by their newspapers, the members of those families that control major media corporations have almost immediate access to most elected officials. In this regard, individual newspapers undoubtedly have a greater influence on politics at the local and state levels than at the national level. The local political influence of newspapers stems from the fact that only a few of the very largest cities in America have more than one newspaper. Metropolitan newspapers have usually created local monopolies by acquiring competing newspapers in order to increase their profits. Newspapers that have local monopolies are generally more profitable than other newspapers because they can charge higher advertising rates.

Certainly the most influential newspaper in America is *The New*

York Times. Adolph Ochs acquired the struggling *New York Times* in 1896 and gradually transformed it into one of the most respected and profitable newspapers in the nation. Almost a century later, the newspaper is still under family control. Iphigene Ochs Sulzberger, the daughter of the founder, and her children own 34 percent of the stock in The New York Times Company. However, because they own a majority of a special class of stock, they elect 70 percent of the directors of The New York Times Company. At present, Arthur O. Sulzberger, a grandson of the founder, is the publisher of *The New York Times* and the chairman of The New York Times Company. In addition, the company publishes several magazines and several suburban newspapers and operates three metropolitan television stations. Given the political influence of *The New York Times,* elected officials have often gone to great lengths to remain on good terms with the newspaper and its owners. When Arthur H. Sulzberger, the husband of Iphigene Ochs Sulzberger, died in 1968, President-elect Nixon attended his memorial service. His gesture was widely interpreted as an attempt to restore amicable relations with *The New York Times,* even though he had earlier denounced the newspaper for its attacks on Spiro T. Agnew, his running mate in the presidential campaign. *The New York Times* is probably even more influential at the state and local levels than it is at the national level. In 1976, Arthur O. Sulzberger endorsed Daniel P. Moynihan in his bid for the Senate. This endorsement by the most influential newspaper in the state of New York undoubtedly helped Moynihan win a very close election.

One of the only other major metropolitan newspapers capable of influencing the political agenda on a national scale is *The Washington Post.* This newspaper is also controlled by members of its founding family. *The Washington Post* was acquired by Eugene Meyer, Jr., a successful financier, in 1933. Several years later, he transferred control of the newspaper to his son-in-law, Philip L. Graham. Over the last several decades, *The Washington Post* has espoused a number of liberal causes and has implicitly, if not explicitly, endorsed Democratic presidential candidates. However, the paper did endorse Dwight D. Eisenhower in his 1952 presidential campaign. In fact, Eugene Meyer was one of several influential publishers, most of whom were members of corporate rich families, who had earlier urged Eisenhower to seek the Republican nomination. Philip Graham was also active in presidential politics. In 1960, he helped convince John F. Kennedy to accept Lyndon B. Johnson as his running mate in the presidential campaign. At the Democratic convention, Graham actually carried messages back and forth between Kennedy and Johnson. At the same time, not coincidentally, *The Washington Post* ran a series of articles that suggested that Johnson was a logical running mate for Kennedy. The Washington Post Company, which owns several television stations, a number of suburban newspapers, and *Newsweek* magazine, is now run by Katharine Meyer Graham, the widow of Philip Graham and the daughter of Eugene Meyer. She and her four children currently own over 21 percent of the stock in The Washington Post Company. However, their stockholdings include all of a special class of common stock that elects a majority of the directors.

The New York Times and *The Washington Post* are perhaps the most liberal of the major metropolitan newspapers in the country. Almost all of the other major metropolitan newspapers, particularly those controlled by corporate rich families, are much more conservative. One of the largest and most conservative of these newspapers is the *Chicago Tribune.* Joseph M. Medill acquired majority control of the Tribune Company in 1874. The newspaper was later run by a son-in-law and two of his grandsons. During its early history, the *Chicago Tribune* generally endorsed progressive Republican candidates and causes. However, the newspaper changed its editorial stance under the influence of Robert R. McCormick, a grandson of the founder. Despite the fact that he went to the Groton School with Franklin D. Roosevelt, McCormick denounced President Roosevelt and his policies. In 1948, the newspaper gained lasting fame for printing a headline that proclaimed that Thomas Dewey, the Republican presidential candidate, had defeated Harry Truman, the incumbent Democratic president. Even after Robert McCormick died in 1955, the newspaper continued to denounce successive Democratic presidential candidates as liberals or Communists. Just before the Democratic convention in 1968, the *Chicago Tribune* reported that Hubert Humphrey had been called "Pinkie" as a boy. Although no member of the Medill family is actively involved with the newspaper, family members still own about 48 percent of the stock in the Tribune Company. The Tribune Company also operates several television stations and publishes the New York *Daily News.* Although the *Chicago Tribune* no longer advocates reactionary policies, its editorial stance is still clearly conservative.

Another major metropolitan newspaper, the *Los Angeles Times,* has been generally conservative in its political endorsements until relatively recently. Harry Chandler acquired control of the *Los Angeles Times* from his father-in-law around 1916. Since that time, a son and a grandson of Harry Chandler have served as publishers of the newspaper. For many years, the *Los Angeles Times* almost routinely endorsed conservative Republicans for both state and national offices. Indeed, the newspaper contributed significantly to the political careers of two conservative California politicians: Richard M. Nixon and Ronald Reagan. An endorsement from the *Los Angeles Times,* the largest newspaper in the state of California, undoubtedly helped Richard Nixon win election to the House of Representatives in 1946. Four years later, the newspaper endorsed him in his successful Senate race. Nixon was elected vice president two years later. Norman Chandler, a son of the founder and the publisher of the *Los Angeles Times* during that period, became a friend and informal political adviser to Richard Nixon. At the insistence of several members of the Chandler family, the *Los Angeles Times* later endorsed Ronald Reagan in his successful bid to become governor of California. Through a holding company and two massive trusts, the children and grandchildren of Harry Chandler still own about 33 percent of the stock in The Times Mirror Company. In addition to the *Los Angeles Times,* The Times Mirror Company operates seven television stations and publishes four metropolitan newspapers. It also owns several book and magazine publishers.

A few media corporations are even more conservative than the Tribune Company or The Times Mirror Company. Many smaller media corporations, particularly those that publish daily and weekly newspapers in small cities throughout the nation, do not even attempt to conceal their conservative editorial positions. For example, Copley Newspapers, owned by the widow and three adopted children of James S. Copley, is one of the most conservative newspaper chains in the country. It publishes 41 newspapers across the country, most of them in small cities and suburbs. The company recently ran advertisements proclaiming religious fundamentalism as an editorial position for all of its newspapers. Perhaps the most conservative media corporation of them all is Freedom Newspapers Inc., founded in 1935 by Raymond C. Hoiles. Freedom Newspapers publishes 29 newspapers and operates four television stations, almost all of them in small cities. Harry H. Hoiles, the son of the founder, recently tried to buy the Freedom Newspapers stock owned by his sister and the children of his brother so he could gain control of the company. He was apparently distressed by the fact that the company had strayed even slightly from the conservative and libertarian precepts espoused by the founder. Among other things, the company had violated libertarian principles by establishing a pension plan for its employees. Corporate rich families that control private media corporations sometimes impose their political preferences on the editors of their newspapers. In 1972, for instance, President Nixon received endorsements from every one of the 43 newspapers owned by Cox Enterprises as well as every one of the 40 newspapers owned by the E.W. Scripps Company.

CHARITY AND IDEOLOGY

In recent years, corporate rich families have begun to influence government policy by providing financial assistance to a number of policy-research institutions or "think tanks." By and large, these organizations advocate policies that are consistent with the political goals and economic interests of the corporate rich. In a few cases, the members of wealthy capitalist families have donated their personal funds to these study groups. Most of the time, however, they have used grants from their family foundations to finance these policy-research institutions. In short, corporate rich families have been able to advance their political and social agenda with funds originally designated for charitable purposes. Because these policy-research institutions are ostensibly concerned with conducting social policy research and propagating the results of this research to the public, they qualify as tax-exempt organizations. As such, they can receive charitable contributions from both individuals and private foundations. As a result, a large number of conservative policy-research institutions have been established over the past few years with the financial support of wealthy capitalist families and their foundations. In his study *Who Rules America Now?*, G. William Domhoff found that charitable foundations were "an integral part of the policy-planning process both as sources of funds and as program initiators." Indeed, a staff member of one of these family foundations recently asserted that "foundations have been quietly and extraordinarily effective in the propagation of certain ideas."

One of the best-known policy-research institutions in the nation is the American Enterprise Institute for Public Policy Research. This organization was founded in 1943 in order to educate government officials and the public at large about the benefits of the free-enterprise system and the problems associated with excessive government regulation and taxation. Over the years, it has published a series of studies advocating the implementation of conservative economic policies. AEI was one of the first policy-research institutions to appoint experts in various fields as resident scholars. In the words of one conservative, "AEI made conservatism intellectually respectable." At least 20 of its resident scholars and associates were later appointed to senior positions in the Reagan administration. By 1984, AEI had a staff of 145 and a budget of over $11 million. Although it depends primarily upon donations from major corporations, this nonprofit institution has received large grants from several foundations controlled by conservative corporate rich families. Over the past decade, for example, AEI has received over $7.3 million from the J. Howard Pew Freedom Trust, a foundation controlled by the descendants of the founder of Sun Company. During that same period, AEI also received over $2.1 million from the Smith Richardson Foundation, a foundation controlled by the descendants of the founder of the Richardson-Vicks Company. Another $2.1 million was received from the Lilly Endowment, the Charles S. Mott Foundation, the John M. Olin Foundation, and the J. M. Foundation.

Another influential conservative research institution is the Hoover Institution on War, Revolution, and Peace in Palo Alto, California. Although it is officially affiliated with Stanford University, this policy-research institution has its own staff and its own endowment. Founded in 1919 as an academic research institute, the Hoover Institution first became involved in public policy research about a decade ago. Unlike other policy groups, the Hoover Institution generally refrains from issuing explicit policy recommendations. Instead, it provides research facilities and financial support for scores of conservative scholars. In the last few years, they have produced studies on such issues as Social Security reform and the deregulation of the transportation industry. Many of these scholars later had opportunities to put their ideas into practice. At least 40 former fellows of the Hoover Institution have served as advisers to the Reagan administration. By 1984, the institution had a staff of 200 and a budget of over $10 million. Although it has a substantial endowment of its own, the Hoover Institution has also received funds from a number of foundations. Since 1978, it has received $2.4 million from the J. Howard Pew Freedom Trust. During this same period, it has received another $2.4 million from the Sarah Scaife Foundation, a foundation controlled by Richard M. Scaife, whose grandfather was a major stockholder in Gulf Oil and several other major corporations. In addition, the Hoover Institution has received a total of $1.4 million from the Lilly Endowment, Samuel R. Noble Foundation, the J. M. Foundation, the John M. Olin Foundation, and the Smith Richardson Foundation.

Since the election of President Reagan in 1980, established conservative policy-research institutions, such as the American Enterprise Institute and the Hoover Institution, have been eclipsed to some extent by institutions advocating even more conservative policies. One of the best-known and most influential of these is the Heritage Foundation. This neoconservative policy-research institution was founded in 1973 with a $250,000 donation from Joseph Coors, a grandson of the founder of Adolph Coors Company. By 1984, the Heritage Foundation had a staff of 110, including 35 resident scholars, and a budget of $10 million. Although it now receives contributions from many wealthy individuals and business corporations, this nonprofit institution still receives large grants from a number of foundations controlled by conservative corporate rich families. The Samuel R. Noble Foundation, for example, has contributed over $3.1 million to the Heritage Foundation since 1978. The Sarah Scaife Foundation has contributed another $2.1 million in the past four years alone. In addition, the J. M. Foundation, the J. Howard Pew Freedom Trust, the John M. Olin Foundation, and the Smith Richardson Foundation have contributed at least $1.8 million to the Heritage Foundation since 1978. The Heritage Foundation is now one of the largest and most influential policy-research institutions in the nation. In 1982, the foundation paid $9 million for an eight-story office building in Washington, D.C., not far from the Capitol Building.

The Heritage Foundation has achieved its prominence as a policy-research institution largely through the publication and distribution of countless research reports and recommendations. For example, the Heritage Foundation publishes a quarterly journal, *Policy Review,* and a monthly report, *National Security Record.* It also publishes and disseminates extensive reports on particular issues. Perhaps the best-known publication of the Heritage Foundation was a voluminous tome titled *Mandate for Leadership.* Policy analysts at the foundation began work on this document in 1979, before President Reagan took office. Free copies of this publication, which outlined a conservative agenda for the Reagan administration, were later delivered directly to officials throughout the legislative and executive branches of government. In 1984 alone, the staff at the Heritage Foundation produced more than 200 books, monographs, and reports. At present, the typical Heritage Foundation report is distributed to about 1,000 elected and appointed government officials. Instead of simply being mailed, these reports are often hand delivered to important officials. Another 6,000 copies of these reports are distributed free of charge to journalists and scholars. Although many of the advisers to the Reagan administration during its first term came from either the American Enterprise Institute or the Hoover Institution, many of the advisers appointed during the second term have come from the Heritage Foundation. By 1984, at least twelve resident scholars from the Heritage Foundation had served as advisers to the Reagan administration.

Another influential policy-research institution is the Center for Strategic and International Studies (CSIS) in Washington, D.C. Although it is officially affiliated with Georgetown University, the center maintains a separate staff and facilities. Founded in 1962, CSIS conducts studies of various aspects of foreign policy and national security. Many of these studies appear as articles in *Washington Quarterly,* a public policy journal published by the center. In addition, the center conducts seminars for both senior corporate officers and senior government administrators. However, one of the main activities of CSIS is the formation of public opinion through news reports and broadcasts. Several former cabinet officers, such as Henry Kissinger, James Schlesinger, and Zbigniew Brzezinski, serve as fellows at the center, even though they are rarely in residence. Whenever a foreign policy development or national security issue becomes news, these experts provide newspaper, radio, and television reporters with interviews. By 1984, CSIS had a staff of 160 and a budget of over $7 million. Although the center receives funds from the major media corporations, it also receives large grants from foundations controlled by conservative corporate rich families. In the past decade, the Sarah Scaife Foundation has contributed over $1.6 million to CSIS. The J. Howard Pew Freedom Foundation, the John M. Olin Foundation, the S. R. Noble Foundation, and the H. Smith Richardson Foundation have contributed at least another $1.1 million.

Several other neoconservative policy-research institutions are financed primarily by a few corporate rich families and their foundations. One of the smallest and least-known neoconservative policy groups is the Institute for Contemporary Studies in San Francisco. Two of the directors of this institute eventually became special advisers to President Reagan. Since 1980, this institute has received over $1.1 million from the Sarah Scaife Foundation. It also received relatively small contributions from the Smith Richardson Foundation, the

J. Howard Pew Freedom Trust, the J. M. Foundation, the Adolph Coors Foundation, and the John M. Olin Foundation. Another small but influential conservative policy-research institution is the Pacific Legal Foundation, which has brought suit on behalf of a number of conservative causes. It has received over $1.3 million in grants from the Sarah Scaife Foundation and the Lilly Endowment. Other neoconservative policy-research institutions include the Institute for Research on the Economics of Taxation, which does research on the benefits of minimal taxation; the Institute for Foreign Policy Analysis, which issues conservative foreign policy recommendations; the Manhattan Institute, which advocates the reduction or elimination of many welfare programs; and Freedom House, which monitors the suppression of individual liberties in socialist countries. All of these institutions have received large grants from either the Sarah Scaife Foundation or the J. Howard Pew Freedom Trust. Most of these institutions have also received grants from the Samuel R. Noble Foundation, the J. M. Foundation, and the John M. Olin Foundation.

The conservative and neoconservative policy-research institutions funded in large part by grants from a few private foundations form a diffuse but coherent social network. Most of these institutions once relied on grants from these foundations for their financial survival. As a result, some of the most influential individuals within this policy-formation network are those members of wealthy capitalist families who control the foundations that provide funds to these institutions. Using a combination of personal and foundation funds, these members of the corporate rich have been able to influence the activities of these study groups. One of the most influential individuals within the network of neoconservative policy-research institutions is Richard M. Scaife, chairman of the Sarah Scaife Foundation. This foundation, with assets of $200 million, was founded by his mother, Sarah Mellon Scaife, the daughter of Richard B. Mellon. Since 1973, when Richard Scaife became chairman, the foundation has devoted more and more of its resources to conservative causes. In fact, Cordelia Mellon Scaife, the sister of Richard Scaife, resigned as a trustee because she objected to the fact that the Sarah Scaife Foundation had departed from the original philanthropic goals of its founder. She pointed out that their late mother, Sarah Mellon Scaife, had originally intended the foundation to fund the arts and research on population control. According to one estimate, Richard Scaife has donated a total of $36 million of foundation and personal funds to over twenty different conservative nonprofit organizations. Some of these personal funds have come from the income generated by trusts originally established by his mother for his children.

Several foundations, such as the Samuel R. Noble Foundation, established by Oklahoma oilman Lloyd Noble, and the J. M. Foundation, established by New York financier Jeremiah Milbank, fund conservative causes, but they also fund a large number of other charitable activities. However, there are a few foundations at the center of the neoconservative policy-research network that devote most of their funds to conservative organizations and programs. One of these is the J. Howard Pew Freedom Trust. This foundation is controlled, through the Glenmede Trust Company, by the grandchildren of Joseph N. Pew. In recent years, this foundation has devoted about half of its annual budget to neoconservative organizations. Similarly, the Smith Richardson Foundation devotes roughly half of its grant funds to neoconservative organizations. The Smith Richardson Foundation is controlled by several of the grandchildren of Lunsford Richardson. Its president is R. Randolph Richardson, a grandson of the founder. Last but certainly not least, there is the John M. Olin Foundation, which devotes almost all of its grant funds to neoconservative organizations. Although one member of the Olin family serves as a trustee of the foundation, the president of the John M. Olin Foundation is William E. Simon, a former cabinet member under Presidents Nixon and Ford. These three foundations often collaborate in their efforts to assist neoconservative organizations and causes. In 1981, for example, the John M. Olin Foundation joined with the Sarah Scaife Foundation and the Smith Richardson Foundation to establish *New Criterion,* a neoconservative review of contemporary arts criticism.

POWER PLAYS

The corporate rich are not reluctant to exercise their political power to their own advantage. For example, members of corporate rich families have occasionally lobbied the Congress and the president to enact special legislation for their benefit. A case in point involves the du Pont family. In 1949, the Justice Department filed an antitrust suit against the members of the du Pont family and their various holding companies on the grounds that their control of both E.I. du Pont de Nemours and Company and General Motors violated the Clayton Antitrust Act. At that point, Pierre S. du Pont, his siblings, and their descendants owned, directly and indirectly, over 26 percent of the stock in Du Pont. In turn, Du Pont owned almost 23 percent of the stock in General Motors. Members of the du Pont family also served as directors of both Du Pont and General Motors. Five years later, the presiding judge dismissed the antitrust complaint. However, the Justice Department appealed the decision to the Supreme Court, which overruled the District Court decision in 1957. After five more years of legal skirmishes, the presiding judge finally entered a final judgment that required Du Pont to divest itself of its General Motors stock by 1965. According to the terms of this decree, Du Pont was required to distribute its General Motors stock to its own stockholders in three installments. Similarly, Christiana Securities, the main holding company of the du Pont family, was required to sell some of this General Motors stock and distribute the rest to its stockholders. The judgment also required several members of the du Pont family, particularly those who were large stockholders in Christiana Securities, to sell a portion of this General Motors stock.

The divestiture order raised serious tax problems for the members of the du Pont family. Du Pont was required to distribute General Motors stock then worth approximately $3 billion to its stockholders. Because the members of the du Pont family owned, either directly or indirectly, at least 26 percent of the stock in Du Pont, they were due to receive about $790 million in General Motors stock. Even though this stock was due to be received in three separate installments over a period of four years, this stock distribution would create enormous tax liabilities because the tax laws treated such distributions as income. Specifically, the du Ponts were faced with the prospect of paying as much as $550 million in income taxes on this General Motors stock. Even before the final divestiture order was issued, special bills were introduced in both the House and the Senate to provide Du Pont stockholders, including the du Ponts, with tax relief. In general, these bills required Du Pont stockholders to pay relatively low capital-gains taxes on only a portion of the value of the General Motors stock they received as a result of these distributions. President Kennedy signed the special Du Pont tax-relief bill in 1962. By 1964, however, the du Ponts were seeking additional tax relief. Because General Motors stock had doubled in value since 1962, the tax liabilities of the du Ponts on the last distribution of General Motors stock were also about to double. Yielding to a concerted lobbying effort, the Treasury Department ruled that the final distribution of General Motors stock was a tax-free distribution. In all, the du Ponts probably saved at least $350 million in income taxes as a result of these government actions.

On occasion, individual members of the corporate rich have lobbied Congress to pass special legislation for their benefit alone. One of the most blatant political maneuvers of this sort involved H. Ross Perot, the founder of Electronic Data Systems. In 1975, as the House Ways and Means Committee was about to finish its work on a major tax-reform bill, one of its members introduced a very unusual amendment. This amendment would permit any taxpayers who had capital losses of more than $30,000 in one year to receive a corresponding refund of any taxes they paid on capital gains during the previous three years. A few weeks earlier, the Senate Finance Committee had included a similar amendment in its version of the tax bill. The main beneficiary of this amendment was H. Ross Perot. In fact, the proposed amendment had been prepared by his lawyer, who was also a former commissioner of the Internal Revenue Service. It seems that Perot had paid roughly $18 million in capital-gains taxes on the sale of $57 million worth of Electronic Data Systems stock in 1971. Three years later, he lost approximately $15 million when a brokerage house that he had financed became bankrupt. This amendment would have entitled him to a tax refund of about $15 million in 1974. H. Ross Perot had some reason to believe that his amendment might pass. Earlier in 1974, he had contributed $90,000 to various congressional candidates, more than any other individual. Moreover, $55,000 of this went to members of the House Ways and Means Committee and the Senate Finance Committee. This amendment was eliminated only after the details of the Perot amendment and his campaign contributions were published in several major newspapers.

A more recent and more successful attempt by the members of a corporate rich family to amend the tax laws for their own benefit involves the Gallo family. Ernest and Julio Gallo and their four children are the owners of a large wine company worth roughly $600 million. When the House Ways and Means Committee began considering a tax-reform package in 1985, one of the proposed changes in gift and estate taxes was the imposition of a new "generation-skipping tax." The existing law contained a provision for taxing distributions from generation-skipping trusts, but the proposed law would tax direct gifts and bequests from grandparents to grandchildren as well. However, the proposed law included a $1 million exclusion for each grandparent. Under this law, for example, the Gallo brothers and their wives would have been able to transfer a total of $4 million in company stock to their grandchildren before they had to pay generation-skipping taxes. Ernest and Julio Gallo, who planned to distribute some of their stock in the family company to their twenty grandchildren, wanted a more generous exclusion. An amendment to the proposed generation-skipping tax that would grant an additional $2 million exclusion to each grandparent for each grandchild was introduced. Indeed, a temporary version of the "Gallo Amendment," as it came to be known, was included in the final tax law. The passage of this amendment may have been aided by the fact that Ernest and Julio Gallo and their wives had contributed over $276,000 to various federal campaigns since 1977. In any event, the Gallos now have until 1990 to transfer a total of $84 million worth of stock in the family corporation to their twenty grandchildren without paying any generation-skipping taxes.

Sometimes, special legislation is introduced in order to enable the descendants of a wealthy entrepreneur to maintain control of their family corporation. For example, the Pew family sought to change the tax laws in 1971 so they could retain their control over Sun Company. The Tax Reform Act of 1969 was the first attempt by the federal government to regulate the activities of tax-exempt private foundations. One of the key provisions of this legislation was a minimum payout rate that required private foundations to disburse 6 percent of the market value of their assets each year. One of the foundations threatened by this provision was the Pew Memorial Trust, which was endowed and controlled by members of the Pew family. Indeed, the descendants of Joseph N. Pew have been able to retain almost absolute control over Sun Company through their control of the Pew Memorial Trust, which, in turn, owns about 22 percent of Sun Company stock. The problem facing the Pews was the fact that Sun Company stock paid very small dividends. In 1971, a member of the House of Representatives from Pennsylvania, the home of Sun Company, the Pew Memorial Trust, and the Pew family, introduced a bill that would have greatly reduced the minimum payout requirement as it applied to the Pew Memorial Trust. The Treasury Department later recommended passage of a bill that reduced the minimum payout provision from 6 percent to 5 percent of foundation assets and extended the deadline for full compliance from 1975 to 1978. Although both bills eventually failed to gain passage, the Pews did receive some assistance from the Republican administration. It was the least they could expect, because they had contributed over $142,000 to national Republican organizations in 1968.

The members of corporate rich families are sometimes able to amend the laws of particular states to suit their own purposes. For example, the Getty family had the laws governing estates and trusts in the state of California changed in order to resolve a lingering family feud. By 1984, the three surviving sons and fifteen grandchildren of J. Paul Getty were the beneficiaries of a trust worth roughly $3 billion. One of the sons, Gordon P. Getty, was the sole trustee of this trust. However, many of the beneficiaries, including his brothers and several of his nieces and nephews, did not approve of his management of the trust. To begin with, many of them felt that he had exposed the trust to unnecessary capital-gains taxes when he agreed to the acquisition of Getty Oil Company by Texaco in 1984. Although the trust received just over $4 billion in cash for its Getty Oil stock, it also incurred state and federal tax liabilities of nearly $1 billion as a result of this sale. During this period, several family members brought suit to have Gordon Getty removed as the trustee of the family trust. After months of litigation, the various descendants of J. Paul Getty finally agreed to split the trust into several smaller trusts, one for each branch of the family. This arrangement would enable the members of each branch of the family to choose the trustees for their trusts. There was one problem with this solution. The laws of the state of California did not contain any explicit provision for dividing a trust into a series of separate trusts. Within a matter of weeks, a bill that allowed the Gettys to resolve their family feud by dividing their trust into separate trusts was passed by the state legislature and signed by the governor.

Even though they are major contributors to many political campaigns, it is not easy for the corporate rich to obtain the passage of preferential legislation. Legislative relief in the form of a change in the law requires the cooperation of the members of various congressional committees and the assent of a majority of the members of both the Senate and the House of Representatives. It is difficult to convince a majority of the members of both houses of Congress to vote for a law that benefits only the members of a few wealthy families. They are much more likely to vote for a law that purports to benefit a large segment of the population, even if the bulk of the benefits accrue to the members of corporate rich families. In 1981, for example, President Reagan advocated several changes in both the income tax and the transfer tax that were very beneficial to the corporate rich. In particular, his tax-reform package contained a provision that would eventually reduce the federal transfer tax on gifts and estates from a maximum rate of 70 percent to a maximum rate of 50 percent. In order to gain legislative support for this provision, the proponents of the Economic Recovery Tax Act argued that the small family farm in America was being destroyed because farm families could not afford to pay the transfer taxes incurred whenever a farm passed from one generation of family members to the next. Because the maximum transfer tax rate applied only to gifts and estates in excess of $5 million, however, the family farms that stood to benefit the most from this change in the law were hardly small. Indeed, the main beneficiaries of this reduction in the maximum transfer tax rate were the corporate rich.

THE PRIVILEGED CLASS

The members of corporate rich families are clearly more powerful and influential than the members of most other families. First and foremost, they are principal stockholders in large corporations. In many cases, family members also serve as officers and directors of these corporations. To the extent that they control major corporations, the members of wealthy capitalist families are able to exercise tremendous economic power. For example, corporations have the power to build new plants and close old ones. In this way, they affect the welfare and even the survival of entire communities. Consequently, government officials, at both the state and local levels, are generally very solicitous of these corporations and the families that control them. At the national level, corporations are sometimes able to influence government policy by lobbying members of Congress for or against particular pieces of legislation. The members of corporate rich families also exercise considerable social power by virtue of the fact that they often control large philanthropic foundations. Almost all of the large foundations in America were endowed by members of wealthy capitalist families. Moreover, many of these foundations are still controlled by these donors or their descendants. As a result, corporate rich families often determine which organizations and causes receive grants from these foundations. The control that these families exert over these foundations enables them to influence civic and cultural affairs at the local, regional, and national levels.

Economic power is not always translated directly into political power. Indeed, the political power exercised by the corporate rich is subtle yet pervasive. For example, only a few scions of wealthy capitalist families are actively involved in politics. Those descendants of wealthy entrepreneurs who have entered electoral politics have usually done so as a means of personal fulfillment. In fact, many of the most important decisions are made by elites who occupy formal positions of authority in major institutions and organizations. These elites are usually affluent, but they rarely possess great wealth. Consequently, the corporate rich must exercise their political power primarily by influencing these elites. In the case of elected officials, the members of wealthy capitalist families are able to influence the selection of candidates by their campaign contributions. Large campaign contributions from the members of wealthy capitalist families provide a distinct financial advantage to those candidates who are willing to defer to the economic interests of these families and their corporations. Similarly, the members of corporate rich families sometimes use their foundations to fund conservative policy-research institutions that, in turn, issue reports and studies advocating policies that are consistent with their economic interests.

In terms of political power, it is important to distinguish between the power of the corporate rich as individuals or families and the power of the corporate rich as a class. Although the boundaries between different social classes in America are vague and indeterminate, the corporate rich belong to a distinct and coherent social class. Specifically, corporate rich families form the core of the capitalist class in America. The members of these families constitute an identifiable social class for several reasons. First and foremost, they represent a social class inasmuch as the members of different families share certain economic interests. These shared economic interests stem from the fact that wealthy entrepreneurs and their descendants are typically principal stockholders in large corporations. As a result, they share a common interest in corporate profitability. The members of these families also constitute a distinct social class because their economic interests are often opposed to the economic interests of other large segments of the population. For example, the corporate rich are generally opposed to many of the government regulations enacted on the behalf of workers and consumers, at least to the extent that they impinge upon the profits of their corporations. In this regard, the corporate rich have important allies among the legions of small-business proprietors across the nation. Although they do not possess great wealth, the proprietors of small businesses have many of the same economic interests and political objectives as the members of wealthy capitalist families.

The corporate rich have also forged alliances with other powerful groups in American society. In particular, the members of established corporate rich families have derived certain political advantages from their acceptance into the national upper class. Although the capitalist class and the upper class overlap to a significant extent, they are not identical. On the one hand, the capitalist class is defined in terms of economic interest and comprises primarily the officers, directors, and principal stockholders of corporations. The upper class, on the other hand, is defined in terms of social status and comprises the members of families that have been socially prominent for several generations. The fortunes of many upper-class families have become depleted over the years, and the members of these families are often unable to subsist comfortably on the incomes provided by their investments. Consequently, many of the scions of these established families have been compelled to take positions in business and government. Of course, they usually obtain positions that are commensurate with their social status. For example, scions of upper-class families often become partners in large investment banks, lawyers in prestigious law firms, professors at elite colleges and universities, or senior government officials. Some of these individuals from upper-class families eventually occupy positions of authority in the major institutions and organizations. In short, there is a great deal of overlap between the upper class and the power elite. The integration of corporate rich families into the upper class serves, therefore, to augment their power and influence at the national level.

The essential question is not whether or not the members of corporate rich families exercise an inordinate amount of political power. It is abundantly clear that they are one of the most powerful groups in American society. Rather, it is whether or not these wealthy capitalist families as a class represent a dominant or ruling class. The corporate rich are obviously powerful, but they are far from omnipotent. Indeed, the very existence of progressive income and transfer taxes, for example, demonstrates that the members of wealthy capitalist families have not been able to prevent the passage of legislation inimical to their economic interests. By and large, the corporate rich favor substantial reductions in the level of government expenditures accompanied by corresponding reductions in taxes. At the same time, most of them accept, albeit reluctantly, the necessity for some minimal level of taxation. They understand that government, at the local, state, and national levels, performs many important functions that contribute to the profitability of their corporations. Corporations are dependent upon government at one level or another for the provision of important facilities and services, such as highway construction, police and fire protection, and education. Moreover, state and local governments, with the assistance of the federal government, are responsible for providing social welfare services to ameliorate the effects of unemployment. Last but not least, these corporations also rely on the fiscal and monetary policies of the federal government to maintain stable rates of economic growth.

The members of corporate rich families may be resigned to the necessity of taxes, even to the inevitability of progressive taxes, but they are not about to relinquish their fortunes without a struggle. After all, wealth is the foundation of the corporate rich family and the source of all its privileges. Consequently, the members of these families take every opportunity to preserve their fortunes. As Karl Marx once proclaimed, "tax struggle is the oldest form of class struggle." The corporate rich have conducted their struggle against taxes on two levels. As individuals and families, they have employed elaborate strategies to avoid or reduce the taxes on their gifts and estates. On occasion, they have even sought special legislation or Internal Revenue Service rulings to relieve particular tax problems. Moreover, as a class, the members of corporate rich families have sometimes induced members of Congress, as well as presidents, to endorse tax reforms that have included reductions in the taxes on intergenerational transfers of wealth. Over the years, these efforts have produced a tax system that is formally progressive but still permits wealthy capitalist families to transfer the bulk of their wealth intact from one generation to the next. In the final analysis, the issue is not whether the corporate rich in America have lost any important political battles, but whether they have lost the war. For the members of these families, the most important war is the war for wealth. Although the corporate rich have lost some significant political battles, such as the imposition of progressive transfer taxes, they have certainly not lost the war for wealth.

Appendix

Directory of Major Corporate Rich Families

There are literally hundreds of corporate rich families. This directory lists 160 families that, by even the most conservative estimates, were each worth at least $200 million in 1986. Because of the scarcity of accurate information, no inventory of this sort can claim to be exhaustive. Nevertheless, this directory almost certainly includes the vast majority of the wealthiest capitalist families in America. The fortunes held by these families are generally derived from their stockholdings in large corporations. For various reasons, however, some very wealthy families are not included in this directory. To begin with, those families whose fortunes are based almost exclusively on commercial real estate have purposely been excluded because it is impossible to determine the extent to which their properties are mortgaged. Similarly, many of those families whose fortunes are based on their stockholdings in private corporations have not been included because the extent of their wealth is often a matter of pure conjecture. It is very difficult to estimate the wealth of these families in the absence of any information on the finances of their corporations. Last but not least, those families who have become worth $200 million only in the past year or two have been excluded because their fortunes may be somewhat transitory. The families included in this directory have relatively established fortunes in the sense that they have been worth at least $200 million for each of the past three years.

Some of the corporate rich families included in this directory are small, consisting only of a founder, his wife, and their children. But many of the more established families, which comprise the grandchildren and great-grandchildren of the founder, are quite large. In order to qualify for inclusion in this directory, a family is defined as a *descent group,* comprising the lineal descendants of the founder, in which the eldest members are at least first cousins. In the case of larger and more complex descent groups, it is necessary that each branch of the family meet these kinship and wealth criteria. For example, the du Pont family, comprising the descendants of the siblings of Pierre S. du Pont II, is a very large and complex descent group in which the eldest members are only second cousins. However, the family is composed of eight distinct branches in which the eldest members are at least first cousins. Moreover, each of these branches of the family is worth at least $200 million. Each family is listed under the name of the individual or individuals who were judged to be the most responsible for accumulating the initial family fortune. These individuals are not always the family members who founded the firms that eventually gave rise to these fortunes. Reliable information on the members of corporate rich families is often more difficult to obtain than information on the aggregate wealth of these families. Individuals who are principal stockholders in large public corporations are often compelled by law to disclose information about their stockholdings in these corporations, but they often refuse to reveal much information about themselves or their families.

Estimates of the wealth of each family contained in this directory are based primarily on information contained in corporate reports issued by family corporations at various points in time. In particular, data on the stockholdings of the founder and his descendants have been compiled from registration statements, proxy statements, and other reports filed with the Securities and Exchange Commission. In many instances, these reports span a period of several decades. The degree to which each fortune has been diversified in recent years has been estimated from the stockholdings of those family members who have served as directors of the family corporation. Additional information on the exact composition of these fortunes and their distribution among family members, as well as information about the tax liabilities and charitable contributions of individual family members, has been derived from probate and other court records. Although corporate reports and court records are the primary sources used to estimate the wealth of a family, supplemental information has also been extracted from newspaper and magazine articles and company histories. Biographical information on individual family members has been compiled primarily from obituaries, published biographies, family histories, probate records, and other genealogical sources. In short, the descriptions of these families and their fortunes are based solely on information that is available, in one form or another, in the public domain. Some of the information about the members of these families may not always be current. For example, family members who have died recently may be listed as living and birthdates are not always available. In general, the information contained in this directory is current as of early 1986. For the sake of brevity, only the key documents and publications relevant to each family are listed as sources.

ABERCROMBIE, JAMES S. (d. 1975) Houston, Texas. Founder of J.S. Abercrombie Minerals Company and a founder of Cameron Iron Works Inc. In 1920, James Abercrombie borrowed enough money to buy a drilling rig. Two years later, he and a partner developed the first successful blowout preventer. Using this equipment, he later discovered and developed the Old Ocean field in Texas. In 1946, Abercrombie sold his interest in this field to a major oil company for $54 million in cash. That same year, he organized the J.S. Abercrombie Minerals Company, which later discovered oil in Texas and Louisiana and participated in a major oil concession in Kuwait. In 1968, James Abercrombie and his wife placed their 51 percent of Cameron Iron Works stock in a charitable lead trust for the benefit of Texas Childrens Hospital. This stock, which is now worth $210 million, reverts to their grandchildren after a period of forty years. Josephine Abercrombie, the only daughter of the founder, owns another 8 percent of Cameron Iron Works stock, worth $35 million. She and one of her two sons serve as directors of the company. Although it is a private corporation, J.S. Abercrombie Minerals is probably worth in excess of $100 million. With the Cameron Iron Works stock held by the charitable lead trust, the descendants of James S. Abercrombie are probably worth well over $350 million. SOURCES: *Houston Post,* June 1, 1953; Prospectus, Cameron Iron Works (July 8, 1980); Patrick J. Nicholson, *Mr. Jim: The Biography of James Smithers Abercrombie* (Houston: Gulf Publishing, 1983).

AHMANSON, HOWARD F. (d. 1968) Los Angeles, California. Founder of H.F. Ahmanson & Company. Howard Ahmanson was eighteen years old when his father died. He invested his $20,000 inheritance in the stock market and made enough money to gain control of a small insurance company founded by his father. In 1947, he bought Home Savings and Loan for $162,000. Over the years, he acquired eighteen other savings and loan companies that he later merged together to form H.F. Ahmanson & Company. By the time he died in 1968, Howard Ahmanson had already transferred most of his fortune to a series of trusts for his first wife and their son, Howard F. Ahmanson, Jr. H.F. Ahmanson & Company did not go public until 1972, when the estate of the founder sold 12 percent of the stock in the company for $78 million. His son and his first wife are the income beneficiaries of a series of trusts that recently held 31 percent of H.F. Ahmanson & Company stock, worth $260 million. Ahmanson Foundation, which is controlled by members of the Ahmanson family, owns another 24 percent of the company, worth $210 million. During the past several years, the company has been managed by William and Robert Ahmanson, two nephews of the founder. With accumulated dividend income, the first wife and son of Howard Ahmanson are worth at least $300 million. SOURCES: Seymour Freedgood, "Emperor Howard Ahmanson of S & L," *Fortune* (May 1958); *Forbes* (July 1, 1965); Proxy Statement, H.F. Ahmanson & Company (March 18, 1977).

ALBERTSON, JOSEPH A. (b. 1906) Boise, Idaho. Founder of Albertson's Inc. After managing a grocery store for several years, Joseph Albertson opened his first grocery store in 1939. Albertson's grew into a large chain of grocery stores by building big stores that included bakeries and pharmacies. Although he has retired from management, he and his wife still serve as directors of Albertson's. His only daughter, Barbara Albertson Rasmussen, once served as a director as well. The founder has transferred less than a third of his Albertson's stock to trusts for the benefit of his daughter and grandchildren. Joseph Albertson, his wife, his daughter, and his two grandsons own over 23 percent of Albertson's stock, worth at least $240 million. SOURCES: Prospectus, Albertson's Inc. (November 21, 1969); Proxy Statement, Albertson's Inc. (April 21, 1978); Barry Stavro, "In The Bag," *Forbes* (December 5, 1983).

ALLEN, CHARLES, JR. (b. 1903), and HERBERT A. New York, New York. Founders of Allen & Company and principal stockholders in both Syntex Corporation and Ogden Corporation. Charles and Herbert Allen formed Allen & Company, their own private investment banking firm, in 1928. Allen & Company acquired 33 percent of the stock in Syntex Corporation for less than $800,000 in 1958. At the time, Syntex was a small drug company that had developed a successful birth control pill. Charles and Herbert Allen have since sold much of their Syntex stock. By 1968, Allen & Company owned 15 percent of Syntex stock, worth $100 million. Charles and Herbert Allen sold a majority interest in the investment banking operations of their firm to their five children in 1964. Herbert A. Allen, Jr., a son of one of the founders, serves as the president of Allen & Company Inc., the investment banking operation. On his recommendation, the firm bought 6 percent of Columbia Pictures stock for about $3 million in 1973. Nine years later, Allen & Company sold this stock to Coca-Cola Company for $43 million. Charles and Herbert Allen and their children, either directly or indirectly through Allen & Company, still own over 7 percent of the stock in Syntex, worth $210 million. In addition, they also own almost 11 percent of the stock in Ogden Corporation, worth $60 million. With the proceeds from stock sales and accumulated dividend income, Charles and Herbert Allen and their five children are worth at least $350 million. SOURCES: *Forbes* (November 15, 1968); Proxy Statement, Syntex Corporation (November 14, 1972); Proxy Statement, Ogden Corporation (April 22, 1977); Shawn Tully, "The Man Who Scored in Coca-Columbia," *Fortune* (February 22, 1982); *Business Week* (November 5, 1984).

ANDERSON, ROBERT O. (b. 1917) Roswell, New Mexico. Founder of Hondo Oil and Gas Company, which was later merged into Atlantic Richfield. In 1941, Robert Anderson borrowed $50,000 and bought an interest in a small oil refinery in New Mexico. In 1957, oil was discovered in a field in which he owned a half-interest. That same year, he made a $20 million profit on the sale of a small oil company he had purchased two years earlier. In 1963, he merged Hondo Oil and Gas Company into the predecessor of Atlantic Richfield and became its largest stockholder. Anderson received over 7 percent of the stock in the company, worth $35 million. Two years later he became chairman. He quickly negotiated mergers with two other oil companies and transformed Atlantic Richfield into a major oil company. Anderson had acquired a number of large cattle ranches several years earlier. He soon owned eleven ranches with over 1 million acres in Texas, New Mexico, and Colorado. By 1972, he had disposed of the bulk of his Atlantic Richfield stock, but he still owned over 1 percent of the stock in the company, worth over $40 million. He and his seven children probably still own about 1 percent of the stock in the company, now worth about $120 million. With the proceeds from stock sales and cattle ranches, Robert Anderson and his children are worth at least $200 million. SOURCES: Prospectus, Atlantic Refining Company (August 21, 1963); *Business Week* (May 29, 1965); *Business Week* (April 18, 1970); Senate Committee on Government Operations, *Disclosure of Corporate Ownership* (Washington, D.C.: U.S. Government Printing Office, 1973).

ANNENBERG, MOSES L. (d. 1942) Philadelphia, Pennsylvania. Founder of Triangle Publications, a private media corporation. After working for several years as a newspaper editor, Moses Annenberg borrowed $400,000 in 1922 to purchase the *Daily Racing Form*. He later purchased a number of other publications, including the *Philadelphia Inquirer*. In 1940, Moses Annenberg was convicted of income tax evasion. He died shortly after he was paroled two years later. In his will, he left his Triangle Publications stock in a trust for his son, Walter H. Annenberg, and his seven daughters. The company was deep in debt but solvent. Walter Annenberg, who succeeded his father as chairman of Triangle Publications, started *Seventeen* magazine in 1944. It was edited by a sister, Enid Haupt. In 1953, he started the highly profitable *TV Guide.* During this period, the company also purchased several radio and television stations. Triangle Publications sold the *Philadelphia Inquirer* for $55 million in 1969. Three years later, the company sold its radio and television stations for $87 million. Walter Annenberg and five surviving sisters, as well as the children of two deceased sisters, own almost all of the stock in Triangle Publications. Walter Annenberg owns only about 35 percent of Triangle Publications stock, but he votes the shares held in trust for his sisters and their families. Each of his sisters or their descendants own just over 9 percent of the stock in the company. Although Triangle Publications is a private corporation, the descendants of Moses Annenberg are probably worth over $1.5 billion. SOURCES: *The New York Times,* July 25, 1942; *Fortune* (June 1970); Gaeton Fonzi, *Annenberg: A Biography of Power* (New York: Weybright & Talley, 1970).

BARRON, CLARENCE W. (d. 1928) Boston, Massachusetts. Principal stockholder in Dow Jones & Company. Clarence Barron was the owner of a financial news service when he acquired almost complete control of Dow Jones & Company, publisher of *The Wall Street Journal,* in 1902. He immediately turned his stock in the company over to his wife, Jessie Barron, who served as a director. When she died in 1918, she bequeathed half of her Dow Jones stock to Jane Barron Bancroft, one of her two daughters by a previous marriage, and the other half to her son-in-law, Hugh Bancroft, who later became president of Dow Jones & Company. Hugh Bancroft was largely responsible for expanding *The Wall Street Journal* into a national publication. He also launched *Barron's,* a weekly business periodical. Hugh Bancroft, who died in 1933, was the last member of the family to run the company. With the death of Jane Barron Bancroft in 1949, majority control of the company passed to her three children. After Dow Jones & Company went public in 1964, the children and grandchildren of Jane Barron Bancroft owned, through a series of trusts, 68 percent of the stock in the company, worth $175 million. Jane Bancroft Cook, a granddaughter of Clarence Barron, and four of his seven great-grandchildren serve as directors of the company. Altogether, they still own 56 percent of the stock in Dow Jones & Company, worth over $1.5 billion. With accumulated dividend income and other investments, the descendants of Jane Barron Bancroft are worth at least $1.6 million. SOURCES: Lloyd Wendt, *The Wall Street Journal* (Chicago: Rand McNally, 1982); Proxy Statement, Dow Jones & Company (March 18, 1983).

BASS, PERRY R. (b. 1914) Fort Worth, Texas. Founder of Bass Brothers Enterprises, a private investment partnership. Perry Bass was the only nephew of Sid Richardson, a wealthy Texas oilman. In 1935, Richardson discovered the Keystone field, one of the largest oil fields in west Texas.

In 1945, he brought in Perry Bass as a partner. Richardson was a bachelor, so when he died in 1959, he left over $10 million to the four sons of Perry Bass. He bequeathed the remainder of his $105 million estate to his Sid Richardson Foundation. Perry Bass, who served as a trustee of the foundation, later purchased a controlling interest in a chain of television stations from the foundation. In 1960, Bass turned over most of his fortune to Bass Brothers Enterprises, a family partnership that he created for his sons. His oldest son, Sid R. Bass, took charge of this partnership in 1968. In recent years, Bass Brothers Enterprises has purchased large blocks of stock in scores of companies. In most cases, these blocks of stock have been sold later at a substantial profit. Between 1981 and 1984, the family partnership made a profit of over $600 million on its investments in just two companies: Marathon Oil Company and Texaco Inc. The brothers recently dissolved their partnership, but they still have many investments in common. Before they began selling some of their stock, the Bass brothers owned almost 25 percent of the stock in Walt Disney Productions, worth $830 million. The known stock and real estate investments of the Bass family are worth at least $2 billion. With extensive oil and gas properties, Perry Bass and his four sons are probably worth in excess of $3 billion. SOURCES: Byron Harris, "Portfolio on the Basses," *Texas Business* (September 1984); Kathleen Stauder, "How the Bass Brothers Do Their Deals," *Fortune* (September 17, 1984); *Newsweek* (November 19, 1984); Anthony Bianco, "The Man Behind a $5 Billion Dynasty," *Business Week* (October 20, 1986).

BECHTEL, WARREN A. (d. 1933) San Francisco, California. Founder of Bechtel Group Inc. After working on a series of railroad construction projects, Warren Bechtel used $1,500 in savings to form his own construction company in 1898. He was soon joined by his brother and three sons. The predecessor of Bechtel Group eventually graduated from small railroad construction projects to large dam and pipeline construction projects. In 1933, the founder bought out his brother and sold the company to two sons. One of those sons, Stephen Bechtel, later bought out his brother. Stephen Bechtel built the company into one of the largest engineering and construction companies in the world. Over the years it has managed the construction of several major projects, including nuclear power plants, subway systems, oil refineries, and ore mines. Stephen Bechtel was succeeded as chairman by his son, Stephen D. Bechtel, Jr. In recent years, the company has obtained equity interests in many of its engineering and construction projects. A separate family investment company, Sequoia Ventures Inc., which owns a minority interest in the investment banking firm of Dillon, Read & Co., has invested in a number of oil-exploration partnerships and high-technology companies. Members of the Bechtel family own only 40 percent of Bechtel common stock. The remaining 60 percent is held by senior management officials who must sell their stock back to the company when they quit or retire. However, Stephen Bechtel, Sr.,and his two children and seven grandchildren own all of the preferred stock in the company. Although both Bechtel Group and Sequoia Ventures are private corporations, the descendants of Stephen Bechtel, Sr., are probably worth at least $800 million. SOURCES: *The New York Times,* August 29, 1933; Michael Kolbenschlag, "Bechtel's Biggest Job—Constructing Its Own Future," *Forbes* (December 7, 1981).

BEINECKE, EDWIN J. (d. 1970) and BROTHERS New York, New York. Principal stockholders in Sperry and Hutchinson Inc., which was later merged into Baldwin United. Walter and Frederick Beinecke were brothers who married the daughters of one of the founders of Sperry and Hutchinson, a trading stamp company. In 1923, they and another brother, Edwin Beinecke, purchased the entire Sperry and Hutchinson company, which became highly profitable and diversified into home furnishings, retailing, and insurance. Edwin Beinecke served as chairman of the company for four decades before he was finally succeeded by his nephew, William S. Beinecke. Indeed, all five sons of the three brothers served as officers and directors of the company. Even after Sperry and Hutchinson went public in 1966, the Beinecke family kept over 90 percent of its stock, worth roughly $310 million. By 1972, the family had sold $125 million worth of stock in the company. Even after these sales, however, the six children of the Beinecke brothers owned 60 percent of Sperry and Hutchinson stock. In 1981, the Beinecke cousins sold their remaining 43 percent of Sperry and Hutchinson stock to Baldwin United for $145 million. With the proceeds from stock sales, the descendants of Edwin, Frederick, and Walter Beinecke are worth about $250 million. SOURCES: Prospectus, Sperry and Hutchinson Company (June 6, 1968); *Forbes* (July 1, 1977); Proxy Statement, Sperry and Hutchinson Company (March 20, 1980).

BELFER, ARTHUR B. (b. 1907) New York, New York. The founder of Belco Petroleum Corporation, which was later merged into InterNorth Corporation. An immigrant from Poland, Arthur Belfer started a company that manufactured sleeping bags and bedding for the military. In 1954, he founded a natural gas company that later became Belco Petroleum Corporation. His son, Robert A. Belfer, eventually succeeded him as president of the company. The husbands of his two daughters also served as directors. When Belco Petroleum went public in 1962, Arthur Belfer and his three children owned 80 percent of the stock in the company, worth $55 million. In 1983, Belco Petroleum was merged into InterNorth Corporation, a large gas transmission company. In return for their 43 percent of Belco Petroleum stock, the Belfers received $37 million in cash and $285 million worth of InterNorth preferred stock. Members of the Belfer family currently receive $28 million a year in dividend income from this stock. Moreover, Arthur Belfer and his son serve as directors of InterNorth. Altogether, the founder and his three children are worth $350 million. SOURCES: Prospectus, Belco Petroleum Corporation (May 1, 1962); *Forbes* (April 1, 1976); Proxy Statement, InterNorth Inc. (February 27, 1984).

BLAUSTEIN, LOUIS (d. 1937) Baltimore, Maryland. Founder of American Oil Company, which was later merged into Amoco Corporation. Louis Blaustein and his son, Jacob Blaustein, founded a chain of gasoline service stations in 1922. The following year, they sold half of their company to an oil company that later came under the control of the predecessor of Amoco Corporation. In 1937, the Blausteins sued Amoco for unfair competition. In a settlement reached seventeen years later, the Blausteins agreed to merge their gasoline marketing company with Amoco. In return, they received nearly 4 percent of Amoco stock, worth $63 million. Jacob Blaustein also became a director of Amoco. In addition to his son, Louis Blaustein had two daughters, Ruth Blaustein Rosenberg and Fanny Blaustein Thalheimer. Through a family holding company, American Trading and Production Company, the seven grandchildren and nineteen great-grandchildren of the founder still own about 4 percent of Amoco, worth $780 million. This holding company also owns at least 49 percent of the stock in Crown Central Petroleum, worth $40 million, as well as $30 million in Exxon stock. American Trading and Production and another family holding company, Blaustein Industries, own a number of oil and gas properties, several oil tankers, some small manufacturing companies, and interests in several real estate developments, including two major office buildings in downtown Baltimore. With accumulated dividend income and other investments, the descendants of Louis Blaustein are worth just over $1 billion. SOURCES: Prospectus, Standard Oil Company of Indiana (August 17, 1954); *Forbes* (September 15, 1968); *Forbes* (July 15, 1977).

BLOCH, HENRY W. (b. 1922) and RICHARD A. Kansas City, Kansas. Founders of H.&R. Block Inc. In 1946, Henry Bloch and his brother, Richard A. Bloch, started a business-service company, which provided bookkeeping assistance to small companies. They founded H.&R. Block in 1955 and began franchising tax-preparation offices across the nation. In 1968, they sold 14 percent of the stock in H.&R. Block to the public for $21 million. However, the Bloch brothers and their children kept 50 percent of the stock in the company, worth another $76 million. H.&R. Block has lately acquired a number of computer and management services companies. Over the years, various family members, particularly Richard A. Bloch, have sold much of their H.&R. Block stock. However, Henry W. Bloch and other family members probably still own over 20 percent of the stock in H.&R. Block, worth $170 million. Richard Bloch serves as chairman of the company, and Henry Bloch serves as president. With proceeds from stock sales and accumulated dividend income, Henry and Richard Bloch and their children are worth at least $250 million. SOURCES: Prospectus, H.&R. Block Inc. (September 5, 1968); *Forbes* (October 1, 1968); Proxy Statement, H.&R. Block Inc. (June 26, 1983).

BLOCK, ALEXANDER (d. 1953) New York, New York. Founder of Block Drug Company. Alexander Block owned a drugstore before he went into the wholesale drug business in 1911. In 1925, he acquired a company that manufactured dental products. Over the years, Block acquired a number of small drug companies that marketed nonprescription products. He then increased the sales of those products by spending heavily on advertising. Both of his sons, Melvin and Leonard Block, served as president and chairman of the company. When the company went public in 1971, the two sons and four grandchildren of the founder owned about 89 percent of Block Drug stock, worth $140 million. Leonard Block still serves as chairman of the company and his nephew, James Block, serves as president. After selling roughly 10 percent of their stock in the company over the past decade or so, members of the Block family still own, through trusts and holding companies, at least 79 percent of Block Drug stock, worth $270 million. With the proceeds from stock sales, the descendants of Alexander Block are worth at least $320 million. SOURCES: Prospectus, Block Drug Company (August 4, 1972); *Forbes* (May 29, 1978).

BRADLEY, HARRY L. (d. 1965) and LYNDE Milwaukee, Wisconsin. Founders of Allen-Bradley Company, which was later acquired by Rockwell International. Harry Bradley and his brother, Lynde Bradley, founded their own electrical control company in 1903, with financial assistance from another partner. Lynde Bradley developed various products, and Harry Bradley ran the company that manufactured them. When their partner retired in 1916, the company repurchased his Allen-Bradley stock. In 1945, Harry Bradley established a series of trusts for the benefit of his three children. Because his brother had no children, almost all of the stock in Allen-Bradley eventually went into trusts for the children and grandchildren of Harry Bradley. In recent years, the company has become one of the leading suppliers of automated production equipment. In 1985, Jane Bradley Pettit, the adopted daughter of Harry Bradley, urged that the company be sold to another corporation. Her stepsister, Marion Bradley Via, and her stepbrother, Harry L. Bradley, Jr., reluctantly agreed to the sale of Allen-Bradley to Rockwell International Corporation. Trusts for the descendants of Harry Bradley received roughly $1.5 billion for 93 percent of Allen-Bradley stock. The Allen-Bradley Foundation, which owned the remaining 7 percent of the stock, received over $110 million. With the proceeds from this stock sale, even after capital-gains taxes, the descendants of Harry L. Bradley are worth $1.2 billion. SOURCES: *The New York Times,* March 30, 1965; James B. Stewart, "How a Safe Company Was Acquired Anyway After Bitter Infighting," *The Wall Street Journal,* May 14, 1985.

BROWN, GEORGE G. (d. 1917) Louisville, Kentucky. A founder of Brown-Forman Inc. George Brown and his partner founded a distillery in 1870. George Brown was succeeded as president in 1917 by his eldest son, Owsley Brown, who became the majority stockholder in the company after it was incorporated in 1933. Owsley Brown also expanded the company by acquiring other distilleries. Over the years, his two sons and at least six of his grandsons became officers and directors of the company. The bulk of the Brown-Forman stock held by the descendants of the founder is owned by the grandchildren of Owsley Brown. Most of the other descendants of George Brown own relatively little stock in the company. Altogether, descendants of the founder own, through a series of trusts, at least 44 percent of the stock in Brown-Forman, worth $430 million. However, they own over 60 percent of the voting stock in the company. Currently, five of the grandchildren of Owsley Brown serve as either officers or directors of the company. With accumulated dividend income, the descendants of Owsley Brown are worth about $450 million. SOURCES: Proxy Statement, Brown-Forman Distillers Corporation (June 21, 1971); Proxy Statement, Brown-Forman Inc. (June 30, 1983).

BUSCH, ADOLPHUS (d. 1913) St. Louis, Missouri. A founder of Anheuser-Busch Companies Inc. In 1866, Eberhard Anheuser bought a brewery and hired his son-in-law, Adolphus Busch, to manage it. When the company was incorporated nine years later, Adolphus Busch and his wife received 70 percent of the stock. Even after Anheuser-Busch went public in 1952, the children and grandchildren of Adolphus Busch still owned over 50 percent of the stock in the company, worth $50 million. Adolphus Busch had five daughters and one son, August A. Busch, who later succeeded him as president. The descendants of two of the daughters of Adolphus Busch sold most of their Anheuser-Busch stock soon after the company went public. However, the descendants of other children of the founder, Hazel Busch von Gontard, Edmee Busch Reisinger, Nellie Busch Magnus, and August Busch, have kept much of their Anheuser-Busch stock. August Busch inherited the largest block of stock in the company. As a result, his descendants have run the company for the past four decades. Nevertheless, several sons and grandsons of the daughters of the founder have served as officers and directors. Anheuser-Busch became the largest brewing company in the nation by establishing a distribution system and mounting advertising campaigns. August A. Busch III, a great-grandson of the founder, serves as president of Anheuser-Busch, and three of his cousins serve as directors. At least thirty great-grandchildren of Adolphus Busch and their children still own, through a series of trusts, no less than 20 percent of the stock in the company, worth $1.1 billion. About half of this stock is held by the descendants of August Busch. With accumulated dividend income, the descendants of four children of Adolphus Busch are worth well over $1.2 billion. SOURCES: Roland Krebs, *Making Friends Is Our Business* (St. Louis, Mo.: Anheuser-Busch, 1953); Prospectus, Anheuser-Busch Inc. (October 29, 1952); *Forbes* (March 1, 1968); Proxy Statement, Anheuser-Busch Companies Inc. (March 21, 1983).

CABOT, GODFREY L. (d. 1962) Boston, Massachusetts. Founder of Cabot Corporation. In 1882, Godfrey Cabot and his brother founded Cabot Corporation to manufacture carbon black from natural gas. Several years later, Godfrey Cabot bought out his brother. The company prospered after carbon black became an important ingredient in rubber and plastics. Although his son, Thomas D. Cabot, was largely responsible for diversifying Cabot Corporation into specialty chemicals, Godfrey Cabot did not relinquish control of the company until he was ninety-three years old. By 1968, the four surviving children of Godfrey Cabot and their children owned 55 percent of the stock in Cabot Corporation, worth $97 million. Louis W. Cabot, a grandson of the founder, currently serves as chairman, and two of his cousins serve as directors. As a result of recent stock repurchases by the company, the thirteen grandchildren of the founder and their children still own about 45 percent of Cabot stock, worth $320 million. With accumulated dividend income and the proceeds from stock sales, the descendants of Godfrey Cabot are worth well over $350 million. SOURCES: Prospectus, Cabot Corporation (May 15, 1968); Leon Harris, *Only to God* (New York: Atheneum, 1967); William Bulkeley, "The Cabots," *The Wall Street Journal,* May 7, 1979.

CARGILL, WILLIAM W. (d. 1909) La Crosse, Wisconsin. Founder of Cargill Inc., a private agricultural products corporation. William Cargill purchased his first grain elevators in 1865. In the years that followed, his company became one of the largest grain trading companies in the country. When William Cargill died in 1909, his stock in the predecessor of Cargill Inc. was divided equally among his four children. John H. MacMillan, a son-in-law of the founder, became president. Over the next several years, two of the children of William Cargill sold their Cargill stock to their sister and brother, Edna Cargill MacMillan and Austen S. Cargill. By 1930, Edna Cargill MacMillan and her two sons owned about 63 percent of the stock in the company. Austen Cargill and his two children owned the remaining 37 percent. Since the death of the founder, the company has been run primarily by the descendants of John MacMillan. Both of his sons and one of his grandsons have served as presidents. In recent years, Cargill has diversified into such activities as commodities trading, soybean processing, meatpacking, and steel manufacturing. It is now one of the largest private corporations in the nation. At present, four grandchildren of Edna Cargill MacMillan probably own close to 55 percent of Cargill stock. The two children and three grandchildren of Austen Cargill probably own another 30 percent of the stock in the company. Although Cargill is a private corporation, the descendants of Edna Cargill MacMillan and Austen Cargill are probably worth at least $1.8 billion. SOURCES: John L. Work, *Cargill Beginnings: An Account of the Early Years* (Wayzata, Minn.: Cargill Inc., 1965); *Business Week* (April 16, 1979); Dan Morgan, *The Merchants of Grain* (New York: The Viking Press, 1979).

CARLSON, CURTIS L. (b. 1914) Minneapolis, Minnesota. Founder of Carlson Companies, a private corporation. Curtis Carlson was working as a soap salesman when he decided to enter the trading stamp business. In 1938, he formed Gold Bond Stamp Company, which sold stamps to grocery stores and then redeemed them for merchandise. It was a profitable company that generated large amounts of surplus cash. Beginning in 1960, Carlson began diversifying into catalog showroom stores, restaurants, hotels, and travel agencies. Edwin C. Gage, a son-in-law of the founder, who joined the company almost two decades ago, was recently named president of Carlson Companies. However, the founder still serves as chairman. Although Carlson Companies is a private corporation, Curtis Carlson, his two daughters, and their eight children are probably worth close to $500 million. SOURCES: *Business Week* (June 13, 1983); Maurice Barnfather, "Capital Formation," *Forbes* (March 29, 1982).

CARVER, ROY (d. 1981) Muscatine, Iowa. Founder of Bandag Inc. Roy Carver founded a small pump company in 1939. In 1957, he founded a company to market a process for retreading tires developed by a former general in the German army. Bandag supplies equipment and supplies to a network of shops that retread tires for commercial trucks. When the company went public in 1968, Carver owned 74 percent of Bandag stock, worth $15 million. He gradually sold over $60 million worth of Bandag stock. When he died in 1981, Roy Carver still owned 45 percent of the stock in the company, worth $130 million. He was succeeded as chairman by Martin G. Carver, one of his two sons. Over the past four years, the wife and children of the founder have sold at least $50 million worth of Bandag stock in order to pay the taxes on his estate. At the same time, Bandag has repurchased over a quarter of its stock. As a result, the widow and two sons of the founder still own 45 percent of the stock in Bandag, worth $230 million. With the proceeds from stock sales and accumulated dividend income, the widow and sons of Roy Carver are worth at least

$250 million. SOURCES: *Forbes* (April 1, 1973); Proxy Statement, Bandag Inc. (April 10, 1981); Ruth Simon, "Minding the Store," *Forbes* (November 4, 1984).

CHANDLER, HARRY (d. 1944) Los Angeles, California. Founder of The Times Mirror Company. In 1894, Harry Chandler married the daughter of the publisher of the *Los Angeles Times*. They later inherited control of the newspaper. Harry Chandler went on to become one of the largest landowners in California. For example, he was a founder and major stockholder in the Tejon Ranch Company, which owned 300,000 acres north of Los Angeles. He and his wife eventually transferred the bulk of their Times Mirror stock to a family holding company and two massive trusts for the benefit of their eight children and twelve grandchildren. Harry Chandler was succeeded as chairman by his eldest son, Norman Chandler, who added radio and television stations to the company. Ruth Chandler Boswell, one of the daughters of the founder, later inherited control of J.G. Boswell Company, a major real estate company, from her husband. When Times Mirror went public in 1960, members of the Chandler family owned over 60 percent of the stock in the company, worth $70 million. Otis Chandler, a grandson of the founder, serves as chairman, and several cousins serve as directors of The Times Mirror Company. The family holding company and two family trusts established by the founder and his wife still own about 33 percent of the stock in The Times Mirror Company, worth just over $1 billion. Members of the Chandler family have received over $200 million in dividends from The Times Mirror Company in the past two decades. With accumulated dividend income and real estate holdings, the descendants of Harry Chandler are worth at least $1.2 billion. SOURCES: Robert Gottlieb and Irene Wolt, *Thinking Big* (New York: G.P. Putnam's Sons, 1977); Proxy Statement, The Times Mirror Company (April 24, 1978).

COFRIN, AUSTIN E. (d. 1979) Green Bay, Wisconsin. Founder of Fort Howard Paper Company. Austin Cofrin founded Fort Howard Paper Company in 1919 after being fired by another paper company. Fort Howard Paper later developed a unique process that enabled it to use more waste paper, which is cheaper than virgin wood, to produce its paper products. It also concentrated on producing tissue products that are distributed through wholesalers. As a result of this price advantage, the company has become one of the most profitable and fastest growing paper companies in the nation. The company went public in 1972, after the Cofrins sold about 13 percent of Fort Howard Paper stock for $33 million. At that point, their remaining 20 percent of the company was worth over $60 million. Austin Cofrin was succeeded as president by his eldest son, John P. Cofrin, who died in 1974. Although there are no longer any family members serving as officers of the company, David A. Cofrin, the younger son of the founder, serves as a director. David Cofrin, his children, and the children of John Cofrin own about 12 percent of the stock in Fort Howard Paper, worth at least $400 million. SOURCES: Prospectus, Fort Howard Paper Company (May 8, 1975); *Forbes* (June 12, 1978); Proxy Statement, Fort Howard Paper Company (March 10, 1978).

COORS, ADOLPH (d. 1929) Golden, Colorado. Founder of Adolph Coors Company. Adolph Coors started his brewery in 1873. He was succeeded as president by his son, Adolph Coors, Jr. The company has gradually expanded the distribution of its beer throughout the nation. In order to pay estate taxes and raise cash for various family members, the Coors family sold 12 percent of the nonvoting stock in Adolph Coors Company to the public in 1975. However, trusts for the benefit of the grandchildren and great-grandchildren of the founder kept about 85 percent of the nonvoting stock and all of the voting stock, worth about $900 million. Adolph Coors III, a grandson of the founder, was killed in a kidnap attempt in 1960. William K. Coors, another grandson of Adolph Coors, serves as chairman of the company. Jeffrey H. Coors, one of the great-grandsons of the founder, recently succeeded his father, Joseph Coors, as president. Three surviving grandchildren and at least fifteen great-grandchildren of the founder still own about 76 percent of Adolph Coors stock, worth almost $600 million. With the proceeds from prior stock sales, the descendants of Adolph Coors are worth at least $650 million. SOURCES: *The New York Times,* November 17, 1970; Grace Lichtenstein, "Coors Will Offer Stock to Public," *The New York Times,* May 6, 1975; Prospectus, Adolph Coors Company (June 15, 1975); *Forbes* (June 1, 1976).

COPLEY, IRA C. (d. 1947) Aurora, Illinois. Founder of Copley Newspapers, a private media corporation. Ira Copley was the son of the founder of several Illinois utility companies. Beginning in 1905, he acquired several newspapers in Illinois. In 1926, he sold his stock in the family utility companies and acquired several newspapers in California. When Ira Copley died in 1947, his two adopted sons inherited control of the newspaper chain. Ten years later, one of the sons, James S. Copley, borrowed $14 million to buy out his brother and other minority stockholders. When James Copley died in 1973, his second wife, Helen Copley, and his three adopted children inherited his Copley Newspapers stock. The company now owns thirty-one newspapers, most of them located in small cities. Helen Copley serves as chairman of Copley Newspapers and her son, David C. Copley, serves as a director. Although Copley Newspapers is a private corporation, the widow and three children of James Copley are probably worth $500 million. SOURCES: *The New York Times*, November 3, 1947; *The New York Times,* October 6, 1973; *Forbes* (April 15, 1975).

COWLES, GARDNER (d. 1946) Des Moines, Iowa. Founder of the Des Moines Register and Tribune Company, a private media corporation. In 1903, Gardner Cowles purchased the *Des Moines Register and Tribune.* One of his sons, John Cowles, later purchased the *Minneapolis Star and Tribune.* Another son, Gardner Cowles, Jr., founded Cowles Communications, which once published *Look* magazine. In 1971, Cowles Communications stopped publishing *Look* and sold several other publications to The New York Times Company for 22 percent of the stock in the company. In 1983, Cowles Communications distributed its New York Times stock and the cash that it received from the sale of its television stations to its stockholders. Six children of the founder and their children, who owned 28 percent of Cowles Communications stock, received $52 million in cash and New York Times stock now worth $106 million. In 1985, the Des Moines Register and Tribune Company, in which the Cowles owned the bulk of the stock, sold its newspapers to Gannett Company for $260 million in cash and its television stations for another $90 million. At least eleven grandchildren of Gardner Cowles and their children still own 80 percent of the stock in Cowles Media Inc., which owns the *Minneapolis Star and Tribune* and several other newspapers as well as television stations and cable television systems. Although it is a private corporation, Cowles Media is probably worth over $300 million. One grandson serves as chairman of Cowles Media, and several of his cousins serve as directors. Altogether, the descendants of Gardner Cowles are worth at least $600 million. SOURCES: Proxy Statement, Cowles Communications (April 9, 1969); Lawrence Ingassia, "John Cowles Is Ousted at Cowles Media and as Publisher of Minneapolis Paper," *The Wall Street Journal,* January 31, 1983; Thomas Moore, "Trouble and Strife in the Cowles Empire," *Fortune* (April 4, 1983).

COX, JAMES M. (d. 1957) Dayton, Ohio. Founder of Cox Enterprises, a privately owned media corporation. James Cox bought his first newspaper in 1898. He entered politics in 1905. He served two terms in the House of Representatives and three terms as governor of Ohio before he ran for president in 1920. After retiring from politics, he acquired newspapers and radio stations in several major cities. His only son, James M. Cox, Jr., eventually succeeded him as president of the various family newspaper and broadcasting companies. The newspapers were later consolidated into Cox Enterprises. The radio and television stations were consolidated into Cox Communications, which went public in 1964. Although the founder had four children, only two of them, Barbara Cox Anthony and Anne Cox Chambers, had children of their own. With the death of James Cox, Jr., in 1974, the two sisters became the sole income beneficiaries of trusts established by their father, which own almost all of the stock in Cox

Enterprises. In 1985, Cox Enterprises paid $1.2 billion for the 60 percent of Cox Communications not owned, directly or indirectly, by members of the Cox family. Cox Enterprises now owns forty-three newspapers, including the *Atlanta Journal and Constitution,* three magazines, twelve radio stations, and eight television stations. Although Cox Enterprises is a private corporation, the descendants of James Cox are probably worth over $1.8 billion. SOURCES: Prospectus, Cox Broadcasting Corporation (June 10, 1964); Proxy Statement, Cox Broadcasting Corporation (February 23, 1978).

CROWN, HENRY (b. 1896) Chicago, Illinois. Founder of Material Service Corporation, which was later merged into General Dynamics Corporation. Henry Crown and his brother started their own sand and gravel business in 1919. The company later expanded into coal and other minerals. In 1958, Crown sold Material Service to General Dynamics for $120 million in preferred stock that the company repurchased over the next six years. He used the proceeds to buy large blocks of stock in several corporations. By 1968, he owned $175 million worth of stock in twelve corporations. The following year, he decided to gain control of General Dynamics. By 1977, Henry Crown had paid about $50 million for 18 percent of the stock in General Dynamics. Over the years, Henry Crown has managed to transfer almost all of his fortune to a series of trusts, holding companies, and partnerships owned by his three sons and their children. Lester Crown, one of the sons of the founder, serves as a director of General Dynamics and several other corporations. In 1984, General Dynamics repurchased a fifth of its stock. As a result, the Crown family now owns over 20 percent of General Dynamics, worth nearly $600 million. Various family entities also own over $300 million in the stock of several other companies, including Burlington Northern, Hilton Hotels, and Vulcan Materials. With real estate holdings and the proceeds from previous stock sales, the two surviving sons and thirteen grandchildren of Henry Crown are worth at least $1 billion. SOURCES: *The Wall Street Journal,* April 8, 1965; *Forbes* (July 15, 1968); Proxy Statement, General Dynamics Corporation (March 11, 1977); Howard Rudnitsky, "The Crowning Touch," *Forbes* (December 8, 1980).

CULLEN, H. ROY (d. 1957) Houston, Texas. Founder of Quintana Production Company. After several years as a cotton trader, Roy Cullen entered the oil business in 1917. Over the next decade, he drilled several successful wells. In 1927, he and a partner discovered a large field that they sold to a major oil company five years later. Cullen used his $20 million share of the proceeds to form his own oil company, Quintana Petroleum Company. That same year, he discovered the Tom O'Connor field, one of the largest oil fields in Texas. His only son went to work for Quintana Petroleum, but was killed in a drilling accident in 1936. Two years later, Roy Cullen dissolved Quintana Petroleum Company and distributed its interests in various oil properties to trusts for the benefit of his four surviving children and fifteen grandchildren. He then formed Quintana Production Company to conduct exploration activities on leases owned by his children and grandchildren and their trusts. After the deaths of the founder and his wife, the family used revenues from the Texas fields to pay estate taxes and develop new fields in Louisiana. Quintana Production Company is now managed by the husbands of three of the daughters of Roy Cullen and one of his grandsons. Two estranged grandsons of the founder, who are beneficiaries of family trusts, but who do not own any stock in Quintana Production, recently sued for a larger share of the family fortune. By 1984, members of the Cullen family received over $30 million a year in royalties from their oil and gas wells. Altogether, the oil and gas properties owned by the descendants of Roy Cullen are probably worth nearly $1 billion. SOURCES: Ed Kilman and Theon Wright, *Hugh Roy Cullen* (New York: Prentice-Hall, 1954); Bryan Burrough, "A Bitter Family Feud Over the Cullen Estate Flares Again in Texas," *The Wall Street Journal,* September 2, 1983; Ellyn Spragins, "Houston to Dallas: Move Over, J. R.," *Forbes* (Fall 1983).

DANFORTH, WILLIAM H. (d. 1955) St. Louis, Missouri. Founder of Ralston Purina Company. William Danforth started his own feed and seed company in 1893. Over the years, he developed and marketed a number of special feeds for different farm animals and pets. He later developed and marketed breakfast cereals. By the time the company went public in 1945, William Danforth, his wife, and their two children owned 27 percent of Ralston Purina stock, worth $9 million. The Danforth Foundation, founded by William Danforth, owned another 13 percent of the stock in the company, worth $4 million. William Danforth was succeeded as chairman by his son, Donald Danforth. Over the years, the Danforth Foundation has received over half of the Ralston Purina stock owned by the founder and his wife. By 1974, the Danforth family owned about 5 percent of Ralston Purina stock, worth $90 million. Another 5 percent was held by the Danforth Foundation, which was still controlled by members of the Danforth family. Over the past decade, Ralston Purina has repurchased over a quarter of its stock. As a result, the fourteen grandchildren of the founder and their children probably still own over 4 percent of Ralston Purina stock, worth $160 million. One grandson still serves as a director of the company. Although it has given much of its endowment to Washington University, the Danforth Foundation is still worth $150 million. With the proceeds from stock sales and accumulated dividend income, the descendants of William Danforth are worth at least $200 million.

SOURCES: *Fortune* (January 1948); Prospectus, Ralston Purina Company (May 15, 1945); Proxy Statement, Ralston Purina Company (December 10, 1974).

DAVIS, MARVIN (b. 1924) Denver, Colorado. Principal stockholder in Davis Oil Company. Jack Davis, the father of Marvin Davis, was a promoter of oil-exploration partnerships. Marvin Davis learned geology and went to work for his father. He convinced others to invest in exploratory wells in areas ignored by the major oil companies. Although he invested very little of his own funds in these wells, he always retained an interest in their future production. Over the years, he has accumulated large oil and gas reserves. In 1981, he sold roughly half of his oil properties to a major corporation for $630 million. That same year, Marvin Davis and a partner borrowed $550 million and put up $172 million in cash to purchase all of the stock Twentieth Century–Fox Film Corporation. Davis later bought out his partner, after the partner fled the country to avoid prosecution for violations of federal law. Over the next two years, Davis sold and mortgaged enough of the assets of the film company to retire the $550 million loan and recover his $172 million cash investment. Although Twentieth Century–Fox now carries a heavy debt load, it probably has a net worth of at least $400 million. Marvin Davis, who is no longer in debt, owns all of the stock in the company. With the proceeds from the sale of his oil properties, Marvin Davis, his wife, and his five children are probably worth close to $1 billion. SOURCES: Richard L. Stern, "20th Century Fox," *Forbes* (March 12, 1984); Robert L. Simison, "Apache to Buy Certain Assets of Davis Oil," *The Wall Street Journal,* March 29, 1985; Stratford P. Sherman, "Hollywood's Foxiest Financier," *Fortune* (January 7, 1985); Bill Abrams and Michael Cieply, "Rupert Murdoch Is Said to Be in Talks to Buy Rest of Fox Films from Partner," *The Wall Street Journal,* September 12, 1985.

DAVIS, WILLIAM M. (d. 1934) Jacksonville, Florida. Founder of the predecessor of Winn-Dixie Stores. After closing an unsuccessful grocery store in Idaho, William M. Davis moved to Florida, where he opened another grocery store in 1925. With the help of his four sons, he expanded his store into a chain of grocery stores. By 1954, the five children of the founder and their children owned 44 percent of the stock in Winn-Dixie Stores, worth $9 million. Winn-Dixie is now the largest grocery store chain in the South. The last of the brothers to serve as an officer of the company, James E. Davis, was succeeded as chairman by a nephew in 1983. At least four other family members serve as directors. James Davis is the chairman of American Heritage Life Insurance Company, which he founded in 1956 with the assistance of his brothers. He and other members of the Davis family, through a family holding company, own 30 percent of the stock in American Heritage Life Insurance, worth about $30 million. Members of the Davis family still own about 29 percent of the stock in Winn-Dixie Stores, worth $440 million. Over the last four decades, they have also received over $260 million in dividends. With accumulated dividend income, the descendants of William Davis are worth at least $600 million. SOURCES: Proxy Statement, Winn-Dixie Stores (September 13, 1968); *Forbes* (October 15, 1973); Proxy Statement, Winn-Dixie Stores (September 13, 1974).

DAYTON, GEORGE D. (d. 1938) Minneapolis, Minnesota. Founder of the predecessor of Dayton Hudson Corporation. In 1902, George Dayton opened a dry goods store in downtown Minneapolis. He had two sons and two daughters. One of the sons, George N. Dayton, took control of the store, and later turned it over to his five sons. They expanded the family department store into a chain of department stores. They also acquired other regional department store chains and several specialty store chains. All five sons eventually became officers and directors of Dayton Hudson. By the time they took the company public in 1967, the five Dayton brothers and their children owned about 60 percent of the stock in Dayton Hudson, worth $160 million. Since 1982, the Daytons have sold about a third of their Dayton Hudson stock for a total of $230 million. They still own 18 percent of the stock in Dayton Hudson, worth $780 million. Two members of the Dayton family still serve as directors of the company. With accumulated dividend income and the proceeds from stock sales, the five sons of George N. Dayton and their children are worth just over $1 billion. SOURCES: *Forbes* (August 15, 1968); Prospectus, Dayton Hudson Corporation (July 15, 1969); Proxy Statement, Dayton Hudson Corporation (April 27, 1977).

DEERE, CHARLES H. (d. 1907) Moline, Illinois. A founder of Deere & Company. Charles Deere was the only son of John Deere, the inventor of the steel plow. He and his father, along with a brother-in-law, incorporated Deere & Company in 1868. Charles Deere ran the company for two decades and built it into a major farm machinery company. When he died, most of his Deere stock went into a series of trusts for his two daughters and his two grandsons. By 1938, they owned 35 percent of common stock in Deere & Company, worth over $30 million. One grandson, Charles D. Wiman, served as president of the company for almost three decades. The other grandson, Dwight D. Wiman, became a successful theatrical producer. When the trusts established by John Deere were finally dissolved in 1974, they still held over 12 percent of Deere & Company stock, worth about $180 million. The last family member to run the company, a husband of one of the great-grandaughters of Charles Deere, resigned as chairman in 1982. The descendants of Charles Deere have received over

$200 million in dividends on their Deere & Company stock over the past four decades. The six great-granddaughters of the founder and their children probably still own about 10 percent of Deere & Company stock, worth at least $150 million. With the proceeds from stock sales and accumulated dividend income, the descendants of Charles Deere are worth at least $300 million. SOURCES: Prospectus, Deere & Company (July 14, 1952); Proxy Statement, Deere & Company (April 30, 1974); Charles G. Burck, "For William Hewitt It Was an Easy Ascent," *Fortune* (August 1976); Wayne G. Broehl, Jr., *John Deere's Company* (New York: Doubleday, 1985).

DEMPSEY, JOHN C. (b. 1914) Delaware, Ohio. Principal stockholder in Greif Brothers Corporation. The wife and mother-in-law of John Dempsey were minority stockholders in Greif Brothers Corporation, a major manufacturer of wooden barrels. In 1946, he decided to acquire majority control of the company by purchasing stock from other stockholders. He eventually acquired just over half of the stock in the company. Later, Greif Brothers began manufacturing various types of containers. It is now a major container manufacturer. Dempsey has served as chairman of the company for almost four decades. Altogether, John Dempsey and his six children own almost 47 percent of the stock in the company, worth $300 million. SOURCES: William Baldwin, "Homely Virtues," *Forbes* (July 19, 1983); Annual Report, Greif Brothers Corporation (October 31, 1985).

DISNEY, WALTER E. (d. 1966), and ROY O. Burbank, California. Founders of Walt Disney Productions. In 1923, Walt Disney and his brother, Roy Disney, rented a small office and began producing cartoons. Walt Disney concentrated on the creative aspects of the business, and Roy Disney managed the finances of the company. When Walt Disney died in 1966, members of the entire Disney family owned 38 percent of Disney stock, worth $50 million. Walt Disney had two daughters, and Roy Disney had one son. Ronald W. Miller, a son-in-law of Walt Disney, served as president of Walt Disney Productions for many years. However, Roy E. Disney, the son of Roy Disney, took control of the company in 1984, after it became the object of several acquisition attempts. Three members of the Disney family, representing both branches of the family, now serve as directors. Lillian Disney, the widow of Walt Disney, and her two daughters and their children own about 8 percent of Disney stock, worth $230 million. They also own several real estate and broadcasting properties, which are probably worth close to $50 million. Roy Disney and his children own at least another 6 percent of Disney stock, worth $160 million. In addition, Roy Disney owns Shamrock Holdings, an investment company with interests in broadcasting, ranching, energy, and food processing, which is probably worth at least $300 million. With accumulated dividend income, the descendants of Walter Disney and Roy Disney are worth over $750 million. SOURCES: *The New York Times,* December 22, 1966; Proxy Statement, Walt Disney Productions (January 12, 1968); *The Wall Street Journal,* June 25, 1984; *The Wall Street Journal,* October 10, 1984; *Business Week* (August 5, 1985).

DONNELLEY, THOMAS E. (d. 1955) Chicago, Illinois. Principal stockholder in R.R. Donnelley and Sons Company. Thomas E. Donnelley and his two brothers were partners in a printing company founded in 1871 by their father, Richard R. Donnelley. The company soon became the leading printer of mail-order catalogs and magazines. Thomas Donnelley, the eldest son of the founder, gradually gained control of the company. It later became the largest commercial printer in the country. When the company went public in 1956, his two sons and one daughter owned about 68 percent of the stock in R.R. Donnelley and Sons, worth $43 million. Thomas Donnelley was also a major stockholder in another printing company, Reuben H. Donnelley Company, founded by one of his brothers, before it was acquired by Dun and Bradstreet in 1960. R.R. Donnelley and Sons was run for several decades by the two sons and one son-in-law of Thomas Donnelley. In the last three decades, however, the members of the Donnelley family have sold much of their R.R. Donnelley and Sons stock. Nevertheless, the surviving son and twelve grandchildren of Thomas Donnelley still own at least 21 percent of R.R. Donnelley and Sons, worth $490 million. Two of his grandsons still serve as directors of the company. With the proceeds from stock sales and accumulated dividend income, the descendants of Thomas Donnelley are worth at least $550 million. SOURCES: Proxy Statement, R.R. Donnelley and Sons Company (March 19, 1963); Proxy Statement, R.R. Donnelley and Sons Company (February 18, 1977); Proxy Statement, R.R. Donnelley and Sons Company (February 22, 1983).

DORRANCE, JOHN T. (d. 1930) Camden, New Jersey. Founder of Campbell Soup Company. John Dorrance joined the predecessor of the Campbell Soup Company in 1897. Within a couple of years, he had developed a process for canning condensed soup. John Dorrance later bought the entire company. When he died in 1930, all of the stock in Campbell Soup Company, then worth roughly $150 million, was placed in a series of trusts for his five children. For the next two decades, the company was controlled by the widow of the founder. Campbell Soup finally went public in 1954, and over the next six years the family trusts sold $98 million worth of stock. John T. Dorrance, Jr., the only son of the founder, joined the company in 1946, and has been chairman since 1962. Over the last four decades, the five children and ten grandchildren of John Dorrance, Sr., have received about $950 million in dividends from their Campbell Soup stock. The surviving son and grandchildren of the founder still own over

60 percent of the stock in Campbell Soup Company, worth over $1 billion. With proceeds from stock sales and accumulated dividend income, the descendants of John Dorrance are worth in excess of $1.6 billion. SOURCES: *The New York Times,* October 3, 1930; *Business Week* (November 13, 1954); Prospectus, Campbell Soup Company (November 16, 1954); Proxy Statement, Campbell Soup Company (October 12, 1978); *Forbes* (December 7, 1981).

DOW, HERBERT H. (d. 1930) Midland, Michigan. Founder of Dow Chemical Company. Herbert Dow developed and patented an inexpensive process for making bleach. In 1897, he and several partners formed the Dow Chemical Company to exploit this process. By the time he died in 1930, Herbert Dow and his six children owned 25 percent of the stock in the company. He was succeeded as president by his oldest son, Willard H. Dow, who greatly expanded the research and development activities of the company. In 1951, the Dow family owned over 12 percent of Dow Chemical stock, worth $130 million. At least three grandsons of the founder have served as officers and directors of the company. Herbert D. Doan, the last family member to serve as president, resigned in 1971. At that point, seven family members alone owned nearly 6 percent of Dow Chemical stock. The Herbert H. and Grace A. Dow Foundation, which is still controlled by members of the Dow family, is now worth $100 million. At least fourteen grandchildren of Herbert Dow and their children probably still own at least 6 percent of Dow Chemical stock, worth $480 million. Moreover, members of the Dow family have received over $200 million in dividends on this stock over the last two decades alone. Two grandsons of the founder continue to serve as directors. With the proceeds from stock sales and accumulated dividend income, the descendants of Herbert Dow are worth in excess of $600 million. SOURCES: Don Whitehead, *The Dow Story: The History of the Dow Chemical Company* (New York: McGraw-Hill Book Co., 1968); Prospectus, Dow Chemical Company (December 10, 1951); Senate Committee on Government Operations, *Disclosure of Corporate Ownership* (Washington, D.C.: U.S. Government Printing Office, 1973).

DU PONT, PIERRE S. II (d. 1954) Wilmington, Delaware. Principal stockholder in E.I. du Pont de Nemours and Company and General Motors Corporation. In 1902, Pierre du Pont and two cousins acquired 72 percent of Du Pont stock from four older cousins for $12 million in promissory notes. Thirteen years later, he organized a family holding company, Christiana Securities, to acquire the Du Pont stock held by another cousin. In 1918, Pierre du Pont had Du Pont purchase 23 percent of the stock in General Motors. For several years, he served as president of both companies. Pierre du Pont was childless, and he transferred most of his fortune to his eight brothers and sisters. By 1938, he and his brothers and sisters and their children owned almost 30 percent of Du Pont stock, worth nearly $290 million. Two brothers and a nephew eventually served as presidents of Du Pont, and several other nephews and great-nephews served as directors. In 1962, Du Pont distributed its General Motors stock to its stockholders. Christiana Securities was dissolved in 1977, and 75 percent of its Du Pont stock was distributed among the 34 nieces and nephews of Pierre du Pont and their 107 children. They probably still own about 11 percent of Du Pont stock, worth $1.8 billion. Several members of the du Pont family still serve as directors of Du Pont. After selling roughly half of their stock in General Motors, as required by a court decree, the members of the du Pont family own somewhat less than 2 percent of General Motors stock, worth $400 million. Moreover, they received $1.5 billion in dividends on their stock in Christiana Securities over the past five decades. With the proceeds from stock sales and accumulated dividend income, the descendants of the brothers and sisters of Pierre du Pont are worth close to $4 billion. SOURCES: Temporary National Economic Committee, *The Distribution of Ownership in the 200 Largest Nonfinancial Corporations* (Washington, D.C.: U.S. Government Printing Office, 1940); Prospectus, E.I. du Pont de Nemours and Company (February 4, 1952); *The Wall Street Journal,* December 16, 1974; John D. Gates, *The du Pont Family* (Garden City, N.Y.: Doubleday, 1979).

DU PONT, WILLIAM (d. 1928) Wilmington, Delaware. Principal stockholder in E.I. du Pont de Nemours and Company. William du Pont inherited a small block of Du Pont stock from his father, Henry du Pont, who was once a major stockholder in the company. Although William du Pont had served as an officer and director of Du Pont, he was excluded from the affairs of the company after Pierre S. du Pont gained control. Nevertheless, he kept all of his Du Pont stock. When he died, his Du Pont stock was placed in a trust for his two children, William du Pont, Jr., and Marion du Pont. By 1937, this trust owned over 2 percent of Du Pont stock, worth $32 million. The trust later sold almost all of its General Motors stock, but kept much of its Du Pont stock. When William du Pont, Jr., died in 1966, his five children each received $50 million from his share of the family trust. Marion du Pont had no children, and when she died in 1983, her five nieces and nephews each received another $60 million from the remainder of this trust. Altogether, the descendants of William du Pont, Sr., are worth about $550 million. SOURCES: Temporary National Economic Committee, *The Distribution of Ownership in the 200 Largest Nonfinancial Corporations* (Washington, D.C.: U.S. Government Printing Office, 1940); Gerard C. Zilg, *Du Pont: Behind the Nylon Curtain* (Englewood Cliffs, N.J.: Prentice-Hall, 1974); George Cooper, *A Voluntary Tax?* (Washington, D.C.: Brookings Institution, 1979).

DYSON, CHARLES H. (b. 1909) New York, New York. Principal stockholder in Wallace Murray Corporation, which was later acquired by Household Finance Corporation. In 1954, Charles Dyson invested $10,000 in Dyson-Kissner, a private holding company that he formed with an associate. Ten years later, they purchased a majority of the stock in Wallace Murray Corporation, a small manufacturing company, for roughly $12 million. At that point, Charles Dyson and his four children owned 95 percent of the stock in Dyson-Kissner. Through a series of acquisitions, Charles Dyson and his associate transformed Wallace Murray into a major conglomerate. John Dyson, the son of Charles Dyson, eventually served as a director of Wallace Murray. In 1981, Wallace Murray was acquired by Household International Corporation. Dyson-Kissner and members of the Dyson family then owned about 40 percent of the stock in Wallace Murray. In return for their stock, Charles Dyson and his four children received roughly $125 million in cash and Household International preferred stock. This private holding company, since renamed Dyson-Kissner-Moran, currently has substantial investments in a number of companies, including Esterline Corporation. Solely on the basis of their public investments, Charles Dyson and his four children are worth at least $200 million. SOURCES: *Forbes* (June 1, 1966); Proxy Statement, Esterline Corporation (April 2, 1970); Proxy Statement, Wallace Murray Corporation (March 23, 1978); *The Wall Street Journal,* February 18, 1981.

ENGELHARD, CHARLES W. (d. 1950) New York, New York. Founder of the predecessor of Engelhard Corporation. Charles Engelhard came to America as a sales representative for a German platinum company. He invested in a number of precious metals companies that were later merged to form Engelhard Industries. He was succeeded as president by his only son, Charles W. Engelhard, Jr., who added chemical processing and ore trading operations to the company. By 1969, the Engelhard family owned, through a family holding company, over 44 percent of the stock in Engelhard Minerals and Chemicals. That same year, Charles Engelhard, Jr., sold 70 percent of the stock in this holding company to a South African investment company for roughly $190 million. After he died in 1971, his widow, Jane Engelhard, served as a director of the corporation. The next year, the Engelhard family exchanged stock in Engelhard Minerals and Chemicals for stock in the family holding company. As a result of this transaction, members of the Engelhard family obtained all of the stock in the family holding company, which owned almost 11 percent of Engelhard Minerals and Chemicals. In 1981, this company was split into two separate companies: Engelhard Corporation and Salomon Inc. Although she no longer serves as a director of either company, Jane Engelhard and her five daughters probably still own close to 9 percent of Engelhard stock, worth

$70 million, and nearly 8 percent of Salomon stock, worth $520 million. With the proceeds from stock sales and accumulated dividend income, the descendants of Charles Engelhard are probably worth well over $700 million. SOURCES: Prospectus, Engelhard Industries (July 8, 1960); *Forbes* (August 1, 1965); *The Wall Street Journal,* March 3, 1971; Prospectus, Engelhard Minerals and Chemicals (December 12, 1972).

FIELD, MARSHALL III (d. 1956) Chicago, Illinois. Founder of Field Enterprises, a private media corporation that was recently liquidated. In 1904, when he was only twelve years old, Marshall Field and his younger brother became the sole beneficiaries of a $75 million trust established by his grandfather, Marshall Field, Sr., the founder of the department store chain. Marshall Field III became the sole beneficiary of this trust upon the death of his brother. In 1941, he started the *Chicago Sun-Times.* Over the next several years, Field Enterprises acquired other publishing companies, including the publisher of the *World Book Encyclopedia.* Although he had five daughters, Marshall Field III left the bulk of his Field Enterprises stock in trust for his son, Marshall Field IV. When Marshall Field IV died in 1965, he named his two sons, Marshall Field V and Frederick E. Field, as the primary beneficiaries of this trust. This trust was dissolved in 1977, and both of the sons of Marshall Field IV received roughly 40 percent of Field Enterprises stock. His four daughters shared the remaining 20 percent of the stock in the company. Between 1978 and 1983, Field Enterprises sold its publishing and broadcasting properties for over $450 million in cash. With the proceeds from these sales and other assets, including a real estate company and a paper mill, the two grandsons of Marshall Field III and their five children are worth at least $500 million. SOURCES: Stephen Becker, *Marshall Field III* (New York: Simon & Schuster, 1964); Frederick C. Klein and Harlan Byrne, "Brothers Share Control of Field Enterprises Through Unusual Pact," *The Wall Street Journal,* April 18, 1983; *Forbes* (December 31, 1984).

FIRESTONE, HARVEY S. (d. 1938) Akron, Ohio. Founder of Firestone Tire & Rubber. In 1900, Harvey Firestone and three associates raised $20,000 to establish Firestone Tire & Rubber. The company grew rapidly after it became the major supplier of tires to Ford Motor Company. When Harvey Firestone died in 1938, he and his six children owned 41 percent of the stock in Firestone Tire & Rubber, worth $17 million. Over the next four decades, all five of his sons served as officers and directors of the company. Raymond C. Firestone, the last son to serve as chairman, resigned in 1976. At that point, family trusts and a family holding company still owned over 25 percent of Firestone stock, worth $340 million. The family holding company was not dissolved until 1979. Even after selling over half of their Firestone stock in recent years, the two surviving children and sixteen grandchildren of the founder still own roughly 20 percent of the stock in the company, worth $170 million. Moreover, members of the Firestone family have received over $300 million in dividends on their Firestone stock over the past five decades. With the proceeds from stock sales and accumulated dividends, the descendants of Harvey Firestone are worth at least $450 million. SOURCES: Temporary National Economic Committee, *The Distribution of Ownership in the 200 Largest Nonfinancial Corporations* (Washington, D.C.: U.S. Government Printing Office, 1940); Prospectus, Firestone Tire & Rubber Company (May 13, 1952); *The Wall Street Journal,* October 27, 1983.

FORBES, BERTIE C. (d. 1954) New York, New York. Founder of Forbes Inc., a private corporation. After working several years as the editor of a financial newspaper, B. C. Forbes borrowed enough money from several prominent businessmen to start *Forbes,* a fortnightly business magazine, in 1916. After the founder died in 1954, his four sons inherited almost all of the stock in Forbes Inc. However, the magazine was run by Bruce and Malcolm Forbes, the two sons who had inherited 60 percent of the stock in the company. When Bruce Forbes died ten years later, Malcolm Forbes took charge of the magazine. He soon purchased all of the stock in the company from the widow of Bruce Forbes and his two other brothers. He also increased the circulation of the magazine. In 1969, he paid roughly $4 million for a 174,000-acre ranch in the mountains of Colorado that he later developed as a vacation resort. Malcolm Forbes has already transferred much of his stock in Forbes Inc. to his five children. His eldest son, Malcolm Forbes, Jr., who serves as president of Forbes Inc., will someday become the majority stockholder in the company. Although Forbes Inc. is a private corporation, Malcolm Forbes and his five children are probably worth at least $300 million. SOURCE: Arthur Jones, *Malcolm Forbes: Peripatetic Millionaire* (New York: Harper & Row, 1977).

FORD, HENRY (d. 1947) Detroit, Michigan. Founder of Ford Motor Company. Henry Ford founded Ford Motor Company in 1903. Several investors supplied $56,000, which was the entire capital, but Henry Ford received 25 percent of the stock in the company in return for his patents and expertise. Due to the low price and reliability of its automobiles, the company was an immediate success. Over the next sixteen years, Henry Ford spent over $104 million to acquire all of the Ford Motor stock issued to the original investors. In order to avoid estate taxes, he and his only son, Edsel Ford, later bequeathed almost all of their nonvoting stock in the company, which represented 95 percent of the total, to the Ford Foundation, and all of their voting stock to other family members. Henry Ford, who was still chairman of the company when his son died, was eventually succeeded by his grandson, Henry Ford II. When the company went public in 1956, the widow and four children of Edsel Ford received 12 percent of Ford Motor stock, worth over $400 million. Over the years, members of the Ford family have sold over $300 million worth of Ford Motor stock. However, as a result of recent stock repurchases, the three surviving grandchildren and thirteen great-grandchildren of the founder still own over 9 percent of the stock in Ford Motor Company, worth at least $800 million. In the past four decades alone, members of the Ford family have received over $900 million in dividends on their Ford Motor stock. Henry Ford II recently resigned as chairman of the company, but he and one of his brothers still serve as directors. No family members are now associated with the Ford Foundation, which has assets of over $3 billion. With the proceeds from stock sales and accumulated dividend income, the descendants of Henry Ford are worth in excess of $1.5 billion. SOURCES: Prospectus, Ford Motor Company (January 17, 1956); Proxy Statement, Ford Motor Company (March 26, 1975); Robert Lacey, *Ford: The Men and the Machine* (Boston: Little, Brown, 1986).

GALLO, ERNEST (b. 1909), and JULIO Modesto, California. Founders of E.&J. Gallo Winery. In 1933, Ernest and Julio Gallo, whose father had been a grape grower, used $5,900 in savings to start a winery. The brothers divided their responsibilities: Ernest was in charge of marketing, and Julio supervised the actual winemaking. They concentrated first on bulk wine, then developed various wine beverages. In recent years, they have added vintage wines. E.&J. Gallo Winery is now the largest producer of wines in the country. All three sons and the one son-in-law of the two founders work for the company. The Gallo brothers lobbied successfully for an amendment to the recent tax-reform legislation, which enables them to transfer $84 million worth of stock in the family company to their twenty grandchildren without paying any gift taxes. Although E.&J. Gallo Winery is a private corporation, Ernest and Julio Gallo, and their four children and twenty grandchildren, are probably worth at least $600 million. SOURCES: *Forbes* (October 1, 1975); Jaclyn Fierman, "How Gallo Crushes the Competition," *Fortune* (September 1, 1986).

GALVIN, PAUL V. (d. 1959), and JOSEPH E. Chicago, Illinois. Founders of Motorola Inc. The Galvin brothers started their own manufacturing company in 1928 with only $1,315 in capital. Until 1934, they produced all of the radios installed in automobiles. The company was also a major producer of television sets for many years. Motorola went public in 1943, and within a decade, the 31 percent of company stock held by the Galvins was worth $21 million. Most of this stock was owned by Paul Galvin, who supplied much of the initial capital for the company. Motorola eventually became a major producer of communications equipment and semiconductor devices. Paul Galvin was succeeded in 1948 by his only son, Robert W.

Galvin, who still serves as chairman. Robert Galvin, his wife and their three children, and his three cousins probably own about 12 percent of the stock in Motorola, worth over $550 million. Including the proceeds from earlier stock sales, the descendants of Paul and Joseph Galvin are worth at least $650 million. SOURCES: Harry M. Petrakis, *The Founder's Touch: The Life of Paul Galvin of Motorola* (New York: McGraw-Hill Book Co., 1965); Prospectus, Motorola Inc. (April 22, 1946); Robert Sheehan, "What Makes Motorola Roll?" *Fortune* (August 1954); Proxy Statement, Motorola Inc. (March 20, 1986).

GATES, CHARLES C. (d. 1961) Denver, Colorado. Founder of Gates Corporation, a private manufacturing corporation. Charles Gates began manufacturing automobile tires in 1911. The company later expanded into other rubber products. He was succeeded as chairman by his son, Charles C. Gates, Jr. Under his guidance, Gates Corporation stopped making tires and diversified into other products. In 1967, Gates Corporation purchased 65 percent of the stock in Learjet Industries, an unprofitable aircraft company. It eventually became the leading manufacturer of business jet aircraft. Gates Corporation recently sold its stock in Gates Learjet for $63 million. However, Gates Corporation is still a major producer of rubber products and batteries. All of the stock in Gates Corporation is owned, either directly or indirectly through trusts, by five of the children of the founder and the Gates Foundation. Although Gates Corporation is a private corporation, the descendants of Charles C. Gates and their children are probably worth at least $400 million. SOURCES: Proxy Statement, Gates Learjet Corporation (August 18, 1978); Ellyn Spragins, "Have Gun, Might Shoot," *Forbes* (November 8, 1982).

GETTY, GEORGE F. (d. 1930) Los Angeles, California. Founder of Getty Oil Company, which was later acquired by Texaco Inc. George Getty drilled his first oil well in Oklahoma in 1903. Three years later, he moved to California, where he soon discovered a major oil field. He was succeeded as president of Getty Oil Company by his only son, J. Paul Getty, who had the company acquire stock in other oil companies. By 1937, Getty Oil Company owned a majority of the stock in Pacific Western Oil Company, which, in turn, owned almost half of the stock in a holding company that owned large blocks of stock in two major oil companies, Tidewater Oil Company and Skelly Oil Company. The predecessor of Getty Oil Company went public in 1946 by merging with Pacific Western. At that point, J. Paul Getty and a trust established by his mother owned over 85 percent of Getty Oil stock, worth about $40 million. Over the next four decades, the companies controlled by J. Paul Getty used the dividends they received from Tidewater and Skelly to purchase more stock in those companies. One by one, these oil companies were then merged into Getty Oil Company. By the time the last oil company was merged into the parent company in 1976, J. Paul Getty and a trust for his children owned 58 percent of the stock in Getty Oil Company, worth $2 billion. J. Paul Getty bequeathed virtually all of his Getty Oil stock, worth roughly $700 million, to his J. Paul Getty Museum. The family trust for the benefit of the three surviving sons and sixteen grandchildren of J. Paul Getty owned $1.3 billion worth of Getty Oil stock. In 1985, this trust sold its 40 percent of Getty Oil stock to Texaco Inc. for just over $4 billion. With accumulated dividend income and the proceeds from this stock sale, even after paying capital-gains taxes, the descendants of George F. Getty are worth well over $3 billion. SOURCES: Proxy Statement, Getty Oil Company (March 26, 1976); Robert Lenzner, *The Great Getty* (New York: Crown Publishers, 1985); Carol J. Loomis, "The War Between the Gettys," *Fortune* (January 21, 1985).

HAAS, OTTO (d. 1960) Philadelphia, Pennsylvania. Founder of Rohm and Haas Company. Otto Haas and his partner founded an industrial chemical company in 1907. After his partner retired, Otto Haas became the majority stockholder in the company. When the company went public in 1949, Otto Haas, his two sons, and a family foundation owned about half of the stock in Rohm and Haas, worth $20 million. The founder was eventually succeeded by his son, Fritz O. Haas. His other son, John C. Haas, served as director for several years. The company recently repurchased over 20 percent of its stock, almost half of it from the family foundation, the William Penn Foundation. The two sons and nine grandchildren of the founder own about 16 percent of Rohm and Haas stock, worth $300 million. Another 15 percent of Rohm and Haas stock, worth $280 million, is held by two charitable trusts, established three decades ago by Otto Haas. These are probably charitable lead trusts. In that case, the Rohm and Haas stock held by these trusts will revert to the grandchildren of the founder at some point in the next couple of decades. The William Penn Foundation, which is controlled by members of the Haas family, still owns 15 percent of Rohm and Haas stock, worth $260 million. With accumulated dividend income and the stock held in the two charitable trusts, the descendants of Otto Haas are worth at least $600 million. SOURCES: Sheldon Hochheiser, *Rohm and Haas: History of a Chemical Company* (Philadelphia, Pa.: University of Pennsylvania Press, 1986); Proxy Statement, Rohm and Haas Company (March 21, 1975).

HAAS, WALTER A. (d. 1979) San Francisco, California. Principal stockholder in Levi Strauss & Co. In 1919, Walter Haas went to work for the clothing company founded several decades earlier by his great-uncle. With the assistance of his brother, Charles W. Haas, and his brother-in-law, Daniel E. Koshland, he later gained majority control of the company. By the time the company went public in 1971, they and their descendants owned over half of the stock in Levi Strauss & Co., worth about $250 million. Members of the Haas and Koshland families gradually sold over $100 million worth of Levi Strauss stock. Walter A. Haas, Jr., and Peter E. Haas, the sons of Walter Haas, have both served as president and chairman of the company. In 1985, members of the Haas and Koshland families, who owned over 40 percent of Levi Strauss stock, formed a private corporation that borrowed over $1.4 billion to acquire Levi Strauss & Co. Family members received roughly $340 million in cash for almost half of their Levi Strauss stock. They exchanged the remainder of their Levi Strauss stock for 92 percent of the stock in the private corporation. One of the sons of Walter Haas serves as chairman of this corporation and one of his grandsons serves as president. Although Levi Strauss & Co. is now a private corporation, the three children and eight grandchildren of Walter Haas, Sr., are probably worth at least $600 million. Three nieces and a nephew of Walter Haas, Sr., and their children are probably worth another $150 million. SOURCES: Prospectus, Levi Strauss & Co. (March 29, 1977); Victor F. Zonana, "Philanthropic Haas Family Embraces a New Cause—Total Control of Levi," *Los Angeles Times,* July 28, 1985.

HALL, JOYCE C. (d. 1982) Kansas City, Missouri. Founder of Hallmark Cards Inc. After selling postcards for a few years, Joyce Hall began distributing greeting cards in 1910. His two brothers joined the company and served as officers for several years. He built Hallmark Cards into the largest greeting card company in the country by providing stores with display racks supplied and maintained by his salesmen. Joyce Hall was succeeded as chairman by his son, Donald J. Hall, who has expanded the company into publishing and broadcasting. Donald Hall and his two sisters, Barbara Hall Marshall and Elizabeth Ann Reid, own all of the voting common stock in Hallmark, probably worth at least $600 million. The son of the founder votes a majority of this stock. An employee stock ownership plan owns all of the nonvoting participating preferred stock in the company, probably worth another $300 million. Although Hallmark is a private corporation, the three children and grandchildren of Joyce Hall are probably worth $650 million. SOURCES: Seymour Freedgood, "Joyce Hall Is Thinking of You," *Fortune* (December 1958); Robert McGough, "Pansies Are Green," *Forbes* (February 10, 1986).

HARBERT, JOHN M. III (b. 1921) Birmingham, Alabama. Founder of Harbert Corporation, a private construction company. In 1946, John Harbert invested $6,000 in equipment to form his own construction company. He started by building bridges but eventually expanded into such large-scale projects as dams and pipelines. In recent years, he has become involved in large international construction projects as well. In 1970, Harbert began acquiring and developing extensive coal properties in Kentucky. He sold his coal and limestone properties to Amoco Corporation for $260 million in stock in 1981. The Amoco stock held by Harbert Corporation is now worth $300 million. John Harbert and his three children own 75 percent of Harbert stock. Although Harbert Corporation is a private corporation, John Harbert and his three children are probably worth at least $350 million. SOURCES: *The Wall Street Journal,* August 24, 1981; Jay Gissen, "Poker Player," *Forbes* (March 26, 1984).

HEARST, WILLIAM R. (d. 1951) San Francisco, California. Founder of Hearst Corporation, a private media corporation. William Hearst, the only son of a wealthy mining speculator, bought his first newspaper in 1887. He later acquired or established newspapers in major cities across the nation. The newspapers were not always profitable, and the company was often on the verge of bankruptcy. When William Hearst died, he left the bulk of his estate, which was worth roughly $59 million, to a family foundation. He left less than $3 million worth of preferred stock in Hearst Corporation to a trust for the benefit of his five sons. Consequently, two family foundations owned all of the nonvoting common stock in Hearst Corporation, but the family trust owned all of the voting preferred stock. The company gradually acquired a number of book publishers, magazines, and radio and television stations. Although the children and grandchildren of the founder controlled Hearst Corporation, they received relatively little income from their preferred stock in the company. In 1975, at the instigation of members of the Hearst family, Hearst Corporation acquired all of its nonvoting common stock from the two family foundations for $135 million. The voting preferred stock owned by the family trust was then converted into voting common stock. As a result of this transaction, all of the stock in Hearst Corporation is now owned by trusts for the benefit of the three surviving sons and fifteen grandchildren of William Hearst. Although Hearst Corporation is a private corporation, the descendants of William Hearst are probably worth at least $2 billion. SOURCES: *Business Week* (September 15, 1980); Lindsay Chaney and Michael Cieply, *The Hearsts: Family and Empire—The Later Years* (New York: Simon & Schuster, 1981).

HEINZ, HENRY J. (d. 1919) Pittsburgh, Pennsylvania. Founder of H.J. Heinz Company. In 1896, Henry Heinz and his partner founded a company that prepared and sold bottled condiments. Several other partners later joined the firm, but Henry Heinz gradually bought out most of them. When the founder died in 1919, one of his sons, Howard C. Heinz, became chairman. By 1946, the daughter of the founder, the widows of his two sons, and three of his grandchildren owned 72 percent of H.J. Heinz stock, worth $43 million. Over the years, the members of the Heinz family have probably sold roughly half of their H.J. Heinz stock. After Howard Heinz died in 1941, his son, Henry J. Heinz II, became president of the company. Vira I. Heinz, the widow of one of the sons of the founder, also served as a director for many years. By 1968, these two family members owned, either directly or through trusts, over 18 percent of the stock in the company, worth $64 million. They also served as trustees of the Howard Heinz Endowment, which owned another 16 percent of the stock, worth $56 million. Six grandchildren of the founder and their children probably still own about 12 percent of H.J. Heinz stock, worth $550 million. With the proceeds from earlier stock sales and accumulated dividend income, the descendants of Henry Heinz are worth roughly $650 million. SOURCES: Prospectus, H.J. Heinz Company (October 10, 1946); Proxy Statement, H.J. Heinz Company (August 9, 1968); Robert C. Alberts, *The Good Provider* (Boston: Houghton Mifflin, 1973); Proxy Statement, H.J. Heinz Company (August 5, 1974).

HESS, LEON (b. 1914) New York, New York. Founder of the predecessor of Amerada Hess Corporation. Leon Hess began driving a fuel delivery truck with his father when he was eighteen years old. He gradually built Hess Oil into a major oil refiner and distributor. When the company went public in 1962, the Hess family and the Hess Foundation owned 68 percent of Hess Oil stock, worth $165 million. In 1969, he merged the company with Amerada Oil to form Amerada Hess. The company has a competitive advantage over most refiners because it operates a giant refinery in the Virgin Islands. Leon Hess has a son and three daughters. The son, John B. Hess, is an officer and director of the company. The Hess Foundation, which is controlled by members of the Hess family, owns almost 3 percent of Amerada Hess stock, worth $70 million. Leon Hess and his children, either directly or through a series of trusts and holding companies, own about 16 percent of the stock in Amerada Hess, worth $400 million. With accumulated dividend income and other investments, including the New York Jets football team, Leon Hess and his children are worth at least $450 million. SOURCES: *Forbes* (May 15, 1961); Arthur M. Louis, "Leon Hess Never Plays It Safe," *Fortune* (January 1970); Proxy Statement, Amerada Hess Corporation (March 23, 1978); *Business Week* (July 16, 1979).

HEUBLEIN, GILBERT F. (d. 1937) Hartford, Connecticut. Founder of Heublein Inc., which was later acquired by R.J. Reynolds Industries. Gilbert Heublein inherited a hotel and restaurant from his parents. He later began to sell condiments and sauces used in the restaurant. Heublein Inc. was finally incorporated in 1905. He had a son and a daughter, but neither was involved with the family company, and he was finally succeeded as president by one of his grandsons, John G. Martin, who ran the company for almost four decades. When Heublein Inc. went public in

1959, the four grandchildren of the founder owned 64 percent of the stock in the company, worth just over $20 million. Even after selling $5 million worth of Heublein stock, they still owned at least 44 percent of the stock in the company, worth $160 million by 1967. After he resigned as chairman, John Martin continued to serve as a director of Heublein until it was acquired by R.J. Reynolds Industries in 1982. The descendants of the founder, who probably still owned at least 12 percent of Heublein stock, received R.J. Reynolds Industries stock worth over $150 million. With the proceeds from earlier stock sales and accumulated dividend income, the four grandchildren of Gilbert Heublein and their children are worth over $200 million. SOURCES: *The New York Times,* March 22, 1937; Prospectus, Heublein Inc. (September 21, 1959); Proxy Statement, Heublein Inc. (September 20, 1967).

HEWLETT, WILLIAM R. (b. 1913) Palo Alto, California. A founder of Hewlett-Packard Company. In 1939, William Hewlett and his partner, David Packard, began manufacturing electronic equipment. Their initial cash investment in the company was $538. Hewlett concentrated on research and development, and Packard concentrated on finance and marketing. When the company went public in 1957, William Hewlett and his wife, Flora Hewlett, owned 44 percent of Hewlett-Packard stock, worth almost $16 million. Within six years, their 37 percent of Hewlett-Packard stock was worth $74 million. The company gradually expanded into calculators and computers. William Hewlett and David Packard later bought a 20,000-acre cattle ranch near San Jose before land values in the area soared. When Flora Hewlett died in 1977, she bequeathed $230 million worth of Hewlett-Packard stock to their William and Flora Hewlett Foundation. William Hewlett and two of his children serve as trustees of the foundation, which now has assets of $550 million. Over the years, Hewlett has sold roughly a third of his stock in the company. Nevertheless, he still owns about 12 percent of Hewlett-Packard stock, worth $900 million. With the proceeds from stock sales, William Hewlett and his five children are worth at least $1.2 billion. SOURCES: Prospectus, Hewlett-Packard Company (January 27, 1961); Proxy Statement, Hewlett-Packard Company (January 27, 1978).

HILLMAN, JOHN H., JR. (d. 1959) Pittsburgh, Pennsylvania. Founder of Hillman Company, a private corporation. In 1913, John H. Hillman, Jr., founded a coal company with his father and two brothers. However, he gradually became the majority stockholder in the company. The predecessor of the Hillman Company acquired large blocks of stock in a number of coal and chemical companies. He was succeeded as chairman by his son, Henry L. Hillman, who began selling the coal, iron, and chemical subsidiaries and reinvesting the proceeds in various equipment manufacturing companies. By 1969, the Hillman Company was probably worth about $500 million. In recent years, the company has become a major venture-capital firm. By 1982, Hillman Company had invested over $500 million in scores of high-technology companies. The company has lost at least $90 million in these ventures, but it has also received at least $200 million in profits from the sale of the stock in some of these companies. In addition to these venture-capital investments, Hillman Company owns a number of manufacturing firms, as well as major real estate developments in several cities. Although Hillman Company is a private corporation, the seven children of John H. Hillman, Jr., and their children are probably worth in excess of $1 billion. SOURCES: Gary Slutsker, "The Quiet Billionaire," *Forbes* (December 31, 1984); Bryan Burrough and Udayan Gupta, "Pittsburgh Billionaire Finds Venture Capital a Rough Game to Play," *The Wall Street Journal,* September 17, 1986.

HIXON, JOSEPH M. (d. 1946?) Pasadena, California. Principal stockholder in AMP Incorporated. Joseph Hixon founded a family holding company that became a major stockholder in AMP. AMP initially produced electrical components for automobiles but later diversified into electrical terminals and connectors. By 1959, this family holding company owned 45 percent of AMP stock, worth almost $18 million. AMP soon became a leading supplier of electrical connectors and equipment. By 1978, the 13 percent of AMP stock owned by the Hixon family holding company was worth $170 million. Frederick C. Hixon, one of three sons of Joseph Hixon, moved the family holding company to Texas and invested in oil and ranching. He also served as a director of AMP for over three decades. In 1980, the Hixons merged their family holding company into AMP. As a result of this merger, the children and grandchildren of Joseph Hixon received roughly 14 percent of AMP stock, worth $270 million. They probably still own at least 12 percent of the stock in the company, worth over $460 million. A son of Joseph Hixon still serves as a director of AMP. With the proceeds from stock sales, the descendants of Joseph Hixon are worth over $500 million. SOURCES: Prospectus, AMP Incorporated (October 2, 1959); *Forbes* (August 15, 1963); Proxy Statement, AMP Incorporated (March 21, 1978); *The Wall Street Journal,* November 24, 1980.

HOILES, RAYMOND C. (d. 1970) Santa Ana, California. Founder of Freedom Newspapers Inc. R. C. Hoiles founded a chain of newspapers in 1935. His newspapers, most of which are located in small cities, espoused libertarian principles. Freedom Newspapers now owns twenty-nine newspapers and four television stations. The founder was succeeded as chairman by his elder son, Clarence H. Hoiles. He, a brother, and a sister each inherited a third of the stock in the company. However, soon after Clarence Hoiles died in 1981, a dispute arose between the two surviving children of the founder. Harry H. Hoiles, the other son, felt that he was entitled to succeed his brother as chairman. His sister, Mary Jane Hoiles Hardie, had her husband installed as chairman instead. In 1981, she and the children of Clarence Hoiles offered to buy the one-third of Freedom Newspapers stock held by Harry Hoiles for $75 million. He rejected their offer and responded with an offer to buy their two-thirds of Freedom Newspapers stock for $650 million. They rejected his offer. Harry Hoiles has now filed suit to obtain a third of the newspaper and broadcasting properties owned by the company. Although Freedom Newspapers is a private corporation, the two surviving children and ten grandchildren of R. C. Hoiles are probably worth at least $900 million. SOURCES: Marc Beauchamp, "Cut the Baby in Half?" *Forbes* (October 7, 1985); Frederick Rose, "Freedom Newspapers' Harry Hoiles Seeks to Split Up the Wealthy Chain," *The Wall Street Journal,* December 2, 1985.

HOUGHTON, AMORY, JR. (d. 1919) Corning, New York. Founder of Corning Glass Works. Amory Houghton, Jr., incorporated the family partnership, Corning Glass Works, in 1875. He soon acquired most of the stock in the company. His elder son, Alanson B. Houghton, succeeded him as chairman. When the founder died, his stock in the company was divided among his four children. Corning Glass Works grew rapidly after it became the first company to manufacture light bulbs. When the company went public in 1945, the descendants of the founder owned over 66 percent of the stock in Corning Glass Works, worth $58 million. These descendants gradually sold almost half of their stock in the company. The company later became the leading producer of television picture tubes. Over the past eight decades, one son, one grandson, and two great-grandsons of the founder have served as chairman of Corning Glass Works. In addition, several other family members have served as directors. Almost all of the Corning Glass Works stock owned by the family is held in a series of trusts controlled by a few family members. The nine grandchildren of the founder and their children probably still own at least 13 percent of the stock in Corning Glass Works, worth $340 million. With the proceeds from stock sales and accumulated dividend income, the descendants of Amory Houghton are worth well over $450 million. SOURCES: Prospectus, Corning Glass Works (March 22, 1945); Prospectus, Corning Glass Works (March 29, 1955); *Forbes* (November 1, 1968); Proxy Statement, Corning Glass Works (February 24, 1978).

HUNT, HAROLDSON L., JR. (d. 1974) Dallas, Texas. Founder of Placid Oil Company and Hunt Oil Company. In 1930, H. L. Hunt invested about $75,000 in cash to buy leases to land that later proved to hold large oil reserves. Five years later, he formed Placid Oil Company, to operate these properties. At the same time, he put all of his Placid Oil stock in a series of trusts for his six children by his first wife. In 1980, three of these children, N. Bunker, W. Herbert, and Lamar Hunt, speculated unsuccessfully in the silver market. With other family members, they had to pledge Placid Oil stock and other assets worth $3.2 billion to secure a $1.1 billion loan in order to repay their creditors. In 1983, the two daughters of the founder, Margaret Hunt Hill and Caroline Hunt Schoellkopf, decided to separate their assets from those of their brothers. Their trusts and one for a mentally incompetent brother received title to roughly 40 percent of the oil properties and other assets owned by Placid Oil. Despite recent financial problems, Bunker, Herbert, and Lamar Hunt are far from insolvent. Their trusts own all of the stock in Placid Oil Company, which still has extensive oil reserves and silver holdings. Although it has recently defaulted on certain loans, Placid Oil still has a net worth of over $1 billion. With personal assets, the three Hunt brothers are probably worth over $1.5 billion. Their sisters and brother own oil properties and real estate worth at least another $2 billion. Altogether, the six children and twelve grandchildren of H. L. Hunt by his first wife are worth over $3.5 billion. When H. L. Hunt died in 1974, he left all of his stock in another oil company, Hunt Oil Company, to his second wife. Ray L. Hunt, the only son of H. L. Hunt by this marriage, has expanded its oil exploration activities and diversified into real estate. As a result, the widow of H. L. Hunt and her four children are worth roughly $1 billion. SOURCES: Harry Hurt III, *Texas Rich* (New York: W.W. Norton, 1981); G. Christian Hill, "Texas's Hunt Brothers Discuss Their Worth," *The Wall Street Journal,* August 27, 1985; Thomas C. Hayes, "The Wealthiest Woman in America," *The New York Times,* October 26, 1986.

INGRAM, ORRIN H. (d. 1963) Nashville, Tennessee. Founder of Ingram Industries, a private marine transportation, energy, and publishing company. Orrin H. Ingram was the grandson of a wealthy lumberman who was one of the founders of Weyerhaeuser Company. In 1951, he founded an oil transportation and distribution company. Ten years later, he merged his company with Murphy Oil Company, in return for 11 percent of Murphy Oil stock. In 1962, he founded Ingram Corporation, an oil refining and transportation company. He was succeeded as chairman by his eldest son, Frederic B. Ingram. Frederic Ingram and his brother, E. Bronson Ingram, eventually acquired 90 percent of the stock in the company. In recent years, Ingram Corporation has diversified into book publishing and distribution. Bronson Ingram now serves as president of Ingram Industries. Frederic B. Ingram, Jr., a grandson of the founder, serves as an officer of another family company. Although Ingram Industries is a private corporation, the two sons of Orrin H. Ingram and their six children are probably worth about $400 million. SOURCES: Prospectus, Murphy Oil Company (October 25, 1961); *Forbes* (November 1, 1976).

IRELAND, C. EUGENE (d. 1960), and BROTHERS Birmingham, Alabama. Principal stockholders in Vulcan Materials. C. Eugene Ireland and his two brothers, C. B. and H. B. Ireland, took over the predecessor of Vulcan Materials after it was purchased by their father in 1916. Originally, the company crushed slag and sold it as aggregate for use in road construction. By 1962, the eleven children of the three Ireland brothers owned, through a series of trusts, over 34 percent of Vulcan Materials stock, worth $23 million. The company later expanded into other aggregates, industrial chemicals, and scrap metals reclamation. Four of the sons of the three brothers eventually served as officers and directors of the company. Trusts established for the eleven children and twenty-seven grandchildren of the Ireland brothers still own about 32 percent of the stock in Vulcan Materials, worth over $320 million. One member of the Ireland family now serves as a director of the company. With accumulated dividend income, the descendants of Eugene, C. B., and H. B. Ireland are worth well over $350 million. SOURCES: *Fortune* (January 1960); Prospectus, Vulcan Materials Company (April 20, 1962); *Forbes* (July 1, 1975); Proxy Statement, Vulcan Materials Company (March 24, 1977).

IRWIN, WILLIAM G. (d. 1943) Columbus, Indiana. Founder of Cummins Engine Company. In 1919, William Irwin, who ran a local bank established by his father, aided his former chauffeur, Clessie L. Cummins, to develop a commercial diesel engine. Over the next eighteen years, he invested over $2 million in the Cummins Engine Company. William Irwin never married. When he died in 1943, J. Irwin Miller and Clementine Miller Tangemann, the two children of a niece of William Irwin, inherited his stock in the company. When the company went public in 1947, they owned roughly 80 percent of the stock in Cummins Engine, worth $13 million. Irwin Miller served as chairman of the company for over three decades. Cummins Engine became the major supplier of diesel engines for heavy-duty trucks. Although the descendants of the founder have sold much of their Cummins Engine stock over the years, they still own almost 30 percent of the stock in the company, worth over $200 million. With proceeds from stock sales and accumulated dividends, Irwin Miller, his sister, and his five children are worth at least $300 million. SOURCES: Prospectus, Cummins Engine Company (July 16, 1956); T. George Harris, "Egghead in the Diesel Industry," *Fortune* (October 1957); Prospectus, Cummins Engine Company (May 6, 1971); Proxy Statement, Cummins Engine Company (March 8, 1983).

JOHNSON, HERBERT F. (d. 1928) Racine, Wisconsin. Founder of S. C. Johnson and Son. Herbert F. Johnson took control of the family parquet flooring firm, established by his father in 1886, and transformed it into a leading manufacturer of household waxes. He was succeeded as president by his son, Herbert F. Johnson, Jr., who was eventually succeeded, in turn, by his son, Samuel C. Johnson II. Over the years, the company has diversified into household pesticides and personal care products. About 90 percent of the stock in S.C. Johnson and Son is owned by the five grandchildren of the founder and their children. The remaining 10 percent is held by senior officers who must sell their stock back to the company when they quit or retire. Samuel Johnson, who votes over 50 percent of the stock in the company, serves as chairman. In addition, two of his children are officers of the company. John J. Louis, the husband of the daughter of the founder, was a principal stockholder in Combined Communications Corporation. In 1979, when Combined Communications was merged into Gannett Company, his three sons exchanged their 13 percent of Combined Communications stock for $40 million worth of Gannett stock. This stock is now worth over $110 million. Although it is a private corporation, the 90 percent of S.C. Johnson and Son stock owned by the grandchildren of the founder and their children is probably worth over $1 billion. Altogether, the descendants of Herbert Johnson are worth at least $1.1 billion. SOURCES: *Forbes* (May 15, 1975); Proxy Statement, Combined Communications Corporation (March 30, 1978); *Forbes* (July 9, 1979); Harlan S. Byrne, " 'Johnson Wax' Puts Out More than Wax and It May Soon Diversify Even Further," *The Wall Street Journal,* December 26, 1980.

JOHNSON, ROBERT W. (d. 1910) New Brunswick, New Jersey. Founder of Johnson & Johnson. In 1873, Robert W. Johnson joined his two brothers in manufacturing bandages. His two sons, Robert W. Johnson, Jr., and J. Seward Johnson, eventually inherited 84 percent of the stock in Johnson & Johnson. The brothers took the company public in 1944, but kept roughly 70 percent of the stock in the company, worth nearly $21 million. As late as 1961, they and a series of trusts that they had created for their children owned over 55 percent of Johnson & Johnson stock, worth $240 million. Seward Johnson served as a director of the company for five decades. However, Robert Johnson, Jr., served as president during most of this period. He appointed his son, Robert W. Johnson III, president of the company, but later forced him to resign. When Robert Johnson, Jr., died in 1968, he left nearly $1 billion in Johnson & Johnson stock to the Robert Wood Johnson Foundation. No family members are currently associated with the foundation. In 1972, trusts for various members of the Johnson family sold $150 million worth of Johnson & Johnson stock. When Seward Johnson died in 1983, he left almost all of his $600 million in Johnson & Johnson stock to his third wife, Barbara P. Johnson. His six children sued her for part of his estate. In accordance with the settlement, she will eventually inherit about $300 million, and most of the rest will go to a family foundation. Trusts for the benefit of the six surviving children and twenty-five surviving grandchildren of Seward Johnson and Robert

Johnson, Jr., probably still own about 8 percent of Johnson & Johnson stock, worth $800 million. With the proceeds from stock sales, the widows and descendants of Robert Johnson, Jr., and Seward Johnson are worth at least $1.2 billion. SOURCES: Prospectus, Johnson & Johnson (August 23, 1944); Proxy Statement, Johnson & Johnson (May 13, 1961); *The Wall Street Journal,* August 17, 1972; David Margolick, "A Famous Fortune Entangles Family in a Bitter Feud over Bequest," *The New York Times,* June 18, 1985.

KAUFFMAN, EWING M. (b. 1916) Kansas City, Missouri. Founder of Marion Laboratories Inc. After working several years as a drug salesman, Ewing Kauffman started a drug company in 1950. The first successful product marketed by the company was a simple calcium supplement. Although Marion Laboratories has not developed many new drugs, it has grown rapidly as a result of its aggressive marketing efforts. When the company went public in 1965, Ewing Kauffman and his wife owned roughly 35 percent of Marion Laboratories stock, worth about $17 million. Within seven years, their 31 percent of Marion Laboratories stock was worth over $150 million. Although the family has sold about a third of its stock in the company, Ewing Kauffman, his wife, and his three children still own 25 percent of Marion Laboratories stock, worth over $500 million. The founder continues to serve as chairman of the company. He recently agreed to sell the Kansas City Royals baseball team, which he has owned since 1968, for $22 million. With the proceeds from stock sales and other investments, Ewing Kauffman and his family are worth at least $530 million. SOURCES: Prospectus, Marion Laboratories Inc. (December 6, 1968); Allan T. Demaree, "Ewing Kauffman Sold Himself Rich in Kansas City," *Fortune* (October 1972); Proxy Statement, Marion Laboratories Inc. (September 26, 1983).

KECK, WILLIAM M. (d. 1964) Los Angeles, California. Founder of Superior Oil Company, which was later acquired by Mobil Corporation. William Keck, an independent oilman, founded Superior Oil in 1921. By focusing solely on exploration and production, Superior Oil amassed large domestic reserves of oil and gas. By the time Superior Oil went public in 1956, William Keck and his four children owned 51 percent of the stock in the company, worth $250 million. When William Keck died in 1964, he left most of his Superior Oil stock to his William M. Keck Foundation. For the next two decades, the company was dominated by his youngest son, Howard B. Keck. In 1982, Willametta Keck Day disagreed publicly with the policies of her brother. Two years later, Howard Keck was forced to accept an acquisition offer from Mobil Corporation. The two surviving children and nine grandchildren of the founder, who still owned about 16 percent of Superior Oil stock, received over $900 million in cash. Willametta Keck Day died later that same year. Descendants of the founder still control the William M. Keck Foundation, which has assets of $490 million. Even after estate and capital-gains taxes, the descendants of William Keck are worth $700 million. SOURCES: Prospectus, Superior Oil Company (July 18, 1956); Proxy Statement, Superior Oil Company (December 31, 1969); Jefferson Grigsby, "The Founder's Son," *Forbes* (September 15, 1976); Susan Fraker, "Brawl in the Family at Superior Oil," *Fortune* (May 30, 1983).

KERKORIAN, KIRK (b. 1917) Los Angeles, California. Principal stockholder in United Artists Corporation. Kirk Kerkorian began renovating and selling surplus military airplanes in 1945. He then built a charter airline that he later sold to Transamerica Corporation for $85 million. During this same period, he borrowed $30 million to build two casinos in Las Vegas that he eventually sold for a total of $72 million. Even before he had sold the casinos, Kerkorian borrowed heavily to purchase 40 percent of Metro-Goldwyn-Mayer for $84 million. MGM soon entered the casino business. The company was later split into two separate companies: MGM Films and MGM Grand Hotels. At that point, Kerkorian owned 47 percent of the stock in both companies. In 1981, MGM Films acquired United Artists. Three years later, MGM Grand Hotels repurchased 28 percent of its stock. In 1985, Kerkorian sold his 69 percent of MGM Grand Hotel stock to Bally Manufacturing Company for $286 million. That same year, he also sold his 50 percent of MGM/UA Entertainment stock to Turner Broadcasting for $750 million. As part of this transaction, he repurchased United Artists for $470 million. After selling some of his stock to the public, Kirk Kerkorian owns 78 percent of the stock in United Artists, worth $600 million. All of this stock is held by Tracinda Corporation, a family holding company. With the proceeds from recent stock sales, Kirk Kerkorian and his two daughters are worth at least $700 million. SOURCES: Dial Torgerson, *Kerkorian: An American Success Story* (New York: Dial Press, 1974); Alex Ben Block, "Kerkorian's Master Plan," *Forbes* (May 20, 1985); Thomas C. Hayes, "Charting Kerkorian's Course," *The New York Times,* August 29, 1985.

KETTERING, CHARLES F. (d. 1958) Dayton, Ohio. Principal stockholder in General Motors Corporation. Charles Kettering developed a series of automotive inventions. In 1916, his engineering laboratory was acquired by General Motors. Kettering eventually became an officer and director of the company as well as a major stockholder. In 1939, he owned just over 1 percent of the stock in General Motors, worth $18 million. Almost all of this stock was held by a family holding company. By the time he died in 1958, this holding company owned almost $200 million worth of General Motors stock. He bequeathed his 30 percent share of the family holding company to his Charles F. Kettering Foundation. The remaining 70 percent of the stock in the family holding company was already held directly or indirectly by his son and three grandchildren. His son, Eugene W. Kettering, served only briefly as an officer of General Motors. With the proceeds from stock sales and accumulated dividend income, the descendants of Charles F. Kettering are probably worth in excess of $200 million. SOURCES: Prospectus, General Motors Corporation (April 30, 1956); Stuart W. Leslie, *Boss Kettering* (New York: Columbia University Press, 1983).

KIECKHEFER, JOHN W. (d. 1965), and BROTHERS Prescott, Arizona. Founders of Kieckhefer Container Company, which was later merged into Weyerhaeuser Company. John Kieckhefer and two of his brothers, Herbert and Walter, founded Kieckhefer Container Company in 1905. The company later became a major producer of milk cartons. Kieckhefer Container and its affiliate, Eddy Paper Corporation, were merged into Weyerhaeuser Company in 1957. As a result of this merger, the Kieckhefers wound up with roughly 14 percent of the stock in Weyerhaeuser, worth $140 million. Over half of this stock went to John Kieckhefer and his son, Robert H. Kieckhefer. Several years later, Robert Kieckhefer also became a major stockholder in Belco Petroleum. When this company was acquired by InterNorth, a major gas transmission company, in 1984, he wound up with $37 million worth of InterNorth preferred stock. John Kieckhefer has served as a director of Weyerhaeuser for almost three decades. Even after selling much of their Weyerhaeuser stock, the children and grandchildren of John Kieckhefer and his two brothers probably still own about 6 percent of Weyerhaeuser stock, worth $270 million. With accumulated dividend income and proceeds from stock sales, the descendants of John Kieckhefer and two his brothers are worth in excess of $350 million. SOURCES: Proxy Statement, Kieckhefer Container Company (March 22, 1957); Ralph W. Hidy, Frank E. Hill, and Allan Nevins, *Timber and Men: The Weyerhaeuser Story* (New York: The Macmillan Company, 1963); Proxy Statement, Weyerhaeuser Company (March 14, 1975).

KIRBY, FRED M. (d. 1940) Wilkes-Barre, Pennsylvania. A founder of F.W. Woolworth Company. Fred Kirby established a chain of variety stores that he merged into F.W. Woolworth Company in 1912. He transferred most of this wealth, through a network of family holding companies, to one of his two sons, Allan P. Kirby. By 1939, they owned, directly and indirectly, over 6 percent of Woolworth stock, worth $22 million. In 1937, Allan Kirby and several other financiers acquired control of Alleghany Corporation, a bankrupt railroad holding company. He had Alleghany Corporation sell its railroad stock and acquire majority control of Investors Diversified Services, a financial services company. He lost control of Alleghany in a proxy contest in 1961, but he bought additional stock and regained majority control two years later. His eldest son, Fred M. Kirby II, eventually succeeded him as president of Alleghany. By 1978, the widow and four children of Allan Kirby owned 35 percent of Alleghany stock, worth $65 million. They also owned close to 3 percent of the stock in F.W. Woolworth Company, worth $10 million. In 1984, Alleghany sold Investors Diversified Services to American Express Company for roughly $1 billion in cash and stock. The four grandchildren of Fred M. Kirby and their children own 38 percent of Alleghany stock, worth $220 million. They also control the F. M. Kirby Foundation, which has assets of $70 million. With accumulated dividend income and the proceeds from stock sales, the descendants of Allan Kirby are worth at least $300 million. SOURCES: Temporary National Economic Committee, *The Distribution of Ownership in the 200 Largest Nonfinancial Corporations* (Washington, D.C.: U.S. Government Printing Office, 1940); Howard Rudnitsky, "Polishing the Family Jewels," *Forbes* (December 7, 1971); Proxy Statement, Alleghany Corporation (April 6, 1978); Proxy Statement, F.W. Woolworth Company (May 9, 1977).

KLEBERG, ROBERT J. (d. 1932) Kingsville, Texas. Principal stockholder in King Ranch Inc. In 1886, Robert J. Kleberg married Alice King, one of the daughters of Richard King, the founder of the enormous King Ranch in Texas. He eventually became the manager of the ranch, and in 1924, he and his wife inherited a third of the ranch. Over the next several years, they acquired additional ranchland from several members of the King family and others. In 1934, Alice King Kleberg incorporated the King Ranch and sold her shares in the family corporation to trusts for the benefit of her five children. At that point, the ranch comprised over 800,000 acres. Her son, Robert J. Kleberg, Jr., served as president of King Ranch for three decades. A major oil and gas field was discovered on the ranch in 1945. In 1956, Alice Kleberg East, one of the daughters of the founder, sold her King Ranch stock back to the corporation in exchange for a 150,000-acre ranch. Some twenty years later, Robert R. Sheldon and Belton K. Johnson, two sons of another daughter of Robert Kleberg, sold their King Ranch stock back to the corporation for approximately $100 million. They recently went to court to obtain a share of the increased oil royalties paid to the King Ranch by Exxon Corporation. All of the King Ranch stock is now held by nine grandchildren of the founder and their children. Several family members serve as officers and directors of the company. Although it is a private corporation, the nine grandchildren of Robert Kleberg who own King Ranch stock are worth at least $600 million. The other five grandchildren of the founder own ranches and other investments that are probably worth at least another $200 million.

APPENDIX

SOURCES: Tom Lea, *The King Ranch* (Boston: Little, Brown, 1957); Anne Bagamery, "In the Best of Families," *Forbes* (June 22, 1981); Bryan Burrough, "Lawsuits Offer Peek at Texas Family's Feud over the Wealth of World's Largest Ranch," *The Wall Street Journal,* June 18, 1982.

KLINE, MAHLON N. (d. 1909) Philadelphia, Pennsylvania. A founder of SmithKline Beckman. In 1875, Mahlon Kline and two partners founded a small drug company that was the predecessor of SmithKline Beckman. Mahlon Kline was succeeded as chairman by his only son, C. Mahlon Kline, who served in that capacity for several decades. By 1958, the three children and five grandchildren of Mahlon Kline owned over 21 percent of the stock in the company, worth almost $70 million. Two grandsons and one great-grandson of the founder eventually served as officers and directors. C. Mahlon Kline never married, and his two sisters, Elizabeth Kline Jordan and Isadora Kline Valentine, and their five children eventually received most of the SmithKline Beckman stock held in a trust created by the founder. Although no family members are currently associated with the company, the Klines probably still own about 6 percent of the stock in SmithKline Beckman, worth at least $360 million. With proceeds from stock sales and accumulated dividend income, the descendants of Mahlon N. Kline are worth at least $450 million. SOURCES: Proxy Statement, Smith, Kline & French Company (April 15, 1958); Proxy Statement, SmithKline Corporation (March 21, 1975); John F. Marion, *The Fine Old House* (Philadelphia: SmithKline Corporation, 1980).

KLUGE, JOHN W. (b. 1914) New York, New York. Principal stockholder in Metromedia Inc. John Kluge first amassed a small fortune in the food distribution business. In 1958, he purchased a large block of stock in the predecessor of Metromedia Inc., a struggling broadcasting company. He later became chairman of the company. By 1964, Kluge owned 10 percent of Metromedia stock, worth $8 million. During the next decade, Metromedia went into debt to acquire several radio and television stations, as well as a major outdoor advertising company. Beginning in 1977, Metromedia spent almost $290 million to repurchase its stock. As a result, Kluge owned 26 percent of Metromedia stock, worth $158 million by 1982. In 1983, Metromedia borrowed $1.3 billion in order to repurchase almost all of its stock. Kluge received $114 million for part of his Metromedia stock, but he exchanged his remaining stock for more than 75 percent of the stock in the new company. Two years later, Metromedia, now a private corporation, sold its seven television stations. In exchange for these stations, the company was relieved of its $1.3 billion in debt and received an additional $650 million in cash. Metromedia has recently disposed of its radio stations, its outdoor advertising company, and its cellular phone operations for a total of over $1.7 billion. Although it is a now private corporation,

John Kluge, his wife, and his three children are worth in excess of $1.5 billion. SOURCES: Joel F. Olesky, "Metromedia's Creative Financier," *Dun's Review* (December 1965); Proxy Statement, Metromedia Inc. (April 15, 1968); Allan Sloan, "The Magician," *Forbes* (April 23, 1984); Bill Abrams, "Metromedia's Kluge's Moves Made Him Wealthy," *The Wall Street Journal,* May 8, 1985.

KNIGHT, CHARLES L. (d. 1933) Akron, Ohio. Founder of the predecessor of Knight-Ridder Newspapers, Inc. Charles Knight purchased the *Akron Beacon-Journal* in 1915. He was succeeded by his son, John S. Knight, who served as chairman of Knight Newspapers for over three decades. James L. Knight, the younger son of the founder, also served as an officer and director of the company. Over the years, Knight Newspapers acquired newspapers in such major cities as Miami, Detroit, and Philadelphia. When the company went public in 1969, the two sons of the founder sold almost 20 percent of Knight Newspapers stock to the public for $28 million. However, they kept 55 percent of the stock, worth $83 million. Five years later, Knight Newspapers was merged with Ridder Publications to form Knight-Ridder Newspapers. After this merger, John and James Knight and their children owned 34 percent of Knight-Ridder stock, worth $195 million. C. Landon Knight, the only surviving child of John Knight, served only briefly as an officer and director of the company. When John Knight died in 1981, he bequeathed part of his estate to the Knight Foundation and the rest to his widow and son. Four years later, Knight-Ridder purchased 15 percent of its stock held by the estate of John Knight and trusts for his family for $330 million. James L. Knight, the other son of the founder, still serves as a director of the company. He and his family, including trusts for the benefit of his four daughters, own about 15 percent of Knight-Ridder stock, worth $320 million. With the proceeds from stock sales, the descendants of Charles Knight are worth in excess of $400 million. SOURCES: *The New York Times,* September 27, 1933; Prospectus, Knight Newspapers Inc. (June 13, 1969); *Business Week* (August 25, 1970); Proxy Statement, Knight-Ridder Newspapers Inc. (March 17, 1976).

KNIGHT, PHILIP H. (b. 1938) Beaverton, Oregon. Founder of Nike Inc. In 1964, Philip Knight formed a partnership with his former college track coach to design and market track shoes. In 1972, they began marketing their own brand of shoes. When the company went public eight years later, Knight kept 46 percent of Nike stock, worth about $200 million. Nike now markets a variety of athletic shoes and clothing. The founder serves as both president and chairman of the company. With the proceeds from stock sales, Philip Knight, his wife, and their two children are worth at least $210 million. SOURCES: John Merwin, "Nike's Fast Track," *Forbes* (November 23, 1981); Proxy Statement, Nike Inc. (September 24, 1984).

KOCH, FRED C. (d. 1967) Wichita, Kansas. Founder of Koch Industries, a private corporation engaged primarily in oil refining and marketing. Fred Koch founded his own engineering company in 1925. Within four years, he was marketing an efficient process for refining gasoline. He gradually acquired a small oil refinery and a network of pipelines and terminals. He was succeeded as chairman of Koch Industries by his son, Charles Koch, who greatly expanded the company. In the last two decades, he has acquired another refinery and a number of chemical and mining operations. Two of the other three sons of the founder eventually became officers and directors of the company. Altogether, the four sons of the founder owned, largely through a series of trusts, about 75 percent of Koch Industries stock. In 1980, two of the brothers tried unsuccessfully to wrest control of the family corporation from their brothers. After three years of legal skirmishes, the two dissident brothers, William Koch and Fred Koch, Jr., sold their 35 percent of Koch Industries back to the company for roughly $1 billion. As a result of this transaction, the two other brothers, Charles and David Koch, now own about 65 percent of the stock in the company, worth at least another $1 billion. Even after the payment of capital-gains taxes, the four sons of Fred Koch and their children are probably worth in excess of $1.8 billion. SOURCES: *Forbes* (August 1, 1968); Louis Kraar, "Family Feud at Corporate Colossus," *Fortune* (July 26, 1982); Leslie Wayne, "Brothers at Odds," *The New York Times*, December 7, 1986.

KREHBIEL, JOHN H. (b. 1906) Lisle, Illinois. Founder of Molex Inc. In 1938, John H. Krehbiel and his brother formed a company to manufacture molded products from a cheap plastic made from coal tar by-products and waste asbestos fibers. John Krehbiel became president of Molex in 1947. The company later began manufacturing special electrical connectors and now supplies a variety of specially designed connectors, cables, and switches to electrical manufacturers. When the company went public in 1972, the 50 percent of Molex stock held by John Krehbiel was worth $40 million. He is still chairman even though his two sons, John H. Krehbiel, Jr., and Frederick A. Krehbiel, both serve as senior officers and directors of the company. The founder, his two sons, and trusts for the benefit of his grandchildren still own over 50 percent of Molex stock, worth at least $350 million. With the proceeds from stock sales, John Krehbiel and his family are worth $370 million. SOURCES: *Forbes* (May 17, 1979); Proxy Statement, Molex Inc. (October 30, 1980).

KROC, RAY A. (d. 1984) Oak Brook, Illinois. Founder of McDonald's Corporation. Ray Kroc was selling milk-shake machines in 1954 when he discovered two popular drive-in restaurants in California. He then convinced the owners to let him franchise other restaurants. He was able to maintain quality and control costs in these restaurants because he leased the buildings and the equipment to the franchise operators. In 1961, Kroc borrowed $2.7 million to buy out the original owners. By the time McDonald's went public in 1965, he owned 53 percent of the stock in the company, worth $18 million. Ray Kroc sold about $100 million in McDonald's stock over the years. By the time he died in 1984, however, he still owned over 11 percent of the stock in the company, worth $480 million. His widow, Joan Kroc, and a stepdaughter still own, through a series of trusts, about 9 percent of McDonald's stock, now worth about $600 million. Joan Kroc has served as a director of McDonald's. She also owns the San Diego Padres baseball team, which Ray Kroc acquired in 1974. With the proceeds from stock sales and other investments, the widow and stepdaughter of Ray Kroc are worth well over $700 million. SOURCES: *The Wall Street Journal,* April 12, 1965; *Forbes* (January 15, 1973); Proxy Statement, McDonald's Corporation (March 29, 1976); Ray Kroc, *Grinding It Out* (Chicago: Contemporary Books, 1977).

LAUDER, ESTEE (b. 1907?) New York, New York. Founder of Estee Lauder Inc., a private cosmetics corporation. Estee Lauder and her husband started manufacturing and selling cosmetics in 1946. Because they did not have the money to advertise their products, they relied on the distribution of free samples at fashion shows and mail-order sales. In recent years, the company has sold its products exclusively at the cosmetics counters of major department stores. Leonard A. and Ronald S. Lauder, the two sons of the founder, have both served as officers and directors of the company. By 1975, the Estee Lauder stock owned by the founder and her two sons was probably worth over $100 million. Estee Lauder still serves as chairman of the company; however, it has been managed for many years by her elder son, Leonard Lauder, who serves as president. Members of the Lauder family still own virtually all of the stock. Although Estee Lauder Inc. is a private corporation, Estee Lauder, her two sons, and her four grandchildren are probably worth in excess of $1 billion. SOURCES: *Forbes* (July 15, 1975); Subrata N. Chakravarty, "Not by Style Alone," *Forbes* (November 18, 1985).

LILLY, ELI (d. 1898) Indianapolis, Indiana. Founder of Eli Lilly and Company. Eli Lilly started a pharmaceutical firm in 1876 and was soon joined by his brother and a cousin. Eli Lilly and Company was incorporated five years later. After buying out two early investors, Eli Lilly eventually wound up with 85 percent of the stock in the company. Later, he turned the company over to his only son, Josiah K. Lilly, who built it into a major drug company. Eli Lilly II, a grandson and namesake of the founder, was the last family member to serve as president of the company. Even after his death in 1977, members of the Lilly family owned nearly 10 percent of the stock in the company, worth $350 million. The Lilly Endowment, a foundation endowed by Josiah K. Lilly, still owns 17 percent of Lilly stock, worth about $800 million, but only one family member serves as a trustee. The two surviving great-grandchildren and seven great-great-grandchildren of the founder probably still own about 6 percent of the stock in the company, worth $450 million. However, none of them is associated with the company any longer. With the proceeds from earlier stock sales, the descendants of Eli Lilly are worth at least $550 million. SOURCES: Proxy Statement, Eli Lilly and Company (March 22, 1968); E. J. Kahn, *All in a Century* (Indianapolis, Ind.: Eli Lilly and Company, 1975); Proxy Statement, Eli Lilly and Company (March 26, 1976).

LINDNER, CARL H. II (b. 1919) Cincinnati, Ohio. A founder of American Financial Corporation. Carl Lindner and his two brothers operated the family dairy store, which they expanded into a chain. In 1959, Carl Lindner convinced his brothers that they should go into debt in order to buy three small savings and loan associations. They then combined them into a single savings and loan association. American Financial Corporation, their financial holding company, went public two years later. In 1972, American Financial acquired the parent company of Great American Insurance Company, a large casualty insurance company, by issuing additional stock. At that point, Carl Lindner and one of his brothers, Robert Lindner, owned only 25 percent of American Financial stock, worth $35 million. Over the next several years, American Financial repurchased over 58 percent of its common stock in exchange for $144 million in debentures and preferred stock. By 1979, members of the Lindner family owned 48 percent of the stock in American Financial, but this stock was worth only $44 million. In 1981, Lindner and his family acquired the remaining 52 percent of American Financial common stock in exchange for $231 million in cash and preferred stock. Carl Lindner, his wife, and their three sons own 91 percent of American Financial stock, and three of his nephews own the remaining 9 percent. Lindner is chairman of the company and two of his sons serve as officers. Although American Financial is a private corporation, Carl Lindner and his family are probably worth at least $400 million. SOURCES: Proxy Statement, American Financial Corporation (May 2, 1975); Carol J. Loomis, "Carl Lindner's Singular Financial Empire," *Fortune* (January 1977); Carol J. Loomis, "Carl Lindner's Disappearing Act," *Fortune* (July 13, 1981).

LONG, JOSEPH M. (b. 1912), and THOMAS J. Walnut Creek, California. Founders of Longs Drug Stores Corporation. In 1938, Joseph M. Long and his brother, Thomas J. Long, borrowed $15,000 to open their own drugstore. Their stores have relied on high sales volume and highly motivated store managers. After the company went public in 1961, J. M. and T. J. Long owned 65 percent of Longs Drug Stores stock, worth $9 million. Ten years later, they and their five children owned 48 percent of the stock in the company, worth over $120 million. R. M. Long, the son of one of the founders, now serves as president of the company. Although members of the Long family have sold roughly half of their stock in the company, they still own about 32 percent of Longs Drug Stores stock, worth $200 million. With the proceeds from stock sales, Joseph M. and Thomas J. Long and their five children are worth at least $240 million. SOURCES: Prospectus, Longs Drug Stores (October 25, 1971); *Forbes* (February 1, 1975); Proxy Statement, Longs Drug Stores (April 15, 1983).

MCCONNELL, DAVID H. (d. 1937) New York, New York. Founder of Avon Products. David H. McConnell started making and marketing perfumes in 1886. His company was successful because it paid women commissions to sell cosmetics to their friends and neighbors. When the company went public in 1946, the descendants of David McConnell owned 56 percent of the Avon stock, worth about $10 million. The founder was succeeded as president by his only son, David H. McConnell, Jr. He was succeeded, in turn, by W. Van Alan Clark, who was married to Edna McConnell Clark, one of the two daughters of the founder. Although other descendants of the founder sold most of their Avon stock, Edna McConnell Clark kept most of hers. W. Van Alan Clark served as chairman of the company for almost two decades, and two of his three sons served as directors. By 1965, Edna McConnell Clark and her family still owned over 13 percent of the stock in Avon Products, worth $260 million. The Edna McConnell Clark Foundation, which is largely controlled by members of the Clark family, has assets of $200 million. A son of Edna McConnell Clark still serves as a director. Moreover, her three sons and twelve grandchildren probably still own about 6 percent of Avon stock, worth nearly $140 million. Over the years, they have also received over $170 million in dividends on this stock. With the proceeds from stock sales and accumulated dividend income, the descendants of Edna McConnell Clark are worth at least $250 million. SOURCES: Prospectus, Avon Products (April 15, 1946); Proxy Statement, Avon Products (March 26, 1965); *Forbes* (July 1, 1973).

MCDONNELL, JAMES S., JR. (d. 1980) St. Louis, Missouri. Founder of McDonnell Douglas Corporation. James S. McDonnell, Jr., started building airplanes in 1939. His company expanded rapidly during the war. In 1968, he merged his company, which built warplanes, with a major manufacturer of commercial airliners to form McDonnell Douglas Corporation. At that point, he and his two sons owned 17 percent of McDonnell Douglas stock, worth $190 million. Both sons have served as officers and directors of the company and one of them is now president. However, the chairman is a nephew of the founder, who worked his way up through the company. The two sons of the founder and their children still own about 11 percent of McDonnell Douglas stock, now worth at least $330 million. The McDonnell Foundation, which is largely controlled by members of the McDonnell family, owns over 3 percent of McDonnell Douglas stock, worth nearly $110 million. With accumulated dividend income, the descendants of James S. McDonnell, Jr., are worth over $350 million. SOURCES: Prospectus, McDonnell Aircraft Company (February 23, 1959); *Forbes* (December 1, 1974); Proxy Statement, McDonnell Douglas Corporation (March 24, 1975); William M. Carley and David P. Garino, "Big Changes Lie Ahead in Management, Board of McDonnell Douglas," *The Wall Street Journal,* September 8, 1980.

MCGRAW, JAMES H. (d. 1948) New York, New York. Founder of McGraw-Hill Inc. In 1886, James McGraw acquired an interest in a magazine publishing company. In 1909, he and a partner established a book publisher that was later merged with the magazine publishing company. Three of his four sons eventually served as president of the company. By 1953, three sons of the founder owned, directly and through a trust, 40 percent of McGraw-Hill stock, worth less than $20 million. By that time, the two other children of the founder had sold most of their stock in the company. Three of the grandsons of James McGraw later served as officers and directors of the company. By 1971, one surviving son and six grandchildren of the founder owned over 28 percent of the stock in McGraw-Hill, worth $150 million. One of the grandsons now serves as chairman of the company. Six grandchildren and twenty-two great-grandchildren of the founder still own about 25 percent of McGraw-Hill stock, worth over $600 million. With accumulated dividend income, the descendants of three of the five children of James McGraw are worth in excess of $650 million. SOURCES: Prospectus, McGraw-Hill Publishing Co. (July 23, 1953); Proxy Statement, McGraw-Hill Inc. (March 30, 1970); Donald D. Holt, "The Unlikely Hero of McGraw-Hill," *Fortune* (May 21, 1979).

MCKNIGHT, WILLIAM L. (d. 1978) St. Paul, Minnesota. Principal stockholder in Minnesota Mining and Manufacturing Company. In 1907, William McKnight went to work for the Minnesota Mining and Manufacturing Company, which manufactured sandpaper. He became president ten years later. Over the years, he accumulated enough stock in the company to become its largest stockholder. By 1949, he owned 14 percent of the stock in the company, worth $18 million. In all, McKnight served as president of Minnesota Mining and Manufacturing for almost five decades. He had one daughter, Virginia McKnight Binger, whose husband became the chairman of another major corporation. By 1972, McKnight, his wife, his daughter, and his grandchildren owned over 8 percent of Minnesota Mining and Manufacturing stock, worth at least $650 million. McKnight and his wife bequeathed most of their estates to the McKnight Foundation. This foundation, which has assets of about $450 million, is controlled by Virginia McKnight Binger and her three children. They probably still own nearly 2 percent of Minnesota Mining and Manufacturing stock, worth over $200 million. They also own Tartan Farms, a successful thoroughbred breeding farm and racing stable. With the proceeds from stock sales and accumulated dividend income, the descendants of William McKnight are worth in excess of $300 million. SOURCES: *Fortune* (March 1949); Proxy Statement, Minnesota Mining and Manufacturing Company (April 11, 1958); Proxy Statement, Minnesota Mining and Manufacturing Company (April 11, 1975); *St. Paul Dispatch,* May 9, 1977.

MCNEIL, ROBERT L. (d. 1955) Philadelphia, Pennsylvania. Founder of McNeil Laboratories, which was later merged into Johnson & Johnson. After working in a drugstore owned by his father, Robert McNeil founded a drug company in 1914. McNeil Laboratories grew rapidly after it introduced a substitute for aspirin. His two sons, Henry S. McNeil and Robert L. McNeil, Jr., later served as president and chairman of the company. In 1959, McNeil Laboratories was acquired by Johnson & Johnson for roughly $50 million worth of company stock. Both of the brothers served for several years as officers and directors of Johnson & Johnson. By 1975, the two sons of the founder and their eight children owned about 5 percent of Johnson & Johnson stock, worth over $250 million. Although they have sold much of their stock in the company in recent years, members of the McNeil family probably still own about 3 percent of Johnson & Johnson stock, worth $250 million. With the proceeds from stock sales, the descendants of Robert McNeil, Sr., are worth over $300 million. SOURCES: Proxy Statement, Johnson & Johnson (March 13, 1961); *Forbes* (June 1, 1972); Proxy Statement, Johnson & Johnson (March 11, 1975).

MANOOGIAN, ALEX (b. 1901) Taylor, Michigan. Founder of Masco Corporation. Alex Manoogian began supplying nuts and bolts to the automobile industry in 1929. As a means of diversifying his product line, he developed and sold the first single-handle faucets in 1955. By 1971, Alex Manoogian and his son, Richard A. Manoogian, owned over 24 percent of Masco stock, worth about $12 million. Richard Manoogian has served as president of Masco since 1968, but his father still serves as chairman. Over the years, Alex Manoogian has transferred most of his stock in the company to his son. Richard Manoogian has continued to diversify Masco by acquiring companies that sell a variety of consumer products and construction materials. Both father and son have sold much of their Masco stock in the last few years. However, they still own close to 10 percent of Masco stock, worth $220 million. With proceeds from stock sales and accumulated dividend income, Alex Manoogian, his son, and his grandchildren are worth roughly $290 million. SOURCES: Proxy Statement, Masco Corporation (April 19, 1971); Steven Flax, "Faucets That Drip Money," *Forbes* (March 16, 1981); Proxy Statement, Masco Corporation (April 27, 1984).

MARRIOTT, J. WILLARD (d. 1985) Washington, D.C. Founder of Marriott Corporation. In 1927, J. Willard Marriott and his wife opened their first coffee shop. They eventually built a coffee shop chain that also owned several hotels and an airline catering service. The predecessor of Marriott Corporation went public in 1952. Willard Marriott and his family, including three brothers, kept 65 percent of the stock in the company, worth almost $5 million. J. Willard Marriott, Jr., the eldest son of the founder, succeeded his father as president in 1964. However, his father continued to serve as chairman for two more decades. Under Willard Marriott, Jr., the company became one of the largest hotel chains in the nation. Over the next two decades, the Marriotts sold nearly half of their stock in Marriott Corporation. By 1972, they owned about 23 percent of Marriott stock, worth $240 million. The bulk of the stock held by the Marriott family was owned by Willard Marriott, his wife, and their two sons. As a result of recent stock repurchases by the company, the various members of the Marriott family still own almost 25 percent of the stock in Marriott Corporation, worth about $670 million. With the proceeds from stock sales, the descendants of J. Willard Marriott and his three brothers are worth in excess of $700 million. SOURCES: *Forbes* (February 1, 1971); Proxy Statement, Marriott Corporation (October 13, 1972); Robert O'Brien, *Marriott: The J. Willard Marriott Story* (Salt Lake City, Utah: Deseret Book Company, 1977).

MARS, FRANK C. (d. 1934) McLean, Virginia. Founder of Mars Inc. Frank Mars and his wife began making and selling candy in 1911. The founder sent his only son, Forrest E. Mars, to Europe in 1932 to establish subsidiaries. After Frank Mars died, the company was run for a decade by his widow. By 1945, the two children of the founder, Forrest Mars and Patricia Mars, each owned about 33 percent of the stock in the company. The rest of the stock was owned by an uncle and a number of senior officers. In 1962, Forrest Mars and his sister bought the 16 percent of Mars stock held by their uncle for $5 million. Two years later, Forrest Mars convinced his sister to exchange her 41 percent of Mars common stock for a large block of preferred stock in the company. During this period, Mars Inc. acquired a packaged rice company and a pet food company. Forrest Mars and his three children probably own, either directly or through trusts, over 80 percent of the common stock in Mars Inc. Forrest Mars recently retired from Mars Inc. and moved to Las Vegas, where he established a small gourmet candy company. Forrest E. Mars, Jr., and John F. Mars, the two sons of Forrest Mars, now share the title of company president. They and their sister, Jacqueline Mars Badger, are the only directors of Mars Inc. Altogether, Forrest Mars and his three children are probably worth in excess of $2 billion. SOURCES: Harold B. Meyers, "The Sweet Secret World of Forrest Mars," *Fortune* (May 1967); Thomas W. Lippman, "More Than Candy at Mars Inc.," *Sacramento Bee,* January 18, 1982.

MEAD, GEORGE W. (d. 1961) Wisconsin Rapids, Wisconsin. Founder of Consolidated Papers Inc. George Mead gained control of the predecessor of Consolidated Papers in 1902. Under his guidance, the company developed an efficient process for manufacturing coated papers. George Mead served as chairman of the company for almost five decades. He eventually turned over all of his Consolidated Papers stock to a family holding company. The stock in this holding company is owned entirely by his three children and several grandchildren. By 1975, the 43 percent of Consolidated Paper stock held by the Mead family holding company was worth $50 million. One of his sons, Stanton W. Mead, served as chairman of Consolidated Papers for many years. He was succeeded as chairman by his own son, George W. Mead II. In addition, one other grandson of the founder serves as a director. The Mead family holding company currently owns 41 percent of the stock in Consolidated Papers, worth $460 million. With accumulated dividend income, the descendants of George W. Mead are worth at least $500 million. SOURCES: *Forbes* (March 15, 1967); Proxy Statement, Consolidated Papers Inc. (March 17, 1978).

MEDILL, JOSEPH M. (d. 1899) Chicago, Illinois. One of the founders of the Tribune Company. Joseph Medill acquired an interest in the *Chicago Tribune* in 1855. He later became its editor and majority stockholder. When he died in 1899, he left his Tribune Company stock to a series of trusts for the benefit of his two daughters and four grandchildren. The husband of one of his daughters and all four of his grandchildren served as officers and directors of the company at some point. In 1932, the descendants of the founder placed their 53 percent of Tribune Company stock in a voting trust. This trust was not terminated until 1975. Consequently, only a few descendants of the founder have sold any of their Tribune Company stock. By the time the company went public in 1983, members of the Medill family owned just over 20 percent of the stock in the Tribune Company, worth at least $200 million. Another 18 percent of the stock was held by charitable trusts established by Robert R. McCormick, one of the grandsons of the founder. Seven great-grandchildren of

Joseph Medill and their children probably still own about 20 percent of Tribune Company stock, worth $400 million. One of these great-grandchildren, Alicia Patterson Guggenheim, founded *Newsday,* which was later acquired by The Times Mirror Company for stock. The Times Mirror stock she bequeathed to four nieces and nephews in 1963 is now worth $100 million. With accumulated dividend income, the descendants of Joseph Medill are worth roughly $550 million. SOURCES: Frank C. Waldrop, *McCormick of Chicago* (Englewood Cliffs, N.J.: Prentice-Hall, 1966); Prospectus, The Times Mirror Company (March 28, 1972); Paul W. Sturm, "Is There an Exorcist in the House?" *Forbes* (September 1, 1977); Prospectus, Tribune Company (October 12, 1983).

MELLON, ANDREW W. (d. 1937) and RICHARD B. Pittsburgh, Pennsylvania. Principal stockholders in Aluminum Company of America, Mellon National Corporation, and Gulf Oil Company, which was later acquired by Chevron Corporation. In 1882, A. W. Mellon and his brother, R. B. Mellon, took over the bank founded by their father. The bank later became Mellon National Corporation. They also invested in many companies that received loans from the bank. In 1889, they invested in the predecessor of Aluminum Company of America. Twelve years later, they invested in the predecessor of Gulf Oil Company. By 1937, the four children of the two Mellon brothers owned 35 percent of Aluminum Company of America stock and 70 percent of Gulf Oil stock, worth a total of $310 million. They also owned large blocks of stock in Koppers Company, Mellon National Corporation, and several smaller corporations. For the next three decades, the Mellon companies were controlled by Richard K. Mellon, the oldest of the four Mellon cousins. Over the past four decades, the children and grandchildren of the Mellon brothers sold over $600 million worth of stock in various Mellon corporations. In 1984, they sold their remaining 12 percent of Gulf Oil stock to Chevron for $1.5 billion. The surviving child and eight surviving grandchildren of A. W. and R. B. Mellon still own about 17 percent of Aluminum Company of America stock and 23 percent of Mellon National stock, worth a total of $850 million. Foundations endowed by members of the Mellon family, including the Andrew W. Mellon Foundation, the Richard King Mellon Foundation, and the Sarah Scaife Foundation, have assets in excess of $1.8 billion. With the proceeds from stock sales and accumulated dividend income, the descendants of A. W. and R. B. Mellon are worth at least $6 billion. SOURCES: Michael C. Jensen, "An Old Fortune Moves On," *The New York Times,* May 2, 1971; *The Wall Street Journal,* October 3, 1972; *The Wall Street Journal,* March 22, 1973; David E. Koskoff, *The Mellons* (New York: Thomas Y. Crowell, 1978).

MEYER, EUGENE, JR. (d. 1959) Mount Kisco, New York. Founder of The Washington Post Company. Eugene Meyer was a successful financier who was one of the founders of Allied Chemical Company. In 1933, he bought the failing *Washington Post* at auction for $825,000. Later, he appointed his son-in-law, Philip L. Graham, as its editor. In 1948, he put all of his voting stock in The Washington Post Company in a trust for the benefit of one of his daughters, Katharine Meyer Graham, and her husband. Before Eugene Meyer died in 1959, he gave much of his nonvoting Washington Post stock to his other four children. After her husband committed suicide in 1963, Katharine Graham took control of the newspaper. When the company went public in 1971, Katharine Graham and her four children owned about 15 percent of the stock in The Washington Post Company, worth $9 million. As the result of recent stock repurchases by the company, they now own over 21 percent of Washington Post stock, worth $310 million. Moreover, Katharine Graham and her children own all of a special class of common stock that enables them to elect a majority of the directors. Katharine Graham has appointed one of her sons, Donald E. Graham, publisher of *The Washington Post,* but she still serves as chairman of The Washington Post Company. With accumulated dividend income and other investments, Katharine Meyer Graham and her children are worth in excess of $320 million. SOURCES: Proxy Statement, The Washington Post Company (April 1, 1977); Howard Bray, *The Pillars of the Post* (New York: W.W. Norton, 1980).

MILLIKEN, SETH M. (d. 1920) Spartanburg, South Carolina. Founder of Milliken & Co. Seth Milliken founded a textile sales company in 1865. He was succeeded as chairman by his son, Gerrish H. Milliken. In the course of its business, the company lent money to scores of small textile mills. When many of these mills went bankrupt during the Depression, Milliken & Co. acquired a controlling interest in some of them. During this same period, the Millikens also acquired a large block of stock in Mercantile Stores Company. Roger Milliken, a son of Gerrish Milliken, became president of the textile company in 1947. He bought out the minority stockholders in the mills operated by the company and combined them into a single corporation. Milliken & Co., which has invested heavily in research and development, is now one of the largest textile companies in the country. Roger Milliken reportedly owns half of the stock in the company. The other major stockholders include his brother, Gerrish H. Milliken, Jr., two sisters, and a first cousin, Minot K. Milliken. Both his brother and his cousin serve as officers and directors of the company. Although it is a private corporation, the Milliken & Co. stock owned by these members of the Milliken family is probably worth at least $600 million. They also own close to 40 percent of Mercantile Stores stock, worth another $400 million. Altogether, these five grandchildren of Seth Milliken and their children are probably worth over $1 billion. SOURCES: *The New York Times,* February

20, 1924; *Business Week* (January 19, 1981); Howard Rudnitsky, "No Superior Oil Situation Here," *Forbes* (July 4, 1983).

MITCHELL, GEORGE (b. 1919) Houston, Texas. Founder of Mitchell Energy and Development. In 1946, George Mitchell and his brother began drilling oil wells in Texas for others in return for a percentage of any production. Six years later, George Mitchell paid $55,000 for the lease to a ranch that had produced only one gas well. Almost every well they drilled on the ranch produced gas. They immediately bought leases on adjoining properties. This field later became one of the largest gas fields in the state. George Mitchell eventually bought out most of his partners, except his brother. By the time he took his company public in 1972, his 71 percent of the stock was worth $42 million. About this time, he also began developing Woodlands, a 23,000-acre planned community outside Houston. Although he has ten children, Mitchell has transferred relatively little of his stock in the company to them. George Mitchell and his wife still own 62 percent of Mitchell Energy and Development stock, worth nearly $400 million. SOURCES: James Presley, *The Saga of Wealth* (New York: G. P. Putnam's Sons, 1978); Lawrence Minard, "George Mitchell and His Edifice Complex," *Forbes* (July 1, 1977); Proxy Statement, Mitchell Energy and Development Corporation (June 26, 1985).

MOORE, GORDON E. (b. 1921) Santa Clara, California. A founder of Intel Corporation. Gordon Moore was one of the inventors of the transistor. In 1957, he became one of the founders of Fairchild Semiconductors. In 1967, he and a partner started Intel Corporation with $1 million they had amassed in Fairchild Semiconductor stock. They later raised $2.5 million from a group of venture capitalists. By the time the company went public in 1971, Moore owned 14 percent of Intel stock, worth $13 million. Within two years, this stock was worth $48 million. Moore, who still serves as chairman of the company, has sold very little of his stock. Gordon Moore, his wife, and their two children still own over 5 percent of Intel stock, worth about $200 million. SOURCES: Prospectus, Intel Corporation (May 10, 1973); Gene Bylinsky, "How Intel Won Its Bet on Memory Chips," *Fortune* (November 1973).

MOTT, CHARLES S. (d. 1973) Flint, Michigan. Principal stockholder in General Motors Corporation, United States Sugar Corporation, and Continental Water Corporation. Charles Mott took over the family manufacturing company and began producing wheels for automobiles. In 1913, he sold the company to General Motors for stock. As a result, he became one of the largest individual stockholders in General Motors. He later invested in a sugar company and several water supply companies. In 1937, he owned over 1 percent of the stock in General Motors, worth $18 million.

Over the years, he established a series of trusts for his six children that held large blocks of stock in General Motors, United States Sugar, and Continental Water. In 1963, he gave almost all of his remaining stock in these companies, worth $195 million, to his Charles Stewart Mott Foundation. His children probably still own at least $75 million worth of General Motors stock. United States Sugar recently repurchased $50 million worth of its stock from members of the Mott family. However, family members and family foundations still own a majority of the stock in the company. Members of the Mott family probably also own almost all of the stock in Continental Water, which owns and operates water systems in five cities. Although it is a private corporation, the Continental Water stock owned by the children of Charles Mott is probably worth at least $150 million. With the proceeds from stock sales and accumulated dividend income, the descendants of Charles Mott are worth at least $300 million. SOURCES: Prospectus, General Motors Corporation (April 17, 1954); *The New York Times,* February 19, 1973; Irwin Ross, "The View from Stewart Mott's Penthouse," *Fortune* (March 1974); Thomas E. Ricks, "U.S. Sugar Corp.'s Bid for 73% of Its Stock Lets the Motts Raise Money, Keep Control," *The Wall Street Journal,* September 23, 1983.

MURCHISON, CLINT W. (d. 1969) Dallas, Texas. Principal stockholder in several oil companies and insurance companies. Clint Murchison became an independent oil producer in 1919 and later formed a number of small oil and gas companies. In 1936, he began acquiring controlling interests in several small life insurance companies. Almost all of these companies were later sold to other companies or liquidated. Between 1961 and 1972, the family sold their stock in several insurance companies for $50 million in cash and stock that is now worth another $50 million. By the time he died, Clint Murchison had transferred most of his assets to a family partnership owned by his two sons, John D. Murchison and Clint W. Murchison, Jr., and trusts for their seven children. In 1955, the family acquired a 50 percent interest in Centex, a small Texas home-building company, by simply guaranteeing some loans. In 1978, several family trusts sold 22 percent of Centex stock back to the company for $52 million. Their remaining 35 percent of the stock in Centex and Cenergy, its energy affiliate, is now worth $190 million. Clint Murchison III, a grandson of the founder, serves as a director of Centex. In addition, members of the Murchison family recently sold their 11 percent of Delhi International stock for $66 million. In 1984, they sold the Dallas Cowboys for $60 million. Clint Murchison, Jr., the surviving son of the founder, recently filed for bankruptcy. However, he and his brother had long ago transferred the bulk of their wealth to their children. With the proceeds from stock sales and other investments, the descendants of Clint Murchison, Sr., are probably worth in excess of $450 million. SOURCES: Freeman Lincoln, "Big Wheeler-Dealer from Dallas," *Fortune* (January 1963); Richard Carry, "Murchisons Thrive on Anonymity," *The New York Times,* June 20, 1971; Howard Rudnitsky, "The Centex Story," *Forbes* (February 6, 1978); Proxy Statement, Centex Corporation (June 8, 1983).

MURPHY, CHARLES H. (d. 1954) El Dorado, Arkansas. Founder of Murphy Oil Corporation. Charles Murphy was a banker, who acquired cotton plantations and timberland. His only son, Charles H. Murphy, Jr., drilled his first oil well when he was only eighteen years old. Three years later, he became president of the family holding company and began transforming it into an oil company. Murphy Oil became a major producer after it discovered oil in Louisiana. Several years later, the company added a refinery. By 1961, Charles Murphy, Jr., and his three sisters owned roughly 45 percent of Murphy Oil stock, worth $50 million. The four children and at least eleven grandchildren of the founder still own 35 percent of the stock in the company, worth about $390 million. Charles Murphy, Jr., continues to serve as chairman, and five other family members serve as directors. With accumulated dividend income, the descendants of Charles Murphy, Sr., are worth at least $420 million. SOURCES: Prospectus, Murphy Oil Corporation (October 25, 1961); Neil A. Martin, "A Maverick Named Murphy," *Dun's Review* (October 1972); Proxy Statement, Murphy Oil Corporation (March 17, 1978).

NEWHOUSE, SAMUEL I. (d. 1979) New York, New York. Founder of Advance Publications Inc., a private media corporation. After working several years as an editor, S. I. Newhouse purchased his first newspaper in 1922. He gradually added newspapers in cities across the country. Advance Publications now owns twenty-eight newspapers, nine magazines, and a major book publisher. At least four decades ago, the founder transferred all of the preferred stock in the company to his wife, his two sons, and his two brothers. He kept all of the common stock. When S. I. Newhouse, Sr., died, he bequeathed all of his common stock in Advance Publications to his wife and six grandchildren. The Newhouse family is appealing the tax assessment on his estate. The Internal Revenue Service claims that the Advance Publications common stock owned by S. I. Newhouse was worth $610 million. The family maintains that it was worth only $47 million. Both sons of the founder serve as officers and directors of the company: Samuel I. Newhouse, Jr., is chairman, and Donald E. Newhouse is president. Their two uncles are also officers and directors. Although Advance Publications is a private corporation and the tax liabilities of the estate are as yet undetermined, the widow, two sons, and six grandchildren of S. I. Newhouse are probably worth in excess of $1.2 billion. SOURCES: Jefferson Grigsby, "Newhouse, after Newhouse,"

Forbes (October 28, 1979); David Henry, "Tax Collector's Vengeance," *Forbes* (November 5, 1984).

NIELSEN, ARTHUR C. (d. 1980) Northbrook, Illinois. Founder of A.C. Nielsen Company, which was later merged with Dun & Bradstreet Corporation. After working as an engineer for several years, Arthur Nielsen borrowed $45,000 to form his own product research firm in 1923. He later became a pioneer in the field of market research. Instead of relying on consumer surveys, he conducted inventories of stores. When the company went public in 1958, Nielsen and his five children owned 24 percent of A.C. Nielsen stock, worth $3 million. The founder was eventually succeeded as president and chairman by his son, Arthur C. Nielsen, Jr. By 1980, Arthur Nielsen, Sr., and a series of trusts for his five children owned 16 percent of the stock in the company, worth about $70 million. However, because they owned all of a special class of stock, they cast 56 percent of the votes. In 1984, A.C. Nielsen Company was merged with Dun & Bradstreet Corporation. The children and grandchildren of A. C. Nielsen, Sr., received over 3 percent of Dun & Bradstreet stock, worth about $170 million. With the proceeds from stock sales, the descendants of Arthur Nielsen, Sr., are worth $200 million. SOURCES: *The Wall Street Journal,* November 21, 1958; Proxy Statement, A.C. Nielsen Company (January 17, 1980); Barry Stavro, "Rating Nielsen," *Forbes* (December 17, 1984).

NORDSTROM, JOHN W. (d. 1964) Seattle, Washington. Founder of Nordstrom Inc. John Nordstrom and a partner founded a shoe store in Seattle in 1901. Three decades later, Nordstrom bought out his partner and sold the store to his three sons: Everett, Lloyd, and Elmer Nordstrom. They expanded the original shoe store into a chain of clothing and shoe stores. The company is now run by the three grandsons of the founder and the husband of one of his granddaughters. By 1976, members of the Nordstrom family owned 64 percent of Nordstrom's stock, worth $50 million. They have since expanded the fashion apparel chain to other states in the West. The family still owns 57 percent of the stock in the company, worth $530 million. In 1965, four members of the Nordstrom family and a family trust purchased 51 percent of the Seattle Seahawks football franchise for $16 million. Altogether, the descendants of John Nordstrom are worth at least $550 million. SOURCES: Proxy Statement, Nordstrom Inc. (April 21, 1978); *Forbes* (May 29, 1978).

OCHS, ADOLPH S. (d. 1935) New York, New York. Founder of The New York Times Company. Adolph Ochs borrowed $75,000 to buy the struggling *New York Times* in 1896. In the years that followed, he transformed it into one of the most staid and respected newspapers in the country. When Adolph Ochs died in 1935, all of his stock in The New York Times

Company went into a trust for the benefit of his daughter, Iphigene Ochs Sulzberger, and her four children. Arthur H. Sulzberger, the son-in-law of the founder, served as publisher of *The New York Times* and chairman of The New York Times Company for over two decades. He was eventually succeeded by his son, Arthur O. Sulzberger. Since 1968, the Adolph Ochs trust has sold over $52 million in New York Times stock. Although the family no longer owns a majority of the stock in the company, it does own a majority of a special class of common stock that elects 70 percent of the directors. As a result, all four of the grandchildren of the founder have served as directors. The trust created by the founder still owns about 34 percent of The New York Times stock, worth nearly $650 million. With proceeds from stock sales and accumulated dividend income, the descendants of Adolph Ochs are worth in excess of $700 million. SOURCES: *The Wall Street Journal,* December 4, 1968; Gay Talese, *The Kingdom and the Power* (New York: World Publishing, 1969); Proxy Statement, The New York Times Company (March 31, 1976).

OLIN, FRANKLIN W. (d. 1953) Alton, Illinois. Founder of Olin Corporation. Franklin Olin founded the Olin Corporation in 1908. He was succeeded as president of the company by his son, John M. Olin. His other son, T. Spencer Olin, served as an officer and director as well. When Franklin Olin died, he left his 30 percent of Olin stock to his Olin Foundation. The company immediately repurchased this stock from the foundation. In 1954, Olin Corporation distributed stock in its oil and gas subsidiary to its stockholders. This oil and gas company was eventually merged into Exxon. Later that same year, Olin Corporation was merged with another major chemical company. At that point, the two sons of the founder and their children owned over 21 percent of Olin stock, worth at least $40 million. In 1968, Olin Corporation distributed stock in a subsidiary, Squibb Corporation, to its stockholders. Consequently, at that point, the two sons of the founder and their children owned 10 percent of Olin stock, worth $110 million, and 5 percent of Squibb stock, worth $90 million. When John M. Olin died in 1982, he left at least $50 million to his John M. Olin Foundation. The one surviving son and seven grandchildren of Franklin Olin probably still own nearly 8 percent of Olin stock, worth $65 million, and approximately 3 percent of Squibb stock, worth another $125 million. The husband of one of the granddaughters of the founder serves as a director of both Olin Corporation and Squibb Corporation. In addition, members of the Olin family may own as much as $120 million in Exxon stock. With the proceeds from stock sales and accumulated dividend income, the descendants of Franklin Olin are probably worth close to $300 million. SOURCES: Richard A. Smith, "The Rise of the House of Olin," *Fortune* (December 1953); Proxy Statement, Olin Mathieson Chemical Company (March 28, 1955); Proxy Statement, Olin Corporation (March 21, 1969); Proxy Statement, Olin Corporation (March 22, 1983).

OLSEN, KENNETH H. (b. 1926) Lincoln, Massachusetts. Founder of Digital Equipment Corporation. After working for several years as an electronics engineer at the Massachusetts Institute of Technology, Kenneth Olsen and a partner founded a computer company. They borrowed $70,000 from a group of venture capitalists and set up their production facilities in an old textile mill. Olsen, who served as president, received 13 percent of the stock in the company. The company was the first to develop and market minicomputers suitable for use in small offices. By 1972, Kenneth Olsen owned almost 9 percent of Digital Equipment stock, and his brother, Stanley C. Olsen, owned almost another 2 percent, worth a total of $120 million. Kenneth Olsen has not sold any of his stock in the company, but he has donated half of it to a foundation that funds religious charities. He still owns over 2 percent of Digital Equipment stock, worth about $200 million. The founder continues to serve as president, but none of his children is associated with the company. Kenneth Olsen, his wife, and his three children are worth at least $200 million. SOURCES: Proxy Statement, Digital Equipment Corporation (October 6, 1972); Peter Petre, "America's Most Successful Entrepreneur," *Fortune* (October 27, 1986).

ORDWAY, LUCIUS P. (d. 1948) St. Paul, Minnesota. Early investor in Minnesota Mining and Manufacturing Company. Lucius Ordway was operating a plumbing-supply company when he invested in Minnesota Mining and Manufacturing Company, a struggling mining company, in 1905. The company became profitable after it began manufacturing abrasive products. Later, it developed a highly successful brand of cellophane tape. In 1915, Lucius Ordway placed all of his Minnesota Mining and Manufacturing stock in a trust for the benefit of his five children and their children. After the company went public in 1945, this trust owned about 14 percent of Minnesota Mining and Manufacturing stock, worth $18 million. Two sons and one grandson of Lucius Ordway eventually served as directors of Minnesota Mining and Manufacturing. The Ordway family trust was dissolved in 1979. Nevertheless, the fourteen grandchildren of Lucius Ordway and their children probably still own close to 7 percent of the stock in the company, worth nearly $700 million. Over the last two decades alone, members of the Ordway family have received roughly $300 million in dividends on their Minnesota Mining and Manufacturing stock. With proceeds from stock sales and accumulated dividend income, the descendants of Lucius Ordway are worth at least $900 million. SOURCES: *Fortune* (March 1949); Prospectus, Minnesota Mining and Manufacturing

Company (March 18, 1952); Proxy Statement, Minnesota Mining and Manufacturing Company (April 7, 1978).

PACKARD, DAVID (b. 1912) Palo Alto, California. Founder of Hewlett-Packard Company. David Packard and his partner, William R. Hewlett, began manufacturing electronic equipment in a garage in 1939. David Packard concentrated on business details, and William Hewlett concentrated on technical innovations. When Hewlett-Packard went public in 1957, David Packard and his wife owned 44 percent of the stock in the company, worth almost $16 million. The company gradually expanded into calculators and later into computers. David Packard and William Hewlett bought a 20,000-acre cattle ranch near San Jose. By 1978, David Packard owned 22 percent of Hewlett-Packard stock, worth at least $500 million. Over the years, he has sold roughly a third of his stock in the company. However, he still owns over 17 percent of Hewlett-Packard stock, worth $1.8 billion. He also serves as chairman of the company. With the proceeds from stock sales, David Packard, his wife, and their four children are worth at least $2.1 billion. SOURCES: Prospectus, Hewlett-Packard Company (January 27, 1961); *Forbes* (April 1, 1966); Proxy Statement, Hewlett-Packard Company (January 7, 1986).

PALEY, WILLIAM S. (b. 1901) New York, New York. Founder of CBS Inc. In 1928, William Paley left the family cigar business to run a struggling radio network. He, his father, and his uncle bought majority control of the Columbia Broadcasting System from its founder for $500,000. He expanded the radio network and made it profitable by hiring famous performers for his broadcasts. After the company went public in 1940, William Paley owned 20 percent of CBS stock, worth $8 million. The company later expanded into television and records. He ran the company, first as president and then as chairman, for over five decades. In the past couple of decades, he has chosen and subsequently dismissed a series of CBS presidents. None of his children has any affiliation with the company. Over the years, he has sold much of his stock in the company. Nevertheless, he still owns almost 8 percent of CBS stock, worth $220 million. His six children, including two stepchildren and two adopted children, probably own at least another 3 percent of CBS stock, worth $90 million. Paley recently purchased an interest in a partnership founded by his late brother-in-law, John H. Whitney, which owns Whitney Communication Corporation. Altogether, with accumulated dividend income and the proceeds from stock sales, William Paley and his children are worth in excess of $350 million. SOURCES: *The New York Times,* February 23, 1940; *Forbes* (January 15, 1964); William S. Paley, *As It Happened* (Garden City, N.Y.: Doubleday, 1979).

PAULSON, ALLEN E. (b. 1922) Savannah, Georgia. Principal stockholder in Gulfstream Aerospace, which was later acquired by Chrysler Corporation. After working several years as an airplane mechanic, Allen Paulson began buying, renovating, and selling used airliners in 1954. In 1978, he borrowed $52 million to purchase Gulfstream, a manufacturer of private jets, from a large defense contractor. Three years later, he borrowed another $25 million to purchase the general aviation subsidary of another defense contractor. Gulfstream Aerospace sold $64 million worth of stock when it went public in 1983. Paulson sold another $85 million worth of Gulfstream Aerospace stock, but kept the remaining 71 percent of the stock, worth $461 million. Paulson later purchased almost 34 percent of the stock in Wheeling-Pittsburgh, a small steel company, for roughly $50 million. By the time Wheeling-Pittsburgh filed for bankruptcy in 1985, his stock in the company was worth less than $15 million. Later that same year, Paulson sold his remaining 71 percent of Gulfstream Aerospace stock to Chrysler Corporation for $127 million in cash and $325 million in notes. He reportedly used some of the proceeds to repay as much as $160 million in personal debt. Even after paying capital-gains taxes and repaying debts, Allen Paulson and his four sons are worth at least $300 million. SOURCES: *Newsweek* (January 13, 1969); Kenneth Labich, "The Turkey That Learned to Soar," *Fortune* (May 30, 1983); Jim Montgomery, "Paulson's Decision to Sell May Stem from Steel Firm," *The Wall Street Journal,* June 3, 1985.

PEROT, H. ROSS (b. 1930) Dallas, Texas. Founder of Electronic Data Systems, which was later acquired by General Motors. In 1962, Ross Perot quit his job as a computer salesman and began selling computer services to companies that did not have their own computers. The company grew rapidly after it began getting contracts from several states to process Blue Cross claims. After Electronic Data Systems went public in 1968, Perot owned over 81 percent of the stock in the company, worth $150 million. The value of his Electronic Data Systems stock tumbled from a high of $1.5 billion in 1970 to a low of $100 million in 1974. In addition, Perot probably lost at least $15 million when he attempted to salvage a failing brokerage house in 1974. Over the years, he sold roughly $190 million worth of Electronic Data Systems stock. In addition, he sold a third of his stock to a family trust for $100 million in 1981. In 1984, he agreed to sell the 46 percent of Electronic Data Systems stock held by him and other members of his family to General Motors for $930 million in cash and $230 million worth of special General Motors stock. They later sold this special stock back to General Motors for $700 million. Although they have paid nearly $400 million in capital-gains taxes on the proceeds of their sales of Electronic Data Systems stock over the years, H. Ross Perot, his wife, and their five children are still worth at least $1.4 billion. SOURCES: Jan Nordheimer, "Billionaire Texan Fights Social Ills," *The New York Times,* November 28, 1969; *Forbes* (June 15, 1972); Proxy Statement, Electronic Data Systems Corporation (August 31, 1972); *The Wall Street Journal,* August 15, 1984.

PETRIE, MILTON J. Secaucus, New Jersey. Founder of Petrie Stores Corporation. Milton Petrie founded the predecessor of Petrie Stores in 1927. After going bankrupt selling hosiery, he concentrated on selling clothes to young women. He has maintained high profit margins by renting store locations and spending very little on advertising. When the company went public in 1971, he owned 63 percent of Petrie Stores stock, worth $170 million. He has sold very little of his stock in the company since then. He has also transferred relatively little of his Petrie Stores stock to his three children. Over the last few decades, the company has expanded by acquiring other chains. A grandson of the founder serves as an officer of the company. Milton Petrie owns 56 percent of Petrie Stores stock, worth over $550 million. With the proceeds from stock sales and accumulated dividend income, Milton Petrie, his wife, and his three children are worth approximately $700 million. SOURCES: Proxy Statement, Petrie Stores Corporation (April 30, 1971); *Forbes* (December 1, 1976); Isadore Barmash, "The Acquisition King of Women's Wear," *The New York Times,* March 31, 1985.

PEW, JOSEPH N. (d. 1912) Philadelphia, Pennsylvania. Founder of Sun Company Inc. Joseph Pew started a small oil company in 1886. Sun Company grew rapidly after it bought leases in the giant Spindletop field in Texas in 1902. The four surviving children and nine grandchildren of the founder owned 69 percent of the Sun Company stock, worth $75 million in 1938. All three sons of the founder became officers and directors of the company. Two of them, J. Newton Pew, Jr., and J. Howard Pew, served either as chairman or president for almost four decades. Later, three grandsons also served as officers and directors. In 1948, the four surviving children of Joseph Pew endowed the Pew Memorial Trust, a family foundation, with $50 million worth of Sun Company stock. Three of them eventually established foundations of their own as well. The Glenmede Trust Company, which is controlled by members of the Pew family, is the sole trustee of all four foundations. Altogether, the J. Newton Pew Charitable Trust, the J. Howard Pew Freedom Trust, the Mabel Myrin Pew Trust, and the Pew Memorial Trust own about 26 percent of the stock in Sun Company, worth over $1.3 billion. The nine grandchildren of Joseph Pew and their children still own at least 6 percent of the stock in Sun Company, worth $300 million. R. Anderson Pew, a great-grandson of the founder, serves as a director of Sun Company and Glenmede Trust Company. With the proceeds from stock sales and accumulated dividend income, the descendants of Joseph Pew are worth at least $500 million. SOURCES: Prospectus, Sun Oil Company (March 21, 1947); *Forbes* (January 15, 1977); David Diamond, "The Pews of Philadelphia," *The New York Times,* October 25, 1981.

PHIPPS, HENRY (d. 1930) Pittsburgh, Pennsylvania. Founder of Bessemer Securities Corporation and Bessemer Trust Company. Henry Phipps was one of the original partners in Carnegie Steel. When the company was acquired by United States Steel Corporation in 1911, he received roughly $50 million for his Carnegie Steel stock. Ten years later, he established Bessemer Securities, a family holding company, with an initial investment of $5 million. The five children of the founder kept all of the preferred stock in this company, but they placed all of its common stock in a series of trusts for their children. By 1932, Bessemer Securities was worth $40 million in corporate securities and real estate. A little over two decades later, it was worth $260 million. Most of the Phipps fortune is now managed by Bessemer Trust Company, a separate trust company owned by the descendants of Henry Phipps. By 1982, Bessemer Trust Company held roughly $700 million worth of assets for the seventeen grandchildren of Henry Phipps and their children. Another $550 million in assets was held for family members by Bessemer Securities Corporation. In recent years, Bessemer Securities has begun to invest in oil exploration partnerships and high-technology companies. In addition, it has become involved in a number of large real estate developments. Although Bessemer Securities is a private investment company, the descendants of Henry Phipps are probably worth in excess of $1.5 billion. SOURCES: Richard A. Smith, "The Heir Who Turned on the House of Phipps," *Fortune* (October 1960); *Forbes* (February 15, 1971); James O'Hanlon, " 'Family Doctor' for the Rich," *Forbes* (March 19, 1979); *Business Week* (August 23, 1982).

PIGOTT, WILLIAM (d. 1929) Seattle, Washington. A founder of PACCAR Inc. William Pigott and a partner founded a company to manufacture rail cars in 1905. After a merger with another rail car manufacturer in 1917, Pigott owned 32 percent of the stock in the predecessor of PACCAR. He served as president and later chairman of the company. PACCAR was acquired by a larger corporation in 1924, but the original stockholders regained control of the company ten years later, after it almost went bankrupt. Paul Pigott, one of the two sons of the founder, served as chairman of PACCAR for almost three decades. The company later diversified into the production of heavy trucks. By 1974, the descendants of the founder owned 30 percent of PACCAR stock, worth roughly $50 million. The eight grandchildren of the founder and their children still own at least 25 percent of PACCAR stock, worth $220 million. Charles M. Pigott, a grandson of the founder, serves as president and another grandson serves as a director. With accumulated dividend income and the proceeds from stock sales, the descendants of William Pigott are worth at least $250 million. SOURCES: *Forbes* (September 1, 1974); Proxy Statement, PACCAR Inc. (March 21, 1978); Alex Groner, *PACCAR* (Bellevue, Wash.:

Documentary Book Publishers Co., 1984); Dero A. Saunders, "In the Passing Lane," *Forbes* (September 10, 1984).

PITCAIRN, JOHN (d. 1916) Bryn Athyn, Pennsylvania. Founder of PPG Industries Inc (formerly Pittsburgh Plate Glass). In 1883, John Pitcairn and several partners founded a glass company. The three sons of the founder formed Pitcairn Company, a family holding company, in 1923. By 1938, Pitcairn Company held 34 percent of the stock in PPG Industries, worth $64 million. Two of the sons of John Pitcairn eventually served as directors of the company, but neither of them served as an officer. The three sons had a total of twenty-four children. A husband of one of the granddaughters of the founder served as a director of PPG Industries for many years. PPG Industries later expanded into the production of paints and chemicals. Over the years, Pitcairn Company sold much of its PPG Industries stock in order to build a diversified investment portfolio. For example, it sold 10 percent of the stock in PPG Industries for $90 million in 1972. Finally, in 1985, Pitcairn Company sold its remaining 13 percent of PPG Industries stock back to the company for $430 million. By that time, PPG Industries had paid approximately $300 million in dividends to Pitcairn Company. With the proceeds from stock sales and accumulated dividend income, the descendants of John Pitcairn are worth roughly $600 million. SOURCES: Temporary National Economic Committee, *The Distribution of Stock Ownership in the 200 Largest Nonfinancial Corporations* (Washington, D.C.: U.S. Government Printing Office, 1940); Prospectus, Pittsburgh Plate Glass (March 19, 1952); *The Wall Street Journal,* May 5, 1972;

PRITZKER, ABRAM N. (d. 1986), and JACK N. Chicago, Illinois. Founders of Hyatt Corporation and The Marmon Group Inc. A. N. Pritzker and his brother, Jack N. Pritzker, were law partners who became involved in real estate development. A. N. Pritzker acquired his first manufacturing company in 1942. Over the years, the Pritzkers and their sons have repeatedly borrowed money from banks to purchase controlling interests in a series of companies that they have later taken private. In 1957, the Pritzkers bought a hotel that formed the basis of the Hyatt Corporation. They finally took Hyatt Corporation private in 1979. The main family corporation, The Marmon Group, was founded in 1953. It has acquired a number of large corporations, including Cerro Corporation in 1976 and Trans Union Corporation in 1981. The Marmon Group is now a major industrial corporation with over sixty-five plants that manufacture a variety of products. It is managed by the two surviving sons of the founder. Jay A. Pritzker, who serves as chairman, is in charge of finances and acquisitions, and Robert A. Pritzker, who serves as president, is in charge of operations. Another son, Robert N. Pritzker, was president of Hyatt Corporation until he died in 1972. The Pritzker family recently purchased Braniff Airlines. In addition, the family has major interests in publishing, tobacco products, amusement parks, forest products, and real estate development. Although The Marmon Group and Hyatt Corporation are private corporations, the two surviving sons and twelve grandchildren of A. N. Pritzker, with the son and two grandchildren of Jack N. Pritzker, are probably worth in excess of $1.5 billion. SOURCES: *Business Week* (May 5, 1975); Proxy Statement, The Marmon Group (May 1, 1978); *Business Week* (March 7, 1983).

PULITZER, JOSEPH (d. 1911) St. Louis, Missouri. Founder of Pulitzer Publishing Company, a private media corporation that owns the *St. Louis Post-Dispatch,* a number of small newspapers, and several radio and television stations. Joseph Pulitzer purchased a bankrupt newspaper in St. Louis for $2,500 in 1978. He gradually transformed it into the highly successful *St. Louis Post-Dispatch.* When the founder died, all of the stock in Pulitzer Publishing Company was placed in a trust in which his three sons were the income beneficiaries. When the trust was dissolved after the death of the last surviving son in 1957, this Pulitzer Publishing stock was distributed among the male descendants of the founder. As a result, neither of the two daughters nor any of the six granddaughters of the founder inherited any stock in the company. Over the years, three of the grandsons sold their Pulitzer stock back to the company or to other family members. By 1985, virtually all of the stock in Pulitzer Publishing was still owned by descendants of Joseph Pulitzer. The company was controlled by three of the grandsons of the founder—Joseph Pulitzer III, Michael Pulitzer, and David Moore—who owned 54 percent of Pulitzer Publishing stock. The following year, Pulitzer Publishing agreed to repurchase 43 percent of its stock from four other grandchildren and five great-grandchildren of the founder for $185 million. Joseph Pulitzer III, a grandson of the founder, serves as chairman of the company. Altogether, seven of the grandchildren of Joseph Pulitzer and their children are worth at least $450 million. SOURCES: W. A. Swanberg, *Pulitzer* (New York: Charles Scribner's Sons, 1967); Alex S. Jones, "And Now the Pulitzers Go to War," *The New York Times,* April 13, 1986.

REYNOLDS, DONALD W. (b. 1906) Las Vegas, Nevada. Founder of Donrey Media Group, a private media corporation that owns scores of small newspapers and seven radio stations. After working as an editor, Donald Reynolds bought a small newspaper. Without going into debt, he gradually acquired fifty-four daily and fifty-five weekly newspapers, most of which are published in small cities. Reynolds has always concentrated more on controlling costs than on editorial policy. His Donrey Media Group also owns seven radio stations, a television station, several cable television systems, and thousands of billboards. He has transferred very little of his wealth to his three children. Although Donrey Media Group is a private corporation, Donald Reynolds is worth at least $600 million. SOURCE: Richard Behar, "Games Others Play," *Forbes* (May 19, 1986).

REYNOLDS, RICHARD J. (d. 1918), and WILLIAM N. Winston-Salem, North Carolina. Founders of R.J. Reynolds Industries. In 1875, Richard J. Reynolds and his brother, William N. Reynolds, founded a tobacco company. It gradually became one of the leading cigarette companies in the country. When R. J. Reynolds died in 1918, he left an estate worth $60 million for his four children. By 1938, the three surviving children of R. J. Reynolds and their uncle owned about 12 percent of the stock in R.J. Reynolds Industries, worth $57 million. William Reynolds, the brother of the founder, was the last member of the family to serve as president of the company. However, Richard J. Reynolds, Jr., the surviving son of the founder, later served as a director. He also owned over 10 percent of the stock in Delta Air Lines in 1957. Although the descendants of the founder have sold most of their R.J. Reynolds Industries stock over the years, they still owned about 6 percent of the stock in the company, worth over $150 million by 1971. The fifteen grandchildren of R. J. Reynolds and their children probably still own about 3 percent of R.J. Reynolds Industries stock, worth $250 million. In addition, they have received about $100 million in dividend income on that stock over the last two decades. Several foundations, endowed by members of the Reynolds family, have assets of almost $200 million. With the proceeds from stock sales and accumulated dividend income, the descendants of R. J. Reynolds are worth nearly $400 million. SOURCES: Temporary National Economic Committee, *The Distribution of Ownership in the 200 Largest Nonfinancial Corporations* (Washington, D.C.: U.S. Government Printing Office, 1940); Prospectus, Delta Air Lines Inc. (March 12, 1957); *Forbes* (December 1, 1971).

RICHARDSON, LUNSFORD (d. 1919) Greensboro, North Carolina. Founder of Richardson-Vicks Inc., which was later acquired by Procter & Gamble Company. In 1905, Lunsford Richardson sold his drugstore and began marketing his own cold remedies. In 1930, Richardson-Vicks was merged with several other drug companies. However, the combined company was dissolved after only three years. As a result, the five children of Lunsford Richardson received large blocks of stock in several drug companies, including Bristol-Myers and Sterling Drug, as well as Richardson-Vicks. Both sons of the founder, three of his grandsons, and one of his great-grandsons have served as officers and directors of the company. In 1981, the company sold a drug subsidiary to Dow Chemical for stock that it then distributed to its stockholders. As a result, members of the Richardson family received Dow Chemical stock that is now worth over $50 million. In 1985, at least sixteen grandchildren of Lunsford Richardson and their children sold their 24 percent of Richardson-Vicks stock to Procter & Gamble Company for $340 million in cash. Several family members also own about 50 percent of the stock in Piedmont Management Company, worth another $25 million. Although they have undoubtedly sold the bulk of their Bristol-Myers and Sterling Drug stock, members of the Richardson family probably still own $150 million worth of stock in these companies. The Smith Richardson Foundation, established by one of the sons of the founder, has assets of $100 million. With the proceeds from stock sales, accumulated dividend income, and stock in other companies, the descendants of Lunsford Richardson are worth in excess of $500 million. SOURCES: Proxy Statement, Richardson-Merrell Inc. (September 23, 1947); Proxy Statement, Richardson-Merrell Inc. (September 12, 1978); James B. Stewart and Michael Waldholz, "How Richardson-Vicks Fell Prey to Takeover Despite Family's Grip," *The Wall Street Journal,* October 30, 1985.

ROBINS, CLAIBORNE (d. 1912) Richmond, Virginia. Founder of A.H. Robins Company Inc. Claiborne Robins began by producing drugs for the family pharmacy. When the founder died in 1912, his wife ran A.H. Robins Company for two decades until their son, E. Claiborne Robins, was old enough to take over. E. Claiborne Robins expanded the company by developing new products and a national sales force. When the company went public in 1965, E. Claiborne Robins and his three children owned 82 percent of A.H. Robins stock, worth $155 million. Within five years, their A.H. Robins stock was worth almost $500 million. However, the value of this stock plummeted after A.H. Robins Company was sued by thousands of women who had used a contraceptive device marketed by the company. The potential liability claims became so large that the company filed for protection under the bankruptcy laws. Even after filing for bankruptcy, the 52 percent of A.H. Robins stock held by the founder and his children is worth over $170 million. Although the son of the founder still serves as chairman, his son, E. Claiborne Robins, Jr., serves as president. With accumulated dividend income and the proceeds from stock sales, Claiborne Robins and his children are worth well over $200 million. SOURCES: Prospectus, A.H. Robins Company Inc. (March 18, 1965); Proxy Statement, A.H. Robins Company Inc. (March 29, 1978).

ROCKEFELLER, JOHN D. (d. 1937) New York, New York. Founder of the Standard Oil Company. J. D. Rockefeller and his partners began operating their first refinery in 1863. By 1900, his Standard Oil Company controlled over 80 percent of the refinery capacity in the nation. When this company was finally dissolved in 1911, J. D. Rockefeller became the largest stockholder in several major oil companies, including the predecessors of Exxon, Chevron, Amoco, and Mobil. By the time he died in 1937, he had passed on to his son, John D. Rockefeller, Jr., most of his fortune, including at least $250 million worth of stock in various oil companies. He gave relatively little of his fortune to his three daughters or their children. J. D. Rockefeller, Jr., gradually sold most of the oil company stock he received from his father, and invested the proceeds in other stocks, bonds, and real estate. As part of this diversification effort, he developed Rockefeller Center in New York City. By 1974, the six children of J. D. Rockefeller, Jr., and their children were worth over $1 billion in stocks and bonds. They recently sold a 71 percent interest in much of their Rockefeller Center property to the public for $1.3 billion. The Rockefeller Foundation, which has assets of $1 billion, was founded by J. D. Rockefeller, Sr., but it is now entirely independent of his family. However, members of the Rockefeller family control the smaller Rockefeller Brothers Fund, established by J. D. Rockefeller, Jr., and his children. In all, the two remaining children and twenty-two grandchildren of John D. Rockefeller, Jr., are worth nearly $5 billion. SOURCES: Peter Collier and David Horowitz, *The Rockefellers: An American Dynasty* (New York: Holt, Rinehart & Winston, 1976); Kathleen Teltsch, "The Cousins: The Fourth Generation of Rockefellers," *The New York Times,* December 30, 1984; Carol J. Loomis, "The Rockefellers, End of a Dynasty?" *Fortune* (August 4, 1986).

ROLLINS, O. WAYNE (b. 1912) Atlanta, Georgia. Founder of Rollins Inc. In 1948, Wayne Rollins and his brother acquired a radio station that they built into a broadcasting company. After the company went public in 1962, the two brothers owned over 80 percent of Rollins Inc. stock, worth at least $12 million. His brother later left Rollins Inc. and founded a leasing company. With Wayne Rollins as president, Rollins Inc. acquired a pest control company and an oil-field services company. By 1983, Wayne Rollins and his two sons owned over 45 percent of the stock in Rollins Inc., worth about $240 million. The following year, Rollins Inc. issued stock in two subsidiaries, Rollins Communications and RPC Energy Services, to its stockholders. Wayne Rollins remained as chairman of all three companies. One son, Gary W. Rollins, became president of Rollins Inc. and the other son, R. Randall Rollins, became president of Rollins Communications. Within a few months, however, the Rollins family sold its 43 percent of Rollins Communications stock to another company for $260 million in cash and notes. Wayne Rollins and his two sons still own at least 43 percent of the stock in both Rollins Inc. and RPC Energy Services, worth a total of $160 million. With the proceeds from stock sales, Wayne Rollins, his two sons, and their children are worth at least $400 million. SOURCES: Proxy Statement, Rollins Inc. (July 9, 1971); Thomas J. Bray, "John Rollins, Farm Boy, Is Becoming a Legend as He Amasses Riches," *The*

Wall Street Journal, September 4, 1973; Proxy Statement, Rollins Inc. (September 12, 1983); *The Wall Street Journal,* May 14, 1986.

ROSENWALD, JULIUS (d. 1932) Chicago, Illinois. Principal stockholder in Sears, Roebuck and Co. Julius Rosenwald was a clothing manufacturer who supplied merchandise for Sears, Roebuck and Co., a mail-order company. In 1895, he paid $75,000 for 23 percent of Sears, Roebuck stock. The company grew rapidly. Six years later, he paid over $600,000 for another 11 percent of Sears, Roebuck stock. Julius Rosenwald succeeded the founder of the company as president in 1908. Over the next several years, Sears, Roebuck and Co. opened a chain of retail stores. Julius Rosenwald was succeeded by his son, Lessing Rosenwald, who resigned after only four years. By 1937, the five children of Julius Rosenwald owned 13 percent of Sears, Roebuck stock, worth $40 million. Two grandsons of Julius Rosenwald served as directors of the company for nearly four decades. William Rosenwald, one of the sons of Julius Rosenwald, became a venture capitalist. By 1970, the five children and sixteen grandchildren of Julius Rosenwald probably owned at least 4 percent of Sears, Roebuck stock, worth $400 million. No members of the Rosenwald family currently serve as directors of the company. With the proceeds from stock sales and accumulated dividend income, the descendants of Julius Rosenwald are probably worth in excess of $400 million. SOURCES: Temporary National Economic Committee, *The Distribution of Stock Ownership in the 200 Largest Nonfinancial Corporations* (Washington, D.C.: U.S. Government Printing Office, 1940); *Forbes* (September 15, 1968); Proxy Statement, Sears, Roebuck and Co. (April 15, 1969).

ROUSH, GALEN J. (d. 1976) Akron, Ohio. Founder of Roadway Express Inc. In 1930, Galen Roush joined his younger brother in the trucking business. The company grew because it acquired very profitable routes and employed strict financial controls. Galen Roush became chairman in 1956, after his brother sold his half of the stock in the company to the public for $5 million. By the time he died in 1976, Galen Roush and members of his family owned 42 percent of Roadway Express stock, worth $320 million. He gave much of his stock in the company to his foundation. His four children still own at least 20 percent of the stock in Roadway Express, worth $270 million. Although none of his children has served as an officer of the company, two of them serve as directors. With accumulated dividend income, the four children of Galen Roush and their children are worth roughly $300 million. SOURCES: *Forbes* (December 1, 1975); Proxy Statement, Roadway Express Inc. (April 12, 1976); Proxy Statement, Roadway Services (April 11, 1983).

SCRIPPS, EDWARD W. (d. 1926) San Diego, California. Founder of E.W. Scripps Company, a privately owned media corporation. Edward Scripps founded his first newspaper, the *Cleveland Press,* in 1878 with financial assistance from his two older brothers. By 1895, he was a stockholder in eight different metropolitan newspapers. Edward Scripps also acquired stock in a large number of small city newspapers. He later turned his stock in some of these newspapers over to his two oldest sons, John P. Scripps and James G. Scripps. Four years before he died, however, he turned over control of the remaining newspapers to his youngest son, Robert P. Scripps. In 1922, he organized E.W. Scripps Company as a holding company for all his remaining newspaper stock and placed all of the stock in this holding company in a trust for the benefit of the six children of Robert Scripps. This trust now owns over 88 percent of the stock in E.W. Scripps Company, which publishes nineteen daily and twenty-four weekly newspapers. The company also owns 80 percent of the stock in Scripps-Howard Broadcasting Company, which owns six television stations and seven radio stations. Charles E. Scripps, one of the four grandsons of the founder, has served as chairman of the company for the past three decades. Although E.W. Scripps is a private corporation, the six children and twenty-eight grandchildren of Robert P. Scripps are probably worth about $1.2 billion. SOURCES: Negley D. Cochran, *E. W. Scripps* (New York: Harcourt, Brace, 1933); Michael L. King, "Weakened Chain," *The Wall Street Journal,* November 28, 1980.

SEARLE, CLAUDE H. (d. 1936) Chicago, Illinois. Founder of G.D. Searle and Company, which was later merged into Monsanto. Claude Searle and his father, Gideon D. Searle, founded a drug company in 1888. Claude Searle was succeeded as president by his son, John G. Searle, who introduced a series of highly profitable products. By the time the company went public in 1963, John Searle and a series of trusts established for his three children owned 51 percent of the stock in the company, worth $350 million. John Searle resigned in 1966 and turned the management of the company over to his two sons and his son-in-law. After several unsuccessful acquisitions, they resigned as officers of the company, although they continued to serve as directors. By 1984, Daniel C. Searle, William L. Searle, and Suzanne Searle Dixon, the three grandchildren of the founder, and their children still owned over 33 percent of the stock in Searle. In order to diversify the family fortune, the Searles had the company repurchase $388 million worth of their Searle stock in 1985. Later that same year, they sold their remaining Searle stock to Monsanto for $578 million. With the proceeds from these sales and accumulated dividend income, the descendants of John Searle are worth at least $800 million. SOURCES: Prospectus, G.D. Searle and Company (December 9, 1963); *Forbes* (February 6, 1978); Proxy Statement, G.D. Searle and Company (May 3, 1984); *The Wall Street Journal,* April 26, 1985.

SINGLETON, HENRY E. (b. 1916) Los Angeles, California. Founder of Teledyne Inc. After working several years for another corporation, Henry Singleton and a partner each contributed $225,000 in capital to form Teledyne in 1960. Two years later, they acquired another company with Teledyne stock. At that point, Singleton owned 24 percent of the stock in the company, worth $5 million. Over the next decade, Teledyne acquired another ninety companies with stock. It eventually became a large conglomerate operating in such diverse fields as consumer products, specialty chemicals, electronics, industrial equipment, and insurance. However, all of these acquisitions diluted the equity interests of the original partners in the company. By 1972, Singleton owned only 2 percent of Teledyne stock, worth $12 million. Teledyne then began repurchasing its own stock. Most stockholders were willing to sell their Teledyne stock because it never paid a cash dividend. Between 1972 and 1984, the company repurchased over 85 percent of its stock at a total cost of roughly $2.6 billion. In this way, the company increased the proportion of Teledyne stock owned by its remaining stockholders as well as the market value of that stock. Singleton, who still serves as chairman of the company, has sold very little of his stock. As a result, he now owns over 14 percent of Teledyne stock, worth at least $490 million. Altogether, Henry Singleton and his five children are worth in excess of $500 million. SOURCES: Proxy Statement, Teledyne Inc. (February 24, 1968); *Forbes* (April 1, 1966); Robert J. Flaherty, "The Singular Henry Singleton," *Forbes* (July 9, 1979); Proxy Statement, Teledyne Inc. (March 24, 1983).

SKAGGS, LEONARD S. (d. 1950) Salt Lake City, Utah. Founder of Skaggs Pay Less Drug Stores, the predecessor of American Stores. The son of a storekeeper, Leonard Skaggs and five of his brothers started Safeway Stores. They eventually sold out, and Leonard Skaggs used his share of the proceeds to buy Pay Less Drug Stores in 1939. When he died in 1950, his son, Leonard S. Skaggs, Jr., took over the company and built Skaggs Pay Less Stores into a major discount drugstore chain. For several years, he and Joseph Albertson owned a series of combination grocery and drugstores. They later parted company. After Skaggs Pay Less Stores went public in 1965, the widow and two children of the founder owned over 50 percent of the stock in Skaggs Pay Less Stores, worth about $5 million. In 1979, Leonard Skaggs, Jr., merged Skaggs Companies with American Stores. He serves as chairman of American Stores, and his wife serves as a director. The two children of the founder and trusts for the benefit of their children own about 25 percent of the stock in American Stores, worth $500 million. SOURCES: Proxy Statement, Skaggs Companies (November

379

8, 1972); Proxy Statement, American Stores (April 28, 1983); *Business Week* (June 18, 1984).

SMITH, PHILIP (d. 1961) Chestnut Hill, Massachusetts. Founder of General Cinema. Philip Smith started building drive-in movie theaters in 1935. After he died in 1961, his son, Richard A. Austin, became chairman of General Cinema. On his initiative, the company began building small movie theaters in shopping centers. Later, the company also acquired several bottling companies. By 1977, Richard Smith and his sister, Nancy Smith Marks, and their children owned 25 percent of the stock in General Cinema, worth $55 million. In 1982, the members of the Smith family converted their common stock into a special class of stock that casts 80 percent of the votes. As the result of recent stock repurchases by the company, the descendants of the founder now own 30 percent of the stock in General Cinema, worth at least $440 million. With the proceeds from stock sales, the descendants of Philip Smith are worth $450 million. SOURCES: *Forbes* (April 15, 1968); Proxy Statement, General Cinema Corporation (March 14, 1977); Paul B. Brown, "Technology Isn't Everything," *Forbes* (October 12, 1981).

STEINBERG, SAUL P. (b. 1939) New York, New York. Principal stockholder in Reliance Group Holdings. In 1961, Saul Steinberg borrowed $100,000 from his father and his uncle to start Leasco, a computer leasing business. Leasco grew rapidly because it offered low-cost long-term leases. Two years after the company went public in 1965, the 40 percent of Leasco stock owned by Saul Steinberg, his father, and his uncle was worth $20 million. In 1968, Leasco acquired Reliance Insurance Company, a major insurance company, by issuing $292 million in Leasco preferred stock. The combined corporation was named Reliance Group. Over the next several years, Reliance Group spent over $300 million repurchasing its own stock. By 1981, the Steinbergs owned over 15 percent of the stock in Reliance Group. They also owned a majority of the stock in a corporation that owned another 25 percent of Reliance Group stock. That same year, Saul Steinberg and his family acquired the remaining stock in Reliance Group. They financed the bulk of the acquisition by issuing $434 million worth of debentures and preferred stock in a new corporation, Reliance Group Holdings. The new company carried a very heavy debt load, but Saul Steinberg and his relatives owned all of its common stock. In order to reduce this debt load, Steinberg recently took Reliance Group Holdings public again by selling 18 percent of the stock in the company. Consequently, the 82 percent of Reliance Group Holdings owned by Saul Steinberg and his relatives is worth about $650 million. SOURCES: *Forbes* (April 1, 1975); Peter W. Bernstein, "Fear and Loathing in the Boardrooms,"

Fortune (December 15, 1980); Abraham J. Briloff, "Saul Steinberg's Pyramid," *Barron's* (November 12, 1984).

STERN, MAX (d. 1982) Harrison, New Jersey. Founder of Hartz Mountain Corporation. In 1926, Max Stern and his two brothers began selling birds and tropical fish. They later formed separate companies to market fish and bird foods and other pet supplies. By 1959, Max Stern had bought out both of his brothers. In a complicated financial transaction involving a family holding company, Max Stern later sold most of his stock in these companies to his three children. One of them, Leonard Stern, became the largest stockholder in these companies and eventually bought out his brother and sister. In 1966, Leonard Stern took Hartz Mountain Corporation into real estate by buying and developing 1,000 acres in the Meadowlands area of New Jersey. By 1978, Leonard Stern owned, through a holding company, about 73 percent of the stock in Hartz Mountain Corporation, worth nearly $400 million. The next year, his holding company acquired the remaining 27 percent of Hartz Mountain for $67 million. The company is now the largest manufacturer of pet supplies and a major developer of real estate in New York and New Jersey. In 1985, Leonard Stern bought *The Village Voice* for $55 million. Although Hartz Mountain is a private corporation, Leonard Stern is probably worth close to $1 billion. Neither his former wife nor any of their three children owns much stock in the company. SOURCES: Proxy Statement, Hartz Mountain Corporation (March 24, 1978); Paul Blustein and Richard Greene, "The Public Be Damned? In 1979?" *Forbes* (April 2, 1979); Gigi Mahon, "Hartz Content: The Good Life of Leonard Stern," *New York* (May 5, 1986).

STONE, JOSEPH H. (d. 1936) Chicago, Illinois. Founder of Stone Container Corporation. Joseph Stone founded Stone Container, which manufactured paperboard and corrugated containers, in 1926. His three sons, Norman, Jerome, and Marvin Stone, later joined him as partners. After the company went public in 1946, the descendants of the founder owned more than 62 percent of the stock in Stone Container, worth about $10 million. Norman Stone, the eldest son of the founder, served as chairman for roughly three decades before he was succeeded by his brother, Jerome Stone. In recent years, the company has used large amounts of debt to finance acquisitions and invest in new facilities. Moreover, the three sons of Joseph Stone and their eight children have sold very little of their Stone Container stock. As a result, members of the Stone family still own over 40 percent of the stock in Stone Container, worth almost $220 million. Roger Stone, a grandson of the founder, currently serves as chairman, and a brother and several cousins serve as directors. With accumulated dividend income, the descendants of Joseph Stone are worth at least $240 million. SOURCES: Prospectus, Stone Container Corporation (April 1,

APPENDIX

1946); Proxy Statement, Stone Container Corporation (April 4, 1978); John A. Byrne, "Guess Who Gets the Last Laugh," *Forbes* (June 20, 1983).

STRANAHAN, ROBERT A. (d. 1962), and FRANK D. Toledo, Ohio. Founders of Champion Spark Plug Company. In 1908, Robert and Frank Stranahan began manufacturing spark plugs and other electrical parts for automobiles. For many years, they were the sole supplier of spark plugs to Ford Motor Company. In 1958, the Stranahan brothers and their ten children owned 76 percent of Champion Spark Plug Company, worth $120 million. Most of this stock was held by forty different trusts. Robert Stranahan served as president of the company for over four decades. He was succeeded by his son, Robert A. Stranahan, Jr. Over the past four decades, members of the Stranahan family have sold over half of their stock in the company. They have also received over $200 million in dividend income on their remaining stock during this period. Nevertheless, family members probably still own about 36 percent of Champion Spark Plug stock, worth over $120 million. A son of one of the founders still serves as chairman, and two of his cousins serve as directors. With the proceeds from stock sales and accumulated dividend income, the ten children of Robert and Frank Stranahan and their children are worth at least $250 million. SOURCES: Prospectus, Champion Spark Plug Company (August 20, 1958); Proxy Statement, Champion Spark Plug Company (March 21, 1969); Proxy Statement, Champion Spark Plug Company (March 19, 1976).

STUART, ELBRIDGE A. (d. 1944) Los Angeles, California. Founder of Carnation Company, which was later acquired by Nestlé. Elbridge A. Stuart founded Carnation in 1899 to sell evaporated milk. The company gradually developed a national distribution system for its dairy products and expanded into other products such as pet foods. The founder was succeeded by his son, Elbridge H. Stuart, who served as chairman of the company for almost three decades. Over the years, the husband of the daughter of the founder, all three of his grandsons, and the husbands of two of his granddaughters have also served as officers and directors of the company. By 1979, a family holding company, created by the founder, owned 44 percent of Carnation stock, worth $450 million. The family also owned another 5 percent of Carnation stock directly, worth an additional $60 million. That same year, the family holding company was dissolved and its Carnation stock was distributed to the five children of Elbridge H. Stuart and the two children of his sister, Katherine Stuart Stibbs. Five years later, Nestlé paid the members of the Stuart family over $1.4 billion in cash for their remaining 46 percent of Carnation stock. By that time, the descendants of the founder had already received roughly $400 million in dividends on their Carnation stock. With the proceeds from this stock sale, even after the payment of capital-gains taxes, the descendants of Elbridge A. Stuart are worth $1.3 billion. SOURCES: James Marshall, *Elbridge A. Stuart* (Los Angeles, Calif.: Carnation Co., 1949); Proxy Statement, Carnation Company (March 22, 1978); *The Wall Street Journal,* September 5, 1984.

TAPER, S. MARK (b. 1901) Beverly Hills, California. Founder of First Charter Financial Corporation, which was later acquired by Financial Corporation of America. Mark Taper founded First Charter Financial in 1955. After the company went public in 1959, he and his wife owned over 50 percent of First Charter Financial stock, worth $52 million. Over the years, he built it into one of the largest savings and loan companies in the nation. In the decade after the company went public, the Taper family sold $94 million worth of First Charter stock. By 1975, Mark Taper and his three children owned, through a series of trusts, 37 percent of the stock in the company, worth $120 million. The founder served as chairman until he was eighty years old, and his two daughters served as directors. In 1983, Taper and his children sold their remaining stock in the company to Financial Corporation of America for $282 million in cash. With the proceeds from these stock sales, Mark Taper and his three children are worth at least $400 million. SOURCES: Prospectus, First Charter Financial Corporation (April 4, 1960); Proxy Statement, First Charter Financial Corporation (March 20, 1975); *The Wall Street Journal,* February 9, 1983.

TEMPLE, THOMAS L. L. (d. 1935) Diboll, Texas. Founder of the predecessor of Temple-Inland Inc. In 1894, Thomas Temple started a sawmill and began acquiring timberland in east Texas. One of his sons, Arthur Temple, eventually served as president of Temple Industries. He was later succeeded, in turn, by his son, Arthur Temple, Jr. By 1973, the descendants of the founder owned 50 percent of the stock in Temple Industries. That same year, they merged their company into Time Inc. In return for their Temple Industries stock, members of the Temple family received 15 percent of Time stock, worth over $60 million. As a result, they became the controlling stockholders in the company. Arthur Temple, Jr., and one of his cousins became directors of Time. Five years later, Time acquired a packaging company, Inland Container. In 1983, Time distributed stock in its Temple-Inland forest products and packaging subsidiary to its stockholders. The descendants of the five children of Thomas Temple still own about 8 percent of Time stock, worth at least $300 million, and nearly 8 percent of Temple-Inland stock, worth over $90 million. Arthur Temple, Jr., now serves as chairman of Temple-Inland. One of his cousins still serves as a director of Time. With accumulated dividend income, the descendants of Thomas Temple are worth in excess of $400 million.

SOURCES: Prospectus, Time Inc. (August 17, 1973); Lee Smith, "The Timber Tycoon of Time Inc.," *Dun's Review* (August 1973); Elisa Wallis, "An East Texas Industry: Temple Eastex," *Texas Historian* (May 1983).

THOMPSON, JOE C., JR. (d. 1961) Dallas, Texas. Principal stockholder in Southland Corporation. In 1934, Joe C. Thompson, Jr., became a principal stockholder in a bankrupt chain of convenience grocery stores. In 1946, he changed the name of the stores to 7-Eleven to emphasize the fact that they stayed open longer than other stores. All three of his sons eventually went to work for the company. He was succeeded as president by his oldest son, John P. Thompson. When the company went public in 1966, the three sons of the founder owned, through a series of family holding companies, about 25 percent of Southland stock, worth $28 million. The company has since added gas stations and automotive parts stores. John P. Thompson now serves as chairman of Southland, and his brother, Jere W. Thompson, serves as president. The youngest brother, Joe C. Thompson III, also serves as an officer and director of the company. The three brothers and their children own over 11 percent of the stock in Southland, worth about $270 million. With accumulated dividend income, the descendants of Jodie Thompson are worth over $280 million. SOURCES: *Forbes* (September 15, 1974); Allen Liles, *Oh, Thank Heaven! The Story of the Southland Corporation* (Dallas, Tex.: Southland Corporation, 1976); Proxy Statement, Southland Corporation (March 28, 1975).

THORNE, OAKLEIGH (d. 1948) New York, New York. Principal stockholder in Commerce Clearing House, Inc. Oakleigh Thorne was the son of a wealthy banker who had purchased an interest in the predecessor of Commerce Clearing House in 1907. The company, which was based in Chicago, soon began publishing legal reporters on a variety of subjects, particularly the tax code. His son, Oakleigh L. Thorne, eventually became the sole stockholder in a family holding company that owned half of the stock in Commerce Clearing House. His two sisters inherited some Commerce Clearing House stock, but they sold most of it years ago. The holding company owned by Oakleigh L. Thorne was merged into Commerce Clearing House in 1976. When he died two years later, Oakleigh L. Thorne owned over 41 percent of the stock in Commerce Clearing House, worth $62 million. His six children owned another 19 percent of the stock, worth $28 million. In order to pay the taxes on his estate, the children of Oakleigh L. Thorne sold half of its Commerce Clearing House stock back to the company. In all, the company repurchased over 27 percent of its stock over a period of two years. As a result, trusts for the benefit of the six children and thirteen grandchildren of Oakleigh L. Thorne now own 55 percent of Commerce Clearing House stock, worth $450 million. Oakleigh B. Thorne, a grandson of Oakleigh Thorne, serves as chairman of the company, and his half-brother, Daniel K. Thorne, serves as a director. With accumulated dividend income, the descendants of Oakleigh L. Thorne are worth at least $480 million. SOURCES: *The New York Times,* May 24, 1948; Proxy Statement, Commerce Clearing House (March 3, 1978); Stratford P. Sherman, "The Company That Loves the U.S. Tax Code," *Fortune* (November 26, 1984).

TISCH, LAURENCE A. (b. 1923), and PRESTON R. New York, New York. Principal stockholders in Loews Corporation. In 1946, Laurence and Preston Tisch convinced their parents to purchase a resort hotel. Over the next several years, the brothers built the hotel into a chain of hotels. In 1958, the family hotel chain began acquiring stock in Loews Theatres. Once they gained control of the company, the Tisch brothers had Loews repurchase a large portion of its stock. As a result, they had to pay only about $10 million for 32 percent of Loews stock. Ten years later, they had Loews Theatres gradually acquire all of the stock in Lorillard Corporation, a cigarette and food company. At that point, the 32 percent of Loews stock owned by the Tisch brothers, through the family hotel company, was worth $110 million. In 1975, Loews acquired a majority interest in CNA, a large financial services company. As the result of stock repurchases by Loews Corporation, Laurence and Preston Tisch owned 44 percent of the stock in the company by 1985. The two brothers recently sold about $210 million worth of Loews stock; however, they kept 36 percent of the stock, worth at least $1.4 billion. With real estate holdings and the proceeds of stock sales, Laurence and Preston Tisch and their children are worth in excess of $1.7 billion. SOURCES: Proxy Statement, Loews Theatres (December 31, 1968); *Business Week* (April 12, 1969); Charles G. Burck, "How the Tisches Run Their 'Little Store,'" *Fortune* (May 1971); *The Wall Street Journal,* February 20, 1985.

UPJOHN, WILLIAM E. (d. 1932) Kalamazoo, Michigan. Founder of The Upjohn Company. William Upjohn and his brothers founded a drug company in 1886. In 1909, William Upjohn bought out his brothers and became the majority stockholder in the company. Over the years, the company developed a number of highly successful proprietary drugs. When the company went public in 1958, the three surviving children and seven grandchildren of William Upjohn owned 71 percent of Upjohn stock, worth $430 million. Even after selling over $175 million worth of company stock, members of the Upjohn family still owned over 44 percent of Upjohn stock in 1964. After the death of the founder, one of his sons-in-law became chairman. This son-in-law was succeeded, in turn, by the husband of one of his daughters. Over the past two decades, members of the Upjohn family have probably sold another $500 million in Upjohn stock. Nevertheless, the seven grandchildren and at least eighteen great-grandchildren of the founder probably own about 30 percent of Upjohn stock, worth at least $1.1 billion. With the proceeds from stock sales and accumulated dividend income, the descendants of William Upjohn are worth at least $1.5 billion. SOURCES: Leonard Engel, *Medicine Makers of Kalamazoo* (New York: McGraw-Hill, 1961); Prospectus, The Upjohn Company (November 26, 1958); Proxy Statement, The Upjohn Company (April 5, 1985).

WALTON, SAM M. (b. 1918), and JAMES L. Bentonville, Arkansas. Founder of Wal-Mart Stores. Sam Walton and his brother, James L. Walton, operated sixteen franchise variety stores before they decided to start their own chain of discount stores. Sam Walton opened his first discount store in 1962. By the time Wal-Mart went public in 1970, there were 30 Wal-Mart stores. At that point, the Walton family owned 68 percent of the stock in the company, worth $16 million. Wal-Mart now operates over 500 discount stores in small cities throughout the South that are supplied by a few large distribution centers. The stores are highly profitable because of strict cost controls. Sam Walton and his four children each own 20 percent of a family holding company, which, in turn, owns almost 39 percent of Wal-Mart stock. With this stock, Sam Walton, his wife, and their four children are worth $3.2 billion. SOURCES: Harold Seneker, "A Day in the Life of Sam Walton," *Forbes* (December 1, 1977); Howard Rudnitsky, "How Sam Walton Does It," *Forbes* (August 16, 1982); Proxy Statement, Wal-Mart Stores (May 7, 1984).

WANG, AN (b. 1920) Lincoln, Massachusetts. Founder of Wang Laboratories. After inventing the magnetic core memory used in computers, An Wang founded his own electronics firm in 1951. At first, the company manufactured calculators. When Wang Laboratories went public in 1967, An Wang, his wife, and a trust for his three children owned about 63 percent of the stock, worth just over $15 million. A few years later, the company began manufacturing small computers suitable for word processing. In 1976, the company issued a new class of common stock, with limited voting rights but a larger dividend, in order to raise additional capital without diluting the control of the founding family. An Wang is still chairman of the company and two of his sons serve as officers. One of them, Frederick A. Wang, is being prepared to succeed his father. The Wang family currently owns about 28 percent of the stock in the company, worth at least $790 million. Much of the Wang Laboratories stock owned by the family is held by a trust for the benefit of the children of the founder. However, the Wang family exercises absolute control over the company by virtue of the fact that it owns a majority of the class of stock that elects 75 percent of the directors. With proceeds from stock sales, An Wang, his wife, and his three children are worth well over $830 million. SOURCES: Proxy Statement, Wang Laboratories (September 12, 1969); Prospectus,

Wang Laboratories (April 9, 1976); An Wang, *Lessons* (Reading, Mass.: Addison-Wesley, 1986).

WATSON, THOMAS J. (d. 1956) Armonk, New York. Principal stockholder in International Business Machines. In 1914, Thomas Watson was hired as the president of a newly formed company that manufactured machines for punching, sorting, and tabulating cards. Ten years later, he renamed the company International Business Machines. As part of his employment contract, Watson received a small block of IBM stock. He later bought additional stock in the company. By 1938, he and his wife owned over 2 percent of IBM stock, worth $3 million. Over the years, they managed to transfer almost all of this stock to their four children. Thomas Watson served as president of IBM for almost four decades, until he was succeeded by his son, Thomas J. Watson, Jr. Another son, Arthur K. Watson, later served as an officer and director of IBM as well. By 1956, the four children and seventeen grandchildren of the founder owned almost 3 percent of IBM stock, worth nearly $80 million. At one point or another, both sons and the husbands of both daughters of the founder served as directors of the company. By 1969, they owned just over 1 percent of the stock in the company, worth over $240 million. In recent years, the members of the Watson family have sold most of their IBM stock. No members of the family are currently associated with the company. With the proceeds from stock sales and accumulated dividend income, the descendants of Thomas Watson are worth in excess of $800 million. SOURCES: Robert Sheehan, "Tom Jr.'s I.B.M.," *Fortune* (September 1956); Proxy Statement, International Business Machines (April 1, 1947); William Rodgers, *Think: A Biography of the Watsons and IBM* (New York: Stein & Day, 1969); Proxy Statement, International Business Machines (April 10, 1969).

WATTIS, EDMUND O. (d. 1934) Ogden, Utah. One of the founders of Utah International, which was later acquired by General Electric Company. In 1901, Edmund Wattis and his brother borrowed $24,000 from a banker to form their own construction company. Over the years, several prominent Utah families invested in the company. Utah International built railroads and dams at first but later diversified into mining. Edmund Wattis was succeeded as president by Leland R. Wattis, the oldest of his seven children. For a number of years, the company was run by descendants of the other early investors. However, Edmund W. Littlefield, a grandson of the founder, became president in 1961. By 1975, four grandsons of Edmund Wattis served as directors of the company. At that point, all nine grandchildren of the founder probably owned at least 14 percent of Utah International stock, worth $300 million. The following year, Edmund Littlefield negotiated the merger of Utah International with General

Electric. In return for their Utah International stock, the nine grandchildren of Edmund Wattis and their children received over 2 percent of the stock in General Electric, worth $320 million. Although they have sold some of this stock, members of the Wattis family probably still own nearly 2 percent of General Electric stock, now worth $640 million. With the proceeds from stock sales and accumulated dividend income, the descendants of Edmund Wattis are probably worth at least $800 million. SOURCES: Louis Kraar, "General Electric's Very Personal Merger," *Fortune* (August 1977); Proxy Statement, Utah International (January 10, 1975); Proxy Statement, Utah International (October 29, 1976).

WEIS, SIGMUND (d. 1962), and HARRY Lewisburg, Pennsylvania. Founders of Weis Markets. Sigmund Weis and his brother, Harry Weis, opened their first grocery store in 1912. They gradually added stores throughout Pennsylvania. The chain is known for its inventory and cost controls. Sigfried and Robert Weis, the two sons of the two founders, went to work for the company in 1947. After Weis Markets went public in 1965, the four children of the two founders owned 77 percent of the stock in the company, worth $50 million. Members of the Weis family still own at least 64 percent of Weis Markets stock, now worth $750 million. With the proceeds from stock sales, the descendants of Sigmund and Harry Weis are worth at least $780 million. SOURCES: Proxy Statement, Weis Markets (March 16, 1971); Eamonn Fingleton, "The Wisdom of Weis," *Forbes* (March 11, 1982).

WEXNER, LESLIE H. (b. 1937) Columbus, Ohio. Founder of The Limited Inc. After working in the family clothing store for two years, Leslie Wexner opened his own clothing store in 1963. The store sold nothing but sportswear for women. When the company went public in 1971, it owned 6 stores. At that point, Leslie Wexner, his parents, and his sister owned 55 percent of The Limited stock, worth only about $3 million. Within eleven years, The Limited had 422 stores. By then, the 40 percent of The Limited stock owned by Leslie Wexner and his family was worth $270 million. The Limited concentrates on merchandising fashionable clothing to young women. In the last few years, The Limited has acquired and renovated two major clothing store chains, Lerner and Lane Bryant. As a result of these acquisitions, The Limited now operates over 1,600 stores. The father of the founder served for a while as chairman of the company. However, Leslie Wexner has always run the company, first as its president and later as its chairman. His mother also serves as an officer and director of the company. Although both his mother and his sister own some of the stock in the company, Leslie Wexner owns most of the stock in The Limited held by the family. Altogether, Leslie Wexner and his family own 39 percent of the stock in The Limited, worth over $1.3 billion. SOURCES:

Bess Gallanis, " 'I See Undervalued Assets,' " *Forbes* (August 2, 1982); Proxy Statement, The Limited Inc. (May 20, 1985); Brian O'Reilly, "Leslie Wexner Knows What Women Want," *Fortune* (August 19, 1985).

WEYERHAEUSER, FREDERICK (d. 1917) Tacoma, Washington. Founder of Weyerhaeuser Company and Potlatch Corporation. In 1900, Frederick Weyerhaeuser and several business associates founded Weyerhaeuser Company. His children later founded another forest products company, Potlatch Corporation. By 1937, the seven children and eleven grandchildren of the founder probably owned about 21 percent of Weyerhaeuser stock, worth at least $17 million. Weyerhaeuser Company eventually became one of the largest and most profitable forest products companies in the world. Over the years, two sons and three grandsons of the founder served as presidents of Weyerhaeuser Company. Two other sons and another grandson also served as presidents of Potlatch Corporation. The Weyerhaeusers have kept almost all of their stock in both family corporations. However, they finally sold their stock in another family company, Arcata Corporation. In 1982, many of the members of the Weyerhaeuser family received over $60 million for about 25 percent of Arcata stock. By 1985, the thirty-three great-grandchildren of Frederick Weyerhaeuser and their children owned about 12 percent of Weyerhaeuser stock, worth $450 million, and over 40 percent of Potlatch stock, worth another $220 million. George H. Weyerhaeuser, a great-grandson of the founder, serves as president of Weyerhaeuser, and a second cousin serves as a director. Three great-grandsons of Frederick Weyerhaeuser serve as directors of Potlatch. Over the past several decades, family members have received almost $300 million in dividend income on their Weyerhaeuser and Potlatch stock. With the proceeds from stock sales and accumulated dividend income, the descendants of Frederick Weyerhaeuser are worth nearly $900 million. SOURCES: Temporary National Economic Committee, *The Distribution of Ownership in the 200 Largest Nonfinancial Corporations* (Washington, D.C.: U.S. Government Printing Office, 1940); Prospectus, Arcata National (December 3, 1968); Prospectus, Potlatch Forests Inc. (October 13, 1969); Marc Beauchamp, "The Tree No Longer Dominates," *Forbes* (December 2, 1985).

WHITEHEAD, EDWIN C. (b. 1919) Greenwich, Connecticut. Founder of Technicon, which was later merged into Revlon Inc. Edwin Whitehead and his father borrowed $5,000 to start their own laboratory-equipment company in 1939. In 1957, they introduced an automated machine for analyzing blood samples. He took the company public in 1969. His 92 percent of Technicon stock was then worth over $800 million. When the price of Technicon plummeted a few years later, his fortune was reduced to less than $150 million. During this period, he transferred almost half of his Technicon stock to a family holding company and a trust for the benefit of his children. In 1979, the Whiteheads sold their remaining 85 percent stake in Technicon to Revlon Inc. for preferred stock that was redeemed four years later for $285 million. In 1981, Edwin Whitehead and the Massachusetts Institute of Technology agreed to establish the Whitehead Institute for Biomedical Research. As part of this agreement, he has donated $35 million to build and equip the institute and has pledged an endowment of $100 million on or before his death. With the proceeds from stock sales, Edwin Whitehead and his three children are worth over $300 million. SOURCES: Prospectus, Technicon Corporation (December 4, 1969); *Forbes* (June 15, 1971); Proxy Statement, Revlon Inc. (March 28, 1983); Dan Rottenberg, "The Education of a Philanthropist," *Town and Country* (December 1984).

WHITNEY, JOHN H. (d. 1982) New York, New York. Founder of Corinthian Broadcasting Company, which was merged into Dun & Bradstreet Corporation, and Whitney Communications Corporation, a private media corporation. John H. Whitney inherited over $40 million from his great-uncle, Oliver H. Payne, who was one of the original partners of John D. Rockefeller. In 1946, Whitney created his own venture-capital firm, J.H. Whitney & Company. Over the years, this partnership invested in a series of companies. In 1954, J.H. Whitney & Company purchased the first of five television stations. Five years later, Whitney combined these stations to form Corinthian Broadcasting Company. When the company went public in 1967, John Whitney owned, either directly or indirectly, 48 percent of Corinthian Broadcasting stock, worth $36 million. Four years later, Corinthian Broadcasting was merged into Dun & Bradstreet Corporation. Whitney received roughly 9 percent of Dun & Bradstreet stock, worth $62 million. He never served as a director of either Corinthian Broadcasting or Dun & Bradstreet. Whitney also founded Whitney Communications, a private media corporation, which acquired twenty-five community newspapers and several magazines. Betsey Whitney, the widow of John Whitney, and her two daughters probably own close to 4 percent of Dun & Bradstreet stock, worth $250 million. They also own, through a partnership, a large block of stock in Whitney Communications. With the proceeds from stock sales and other investments, the widow and two adopted daughters of John Whitney are worth in excess of $350 million. SOURCES: E. J. Kahn, Jr., *Jock: The Life and Times of John Hay Whitney* (Garden City, N.Y.: Doubleday, 1981); Prospectus, Dun & Bradstreet Corporation (February 19, 1970).

WOODRUFF, ERNEST (d. 1944) Atlanta, Georgia. Principal stockholder in Coca-Cola Company. Ernest Woodruff was the chairman of Trust Company of Georgia when he formed a syndicate to acquire Coca-Cola Company from its founder in 1919. He then asked his son, Robert W. Woodruff, to run the company. Robert Woodruff spent heavily on advertising and built a national distribution system. By 1939, Ernest Woodruff and his three sons owned, through a series of holding companies, about 8 percent of Coca-Cola stock, worth about $35 million. One son, Henry F. Woodruff, sold most of his stock in the company. Robert Woodruff exercised absolute control over Coca-Cola Company for almost six decades. Over the years, he and his other brother, George Woodruff, received over $200 million in dividends on their Coca-Cola stock. Robert Woodruff died in 1985. Because he had no children, he left almost his entire estate, worth at least $200 million, to his Robert Woodruff Foundation. George Woodruff and his three daughters still own almost 2 percent of the stock in Coca-Cola, worth $180 million. With accumulated dividend income and the proceeds from stock sales, George Woodruff, his three daughters, and their children are worth $250 million. SOURCES: Temporary National Economic Committee, *The Distribution of Ownership in the 200 Largest Nonfinancial Corporations* (Washington, D.C.: U.S. Government Printing Office, 1940); Proxy Statement, Coca-Cola Company (April 2, 1954); Proxy Statement, Coca-Cola Company (April 2, 1975).

WRIGLEY, WILLIAM, JR. (d. 1932) Chicago, Illinois. Founder of Wm. Wrigley Jr. Company. In 1892, William Wrigley, Jr., began using chewing gum as a premium to sell baking powder. The gum was so popular that he decided to sell chewing gum instead. He advertised his brands heavily, and they soon became the most popular gums in the country. In 1919, he bought Santa Catalina Island off the coast of California and transformed it into a resort. He bought a controlling interest in the Chicago Cubs baseball team two years later. By 1932, the 35 percent of Wrigley stock owned by the founder and his two children was worth $34 million. William Wrigley was succeeded as president of the company by his son, Philip K. Wrigley. In 1981, the Wrigley family sold its 81 percent of the Chicago Cubs for $16 million. The five grandchildren of William Wrigley, Jr., and their children still own at least 35 percent of the stock in Wm. Wrigley Jr. Company, worth $260 million. William Wrigley III, a grandson of the founder, now serves as president and chairman of the company. Over the last five decades, members of the Wrigley family have received over $190 million in dividends on their Wrigley stock. With accumulated dividend income, the descendants of William Wrigley, Jr., are worth well over $300 million. SOURCES: *The New York Times,* August 1, 1935; Proxy Statement, Wm. Wrigley Jr. Company (February 20, 1959); *Forbes* (September 15, 1963); Proxy Statement, Wm. Wrigley Jr. Company (February 11, 1983).

ZIFF, WILLIAM B. (d. 1953) A founder of Ziff Corporation, a private media corporation. William Ziff and a partner founded a magazine publishing company in 1933. When William Ziff died in 1953, the predecessor of Ziff Corporation published eight magazines. Two years later, his older son, William B. Ziff, Jr., took over as president of the company. After he bought out the other founder, William Ziff, Jr., began to expand and diversify the company. He acquired six television stations and a series of special interest magazines devoted to such pursuits as flying, boating, skiing, and backpacking. Over the past three years, however, William Ziff, Jr., has liquidated much of the company. The television stations were sold in 1983 for $100 million. The following year, Ziff Corporation sold twenty-four magazines to two media companies for a total of $710 million. However, the company still owns eleven computer magazines and an electronic information operation. The four children of William Ziff, Sr., own virtually all of the stock in Ziff Corporation, but William Ziff, Jr., votes all of the voting stock. Although Ziff Corporation is a private corporation, the descendants of William Ziff, Sr., are worth in excess of $600 million. SOURCES: *Business Week* (November 29, 1982); *Time* (December 3, 1984); Charles Kaiser, "Murdoch Firm Agrees to Buy 12 Magazines," *The Wall Street Journal,* November 23, 1984.

Notes

1: THE CORPORATE RICH

1 According to the best estimates: James D. Smith and Stephen D. Franklin, "The Concentration of Personal Wealth, 1922–1969," *American Economic Review* (May 1974).

1 As a group, they comprise: Ferdinand Lundberg, *The Rich and the Super-Rich* (New York: Lyle Stuart, 1968).

2 On the basis of his own: C. Wright Mills, *The Power Elite* (New York: Oxford University Press, 1956), p. 94.

3–4 For example, Richard M. Scaife: Karen Rothmyer, "Citizen Scaife," *Columbia Journalism Review* (July 1981).

5 These taxes were never intended: George F. Break and Joseph A. Pechman, *Federal Tax Reform: The Impossible Dream?* (Washington, D.C.: Brookings Institution, 1975), p. 111.

6 Indeed, it was largely the fear: Ronald Chester, *Inheritance, Wealth, and Society* (Bloomington, Ind.: Indiana University Press, 1982), pp. 57–90.

6 In his message to Congress: Gustavus Myers, *The End of Hereditary American Fortunes* (New York: Julian Messner, 1939), p. 363.

7 As a matter of fact: George Cooper, *A Voluntary Tax? New Perspectives on Sophisticated Estate Tax Avoidance* (Washington, D.C.: The Brookings Institution, 1979).

7 Yet when Hunt died in 1974: Harry Hurt III, *Texas Rich* (New York: W.W. Norton, 1981), p. 377.

7 Altogether, the family was able: George Getschow and Roger Thurow, "Hunts in Hock," *The Wall Street Journal,* May 27, 1980.

9 In his classic study: Ferdinand Lundberg, *America's Sixty Families* (New York: Vanguard Press, 1937), p. 8.

9 A somewhat less impassioned observer: E. Digby Baltzell, *Puritan Boston and Quaker Philadelphia* (New York: Free Press, 1969), p. 207.

9 For example, William Randolph Hearst: Lindsay Chaney and Michael Cieply, *The Hearsts: Family and Empire—The Later Years* (New York: Simon & Schuster, 1981), p. 67.

10 Because he apparently died without: Suzanne Finstad, *Heir Not Apparent* (Austin, Tex.: Texas Monthly Press, 1984), pp. 119–33.

10 As George E. Marcus: George E. Marcus, "Law in the Development of Dynastic Families Among American Business Elites," *Law and Society Review* (Summer 1980), p. 861.

11 The reason, of course, is that: Ralph Hewins, *The Richest American* (New York: E.P. Dutton, 1960).

11 In the words of one expert: Bernard Farber, *Kinship and Class* (New York: Basic Books, 1971), p. 99.

11–12 As E. Digby Baltzell: E. Digby Baltzell, *Philadelphia Gentlemen: The Making of a National Upper Class* (Glencoe, Ill.: The Free Press, 1958), p. 7.

13 The classic example of this pattern: Carol Gelderman, *Henry Ford: The Wayward Capitalist* (New York: The Dial Press, 1981), p. 208.

13 More recently, Steven P. Jobs: Bro Uttal, "Behind the Fall of Steve Jobs," *Fortune* (August 5, 1985).

14 Several studies have shown: Michael P. Allen, "Management Control in the Large Corporation," *American Journal of Sociology* (January 1976).

14 In light of this evidence: Maurice Zeitlin, "Corporate Ownership and Control: The Large Corporation and the Capitalist Class," *American Journal of Sociology* (March 1974).

15 One example is the Weyerhaeuser family: Marvin G. Dunn, "The Family Office as a Coordinating Mechanism Within the Ruling Class," in G. William Domhoff, ed., *Power Structure Research* (Beverly Hills, Calif.: Sage Publications, 1980).

17 According to Herbert E. Alexander: Herbert E. Alexander, *Financing the 1972 Election* (Lexington, Mass.: Lexington Books, 1976), p. 396.

19 For example, Henry Ford II: Dan Cordtz, "Henry Ford, Superstar," *Fortune* (May 1973).

19 In order to get media coverage: Ben H. Bagdikian, *The Media Monopoly* (Boston: Beacon Press, 1983), p. 24.

19 As trustees and officers of these: Waldemar A. Nielsen, *The Big Foundations* (New York: Columbia University Press, 1972), p. 406–10.

19 Foundations also enable the corporate: John S. Saloma III, *Ominous Politics: The New Conservative Labyrinth* (New York: Hill & Wang, 1984).

20 Nevertheless, proponents of the ruling: Zeitlin, "Corporate Ownership and Control."

21 As G. William Domhoff puts it: G. William Domhoff, *The Higher Circles: The Governing Class in America* (New York: Random House, 1970), p. 106.

22 The historical evolution of corporate: Pierre Bourdieu and Monique de Saint-Martin, "Le Patronat," *Actes de la Recherche en Sciences Sociales* (March 1978).

22 In his study of upper-class society: Baltzell, *Philadelphia Gentlemen*, pp. 49–69.

23 For example, another observer of: Nathaniel Burt, *The Leisure Class in America* (Boston: Little, Brown, 1963), p. 43.

23 As Nathaniel Burt observed: Ibid., p. 42.

23 In order to accumulate: Lucy Kavaler, *The Private World of High Society* (New York: David McKay, 1960), pp. 94–110.

24 According to E. Digby Baltzell: Baltzell, *Philadelphia Gentlemen*, p. 293.

24 As E. Digby Baltzell notes: Ibid., p. 329.

25 Of course, the most exclusive: Domhoff, *Higher Circles*.

26 For example, John D. Rockefeller: Peter Collier and David Horowitz, *The Rockefellers: An American Dynasty* (New York: Holt, Rinehart & Winston, 1976), pp. 59–65.

27 One extreme example of this: Thomas W. Lippman, "More Than Candy at Mars, Inc.," *The Washington Post,* December 6, 1981.

27 In order to identify the wealthiest: Philip H. Burch, Jr., *The Managerial Revolution Reassessed* (Lexington, Mass.: D.C. Heath, 1972), pp. 20–35.

27 This requirement to identify major: Vic Reinemer, "Stalking the Invisible Investor," *Journal of Economic Issues* (June 1979).

30 Any such historical analysis: Lundberg, *Rich and Super-Rich,* pp. 204–47.

2: THREE DYNASTIES IN TRANSITION

32 According to one official government: Temporary National Economic Committee, *The Distribution of Ownership in the 200 Largest*

Nonfinancial Corporations (Washington, D.C.: U.S. Government Printing Office, 1940), p. 116.

34 At the height of its: Harold F. Williamson, Ralph L. Andreano, Arnold R. Daum, and Gilbert C. Klose, *The American Petroleum Industry* (Evanston, Ill.: Northwestern University Press, 1963), p. 7.

34 The man who had once: *The New York Times,* November 23, 1938.

35 In this study of the: Temporary National Economic Committee, p. 127.

35 Beginning in 1917: Alvin Moscow, *The Rockefeller Inheritance* (Garden City, N.Y.: Doubleday, 1977), p. 95.

36 In the midst of the: Peter Collier and David Horowitz, *The Rockefellers: An American Dynasty* (New York: Holt, Rinehart & Winston, 1976), p. 173.

37 In December of that year: Ibid., p. 204.

37 When he died in 1960: *The New York Times,* May 20, 1960.

38 Between 1958 and 1970: House Committee on the Judiciary, *Nomination of Nelson A. Rockefeller to Be Vice President of the United States* (Washington, D.C.: U.S. Government Printing Office, 1974), pp. 265–66.

38 When he was later asked: Ibid., p. 115.

39 By 1975, he had made a total: Moscow, *The Rockefeller Inheritance,* p. 314.

39 As its first chairman: Collier and Horowitz, *The Rockefellers,* p. 373.

40 To begin with, Nelson: House Committee on the Judiciary, p. 24.

40 In his will, he left: Collier and Horowitz, *The Rockefellers,* p. 447.

40 His will stipulated: *The New York Times,* July 21, 1978.

41 His personal estate was valued: *The New York Times,* February 16, 1979.

41 In all, Jay spent: *The New York Times,* November 2, 1984.

42 The total net worth of: *The Wall Street Journal,* August 2, 1985.

43 In all, they acquired: John D. Gates, *The du Pont Family* (Garden City, N.Y.: Doubleday, 1979), p. 75.

43 For example, when Pierre first: Ibid., p. 89.

43 He then distributed: Alfred D. Chandler, Jr., and Stephen Salsbury, *Pierre S. du Pont and the Making of the Modern Corporation* (New York: Harper & Row, 1971), p. 562.

44 By 1938, the stock in Delaware: Temporary National Economic Committee, p. 869.

44 As John Gates: Gates, *The du Pont Family,* p. 100.

44 As a result of soaring: Chandler and Salsbury, *Pierre S. du Pont,* p. 609.

45 In 1927, he organized: Gates, *The du Pont Family,* p. 129.

45 When he died in 1966: Ibid., p. 136.

46 When he died in 1954: Ibid., p. 140.

46 Under Delaware law: Gerard C. Zilg, *Du Pont: Behind the Nylon Curtain* (Englewood Cliffs, N.J.: Prentice-Hall, 1974), p. 463.

46 One of their four children: *The New York Times,* November 24, 1943.

47 When he died in 1935: Waldemar A. Nielsen, *The Big Foundations* (New York: Columbia University Press, 1972), p. 144.

48 In 1979, the trust: *The Wall Street Journal,* July 28, 1981.

48 When William du Pont, Jr.: Gates, *The du Pont Family,* p. 252.

49 When he first entered: Zilg, *Behind the Nylon Curtain,* p. 548.

50 In explaining the decision: Ibid., p. 547.

51 In the words of: David E. Koskoff, *The Mellons: The Chronicle of America's Richest Family* (New York: Thomas Y. Crowell, 1978), p. 67.

51 According to this same: Ibid.

52 The Mellons gradually increased: Charles C. Carr, *ALCOA: An American Enterprise* (New York: Rinehart, 1952), p. 44.

52 By 1937, the Mellon family: Temporary National Economic Committee, p. 124.

53 In 1907, the Mellons reorganized: Koskoff, *The Mellons,* p. 106.

53 By 1939, the Mellon family: Temporary National Economic Committee, p. 964.

53 Their 52 percent stake: Ibid., p. 1010.

53 The Mellon brothers emerged: Koskoff, *The Mellons,* 77.

54 Nevertheless, he left an estate: Burton Hersh, *The Mellon Family: A Fortune in History* (New York: William Morrow, 1978), p. 334.

54 When he died: Ibid., p. 354.

54 When a reporter asked him: Ibid., p. 452.

55 On returning to America: Ibid., p. 422.

56 According to her own daughter: Ibid., p. 395.

56 A conservative Republican: Karen Rothmyer, "Citizen Scaife," *Columbia Journalism Review* (July 1981).

57 His son, Timothy Mellon: *The Wall Street Journal,* January 6, 1984.

57 By 1937, his 4 percent stake: Temporary National Economic Committee, p. 964.

58 As the result of an exchange: Hersh, *Mellon Family,* p. 379.

59 As one of the younger Mellons: Ibid., p. 566.

3: THE TEST OF TIME

64 The most reliable source: Temporary National Economic Committee, *The Distribution of Ownership in the 200 Largest Nonfinancial*

Corporations (Washington, D.C.: U.S. Government Printing Office, 1940).

64 For example, Ferdinand Lundberg: Ferdinand Lundberg, *America's Sixty Families* (New York: Vanguard Press, 1937).

65 Any estimate of their wealth: Temporary National Economic Committee, p. 115.

65 The founder of this massive: Carol Gelderman, *Henry Ford: The Wayward Capitalist* (New York: The Dial Press, 1981).

65 Finally in 1903, Henry Ford: Ibid., p. 25.

66 At age seventy-two, he still: Temporary National Economic Committee, p. 928.

66 Appalled at the prospect: Robert Lacey, *Ford: The Men and the Machine* (Boston: Little, Brown, 1986), p. 450.

68 After extensive negotiations: *The New York Times,* January 18, 1956.

68 In early 1956, Ford Motor Company: *The New York Times,* January 7, 1956.

68–69 However, as the result of large: *The Wall Street Journal,* November 15, 1985.

69 For example, William Ford: *The Wall Street Journal,* August 25, 1978.

69 John Pitcairn, the founder: *The New York Times,* July 23, 1916.

70 When he died in 1916, John Pitcairn: *The New York Times,* December 19, 1973.

70 By 1938, Pitcairn Company: Temporary National Economic Committee, p. 1224.

70 One son, Theodore Pitcairn: *The New York Times,* December 19, 1973.

70 For example, he sold three: *The New York Times,* November 7, 1967.

70 His brother, Raymond Pitcairn: *The New York Times,* July 13, 1966.

70 The youngest son, Harold Pitcairn: Jacqueline Thompson, *The Very Rich Book* (New York: William Morrow, 1981), p. 73.

71 That same year, it sold: *The Wall Street Journal,* April 12, 1972.

71 Finally, in 1985, the family: *The Wall Street Journal,* September 17, 1985.

71 The family fortune is derived: *The New York Times,* October 25, 1981.

72 Sun Company has been managed: *The New York Times,* October 10, 1971.

72 In 1938, his four living children: Temporary National Economic Committee, p. 1330.

72 As early as 1936, for example: Lundberg, *America's Sixty Families,* p. 484.

72 Between 1956 and 1972: Herbert E. Alexander, *Financing the 1972 Election* (Lexington, Mass.: D.C. Heath, 1976).

72 The oldest and largest: Waldemar A. Nielsen, *The Big Foundations* (New York: Columbia University Press, 1972), p. 124.

73 In order to consolidate: *The New York Times,* October 10, 1971..

73 According to R. Anderson Pew: David Diamond, "The Pews of Philadelphia," *The New York Times,* October 25, 1981.

74 Cyrus H. McCormick is still: Gilbert A. Harrison, *A Timeless Affair: The Life of Anita McCormick Blaine* (Chicago: University of Chicago Press, 1979), p. 10.

74 As of 1937, the descendants: Temporary National Economic Committee, p. 980.

74 One of the daughters: Harrison, *Timeless Affair,* p. 42.

75 After divorcing Edith: Temporary National Economic Committee, p. 980.

75 One of them, Anne Blaine: Harrison, *Timeless Affair.*

76 For example, when Virginia McCormick: *Chicago Tribune,* January 20, 1947.

76 When she died many years later: *The New York Times,* January 14, 1968.

76 The founder of this fortune: Ruth Brandon, *A Capitalist Romance: Singer and the Sewing Machine* (Philadelphia: J.B. Lippincott, 1977).

77 When he died in 1882: *The New York Times,* October 17, 1882.

77 The three surviving sons: Temporary National Economic Committee, p. 1992.

77 When he died in 1957: *The New York Times,* August 24, 1961.

77 He once admitted: *The New York Times,* February 27, 1964.

78 In 1972, they gave over: Alexander, *Financing the 1972 Election.*

78 Two years later, Martin Peretz: *The Wall Street Journal,* March 13, 1974.

79 The Duke fortune was founded: Robert F. Durden, *The Dukes of Durham* (Durham, N.C.: Duke University Press, 1976).

79 James Duke left an estate: *The New York Times,* January 5, 1927.

79 By 1939, she and trusts: Temporary National Economic Committee, p. 862.

80 Instead, Doris Duke devoted: *Time* (September 15, 1947).

80 They gained admittance to upper-class: Nathaniel Burt, *The Perennial Philadelphians* (New York: Arno Press, 1975), p. 54.

81 For example, when Mary Duke Biddle: *The New York Times,* April 21, 1967.

81 The company was founded: *The New York Times,* July 30, 1918.

81 By 1938, the descendants: Temporary National Economic Committee, p. 1266.

81–82 However, Richard Reynolds showed: *The New York Times,* December 16, 1964.

   82 After receiving his inheritance: *The New York Times,* April 19, 1934.

   82 His death in 1932: Hamilton D. Perry, *Libby Holman: Body and Soul* (Boston: Little, Brown, 1983), p. 224.

   82 An early supporter of President Carter: *The New York Times,* August 2, 1979.

   83 Nevertheless, members of the Reynolds: *Forbes* (December 1, 1971).

   83 The founder of this fortune: Edwin P. Hoyt, *That Wonderful A&P!* (New York: Hawthorn Books, 1969).

   84 As late as 1939, family: Temporary National Economic Committee.

   84 When John A. Hartford died: Nielsen, *The Big Foundations,* p. 177.

   84 After the various classes: *Business Week* (December 20, 1958).

   85 Ten years later, when: *The Wall Street Journal,* January 27, 1979.

   85 In an interview published: *Esquire* (March 1961).

   85 After investing a total of: Lisa Gubernick, "That's My Excuse, Anyway," *Forbes* (October 28, 1985).

   85 By the time Huntington Hartford: *The Wall Street Journal,* August 22, 1968.

   86 His father, a successful distillery: Cleveland Amory, *The Last Resorts* (New York: Harper & Brothers, 1952), p. 334.

   86 His son, Edward S. Harkness: *The New York Times,* January 30, 1940.

   87 By 1938, his stockholdings: Temporary National Economic Committee.

   87 In all, Edward Harkness: *The Commonwealth Fund: Historical Sketch 1918–1962* (New York: The Commonwealth Fund, 1963).

   87 The Woolworth fortune was amassed: John K. Winkler, *Five and Ten: The Fabulous Life of F. W. Woolworth* (Freeport, N.Y.: Books for Libraries Press, 1940).

   88 When she died five years later: Gustavus Myers, *The Ending of Hereditary American Fortunes* (New York: Julian Messner, 1939), p. 328.

   88 Altogether, the various members of: Temporary National Economic Committee, p. 1434.

   88 When Barbara Hutton finally came: Philip Van Rensselaer, *Million Dollar Baby: An Intimate Portrait of Barbara Hutton* (New York: G. P. Putnam's Sons, 1979), p. 27.

   89 She had created a trust: *The New York Times,* March 16, 1938.

4: ALL IN THE FAMILY

95 By the time he was eighty-four years old: Howard Rudnitsky, "The Crowning Touch," *Forbes* (December 8, 1980), p. 84.

95 For example, John D. Rockefeller, Jr.: Peter Collier and David Horowitz, *The Rockefellers: An American Dynasty* (New York: Holt, Rinehart & Winston, 1976), p. 204.

95 The primary assets of these: Temporary National Economic Committee, *The Distribution of Ownership in the 200 Largest Nonfinancial Corporations* (Washington, D.C.: U.S. Government Printing Office, 1940), pp. 126–29.

96 In such an arrangement: George Cooper, *A Voluntary Tax?* (Washington, D.C.: Brookings Institution, 1979), p. 57.

96 In the case of the Rockefeller: House Committee on the Judiciary, *Nomination of Nelson A. Rockefeller to Be Vice President of the United States* (Washington, D.C.: U.S. Government Printing Office, 1974), p. 849.

96 Similarly, almost all of the fortune: Harry Hurt III, *Texas Rich* (New York: W.W. Norton, 1981), p. 117.

97 When the young du Pont scion: Gerard C. Zilg, *Du Pont: Behind the Nylon Curtain* (Englewood Cliffs, N.J.: Prentice-Hall, 1974), p. 463.

98 As Rachel Lambert Mellon: Burton Hersh, *The Mellon Family: A Fortune in History* (New York: William Morrow, 1978), p. 520.

98 Conceptions of kinship are also: Bernard Farber, *Conceptions of Kinship* (New York: Elsevier North Holland, 1981).

98 Andrew W. Mellon and Richard B. Mellon: David E. Koskoff, *The Mellons: The Chronicle of America's Richest Family* (New York: Thomas Y. Crowell, 1978), p. 309.

99 In this same manner, Sid W. Richardson: James Presley, *The Saga of Wealth: The Rise of the Texas Oilmen* (New York: G. P. Putnam's Sons, 1978), p. 221.

99 By way of illustration: Hersh, *Mellon Family*, p. 564.

99 As Stanley Lebergott puts it: Stanley Lebergott, *Wealth and Want* (Princeton, N.J.: Princeton University Press, 1975), p. 187.

102 "The presence of a transcendent": Farber, *Conceptions of Kinship*, p. 16.

102 As one of the great-grandchildren: Marvin G. Dunn, "The Family Office as a Coordinating Mechanism Within the Ruling Class," in G. William Domhoff, ed., *Power Structure Research* (Beverly Hills, Calif.: Sage Publications, 1980), p. 30.

102 This network of relatives: Bernard Farber, *Kinship and Class* (New York: Basic Books, 1971).

103 As Bernard Farber observes: Ibid., p. 107.

103 In the words of one keen observer: Nathaniel Burt, *The Perennial Philadelphians* (New York: Arno Press, 1975), p. 40.

103 As the historian Edward Saveth: Edward N. Saveth, "The American Patrician Class: A Field of Research," *American Quarterly* (Summer 1963), p. 259.

104 Despite the fact that she had: Laura D. Riley, "America's Ten Richest Women," *Ladies Home Journal* (September 1957), p. 181.

105 Some of the wealthiest scions: Koskoff, *The Mellons,* p. 474.

105 The Rockefeller family, for example: Kathleen Teltsch, "The Cousins: The Fourth Generation of Rockefellers," *The New York Times,* December 30, 1984.

105 In the same manner, the descendants: James B. Stewart and Michael Waldholz, "Internal Affair: How Richardson-Vicks Fell Prey to Takeover Despite Family's Grip," *The Wall Street Journal,* October 30, 1985.

106 As one of the young Rockefeller cousins: Collier and Horowitz, *The Rockefellers,* p. 509.

106 As Pierre S. du Pont IV: *The Wall Street Journal,* May 24, 1979.

107 In the words of Maurice Zeitlin: Maurice Zeitlin, Lynda Ann Ewen, and Richard Earl Radcliffe, " 'New Princes' for Old: Large Corporations and the Capitalist Class in Chile," *American Journal of Sociology* (July 1974), p. 109.

108 In order to administer: John Train, "Rejuvenating Old Money," *The New York Times,* June 8, 1986.

108 The Rockefellers maintain: Collier and Horowitz, *The Rockefellers,* pp. 556–75.

108 For many years, the Mellons: Koskoff, *The Mellons,* p. 451.

109 The Weyerhaeusers, for example: Dunn, "The Family Office."

109 The Blaustein family of Baltimore: Mark Bowden, "Baltimore's Richest People," *Baltimore Magazine* (July 1978).

109 Indeed, George Marcus, an observer: George E. Marcus, "Law in the Development of Dynastic Families Among American Business Elites," *Law and Society Review* (Summer 1980), p. 859.

110 One of the most celebrated instances: Robert Lenzner, *The Great Getty* (New York: Crown Publishers, 1985), p. 229.

110 One of the most protracted: Richard Austin Smith, "The Heir Who Turned on the House of Phipps," *Fortune* (October 1960).

111 Not one to be easily deterred: James O'Hanlon, "Family Doctor for the Rich," *Forbes* (March 19, 1979).

111 One of the most celebrated: Anne Bagamery, "In the Best of Families," *Forbes* (June 22, 1981).

111 A similar dispute has surfaced: Bryan Burrough, "Grandpa's Billions: A Bitter Family Feud over the Cullen Estate Flares Again in Texas," *The Wall Street Journal,* September 2, 1983.

112 As one knowledgeable observer: *The Wall Street Journal,* August 25, 1978.

113 Around the turn: Ruth Brandon, *The Dollar Princesses* (New York: Alfred A. Knopf, 1980).

113 Perhaps the most celebrated: Edwin P. Hoyt, *The Vanderbilts and Their Fortunes* (Garden City, N.Y.: Doubleday, 1962), pp. 293–97.

113 As Stephen Birmingham notes: Stephen Birmingham, *The Right People* (Boston: Little, Brown, 1968), p. 114.

114 In this same manner, John D. Rockefeller, Jr.: Collier and Horowitz, *The Rockefellers,* p. 92.

114 Indeed, one observer felt justified: Ferdinand Lundberg, *America's Sixty Families* (New York: Vanguard Press, 1937), p. 9.

115 According to one family historian: Zilg, *Behind the Nylon Curtain,* p. 82.

116 As one observer puts it: Birmingham, *The Right People,* p. 114.

116 In almost every case: Collier and Horowitz, *The Rockefellers,* pp. 181–226.

116 The pattern is much the same: Koskoff, *The Mellons,* pp. 461–565.

117 The social status of these: Paul M. Blumberg and P. W. Paul, "Continuities and Discontinuities in Upper-Class Marriages," *Journal of Marriage and the Family* (February 1975).

117 However, he also notes: G. William Domhoff, *The Higher Circles: The Governing Class in America* (New York: Random House, 1970), p. 76.

118 Consequently, half of all the millionaires: Internal Revenue Service, *Statistics of Income, 1972—Personal Wealth Estimated from Estate Tax Returns* (Washington, D.C.: U.S. Government Printing Office, 1976).

118 For example, very few of the women: Ann R. Tickamyer, "Wealth and Power: A Comparison of Men and Women in the Property Elite," *Social Forces* (December 1981).

119 Most of the women from corporate rich: Susan A. Ostrander, *Women of the Upper Class* (Philadelphia: Temple University Press, 1984), pp. 111–39.

119 One of the two founders: Stephen Birmingham, *The Grand Dames* (New York: Simon & Schuster, 1982), p. 238.

119 Ethel M. Dorrance could hardly: *The New York Times,* October 30, 1930.

119 After all, she was the largest: Temporary National Economic Committee, p. 1455.

120 One of the first women to become: Tom Kelly, *The Imperial Post* (New York: William Morrow, 1983).

120 In her first meeting with: David Halberstam, *The Powers That Be* (New York: Alfred A. Knopf, 1979), p. 518.

120 More recently, Helen Copley: *Forbes* (April 15, 1975).

120 There is the example: Carol Gelderman, *Henry Ford: The Wayward Capitalist* (New York: Dial Press, 1981), p. 377.

121 In 1974, Duke Power became: *Forbes* (February 1, 1976).

121 For example, William Butterworth: Wayne C. Broehl, Jr., *John Deere's Company* (Garden City, N.Y.: Doubleday, 1984).

121 According to David Halberstam: Halberstam, *The Powers That Be*, p. 215.

121 More recently, Ronald W. Miller: *Business Week* (August 5, 1986).

122 Even the reclusive Abby Rockefeller Mauze: Alvin Moscow, *The Rockefeller Inheritance* (Garden City, N.Y.: Doubleday, 1977), p. 318.

122 A case in point involved: Waldemar A. Nielsen, *The Big Foundations* (New York: Columbia University Press, 1972), p. 179.

5: FAMILY BUSINESS

125 The transformation of a small company: Edward S. Herman, *Corporate Control, Corporate Power* (New York: Cambridge University Press, 1981), p. 4.

125 Despite its popularity, there is: Maurice Zeitlin, "Corporate Ownership and Control: The Large Corporation and the Capitalist Class," *American Journal of Sociology* (March 1984).

126 This growth has been financed: Robert Sobel, *IBM: Colossus in Transition* (New York: Times Books, 1981).

127 In 1937, Thomas J. Watson: Temporary National Economic Committee, *The Distribution of Ownership in the 200 Largest Nonfinancial Corporations* (Washington, D.C.: U.S. Government Printing Office, 1940), p. 978.

127 By 1939, this trust held: Ibid., p. 862.

129 For example, the Weyerhaeusers: Marvin G. Dunn, "The Family Office as a Coordinating Mechanism Within the Ruling Class," in G. William Domhoff, ed., *Power Structure Research* (Beverly Hills, Calif.: Sage Publications, 1980).

130 Specifically, one of the most valuable investments: Temporary National Economic Committee.

130 By 1974, the stockholdings: House Committee on the Judiciary, *Nomination of Nelson A. Rockefeller to Be Vice President of the United States* (Washington, D.C.: U.S. Government Printing Office, 1974), pp. 848–49.

131 As a result, roughly a quarter: Michael P. Allen, "Management Control in the Large Corporation," *American Journal of Sociology* (January 1976).

131 For example, after the death of his son: Carol Gelderman, *Henry Ford: The Wayward Capitalist* (New York: The Dial Press, 1981), p. 363.

132 At the same time, he stated: Robert O'Brien, *Marriott: The J. Willard Marriott Story* (Salt Lake City, Utah: Deseret Book Company, 1977), p. 269.

133 A notable exception: Ralph W. Hidy, Frank E. Hill, and Allan Nevins, *Timber and Men: The Weyerhaeuser Story* (New York: The Macmillan Company, 1963).

134 There is the example of the Cabot Corporation: Leon Harris, *Only to God: The Extraordinary Life of Godfrey Lowell Cabot* (New York: Atheneum, 1967).

135 For example, Daniel C. Searle: *Forbes* (February 6, 1978).

135 Seven years after they: *The Wall Street Journal,* September 28, 1984.

136 Paul Mellon, for example, could have: David E. Koskoff, *The Mellons: The Chronicle of America's Richest Family* (New York: Thomas Y. Crowell, 1978).

136 Similarly, David Rockefeller was the only: Peter Collier and David Horowitz, *The Rockefellers: An American Dynasty* (New York: Holt, Rinehart & Winston, 1976).

136 For example, the children and grandchildren: Senate Committee on Government Operations, *Disclosure of Corporate Ownership* (Washington, D.C.: U.S. Government Printing Office, 1973), p. 44.

138 As Adolf Berle and Gardiner Means: Adolf A. Berle and Gardiner C. Means, *The Modern Corporation and Private Property* (New York: The Macmillan Company, 1932), p. 75.

138 In recent years, however, researchers: Philip H. Burch, Jr., *The Managerial Revolution Reassessed* (Lexington, Mass.: Lexington Books, 1972), p. 29.

138 Thomas J. Watson is often: Sobel, *IBM: Colossus.*

139 The Watsons never owned: Robert Sheehan, "Tom Jr.'s I.B.M.," *Fortune* (September 1956).

139 This grocery store chain was: *Forbes* (September 15, 1955).

139 As a manager of a competing: *Forbes* (February 18, 1980).

140 One of the most notable examples: Herman, *Corporate Control,* p. 158.

140 One of those sons: John Huey, "Bob Woodruff at 91: The Old Salesman as Country Squire," *The Wall Street Journal,* January 9, 1981.

140–41 For example, McGraw-Hill Inc.: Donald D. Holt, "The Unlikely Hero of McGraw-Hill," *Fortune* (May 21, 1979).

141 Recently, the Richardson family: James B. Stewart and Michael Waldholz, "Internal Affair: How Richardson-Vicks Fell Prey to

Takeover Despite Family's Grip," *The Wall Street Journal,* October 30, 1985.

141 For example, when The Washington Post Company: *The Wall Street Journal,* March 26, 1971.

142 Originally a grain trading firm: Dan Morgan, *Merchants of Grain* (New York: The Viking Press, 1979), pp. 168–75.

143 At last count, there were: Leslie Pittel, "Behind the Paper Curtain," *Forbes* (November 18, 1985).

143 In return for mortgages: *The Wall Street Journal,* April 28, 1980.

143 As a result of these: G. Christian Hill, "Texas's Hunt Brothers Discuss Their Worth," *The Wall Street Journal,* August 27, 1985.

144 As one tax expert, George Cooper: George Cooper, *A Voluntary Tax?* (Washington, D.C.: Brookings Institution, 1979), p. 5.

145 For example, Cargill Inc.: *The Wall Street Journal,* November 13, 1981.

146 As Walter Haas explained: Lawrence Minard, "In Privacy They Thrive," *Forbes* (November 1, 1975), p. 40.

146 In the words of one family member: Victor F. Zonana, "Philanthropic Haas Family Embraces a New Cause," *Los Angeles Times,* July 28, 1985.

147 For example, the descendants of: *The New York Times,* May 6, 1975.

147 For purposes of gift and estate: *The Wall Street Journal,* November 19, 1958.

149 By 1975, the Uihlein family: *The Wall Street Journal,* January 3, 1975.

149 When Schlitz president Robert A. Uihlein, Jr.: Charles G. Burck, "Getting Schlitz Back on the Track," *Fortune* (April 24, 1978).

150 In return for their stock: *The Wall Street Journal,* March 6, 1981.

150 The situation was much the same: *The Wall Street Journal,* March 3, 1981.

150 He explained the mergers by saying: *The Wall Street Journal,* July 6, 1973.

150 Similarly, Edmund W. Littlefield: Louis Kraar, "General Electric's Very Personal Merger," *Fortune* (August 1977).

151 For example, the Sarah C. Getty Trust: *The Wall Street Journal,* April 25, 1984.

151 For example, when Malcolm McLean: *Forbes* (December 1, 1971).

152 After several years of disagreements: Howard Rudnitsky, "The Crowning Touch," *Forbes* (December 8, 1980).

152 In 1963, Anderson sold Hondo Oil and Gas: *Business Week* (April 18, 1970).

153 Similarly, Dwayne O. Andreas and his brother: Irwin Ross,

"Dwayne Andreas's Bean Has a Heart of Gold," *Fortune* (October 1973).

153 The merger between Time Inc.: *Business Week* (August 25, 1973).

6: DEATH AND TAXES

156 Although several states enacted: Gustavus Myers, *The Ending of Hereditary American Fortunes* (New York: Julian Messner, 1939), p. 91.

156 For example, when Philip D. Armour: Ibid., p. 160.

156 In an address to Congress: Ibid., p. 371.

156 It was originally a very modest tax: Internal Revenue Service, *Statistics of Income for 1950* (Washington, D.C.: U.S. Government Printing Office, 1954), p. 338.

157 Even Herbert Hoover, a steadfast: Philip M. Stern, *The Great Treasury Raid* (New York: Random House, 1964), p. 255.

157 Huey Long, a populist senator: Mark H. Leff, *The Limits of Symbolic Reform: The New Deal and Taxation, 1933–1939* (New York: Cambridge University Press, 1984), p. 123.

157 In an address to Congress: Myers, *Ending of Hereditary*, p. 362.

158 In the words of one historian: Leff, *Limits of Symbolic Reform*, p. 8.

158 With two full months: *The New York Times*, October 31, 1935.

159 In general, the vicissitudes of gift: Ira Sharkansky, *The Politics of Taxing and Spending* (New York: Bobbs-Merrill, 1969), p. 173.

159 In 1941, Congress raised the maximum: Internal Revenue Service, p. 339.

159 They were not altered significantly: Edward E. Milam and D. Larry Crumbley, *Estate Planning—After the 1976 Tax Reform Act* (New York: AMACOM, 1978).

159 In 1981, Congress agreed to reduce the maximum: Travis P. Goggans and Ted D. Englebrecht, *Estate Planning and Practice Handbook* (Englewood Cliffs, N.J.: Prentice-Hall, 1982), p. 461.

160 For example, a parent who gave a child: Stern, *Treasury Raid*, p. 261.

161 The disparity between the tax rates: Milam and Crumbley, *Estate Planning*, p. 72.

161 As a result of this legislation: Goggans and Englebrecht, *Estate Planning and Practice*, p. 461.

162 His gift taxes during this ten-year: House Committee on the Judiciary, *Nomination of Nelson A. Rockefeller to Be Vice President of the United States* (Washington, D.C.: U.S. Government Printing Office, 1974), p. 26.

163 During this same period: Ibid.

164 For example, the sum of $100 invested: Lawrence Fisher and James H. Lorie, *A Half Century of Returns on Stocks and Bonds* (Chicago: University of Chicago Graduate School of Business, 1977).

164 In 1940, Mott placed slightly: *The New York Times,* February 7, 1940.

165 When he first joined the company in 1914: William Rodgers, *Think: The Biography of the Watsons and IBM* (New York: Stein & Day, 1969), p. 70.

165 By 1937, the Watson family owned: Temporary National Economic Committee, *The Distribution of Ownership in the 200 Largest Nonfinancial Corporations* (Washington, D.C.: U.S. Government Printing Office, 1940), p. 978.

165 He died with less than $4 million: *The New York Times,* November 14, 1957.

166 At age seventy-nine, Henry Crown: *Business Week* (December 22, 1975), p. 31.

167 As a result of these characteristics: Ronald Chester, *Inheritance, Wealth, and Society* (Bloomington, Ind.: Indiana University Press, 1982), p. 126.

168 The only limitation on the duration: Ibid., p. 141.

168 One of the best-documented examples: George Cooper, *A Voluntary Tax?* (Washington, D.C.: Brookings Institution, 1979), pp. 66–71.

169 Sarah Getty paid a small gift: *The Wall Street Journal,* April 25, 1984.

169 John D. Rockefeller, Jr., for instance: Peter Collier and David Horowitz, *The Rockefellers: An American Dynasty* (New York: Holt, Rinehart & Winston, 1976), p. 560.

170 H. L. Hunt created trusts for each: Harry Hurt III, *Texas Rich* (New York: W.W. Norton, 1981), p. 117.

170 For example, all of the common stock: Lindsay Chaney and Michael Cieply, *The Hearsts, Family and Empire—The Later Years* (New York: Simon & Schuster, 1981), pp. 277–81.

171 For example, the ten children: Stern, *Treasury Raid,* p. 78.

171 As a result of these objections: Milam and Crumbley, *Estate Planning,* p. 160.

172 Many of the oldest corporate rich: Temporary National Economic Committee, pp. 1441–53.

173 Until recently, the largest and best-known: John D. Gates, *The du Pont Family* (Garden City, N.Y.: Doubleday, 1979), p. 89.

173 According to the SEC: *The Wall Street Journal,* December 16, 1974.

174 In general, the *valuation discount* for stock: Cooper, *A Voluntary Tax?,* pp. 44–55.

174 The complexity of this problem: *Tax Court Memorandum Decisions 33* (New York: Commerce Clearing House, 1974).

176 A case in point is the pyramid: *Tax Court Memorandum Decisions 24* (New York: Commerce Clearing House, 1960).

176 In particular, closely held corporations: Cooper, *A Voluntary Tax?*, p. 45.

177 Bessemer Securities was created: Richard A. Smith, "The Heir Who Turned on the House of Phipps," *Fortune* (October 1960).

177 In 1938, the company had two classes: Temporary National Economic Committee, p. 1442.

178 By 1982, Bessemer Securities had a net asset: *Business Week* (August 23, 1982).

178 One of these is the deferred: Goggans and Englebrecht, *Estate Planning and Practice,* p. 470.

180 For example, when Richard K. Mellon died: Burton Hersh, *The Mellon Family: A Fortune in History* (New York: William Morrow, 1978), p. 564.

180 One tactic for transferring wealth: Cooper, *A Voluntary Tax?,* pp. 41–43.

181 When Congress raised the gift: Alfred D. Chandler, Jr., and Stephen Salsbury, *Pierre S. du Pont and the Making of the Modern Corporation* (New York: Harper & Row, 1971), p. 561.

182 In 1967, one of these family partnerships: *Tax Court Reporter 88* (New York: Commerce Clearing House, 1977).

183 In 1979, Nelson Hunt and two: Stephen Fay, *Beyond Greed* (New York: The Viking Press, 1982).

183 In his income tax return for 1980: *The Wall Street Journal,* February 12, 1985.

184 Almost a year later: *The Wall Street Journal,* June 23, 1981.

7: PRACTICAL PHILANTHROPY

185 Fewer than three hundred foundations: *Foundation Directory* (New York: Foundation Center, 1983).

187 Once he had accumulated his fortune: Waldemar A. Nielsen, *The Big Foundations* (New York: Columbia University Press, 1972), p. 32.

187 This consideration may explain: Peter Collier and David Horowitz, *The Rockefellers: An American Dynasty* (New York: Holt, Rinehart & Winston, 1976), p. 64.

188 Similarly, the Annenberg family: John Cooney, *The Annenbergs* (New York: Simon & Schuster, 1982), p. 195.

188 For example, the Ford family: Joseph C. Goulden, *The Money Givers* (New York: Random House, 1971), pp. 42–44.

188 It appears that William R. Hearst: Lindsay Chaney and Michael Cieply, *The Hearsts: Family and Empire—The Later Years* (New York: Simon & Schuster, 1981), p. 278.

189 As a result, his estate: *The New York Times,* July 7, 1984.

189 One example of this pattern: Nielsen, *The Big Foundations,* p. 193.

190 One of the few philanthropists: Horace B. Powell, *The Original Has This Signature—W. K. Kellogg* (New York: Prentice-Hall, 1956).

191 One of these lifetime philanthropists: Nielsen, *The Big Foundations,* p. 236.

192 The most recent example of a large: *The Wall Street Journal,* January 9, 1978.

192 For example, when William M. Keck: *The New York Times,* June 30, 1965.

193 Similarly, the Henry J. Kaiser Family Foundation: Nielsen, *The Big Foundations,* p. 247.

193 Moreover, instead of bequeathing: Harry Hurt III, *Texas Rich* (New York: W.W. Norton, 1981), p. 350.

194 One of the most interesting of these: Travis P. Goggans and Ted D. Englebrecht, *Estate Planning and Practice Handbook* (Englewood Cliffs, N.J.: Prentice-Hall, 1982), pp. 159–73.

194 One of the largest charitable remainder: Arthur M. Louis, "It's Moody Versus Moody in the Struggle for American National," *Fortune* (March 1981).

197 Similarly, when Alfred I. du Pont: John D. Gates, *The du Pont Family* (Garden City, N.Y.: Doubleday, 1979).

197 Another arrangement that enables: George Cooper, *A Voluntary Tax?* (Washington, D.C.: Brookings Institution, 1979), pp. 59–63.

197 One of the largest charitable: Patrick J. Nicholson, *Mr. Jim: The Biography of James Smither Abercrombie* (Houston, Tex.: Gulf Publishing, 1983), p. 340.

198 For example, when William R. Hearst died: Chaney and Cieply, *The Hearsts,* p. 67.

199 While he was alive, Kresge: Nielsen, *The Big Foundations,* p. 236.

199 In a similar manner: *The New York Times,* January 13, 1948.

200 For example, when John A. Hartford: Nielsen, *The Big Foundations,* p. 177.

201 In point of fact, the family: Collier and Horowitz, *The Rockefellers,* p. 253.

201 However, the last family representative: *The New York Times,* January 12, 1977.

202 One example of this pattern: David Diamond, "The Pews of Philadelphia," *The New York Times,* October 25, 1981.

202 In 1962, the House Select Committee: House Select Committee on Small Business, *Tax-Exempt Foundations and Charitable Trusts: Their Impact on Our Economy* (Washington, D.C.: U.S. Government Printing Office, 1962).

203 In response to these and other: William H. Smith and Carolyn P. Chiechi, *Private Foundations Before and After the Tax Reform Act of 1969* (Washington, D.C.: American Enterprise Institute for Public Policy Research, 1974).

203 As late as 1980, the two Pews: Diamond, "The Pews."

204 For example, after the company issued: Burton Hersh, *The Mellon Family: A Fortune in History* (New York: William Morrow, 1978), p. 584.

205 For example, the Robert Wood Johnson: *Source Book Profiles* (New York: Foundation Center, 1982).

205 John Pitcairn was one of the founders: Ibid.

207 For example, the Timken Foundation: Ibid.

207 This foundation was endowed by Otto Haas: Nielsen, *The Big Foundations,* p. 239.

207 The same is true of the McKnight Foundation: Foundation Center, *Source Book Profiles.*

208 In recent years, however: Waldemar A. Nielsen, *The Golden Donors* (New York: E.P. Dutton, 1985), pp. 37–58.

208 In his seminal study: Nielsen, *The Big Foundations,* p. 407.

209 In recent years, the Stern Fund: *Source Book Profiles.*

209 One of the most questionable: Donald L. Bartlett and James B. Steele, *Empire: The Life, Legend, and Madness of Howard Hughes* (New York: W.W. Norton, 1979), pp. 198–202.

211 The Olin Corporation was one: Richard A. Smith, "The Rise of the House of Olin," *Fortune* (December 1953).

211 William R. Hearst, the only son: Chaney and Cieply, *The Hearsts.*

213 The financial reorganization: Ibid., p. 279.

8: MAKING IT BIG

217 Specifically, Thurow argues: Lester C. Thurow, *Generating Inequality: Mechanisms of Distribution in the U.S. Economy* (New York: Basic Books, 1975).

217 As Thurow observes: Ibid., p. 149.

217 Whitehead and his father: *Forbes* (June 15, 1971).

218 In exchange for their Technicon: *The New York Times,* May 25, 1983.

218 By the time the company went: Michael Moritz, *The Little Kingdom: The Private Story of Apple Computer* (New York: William Morrow, 1984), p. 278.

218 His entire estate: *The New York Times,* December 19, 1914.

218 Only ten years later: *Forbes* (June 1, 1972).

219 Paul V. Galvin and his brother: Harry M. Petrakis, *The Founder's Touch: The Life of Paul Galvin of Motorola* (New York: McGraw-Hill, 1965), p. 60.

220 When Anheuser-Busch was incorporated: Roland Krebs, *Making Friends Is Our Business: 100 Years of Anheuser-Busch* (St. Louis, Mo.: Anheuser-Busch, 1953), p. 19.

221 Similarly, Charles Kettering: Stuart W. Leslie, *Boss Kettering* (New York: Columbia University Press, 1983).

221 A more recent example of an inventor: Mark Olshaker, *The Instant Image: Edwin Land and the Polaroid Experience* (New York: Stein & Day, 1978).

222 Henry Ford, for example: Robert Lacey, *Ford: The Men and the Machine* (Boston: Little, Brown, 1986).

223 The original Corning Glass Works: *Forbes* (November 1, 1968).

223 For example, the Donnelley family: *The New York Times,* February 27, 1955.

224 John T. Dorrance joined: *Forbes* (December 7, 1981).

224 For example, the descendants of Henry J. Heinz: Robert C. Alberts, *The Good Provider: H. J. Heinz and His 57 Varieties* (Boston: Houghton Mifflin, 1973), p. 263.

225 There is also the case: Leonard Engel, *Medicine Makers of Kalamazoo* (New York: McGraw-Hill, 1961).

226 Erle P. Halliburton, for example: *The New York Times,* October 14, 1957.

227 Samuel Friedland and his brother: Paul Blustein, "Is All Fair at Food Fair?" *Forbes* (August 21, 1978).

228 One of the oldest electronics companies: *Forbes* (April 1, 1966).

228 The founders of another early: J. McDonald, "Men Who Made Texas Instruments," *Fortune* (November 1961).

229 For example, Robert N. Noyce: Jacqueline Thompson, *Future Rich: The People, Companies, and Industries Creating America's Next Fortunes* (New York: William Morrow, 1985), pp. 106–10.

229–30 While selling milk-shake machines: Ray Kroc, *Grinding It Out: The Making of McDonald's* (Chicago: Contemporary Books, 1977), p. 6.

230 After operating several franchise: Howard Rudnitsky, "How Sam Walton Does It," *Forbes* (August 16, 1982).

231 One of the most recent examples of this pattern: James Presley, *A Saga of Wealth: The Rise of the Texas Oilmen* (New York: G. P. Putnam's Sons, 1978), pp. 240–47.

232 As one associate put it: Robert Lenzner, *The Great Getty* (New York: Crown Publishers, 1986), p. 57.

232 J. Paul Getty once described: J. Paul Getty, *My Life and Fortunes* (New York: Duell, Sloane & Pearce, 1963), p.176.

234 This company was founded in 1960: *Forbes* (April 1, 1966).

234 Over the next four years: Robert J. Flaherty, "The Singular Henry Singleton," *Forbes* (July 9, 1979).

235 In 1984, Teledyne announced: *The Wall Street Journal,* May 30, 1984.

236 He got his start in business: Dial Torgerson, *Kerkorian: An American Success Story* (New York: Dial Press, 1974), p. 76.

237 In 1984, the company exchanged: *The Wall Street Journal,* June 7, 1985.

238 Laurence and Preston Tisch took: William R. Sheldon, "The Tisches Eye Their Next $65 Million," *Fortune* (January 1960).

238 That same year, the Tisch: Charles B. Burck, "How the Tisches Run Their 'Little Store,' " *Fortune* (May 1971).

239 That year, they announced: *The Wall Street Journal,* February 20, 1985.

240 The Lindner brothers started: Carol J. Loomis, "Carl Lindner's Singular Financial Empire," *Fortune* (January 1977).

241 In 1979, Carl Lindner decided: Carol J. Loomis, "Carl Lindner's Disappearing Act," *Fortune* (July 13, 1981).

241 Saul Steinberg became an entrepreneur: *Fortune* (July 1967).

242 The following year, Reliance Group: Peter W. Bernstein, "Fear and Loathing in the Boardrooms," *Fortune* (December 15, 1980).

243 Later that year, Saul Steinberg: *The Wall Street Journal,* July 29, 1981.

243 Kluge was a successful entrepreneur: Joel F. Olesky, "Metromedia's Creative Financier," *Dun's Review* (December 1960).

244 In 1983, John Kluge announced: Allan Sloan, "The Magician," *Forbes* (April 23, 1984).

9: LIFE-STYLES OF THE RICH

248 According to Veblen: Thorstein Veblen, *The Theory of the Leisure Class* (New York: The Macmillan Company, 1905).

249 As one observer of these: Steven B. Levine, "The Rise of American Boarding Schools and the Development of a National Upper Class," *Social Problems* (October 1980), p. 91.

250 Nevertheless, his son attended: Peter Collier and David Horowitz, *The Rockefellers: An American Dynasty* (New York: Holt, Rinehart & Winston, 1976).

250 However, the three grandsons: Robert Lacey, *Ford: The Men and the Machine* (Boston: Little, Brown, 1986).

251 They are often designed by: Merrill Folsom, *The American Mansions and Their Stories* (New York: Hastings House, 1963).

252 During the early part of: Gerard C. Zilg, *Du Pont: Behind the Nylon Curtain* (Englewood Cliffs, N.J.: Prentice-Hall, 1974), pp. 564–68.

252 Pocantico was eventually: Collier and Horowitz, *The Rockefellers*, pp. 250–53.

253 However, Paul Mellon eventually: Burton Hersh, *The Mellon Family: A Fortune in History* (New York: William Morrow, 1978), p. 399.

253 San Simeon was a working ranch: Lindsay Chaney and Michael Cieply, *The Hearsts: Family and Empire—The Later Years* (New York: Simon & Schuster, 1981), p. 153.

253 In all, the castle and guesthouses: W. W. Swanberg, *Citizen Hearst: A Biography of William Randolph Hearst* (New York: Charles Scribner's Sons, 1961), p. 603.

254 For example, when Pierre S. du Pont: Waldemar A. Nielsen, *The Big Foundations* (New York: Columbia University Press, 1972), p. 141.

254 In 1972, J. Seward Johnson: Shawn Tully, "Mr. Johnson's $21 Million Palace," *Town and Country* (May 1976).

254 For example, only a few: Collier and Horowitz, *The Rockefellers*.

254 The major exception is: Lois Romano, "The Rich Tradition of Jay Rockefeller," *The Washington Post,* June 27, 1985.

255 Gordon Getty, for example: Pat Steger, "San Francisco's Shy Tycoon," *San Francisco Chronicle,* September 30, 1983.

256 Many wealthy individuals own: Kathryn Livingston, "Palm Beach: The Greatest Little Beach Town on Earth," *Town and Country* (March 1983).

256 Other members of the corporate: Gloria Greer, "Palm Springs," *Town and Country* (May 1975).

256 One of the most secluded: Lorna Livingston, "Northeast Harbor, Maine," *Town and Country* (July 1985).

257 For example, the scions of several: Judy Ross, "The Lure of the Lakes," *Town and Country* (August 1986).

257 Malcolm Forbes, for example: Arthur Jones, *Malcolm Forbes: Peripatetic Millionaire* (New York: Harper & Row, 1977), p. 149.

257 Perhaps the most eclectic: Norm Shortridge, "The Lilly Legacy," *Indianapolis Magazine* (August 1974).

259 Although his father was not: David E. Koskoff, *The Mellons: The Chronicle of America's Richest Family* (New York: Thomas Y. Crowell, 1978), pp. 330–39.

259 In 1931, he invested: Richard J. Whalen, "Norton Simon Says Thumbs Down," *Fortune* (June 1965).

260 In 1975, Simon offered: Walter McQuade, "Norton Simon's Great Museum Caper," *Fortune* (August 25, 1980).

260 When he divorced his second wife: *The New York Times,* May 14, 1980.

260 Three years later, Paul Mellon: *The New York Times,* November 16, 1983.

260 Geraldine Keen, in her classic: Geraldine Keen, *Money and Art: A Study Based on the Times-Sotheby Index* (New York: G. P. Putnam's Sons, 1971).

261 Norton Simon, for example: Jerry E. Patterson, "Norton Simon 'Refines' His Collections," *ARTnews* (Summer 1973).

261 For example, Barbara Johnson: *ARTnews* (October 1984).

261 In 1982, Daniel J. Terra: *The New York Times,* July 30, 1982.

261 Similarly, Wendell Cherry: *The New York Times,* May 22, 1981.

261 Almost all of the most valuable: Thomas Hoving, "America's 101 Top Collectors," *Connoisseur* (September 1983).

262 The Internal Revenue Service has: Lee Rosenbaum, "Can the Art World Live with the Tax Reform Act?" *ARTnews* (January 1986).

262 According to one biographer: Robert Lenzner, *The Great Getty* (New York: Crown Publishers, 1985), p. 178.

263 Major horse auctions: Patricia Linden, "The Saratoga Season," *Town and Country* (August 1985).

264 The owners of racing stables: Keith Chamblin, "Bills and Taxes," *Blood-Horse* (June 7, 1986).

264 One of the most successful racing: E. J. Kahn, Jr., *Jock: The Life and Times of John Hay Whitney* (Garden City, N.Y.: Doubleday, 1981), p. 193.

265 The first racing enthusiast: *The New York Times,* October 20, 1970.

266 Perhaps the most successful: Hersh, *Mellon Family,* pp. 434–36.

266 One of the first horses: *Thoroughbred Record* (July 18, 1984).

267 Engelhard bought the colt: *The New York Times,* August 16, 1970.

267 In 1978, she sold the last: *Blood-Horse* (April 10, 1978).

267 Perhaps the most extensive: Harry Hurt III, *Texas Rich* (New York: W.W. Norton, 1981), pp. 263–64.

268 In 1978, he sold 18 yearlings: *Blood-Horse* (August 4, 1979).

268 At present, Bluegrass Farms: *Thoroughbred Record* (January 18, 1986).

268 For example, Catoctin Stud: Suzanne Wilding, "The Firestone Phenomenon," *Town and Country* (July 1982).

269 Their best-known horse: *Thoroughbred Record* (August 2, 1986).

269 One of the newest entrants: *The Wall Street Journal,* June 3, 1985.

269 That same year, Paulson: *Thoroughbred Record* (July 26, 1986).

269 Another newcomer to horse: Steven E. Prokesch, "Jack Cooke: Genial but Tough," *The New York Times*, July 27, 1985.

269 In 1984, Cooke bought Elmendorf Farms: *Blood-Horse* (December 29, 1984).

270 Ewing Kauffman, the founder: Sheldon Gallner, *Pro Sports: The Contract Game* (New York: Charles Scribner's Sons, 1974), p. 141.

270 The franchise, which cost: *The New York Times*, January 12, 1968.

270 In 1985, he agreed to sell: *Forbes* (June 3, 1985).

270 In 1984, 10 million fans: Brenton Welling, Jonathan Tansini, and Dan Cook, "Basketball: Business Is Booming," *Business Week* (October 28, 1985).

271 The National Football League, for example: Thomas Moore, "Its 4th and 10—The NFL Needs the Long Bomb," *Fortune* (August 4, 1986).

271 Similarly, major-league baseball: *The New York Times*, April 8, 1983.

271 The National Basketball Association: *Business Week* (October 28, 1985).

271 For example, Leon Hess: *The New York Times*, September 29, 1983.

272 One sports entrepreneur: Gallner, *Pro Sports*, p. 143.

272 Clint Murchison, Jr., a former college: Don Kowet, *The Rich Who Own Sports* (New York: Random House, 1977), pp. 88–97.

272 Indeed, the team has earned: Robert L. Simison and Karen Blumenthal, "Besieged Tycoon: Clint Murchison," *The Wall Street Journal*, January 22, 1985.

273 In 1981, William Wrigley III: *The Wall Street Journal*, June 17, 1981.

273 That same year, Robert R. M. Carpenter III: *The New York Times*, October 30, 1981.

273 She died in 1975: *The New York Times*, January 25, 1980.

273 Professional sports teams, however: Gallner, *Pro Sports*, pp. 150–56.

273 In 1974, for example: *The New York Times*, December 6, 1974.

274 Independent accountants later: Murray Chass, "Accountants Debate Losses," *The New York Times*, July 10, 1985.

274 Recent court decisions have: Kowet, *The Rich*.

274 In 1980, three members of the: *San Francisco Chronicle*, August 24, 1980.

274 In 1976, Turner paid: *The New York Times*, January 7, 1976.

274 The following year, he paid: *The New York Times*, January 4, 1977.

275 Jack Kent Cooke became wealthy: Kowet, *The Rich*.

275 In 1965, Cooke paid just over: *Time* (June 11, 1979).

275 In 1959, at the age of twenty-six: Hurt, *Texas Rich*, p. 212.

276 Hunt is also one of the owners: Art Detman, "The Quiet Success of Lamar Hunt," *Dun's Review* (January 1975).

10: POWER AND PRIVILEGE

279 For example, W. Clement Stone: George Thayer, *Who Shakes the Money Tree?* (New York: Simon & Schuster, 1973), p. 125.

279 As one observer puts it: Ibid., p. 128.

279 In his classic study: Ferdinand Lundberg, *America's Sixty Families* (New York: Vanguard Press, 1937), p. 60.

280 Indeed, the actions that he: Gabriel Kolko, *Triumph of Conservatism* (Chicago: Quadrangle Books, 1967).

280 Using information from a variety: Herbert E. Alexander, *Financing the 1960 Election* (Princeton, N.J.: Citizens' Research Foundation, 1964).

281 As a rule, many: G. William Domhoff, *Fat Cats and Democrats* (Englewood Cliffs, N.J.: Prentice-Hall, 1972).

281 For example, when President: Lundberg, *America's Sixty Families.*

281 In all, the 1,254 largest: Herbert E. Alexander, *Financing the 1972 Election* (Lexington, Mass.: D. C. Heath, 1976).

283 As Mott later boasted: Brooks Jackson, "Loopholes Allow Flood of Campaign Giving by Businesses, Fat Cats," *The Wall Street Journal,* July 5, 1984.

284 They both spent so much money: Peter Collier and David Horowitz, *The Rockefellers: An American Dynasty* (New York: Holt, Rinehart & Winston, 1976), p. 333.

284 In 1984, Jay Rockefeller: Lois Romano, "The Rich Tradition of Jay Rockefeller," *The Washington Post,* June 27, 1985.

284 For example, H. John Heinz III: *Time* (September 27, 1982).

285 In 1982, Mark Dayton: *The Wall Street Journal,* November 4, 1982.

285 During the campaign, Dayton: *The New York Times,* October 12, 1982.

285 Over half of the newspapers: Ben H. Bagdikian, *The Media Monopoly* (Boston: Beacon Press, 1983), p. 8.

286 Indeed, several corporate rich: Tom Goldstein, *The News at Any Cost* (New York: Simon & Schuster, 1985), pp. 100–101.

286 The local political influence of: Bagdikian, *Media Monopoly,* p. 76.

287 Adolph Ochs acquired: Gay Talese, *The Kingdom and the Power* (New York: World Publishing, 1969), p. 160.

287 One of the only: Howard Bray, *The Pillars of the Post* (New York: W.W. Norton, 1980), p. 15.

287 Several years later, he: Ibid., p. 58.

288 One of the largest and most: Lloyd Wendt, *Chicago Tribune: The*

Rise of a Great American Newspaper (Chicago: Rand McNally, 1979), p. 752.

289 Harry Chandler acquired control: Robert Gottlieb and Irene Wolt, *Thinking Big: The Story of the Los Angeles Times* (New York: G. P. Putnam's Sons, 1977), p. 117.

289 Norman Chandler, a son: David Halberstam, *The Powers That Be* (New York: Alfred A. Knopf, 1979), p. 342.

290 For example, Copley Newspapers: *Forbes* (April 15, 1975).

290 The company recently ran: Bagdikian, *Media Monopoly,* p. 86.

290 Perhaps the most conservative: Frederick Rose, "Freedom Newspapers' Harry Hoiles Seeks to Split Up the Wealthy Chain," *The Wall Street Journal,* December 2, 1985.

290 In 1972, for instance: Bagdikian, *Media Monopoly,* p. 102.

290 Most of the time: Bernard Weinraub, "Foundations Assist Conservative Cause," *The New York Times,* January 20, 1981.

291 In his study: G. William Domhoff, *Who Rules America Now?* (New York: Prentice-Hall, 1984), p. 94.

291 Indeed, a staff member of one: Weinraub, "Foundations Assist."

291 One of the best-known: James Bencivenga, "A Voice with Clout," *Christian Science Monitor,* September 28, 1984.

291 In the words of one: Gregg Easterbrook, "Ideas Move Nations," *Atlantic Monthly* (January 1986), p. 70.

291 At least 20 of its resident: Rushworth M. Kidder, "Public Policy Think Tanks," *Christian Science Monitor,* September 25, 1984.

291 Over the past decade, for example: *The Foundation Grants Index* (New York: The Foundation Center, 1984).

292 Another influential conservative: Keith Henderson, "A 3,000 Mile Corridor of Power," *Christian Science Monitor,* October 9, 1984.

292 At least 40 former fellows: Kidder, "Public Policy Think Tanks."

292 Since 1978, it has received: *Foundation Grants Index.*

292 One of the best-known: James Bencivenga, "Young, Brash, and Conservative," *Christian Science Monitor,* October 5, 1984.

293 The Samuel R. Noble Foundation: *Foundation Grants Index.*

294 By 1984, at least twelve resident: Kidder, "Public Policy Think Tanks."

294 Another influential policy-research: Alison Muscatine, "Georgetown's Media Profs," *The Washington Post,* May 11, 1986.

294 In the past decade, the Sarah Scaife: *Foundation Grants Index.*

294 One of the smallest and least-known: *The New York Times,* November 17, 1980.

294 Since 1980, this institute has: *Foundation Grants Index.*

295 One of the most influential: Karen Rothmyer, "Citizen Scaife," *Columbia Journalism Review* (July 1981).

296 This foundation is controlled: Waldemar A. Nielsen, *The Golden Donors* (New York: E. P. Dutton, 1985), p. 174.

296 Last but certainly not least: Richard J. Margolis, "Moving America Right," *Foundation News* (July 1983).

297 In 1949, the Justice Department: Gerard C. Zilg, *Du Pont: Behind the Nylon Curtain* (Englewood Cliffs, N.J.: Prentice-Hall, 1974), pp. 390–99.

298 President Kennedy signed: *The New York Times,* February 4, 1962.

298 In 1975, as the House: Albert H. Hunt, "Perot Would Gain $15 Million Benefit in Tax Panel's Bill," *The Wall Street Journal,* November 7, 1975.

299 Earlier in 1974, he had: Richard D. Lyons, "Bigger Election Fund Role Seen in Specialized Units," *The New York Times,* August 12, 1976.

299 Ernest and Julio Gallo: Jaclyn Fierman, "How Gallo Crushes the Competition," *Fortune* (September 1, 1986).

299 An amendment to the proposed: Brooks Jackson and Jeffrey H. Birnbaum, " 'Gallo Amendment' Backed by Wine Family Opens Multimillion-Dollar Estate-Tax Loophole," *The Wall Street Journal,* October 31, 1985.

300 In 1971, a member of: *The New York Times,* October 14, 1971.

301 After months of litigation: *The Wall Street Journal,* May 5, 1985.

301 In particular, his tax-reform package: *The New York Times,* June 5, 1981.

304 In this regard, the corporate rich: Howard P. Tuckman, *The Economics of the Rich* (New York: Random House, 1973).

305 As Karl Marx once proclaimed: James O'Connor, *The Fiscal Crisis of the State* (New York: St. Martin's Press, 1973), p. 203.

Acknowledgments

C. Wright Mills, the author of *The Power Elite,* once reminded his fellow social scientists that the term *publish* literally means "to make public." In that same tradition, this book is an attempt to make public, in a comprehensive and coherent manner, the facts concerning the accumulation and perpetuation of great wealth within a few hundred families. Very little is known, with any certainty, about the wealthiest capitalist families in America or their fortunes. Consequently, it has taken several years of careful research to compile and analyze the information contained in this study. In order to make these facts and their implications accessible to as large a public as possible, I have endeavored to write a book that is both interesting and informative to the average reader. At the same time, I have tried to include, as unobtrusively as possible, cursory discussions of some of the major theoretical and substantive issues of interest to social scientists and policymakers. These goals are not necessarily incompatible but they are often difficult to reconcile. Furthermore, it is difficult to be entirely dispassionate about the accumulation and perpetuation of large fortunes. As a social scientist, I have strived to present an objective interpretation of the available empirical evidence. I admire the genius and perseverance of some of the entrepreneurs who amassed great wealth as a result of their success in business. At the same time, I deplore the inheritance of great wealth in an ostensibly egalitarian society in which so many people live in poverty.

420

Any attempt to document and analyze the historical evolution of the wealthiest capitalist families in America confronts one almost insurmountable obstacle: the limited availability of accurate information. However, if we wish to understand more fully the dynamics of corporate rich families and their fortunes, we must be willing to proceed on the basis of information that is usually incomplete and occasionally inaccurate. The information contained in this book is derived entirely from documents that are considered to be within the public domain. I have relied exclusively on public documents that are on file in various libraries and courthouses across the country. It should be noted that I tried, at the outset of this research, to elicit the cooperation of various members of several corporate rich families. Without exception, my requests for background interviews were summarily rejected by even the most liberal and outspoken members of these families. Perhaps I might have obtained more cooperation if I had been willing to deceive these individuals about my intentions, but the use of deception in a study of this sort raises serious ethical and legal issues. In the end, I decided to limit my analysis to information that was available, although not always readily accessible, from various public records. I have never regretted this decision. In fact, I am now convinced that public documents are the best source of systematic and reliable information on the historical evolution of corporate rich families and their fortunes.

Although this has been largely a solitary project, I must acknowledge the contributions of many individuals and institutions to this research. To begin with, I am obliged to the staffs of many libraries and courts for their assistance in locating information contained in this book. In particular, I am indebted to the staff of the Baker Library of the Harvard University Graduate School of Business Administration for allowing me unrestricted access to its historical collection of corporate reports. My associates at Washington State University deserve some recognition for keeping faith with a colleague who devoted several years to such an unorthodox research project. Two colleagues in particular, Armand Mauss and Scott Long, discussed many aspects of this project with me and provided me with a number of important insights. Several scholars were kind enough to read parts of the original manuscript. I am grateful to George Cooper, Waldemar Nielsen, Philip Burch, and John Campbell for their comments and suggestions. Above all, I am indebted to Bill Domhoff, whose encouragement and advice were essential to the completion of this research. I am also grateful to Truman M. Talley, my editor and publisher, for taking his chances with this manuscript and helping me turn it into a readable book. In this regard, I must acknowledge the valuable assistance of my copy editor, Susan Thornton. Last but not least, I wish to thank my wife, Jude, and our children, Emily and Patrick, for their patience and understanding.

421

Index

422

INDEX

Center for Strategic and International
Studies (CSIS), 208, 294
Chairman (corporation), 133, 139
Champion Spark Plug, 113, 171
Chandler, Harry, 170, 289, 320
Chandler, Norman, 289
Chandler, Otis, 133
Chandler family, 108, 136, 170, 286
Chandlis Securities, 108
Charitable foundations. *See* Foundations
Charitable holding companies, 198–204,
206
Charitable lead trusts, 197–98
Charitable remainder trusts, 194–97
Charity, 5, 30, 34–35, 82, 185, 189,
190–91; funded by foundations, 205–207;
and ideology, 290–96; tax avoidance and,
192–98; women in, 119; *see also* Lifetime
gifts, to charity; Testamentary bequests
Charles Stewart Mott Foundation, 191,
200, 207, 292
Charlton, Helena McCann Guest, 89
Chase Manhattan Bank, 38, 114
Cherry, Wendell, 261
Chevron Corporation, 34, 35, 58, 87
Chicago Tribune, 21, 114, 288–89
Chief executive officer(s) (CEOs), 135, 152;
family member as, 132, 133, 134, 138;
nonfamily, 136, 137
Chiles, Harrell E., 274
Christian Anti-Communist Crusade, 72
Christiana Securities, 43–44, 45, 46, 47, 50,
173, 175, 179, 181–82, 297
Chrysler, 269
Chrysler Building, 269
Civic activities, 39, 119, 302
Clark, Alfred C., 77
Clark, Edward, 77, 78
Clark, Emory T., 183–84
Clark, F. Ambrose, 77–78, 264
Clark, Robert S., 77
Clark, Stephen C., 77, 78
Clark, Stephen C., Jr., 78, 264
Clark Estates, 78
Clark family, 63, 64, 76–78, 184
Clark fortune, 76–77, 78
Clark Foundation, 78
Clark Oil Company, 183–84
Clan(s), 102, 106, 115
Clayton Antitrust Act, 297
CNA Financial, 238–39
Coalesced Company, 53
Coca-Cola Company, 140
Cofrin, Austin E., 320–21
Collateral relatives, 8, 9, 28, 98–99
Collectors, collections, 257–63
Combined American Insurance Company,
279
Committee for Economic Development,
208
Common stock, 175–76, 239–45
Commonwealth Fund, 87
Community property laws, 180, 194, 195
Conoco, 50
Conservative (political) causes, 72,
208–209, 288–90, 291–96, 303

Consolidated Paper Inc., 108
Consumption patterns (of rich), 247, 248,
250–51
Control of family corporation, 13–15, 59,
71–73, 92, 122, 137, 204, 277, 302; cost
of, 65–69; by family members, 14–15,
16–17, 27, 33, 123–53, 302; foundations
in, 186, 188, 198–200, 201, 202, 210,
211; through holding companies, 173;
lapsed, through lack of interest, 79–86;
loss of, 74–78; and manipulation of stock
valuation, 234–35; media companies,
286–88; mergers and acquisitions and,
151–53; minority, 138–42, 153; through
philanthropy, 195–96; and power of rich,
277, 278; and preservation of family
fortunes, 69–73; special legislation in
maintenance of, 300; *see also* Passive
control
Cooke, Jack Kent, 263, 269, 275
Cooper, George, 144
Coors, Adolph H., 142, 147, 321
Coors, Joseph, 293
Coors, William K., 133, 147
Coors family, 16
Copeland, Charles, 46
Copeland, Lammot du Pont, 12, 46, 49
Copeland, Lammot du Pont, Jr., 46, 97
Copeland, Louisa du Pont, 46
Copley, Helen, 120
Copley, Ira C., 321
Copley, James S., 120, 290
Copley Newspapers, 290
Copley Press, 120
Cornell University, 24
Corning Glass Works, 103, 109, 134, 170,
222–23, 225
Corporate rich, the, 2–3; alliances with
other powerful groups, 304; directory of,
307–92; entrepreneur/inheritor
distinction, 4–8; life-styles of, 246–76;
pattern in accumulation of wealth, 216;
as privileged class, 302–306; and tax
reform, 158–60, 298–302; *see also*
Families, wealthy
Corporations, 156, 216, 219; closely held,
174–77; controlled by trusts, 170–71;
government and, 305; rational
organization of, 125; mature, 92;
recapitalization in taking private,
239–45; tax rates, 178, 179; women at
head of, 120; *see also* Control of family
corporation; Family corporation(s);
Private corporations
Council on Foreign Relations, 208
Cowles, Gardner, 322
Cox, James M., 193–94, 284, 322–23
Cox Enterprises, 284, 290
Cox family, 286
Cromwell, Doris Duke, 281
Crown, Henry, 92, 152, 166, 182, 323
Crown Central Petroleum Company, 175
Crown fortune, 182
Crown Fund, 166
Cullen, Hugh Roy, 111–12, 323–24
Cultural capital, 22–26, 62, 249, 258

INDEX

431

INDEX

Privacy, 2–3, 72; *see also* Anonymity
Private corporations, 7, 107–108, 124, 142–45, 239–45; and family fortunes, 224; going public, 217–18, 224, 225; trading shares in, 147
Private schools, 23–24, 37, 62, 115, 246; and social interaction, 116, 117; *see also* Preparatory schools
Privilege: perpetuation of, 64; wealth and, 277–306
Procter & Gamble Company, 106, 141, 148
Professional sports teams, 251, 269, 270–76
Profitability (corporate), 303, 304, 305
Public opinion, 278, 286, 294
Public policy, 21; influence of corporate rich on, 4, 278, 290–96, 302; influenced through foundations, 208–209
Public policy-research institutions, 208, 278, 290–96
Publishing properties, 213, 214, 285–86
Pulitzer, Joseph, 373
Pulitzer family, 286
Pullman (company), 53, 54

Quintana Petroleum, 111, 112

R.H. Macy & Co. Inc., 158
R.J. Reynolds Industries Inc., 81, 82, 83, 151
R.R. Donnelley and Sons, 136, 223–24, 226
Radio stations, 21, 285–86
Ralston Purina Company, 18, 132, 136, 203, 222
Rapid American Corporation, 261
Reagan, Ronald, 20, 159, 289, 292, 294, 301
Reagan administration, 208, 291, 292, 293–94
Real estate, 2, 39, 69, 178, 179, 204, 251
Recapitalization, 239–45
Reliance Financial Corporation, 261
Reliance Financial Group, 241–43
Reliance Group Holdings, 243
Reliance Insurance Company, 242
Republican National Committee, 280
Republican party, 17, 38, 72, 279, 280, 281, 282, 288, 289
Retailing, 17, 128, 219, 228; discount, 230–31; specialty, 229–31
Retained earnings, 14, 126–28, 217, 223–24, 227–28, 286
Revlon, 151–52, 218
Reynolds, Donald W., 373–74
Reynolds, Richard J., 81, 83, 374
Reynolds, Richard J., Jr., 81–82, 83
Reynolds, Richard J. III, 12
Reynolds, William N., 81, 374
Reynolds family, 64, 81–83
Reynolds fortune, 82–83
Richard K. Mellon and Sons, 108
Richard King Mellon Foundation, 55, 56, 59, 180, 199, 200, 200–208
Richardson, Lunsford, 105–106, 296, 374–75
Richardson, R. Randolph, 296

Richardson, Sid W., 99, 193
Richardson family, 141
Richardson Foundation, 20
Richardson-Vicks Inc., 106, 141, 148, 292
Right People, The (Birmingham), 114
Riklis, Meshulam, 261
Robert S. Clark Foundation, 77, 78
Robert Wood Johnson Foundation, 192, 201, 205
Robertson, Nedenia Hutton (Dina Merrill), 119
Robins, Claiborne, 375
Rockefeller, Abby Aldrich, 114
Rockefeller, David, 1, 38–39, 136
Rockefeller, John D., 4, 11, 26, 34–36, 37, 75, 107, 114, 115, 116, 130, 264; biography, 375–76; descendants of, 10, 12; education of, 250; estate of, 34–35, 164; homes, 252, 254; liftime gifts, 95; philanthropy, 187–88
Rockefeller, John D., Jr., 26, 35–38, 40, 41, 67, 118, 130, 136; art collection, 262; education, 250; estate, 37–38; grandchildren, 117; homes, 252, 257; inheritance, 100; lifetime gifts, 95–96; married Abby Aldrich, 114; philanthropy, 199; trusts, 96, 158, 163, 169
Rockefeller, John D. III, 39, 40–41
Rockefeller, John D. IV ("Jay"), 12, 18, 32, 41, 104, 254, 284
Rockefeller, Laurence, 39, 117
Rockefeller, Martha B., 118
Rockefeller, Nelson, 18, 38, 40, 41, 42, 97, 257, 258, 281; financial disclosure, 162–63, 284
Rockefeller, Rodman, 41
Rockefeller, Winthrop, 18, 39, 40, 41, 117, 250, 284
Rockefeller, Winthrop Paul, 40
Rockefeller Brothers Fund, 37–38, 122, 199, 204
Rockefeller Center, 36, 38, 42, 130
Rockefeller family, 5, 8, 11, 21, 35, 63, 92, 105, 136, 201; continuity and change, 60–62; as dynasty, 32–33, 34–42; family office, 108; generation-skipping trusts, 96; homes, 254; loss of control of family corporation, 130; marriages, 116, 117; political contributions, 280–81, 283–84; preservation of fortune, 160; and Rockefeller Brothers Fund, 204; social status, 12, 114; trusts, 172
Rockefeller Family and Associates, 10, 40, 42, 108
Rockefeller fortune, 4–5, 40, 42, 60, 76, 130, 160, 169
Rockefeller Foundation, 34, 35, 39, 188, 201, 208
Rockefeller Group Inc., 10, 42, 60, 96
Rockefeller Institute, 35
Rockwell, Willard F., Jr., 150
Rockwell family, 150
Rockwell International Corporation, 150
Rockwell Manufacturing, 150
Rockwell Standard, 150

INDEX

Stockholders, major, 4, 302, 304, 308;
control of corporations, 277; disclosure
of identities of, 27–28; family members
as, 14, 16, 18, 22, 23, 36, 136; and
mergers and acquisitions, 152–53;
minority, 123, 124, 138–40; women as,
94, 118, 119–20
Stockholdings, 64, 137; as basis of family
fortunes, 93, 218–26, 307; in companies
in growth industries, 228–30;
concentration of, 14–15, 129, 173;
diluted, 14–15, 125–26, 135; dispersal of,
within family, 14–15, 125, 128–29, 131;
Duke family, 80; du Pont family, 50–51;
Ford family, 69; Getty family, 233–34;
information about, 28–31; inheritance of,
as defining characteristic of corporate
rich family, 102; Mellon family, 51, 52,
53, 54, 57–58, 59; not disclosed in
private corporations, 144; Rockefeller
family, 42, 130; and shared economic
interests, 107–108
Stone, Joseph H., 381–82
Stone, W. Clement, 279, 282
Stranahan, Frank D., 171, 382
Stranahan, Robert A., 171, 382
Stranahan, Robert A., Jr., 171, 382
Strauss, Jesse I., 158
Strauss, Levi, 145
Strauss, Percy S., 158
Stroh Brewing Company, 149
Strong, Bessie Rockefeller, 35
Stuart, Elbridge A., 194, 382–83
Studebaker Corporation, 236
Sulzberger, Arthur H., 121
Sulzberger, Arthur Ochs, 12, 19, 104, 133,
287
Sulzberger, Iphigene Ochs, 121, 287
Sulzberger family, 109, 286
Summa Corporation, 189
Sun Company Inc., 71–72, 73, 199, 202,
203, 291, 300
Superior Oil Company, 192–93, 264
Supreme Court, 34, 182–83, 188, 283, 297
Symbolic estate(s), 11–12, 94, 102–103, 250

T. Mellon and Sons, 51, 52, 53
Taper, S. Mark, 383
Tax advantages: in collecting, 258; in
diversification, 129; in gifts, 160–61,
262–63; in horse breeding/racing, 264,
268; in ownership of professional sports
teams, 273–75; in residential real estate,
251, 257
Tax avoidance, 37–38, 50; through
foundations, 186, 188–89, 192–98;
through holding companies, 173–79; in
mergers and acquisitions, 151; private
corporations and, 144–45
Tax-avoidance strategies, 6–7, 8, 33, 60, 64,
65, 66, 91, 95, 99, 155, 160, 305; effect
of tax reform on, 172; lifetime gifts as,
161–66; transactions between family
members as, 179–84
Tax laws, 46, 196, 278; corporate rich use
of influence to change, 298–302

Tax reform, 158–60, 301–302, 305–306
Tax Reform Act of 1969, 203, 210, 300
Tax Reform Act of 1976, 161, 171–72
Tax system, 5–8, 118, 154–55, 306
Taxes (taxation), 15, 30, 34, 154–84, 291,
299; on foundations, 203; on
generation-skipping trusts, 159, 166–72;
multiple, 179
Technicon Corporation, 152, 217–18
Tektronix, 228
Teledyne (company), 234–35
Teleprompter Corporation, 269, 275
Television stations, 21, 285–86, 287, 289,
290
Temple, Thomas L., 153
Temple, Thomas L. L., 383–84
Temple family, 153
Temple Industries, 153
Temporary National Economic Committee,
35, 64
Testamentary bequests, 160, 161, 162, 163,
189, 192, 210; artworks, 262; for
charitable remainder trusts, 196–97;
endowing foundations, 192–93
Terra, Daniel, 258, 261, 282
Terra Chemicals, 261
Texaco Inc., 110, 151, 169, 301
Texas Childrens Hospital, 197
Texas Instruments Inc., 16, 128, 228–29
Thalheimer, Alvin, 174–76
Thalheimer, Fanny Blaustein, 174
Third generation of corporate rich, 62, 101,
117, 128, 149
Thompson, Joe C., Jr., 384
Thompson, John P., 132
Thorne, Oakleigh, 384–85
Thurow, Lester: *Generating Inequality*, 217
Tidewater Oil Company, 232, 233
Time Inc., 153
Times Mirror Company, The, 17, 108, 133,
136, 170, 285–86, 289
Timken, Henry H., 207
Timken, William R., Jr., 133
Timken Company, The, 133, 207
Timken family, 16
Timken Foundation, 200, 207
Timken Mercy Medical Center, 207
Tisch, Laurence, 238–39, 385
Tisch, Preston, 238–39, 385
Tisch Hotels, 238
Tracinda Corporation, 108, 238
Trans International Airlines, 236
Transamerica Corporation, 236, 237
Transfer taxes, 107, 172, 302, 305, 306;
progressive, 7, 163, 278; uniform, 159,
161
Triangle Publications, 188
Tribune Company, 109, 285–86, 288–89
Truman, Harry, 288
Trustees (foundation), 167, 198, 200–201,
205, 210
Trusts, 10–11, 61, 94, 129, 131, 247;
centralizing control of family fortune
through, 109–10; charitable, 188; Clark
family, 78, 183–84; controlling
corporations, 170–71; Crown family,

436

INDEX